Globalization for Development
Meeting New Challenges

New Edition

D0779089

Globalization for Development

Meeting New Challenges

New Edition

Ian Goldin and Kenneth Reinert

OXFORD

UNIVERSITY PRESS

OXFORD

UNIVERSITY PRESS

Great Clarendon Street, Oxford OX2 6DP

Oxford University Press is a department of the University of Oxford.
It furthers the University's objective of excellence in research, scholarship,
and education by publishing worldwide in

Oxford New York

Auckland Cape Town Dar es Salaam Hong Kong Karachi
Kuala Lumpur Madrid Melbourne Mexico City Nairobi
New Delhi Shanghai Taipei Toronto

With offices in

Argentina Austria Brazil Chile Czech Republic France Greece
Guatemala Hungary Italy Japan Poland Portugal Singapore
South Korea Switzerland Thailand Turkey Ukraine Vietnam

Oxford is a registered trade mark of Oxford University Press
in the UK and in certain other countries

Published in the United States
by Oxford University Press Inc., New York

British Library Cataloguing in Publication Data

Data available

Library of Congress Cataloging in Publication Data

Data available

Typeset by SPI Publisher Services, Pondichery, India
Printed in Great Britain
on acid-free paper by
Clays Ltd, St Ives plc

ISBN 978–0–19–964556–5 (Hbk)
     978–0–19–964557–2 (Pbk)

10 9 8 7 6 5 4 3 2 1

■ ACKNOWLEDGMENTS

Many people have supported us in writing this book, and to all our deep thanks are due. Andrew Beath contributed a great deal in 2005 to our first edition of this book, and more recently Javier Beverinotti, Samantha Burn, David Clark, Johnny Glyn, Ranjit Lall, and Laragh Larsen have provided tremendous support as we have sought to update our literature reviews, data, analysis, and perspectives for this fundamentally revised edition of our book. It was Dominique van der Mensbrugghe who introduced us, so we owe this happy collaboration to his matchmaking. Kemal Derviş, François Bourguignon, Trevor Manuel, Amartya Sen, Nicholas Stern, and Joseph Stiglitz generously gave their time and thoughts to provide comments on the earlier editions of this book. We also are indebted to many other former and current colleagues who have provided very helpful material, comments, and support. They include Amar Bhattacharya, Gerard Caprio, Jean-Jacques Dethier, Desmond Dinan, Sonia Ketkar, Amy Heyman, Bernard Hoekman, Andrew Hughes-Hallett, Michael Klein, Danny Leipziger, David McKenzie, Lant Pritchett, Ramkishen Rajan, Dilip Ratha, Martin Ravallion, William Rex, David Rivero, F. Halsey Rogers, Eric Swanson, Zhen Kun Wang, L. Alan Winters, Xiao Ye, and Shengman Zhang. Carlos Rossel and Santiago Pombo-Bejarano of the Office of the Publisher at the World Bank have been most helpful in the transition of this revised edition to Oxford University Press. OUP have proved to be exemplary partners and we are most grateful for the wide-ranging and always professional editorial, publishing, and marketing support we have received. We particularly have our commissioning editor, Adam Swallow to thank, as through his enthusiasm and timely guidance we chose OUP for the publication of this new edition. In preparing the manuscript for publication David Clark, in addition to providing most helpful insights and research, has proved extraordinarily diligent in ensuring the final manuscript was submitted in a timely manner.

The creation of this substantially revised edition has been undertaken while Ian served as Director of the Oxford Martin School at the University of Oxford. He is most grateful to his colleagues for creating a vibrant and stimulating work environment and for allowing him to carve out the necessary time to work on this volume. Laura Lauer, the School's Administrator has ensured that Ian has had excellent research support.

As this project fell on top of our normal work responsibilities, it is to our families that we are most grateful. Ian's wife Tessa, daughter Olivia, and son Alex, and Ken's wife Gelaye, daughter Ayantu, and son Oda once again demonstrated their unstinting support and patience during the many evenings and weekends that this project invaded. The authors alone take responsibility for the contents of the book, which does not necessarily reflect the views of our colleagues or the institutions with which we are associated.

Ian Goldin, Oxford, England
Ken Reinert, Arlington, USA

June 2011

■ CONTENTS

■ LIST OF FIGURES

■ LIST OF TABLES

■ LIST OF BOXES

■ LIST OF ACRONYMS AND ABBREVIATIONS

ACWL	Advisory Centre on WTO Law
AERC	African Economic Research Consortium
AGOA	African Growth and Opportunities Act (of United States)
AIDS	Acquired Immune Deficiency Syndrome
ALBA	Bolivian Alternative for the Americas
AMR	Anti-Microbial Resistance
APOC	African Program for Onchocerciasis Control
BIS	Bank for International Settlements
CBD	Convention of Biological Diversity
CDD	Community Directed Drug Distributors
CGE	Computable General Equilibrium
CGIAR	Consultative Group for International Agricultural Research
CITIES	Convention on International Trade in Endangered Species
CMA	Capital Markets Authority
CTH	Change in Tariff Heading
DAC	Development Assistance Committee (of OECD)
DALYS	Disability Adjusted Life Years
DBCP	Debromochloropropane
DIME	Development Impact Evaluation Initiative
DOTS	Directly Observed Treatment Short Course
EBA	Everything But Arms
EBRD	European Bank for Reconstruction and Development
EIP	Enhanced Integrated Framework
EPZ	Export-Processing Zone
EU	European Union
FAO	Food and Agriculture Organization (of the United Nations)
FDI	Foreign Direct Investment
FLO	Fairtrade Labelling Organizations International
FTA	Free Trade Association
G-7	Group of Seven
G-8	Group of Eight
G-20	Group of Twenty

G-24	Group of Twenty-Four
GATS	General Agreement on Trade in Services
GATT	General Agreement on Tariffs and Trade
GAVI	Global Alliance for Vaccines and Immunizations
GCIM	Global Commission on International Migration
GDP	Gross Domestic Product
GFMD	Global Forum on Migration and Development
GHG	Greenhouse Gas
GNI	Gross National Income
GNP	Gross National Product
GPNs	Global Production Networks
GSP	Generalized System of Preferences
HDI	Human Development Index
HIPC	Heavily Indebted Poor Country
HIV/AIDS	Human Immunodeficiency Virus / Acquired Immune Deficiency Syndrome
HLD	High Level Dialogue
HTME	High Technology Manufactured Exports
ICT	Information and Communication Technologies
IDPs	Internally Displaced Persons
IF	Integrated Framework
ILO	International Labour Organization
IMF	International Monetary Fund
IOM	International Organization for Migration
IP	Intellectual Property
IQ	Intelligence Quotient
LDC	Least Developed Countries
MA	Masters of Arts
MDG	Millennium Development Goals
MDRI	Multilateral Debt Relief Initiative
MEAs	Multilateral Environmental Agreements
MIT	Massachusetts Institute of Technology
MNE	Multinational Enterprise
MRAs	Mutual Recognition Agreements
NELM	New Economics of Labor Migration
NGO	Non-Governmental Organization
NSE	Nairobi Stock Exchange

OCP	Onchocerciasis Control Programme
ODA	Official Development Assistance
OECD	Organisation for Economic Co-operation and Development
OEM	Original Equipment Manufacturer
PPP	Purchasing Power Parity
PSE	Producer Support Estimate
R&D	Research and Development
RCTs	Randomized Control Trials
REM	Replacement Equipments Manufacturer
ROO	Rules of Origin
SAMIRAD	Saudi Arabia Market Information Resource and Delivery
SCM	Subsidies and Countervailing Measure
STRs	Standards and Technical Regulations
TKDL	Traditional Knowledge Digital Libraries
TMNP	Temporary Movement of Persons
TRIM	Trade-Related Investment Measures
TRIPS	Trade-Related aspects of Individual Property Rights
UAE	United Arab Emirates
UK	United Kingdom
UN	United Nations
UNAIDS	United Nations Programme on HIV/AIDS
UNCTAD	United Nations Conference on Trade and Development
UNDP	United Nations Development Programme
UNHCR	United Nations High Commissioner for Refugees
UNICEF	United Nations Children's Fund
UNWRA	United Nations Relief and Works Agency (for Palestine Refugees in the Near East)
USA	United States of America
USAID	United States Agency for International Development
USSR	Union of Soviet Socialist Republics
WHO	World Health Organization
WIPO	World Intellectual Property Organization
WTO	World Trade Organization
XDR	Extensively Drug Resistant

1 Background and context

The relationship between globalization and poverty is not well understood. For many, globalization is held out as the only means by which global poverty can be reduced. For others, globalization is seen as an important cause of global poverty.[1] To the global citizen trying to understand these issues, such disparate views are a cause of some confusion and concern. In this book, we aim to resolve this confusion. We attempt to provide an understanding of the main dimensions of economic globalization and their impacts on poverty and development. Although rooted in rigorous inquiry, this is not a narrow academic book. Rather, our objective is to inform the wider public and to provide a broad foundation for policy discussions on globalization and poverty.

Many claims about the relationship between globalization and poverty are not well founded. By examining both the processes through which globalization takes place and the effects that each of these processes can have on global poverty alleviation, current discussions can be better informed. The processes we examine in this book constitute the main global economic channels affecting poverty: trade, finance, aid, migration, and ideas.[2] By carefully considering each of these globalization processes, confusion about globalization can, to some extent at least, be resolved.

To that end, this chapter introduces the five dimensions of globalization and considers the problem of global poverty, placing both globalization and poverty in historical context. Our central message is that, with appropriate national and global policies, globalization can be an important catalyst for alleviating global poverty. In the absence of these policies, however, this catalyst role is significantly diminished. In a few particular instances, globalization without corrective policies can actually exacerbate certain dimensions of poverty. We identify what actions are needed to produce more positive global outcomes, reduce systemic risks, and better manage the global commons.

---

[1] For example, consider the following two quotations. Wolf (2004) claimed that "A world integrated through the market should be highly beneficial to the vast majority of the world's inhabitants." In contrast, the International Forum on Globalization (www.ifg.org) claimed that "While promoters of globalization proclaim that this model is the rising tide that will lift all boats, citizen movements find that it is instead lifting only yachts."

[2] Clearly, our coverage is not comprehensive. We do not extensively examine questions of culture, peace, politics, natural disasters, and security, nor global environmental and health issues. We do give some of these issues consideration under the rubric of the *global commons* in this and other chapters.

1.1 **Globalization and global poverty**

Globalization is an often discussed but seldom defined phenomenon. At a broad level, globalization is an increase in the impact on human activities of forces that span national boundaries. These activities can be economic, social, cultural, political, technological, or even biological, as in the case of disease. Additionally, all of these realms can interact. For example, HIV/AIDS is a biological phenomenon, but it affects and is affected by economic, social, cultural, political, and technological forces at global, regional, national, and community levels. In this book, we focus primarily on economic activities, referring to the other realms of globalization only as needed. This no doubt reflects our bias as economists, but also our observation that global poverty is very much (but certainly not exclusively) an economic phenomenon. In adopting this economic focus, we in no way wish to imply that social, cultural, political, technological, and environmental aspects of globalization are unimportant. They are very important indeed. But having cast our net widely already to include multiple dimensions of economic globalization, we consider it unwise to cast it even more broadly.

The changing natures and qualities of the five economic dimensions of globalization characterize its process. These dimensions are:

- trade
- finance
- aid
- migration
- ideas

Trade is the exchange of goods and services among countries. *Finance* involves the exchange of capital or money through assets or financial instruments among countries. *Aid* involves the transfer of loans and grants among countries, as well as technical assistance for capacity building. *Migration* takes place when persons move between countries, either temporarily or permanently, to seek education and employment or to escape adverse natural or political environments. *Ideas* are the broadest globalization phenomenon. They involve the generation and cross-border transmission of intellectual constructs in areas such as technology, management, or governance.

1.2 **Dimensions of poverty**

For each of these five economic dimensions of globalization, the field of investigation is very wide. We will narrow it significantly by considering only those aspects that are most closely tied to issues of poverty alleviation. This process of narrowing our scope requires a large element of judgment. In choosing what to emphasize, we have reflected the issues and concerns of development policy communities as well as our disciplinary backgrounds in economics.

What do we mean by *global poverty*? Although we all have some concept of what it is to be "poor," the notion of *poverty* is not as straightforward as it might first appear. The reason is that poverty is not a *one*-dimensional phenomenon. It is *multi*dimensional. A number of different concepts and measures of poverty relate to its various dimensions. Each of these dimensions has the common characteristic of representing *deprivation* of an important kind. The variety of poverty concepts in use in development policy communities reflects the variety of relevant deprivations. The major measures of poverty we consider here are those that encompass:

- income
- health
- education
- empowerment
- working conditions

The most common measure of poverty is known as *income poverty*, and it derives from a conception of human well-being defined in terms of the consumption of goods and services. In this approach, poverty is viewed as a lack of goods and services consumption due to a lack of necessary income. The World Bank keeps estimates of both the *poor* and the *extremely poor* based on this concept. The former is defined as those living below a US$2.00 per day poverty line (measured using purchasing power parity or PPP methods).[3] The latter is defined as those living below a US$1.25 per day poverty line (again measured using PPP methods).[4] In this book, we use this concept as one important indicator of global poverty.

There is growing recognition that income poverty is not the only important measure of deprivation. For example, poor *health* is now recognized as perhaps the most central aspect of poverty. The fact that nearly 6 million persons die annually from AIDS, tuberculosis, and malaria illustrates this point, as do the annual deaths of a roughly equal number of infants from largely preventable causes such as diarrheal disease. Health deprivation

---

[3] *Purchasing power parity dollars* adjust for differences in the cost of living among the countries of the world. This adjustment is especially important because non-traded services tend to be less expensive at low levels of income.

[4] See, for example, Ravallion, Chen, and Sangraula (2009). For an important work on the role of income growth in development, see Rodrik (2007). For a different perspective on income poverty, defined in terms of basic goods deprivation, see Reinert (2011).

characterizing poverty can be assessed in terms of life expectances, infant and child mortality, and a number of other health-related measures.

Lack of *education* that results in limited literacy and numeracy is a third important deprivation. Indeed, lack of education (particularly female education) is often an important contributor to deprivations in income and health. This dimension of poverty can be assessed in terms of literacy rates, average years of schooling, or enrolment rates. Gender disparities in education are an important and too-often observed component of educational deprivation and represent a key obstacle to development.[5]

Lack of what is sometimes called *empowerment* is a fourth important dimension of poverty. This includes limits on individuals' abilities to enter into and participate in social realms such as work and political processes because of discrimination of various kinds. Gender disparities are an important kind of empowerment deprivation and interact in detrimental ways with consequences for health and educational deprivations. In many countries, for example, women are socially restricted from entering the workforce or from political participation. In some instances, they do not have the same legal rights as men.[6]

One important issue that does not always arise in discussions of poverty concepts is *working conditions*. As emphasized some time ago by Bruton and Fairris (1999), "Because a person fortunate enough to have a full time job will spend at least one half of his/her waking hours at work, it is incumbent on social scientists to investigate the conditions necessary for the maintenance of working conditions that are safe and pleasant and for the creation of jobs that contribute to individual and social well-being."[7] We will turn to these working condition issues at various junctures in this book, especially to considerations of forced labor, health, and safety.

Each of these dimensions of poverty can be assessed in *absolute* or in *relative* terms. For example, income poverty can be assessed in terms of the numbers of individuals living below an income level (absolute) or in terms of the lowest 20 percent of households ranked according to income (relative). Both absolute and relative poverty are important for social outcomes. In this book, however, we will place a greater emphasis on absolute poverty. With regard to income poverty, we will emphasize the *extremely poor* measure. With regard to other dimensions of poverty, we will emphasize illiteracy (including gender disparities) and infant mortality. The ways in which globalization positively or negatively affect absolute poverty is our central concern here.

---

[5] Among development economists, there is a long-standing debate as to whether education can contribute to income growth and thereby to poverty alleviation. The evidence suggests that it can. See Cohen and Soto (2007).

[6] See Nussbaum (2000) for a powerful, book-length discussion of the lack of empowerment of women in developing countries.

[7] Bruton and Fairris (1999), p. 6.

1.3 **A historical view**

Both globalization and poverty have deep historical roots. Although in popular accounts globalization is a recent phenomenon, historians recognize that, in some important respects, it is not at all new.[8] The ever-increasing integration of people and societies around the world has been both a cause and an effect of human evolution, proceeding more in fits and starts than in any simple, linear progression. Technological innovations, whether in the form of the marine chronometer or modern fiber optics, have propelled surges in globalization, while changes in policy, institutions, or cultural preferences have restrained or even reversed it. In the fifteenth century, for instance, the Chinese emperor Hung-hsi banned maritime expeditions, slowing down and even reversing Asian globalization considerably.[9] Similarly, the proliferation of nation states and the imposition of border controls in the early twentieth century generated new obstacles to the movement of goods, capital, persons, and ideas among the countries of the world.

Economic historians date the modern era of globalization to approximately 1870. The period from 1870 to 1914 is often considered to be the birth of the modern world economy, which, by some measures, was as integrated as it is today. A description of this world by John Maynard Keynes can be found in Box 1.1. What historians have observed is that, from the point of view of capital flows (the predominately British foreign direct investment and portfolio investment of the era), the late 1800s were an extraordinary time.[10] The global integration of capital markets was facilitated by advances in rail and ship transportation and in telegraph communication. European colonial systems were at their highest stages of development, and migration was at a historical high point in relation to the global population of the time.

BOX 1.1 JOHN MAYNARD KEYNES ON GLOBALIZATION

Looking back on the end of the nineteenth century, and writing in 1919, John Maynard Keynes described the vanishing world of the British economic empire as follows:

The inhabitant of London could order by telephone, sipping his morning tea in bed, the various products of the whole earth, in such quantity as he might see fit, and reasonably expect their early delivery upon his doorstep; he could at the same moment and by the same means adventure his wealth in the natural resources and new enterprises of any quarter of the world, and share, without exertion or even trouble, in their prospective fruits and

---

[8] See, for example, Osterhammel and Petersson (2005).

[9] Indeed, by 1500 in China, building ships with more than two masts was punishable by death.

[10] See, for example, chapter 1 of James (1996), O'Rourke and Williamson (1999), and chapter 2 of Eichengreen (2008).

advantages; or he could decide to couple the security of his fortunes with the good faith of the townspeople of any substantial municipality in any continent that fancy or information might recommend. He could secure forthwith, if he wished it, cheap and comfortable means of transit to any country or climate without passport or other formality, could despatch his servant to the neighbouring office of a bank for such supply of the precious metals as might seem convenient, and could then proceed abroad to foreign quarters, without knowledge of their religion, language, or customs, bearing coined wealth upon his person, and would consider himself greatly aggrieved and much surprised at the least interference. But, most important of all, he regarded this state of affairs as normal, certain, and permanent, except in the direction of further improvement, and any deviation from it as aberrant, scandalous, and avoidable.

Source: Keynes (1920), pp. 11–12.

This first modern stage of globalization was followed by two additional stages, one from the late 1940s to the mid-1970s and another from the mid-1970s to the present. These, however, were preceded by World War I, the Great Depression, and World War II. During this time, many aspects of globalization were reversed as the world experienced increased conflict, nationalism, and patterns of economic *autarky*. To some extent, then, the second and third modern stages of globalization involved regaining lost levels of international integration.

The second modern stage of globalization began at the end of World War II. It was accompanied by a global, economic regime developed by the Bretton Woods Conference of 1944 establishing the International Monetary Fund (IMF), what was to become the World Bank, and the General Agreement on Tariffs and Trade (GATT). This stage of globalization involved an increase in capital flows from the United States, as well as a US-founded production system known as "Fordism" or "managerial capitalism" that relied on exploiting economies of scale in manufacturing and the advance of US-based multinational enterprises.

This second stage also involved some reduction of trade barriers under the auspices of GATT. Developing countries were not highly involved in this liberalization, however. In export products of interest to developing countries (agriculture, textiles, and clothing), a system of non-tariff barriers in rich countries evolved. Also, a set of key developing countries, especially those in Latin America, pursued import substitution industrialization with their own trade barriers.[11] These developments, along with the Cold War, suppressed the integration of many developing countries into the world trading system.

The third modern stage of globalization began in the late 1970s. This stage followed the demise of Bretton Woods monetary relationships (the advance of

[11] See Bruton (1998) for a review of import substitution industrialization.

more flexible exchange rates) and involved the emergence of the newly industrialized countries of East Asia. Rapid technological progress, particularly in transportation, information, and communication technologies, began to dramatically lower the costs of moving goods, capital, people, and ideas across the globe.[12] Assembly systems in this latest stage of globalization were also significantly modified into a new arrangement characterized by *flexible manufacturing*. In flexible manufacturing systems known as "Toyotism," information and communication technology (ICT) supported computer-aided production and relied less on economies of scale.

In this stage, Japan emerged as an important, new source of foreign direct investment (FDI): between 1960 and 1995, Japan's share of global FDI increased from less than 1 percent to over 10 percent.[13] The thawing of the Cold War, the entry of China into the world economy, and a general reduction of trade barriers in most developing countries beginning in the late 1980s, helped to accelerate global integration during this phase. Beginning in the 1990s, a new set of developing economies emerged, particularly India and China, but also including Mexico, Chile, Brazil, and Vietnam. These changes, too, characterized the third stage of globalization.

The "Great Recession" of 2007–2009 marked the end of a bubble, which more benignly has been referred to as the "golden decade" of recent globalization. Indeed, *The Financial Times* referred to 2008 as "the year the god of finance failed." In our view, while it has been clear that financial dimensions of globalization have slowed, 2010 and 2011 data showed that globalization has not ended. The regulatory race to the bottom and acceleration of technological tools has highlighted the new dangers associated with globalization in terms of complexity and systemic risk. In this book, we highlight the importance of managing systemic risk and the increased dangers of interconnectedness as a vital element to ensure that globalization works for development.

1.4 Modern globalization and global poverty

What has been the historical relationship between globalization and poverty during these three stages? A partial view is found in Figure 1.1. This figure combines a single measure of globalization—exports as a percentage of world *gross domestic product* (GDP), with a single measure of poverty—the number

---

[12] On the transportation revolution involving container shipping, see Levinson (2006). On information and communication technologies (ICT), see Heshmati and Lee (2009).

[13] Japan's share of global FDI outflows subsequently declines to 4 percent in 2008. These figures are taken from various *World Investment Reports* of the United Nations Conference of Trade and Development (UNCTAD).

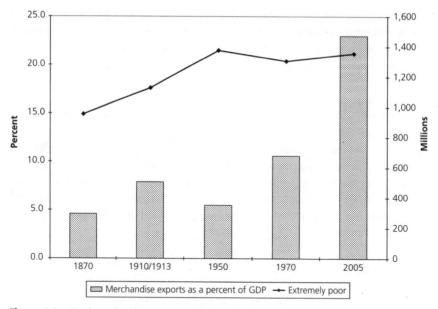

Figure 1.1. Trade and extreme poverty in historical perspective

Note: The 2005 extremely poor measure is estimated using a different methodology than the others.

Sources: Merchandise exports as a percent of GDP from Maddison (2001) for 1870, 1913, and 1950, and from the World Development Indicators (http://databank.worldbank.org) for 1970 and 2005. Extremely poor from Bourguignon and Morrisson (2002) for 1870, 1910, 1950, and 1970, and from World Bank, World Development Indicators for 2005.

of extremely poor people, in a time series from 1870 to 2005.[14] What is clear from this schematic is that, historically, globalization and global poverty can be *either* positively related *or* negatively related to each other. From 1870 through 1910, globalization as measured by trade and global poverty increased together. However, the decline in trade from 1910 to 1950 (and through two world wars and the Great Depression) was accompanied by a *continued* increase in global poverty. More specifically, as merchandise trade as a percent of GDP fell back to nearly the 1870 level, extreme poverty reached a peak of approximately 1.4 billion persons.

From 1950 to 2005, trade as a percent of GDP increased dramatically, from approximately 6 to 23 percent. However, extreme poverty has remained more or less the same over this period. So while retreats from globalization can be accompanied by increases in extreme poverty, advances in globalization do not necessarily reduce extreme poverty. Part of the reason for this is the dramatic increase in global population between 1950 and 2005, but it is

---

[14] At the time of this writing in mid-2011, 2005 is the last year for which the World Bank's World Development Indicators report poverty data.

clear from Figure 1.1 that simple statements about globalization and poverty are not helpful. A key public policy challenge facing humankind is to *eliminate* the still prominent level of extreme poverty. Understanding how to do this requires a deeper understanding of the links between globalization and poverty.

As mentioned above, globalization has the five primary economic dimensions of trade, finance, aid, migration, and ideas. Increases in these dimensions of globalization, if managed in a way that supports development in all countries, can help to alleviate global poverty under certain conditions. We investigate these pathways and conditions in some detail throughout this book. We also consider some particular circumstances where dimensions of globalization can aggravate some dimensions of poverty. Here we define and summarize the five economic dimensions of the relationship between globalization and poverty.

1.4.1 TRADE

Trade is the exchange of both goods and services among the countries of the world economy.[15] The involvement of developing countries as exporters in global trade has increased significantly since the mid-1980s, even in services where their comparative advantage is traditionally perceived to be weak. The regional involvement of developing countries in trade varies widely, with Africa's share of world exports being relatively stagnant compared to other regions, particularly in the case of manufactured exports.

Increased international trade can help to alleviate poverty through job creation, increased competition, improvements in education and in health, and technological learning. The impact of increasing trade openness depends critically on the relationship between trade reforms and other reforms and complementary actions at the national and international levels, particularly in the area of trade related capacity building. Increased exports of petroleum and minerals often (but not always or necessarily) fail to support these activities, as many developing countries have found.[16] Many kinds of manufacturing, agricultural, and service exports, accompanied by complementary infrastructure and training policies, can support these activities, however. In addition, imports of many types—especially health-related imports and imports embodying new technologies—are crucial for alleviating poverty.

---

[15] Goods (or merchandise) are tangible and can be stored over time in inventories, while services are less tangible and cannot be stored. Consequently, the production and consumption of a service happens more or less simultaneously. On the role of services in the world economy, see Francois and Hoekman (2010).

[16] The failure of petroleum and mineral exports to contribute to development has become known as the 'resource curse.' See, for example, Robinson, Torvik, and Verdier (2006).

The exports of developing countries face many kinds of protective barriers, including tariffs, subsidies, quotas, rules of origin, standards and regulations, and increasing security checks. Just the producer-support payments of the rich world reach approximately US$150 billion annually, the same value as foreign aid. A realistic estimate of the impacts of trade liberalization on poverty reduction is an order of magnitude of 100 million.[17] But any increases in market access for developing country exports need to be accompanied by efforts in trade-related capacity building, particularly to support export diversification.[18] Further, to protect the most vulnerable who can sometimes lose as a result of trade liberalization, social safety nets and complementary anti-poverty programs are crucial.[19]

1.4.2 FINANCE

Global finance in the form of capital flows involves the exchange of assets or financial instruments among the countries of the world, either by private or public agents. In this book, we distinguish among four types of capital flows: foreign direct investment or FDI, equity portfolio investment, bond finance, and commercial bank lending. We briefly consider each of these.

Foreign direct investment (FDI) is defined as the acquisition of part of a foreign-based enterprise that exceeds a threshold of 10 percent, implying managerial participation in the foreign enterprise. *Equity portfolio investment* is similar to FDI in that it involves the ownership of shares in foreign enterprises. It differs from FDI, however, in that the share holdings are too small to imply managerial participation in the foreign enterprise. It is thus *indirect* rather than direct investment, undertaken for portfolio reasons rather than for managerial reasons. Its behavior can consequently differ substantially from that of FDI.

Bond finance (also called *debt issuance*) is a second kind of portfolio activity. It involves governments or firms issuing bonds to foreign investors. These bonds can be issued in either the domestic currency or in foreign currencies, and they carry a number of types of default risk. Both bond finance and equity portfolio investments are held by domestic and international investors as a way to manage wealth, and the entire range of portfolio behaviors apply to both. *Commercial bank lending* is another form of debt, but it does not involve a tradable asset as bond finance does.[20]

---

[17] To take one example, van der Mensbrugghe (2006) estimated that even a limited Doha Round trade liberalization scenario would reduce poverty by 60 million. More complete liberalization would exceed that amount. See, for example, Anderson, Martin, and van der Mensbrugghe (2006).

[18] See, for example, Brenton et al. (2009).

[19] This point is made by Winters, McCulloch, and McKay (2004).

[20] Commercial bank loans, including interbank loans, can be short term or long term and can be made with fixed or flexible interest rates. A single bank or a syndicate of banks can be involved in any particular loan package.

Private capital flows to developing countries have increased significantly since the early 1990s, particularly in the case of FDI, which has displaced the previously dominant commercial bank lending in importance. Equity portfolio investment and bond finance flows to developing countries, however, were volatile after the 1997 Asian crisis and after the 2007 to 2009 "Great Recession." Having its roots in the US mortgage markets, the latter has inspired no small amount of rethinking of the role of global finance in development.[21] Official capital flows, reflecting the activities of central banks, are a different story. Since 2000, the government and trade deficits of the United States have involved that country importing over US$500 billion in recent years, structurally claiming the bulk of world savings, which is provided in part by Asian central banks buying US government debt.[22] As a result of these official transactions, the developing world has recently become a net exporter of capital.

From the point of view of alleviating poverty, capital flows have both significant promise and some particular dangers. Capital flows can help to mobilize and deploy savings, develop the financial sector, and transfer technology. They can also manage various types of risk and channel funds in line with the performance of firms' managers. The financial markets involved in some kinds of capital flows, however, are characterized by a number of imperfections that economists refer to as "market failures." In particular, information is less than perfect in these markets, and this can cause significant volatility in flow levels.[23] Commercial bank lending is particularly prone to crises.[24] Consequently, managing these flows poses considerable policy challenges.

Capital flows in the form of FDI can contribute to poverty alleviation when it supports the generation of new employment, promotes competition, improves the education and training of host country workers, and transfers new technology. These benefits are evident in a host of developing countries. Unfortunately, FDI is highly concentrated, and many developing countries receive little or no FDI inflows. FDI that establishes backward links to local suppliers and advances best practices in terms of technology, employment, and social conditions is more beneficial than FDI that remains a low wage enclave within the host country.

Equity portfolio investment, bond finance, and commercial bank lending can help to alleviate poverty under effective exchange rate regimes and properly regulated and developed financial systems. Equity portfolio investment, in particular, has been positively associated with growth through its

---

[21] See, for example, Rodrik and Subramanian (2009) and Goldin and Vogel (2010).

[22] For rich countries as a whole, for example, global capital *imports* exceeded US$500 billion in 2008. The United States actually imported approximately US$700 billion in 2008, with capital exports of Japan, the European Union, and other high-income countries making up the $200 billion difference.

[23] These insights on market failures in finance go at least as far back as Stiglitz and Weiss (1981).

[24] On banking crises and their causes, see chapter 10 of Reinhart and Rogoff (2009).

support of entrepreneurial activity. Bond finance and commercial bank lending can leave developing countries vulnerable to crises that arise from the volatile nature of portfolio investment. Such crises can increase poverty substantially, as happened in Asia during the late 1990s and in Argentina in 2001. Properly managed, however, bond finance and commercial bank lending can be an important part of financial sector development. This aspect of economic globalization must be handled with care.

1.4.3 AID

Aid is the transfer of funds in the form of some combination of loans or grants and the provision of technical assistance or capacity building. The transfer of funds can be in the form of bilateral aid between two countries or in the form of multilateral aid that is channeled through organizations such as the World Bank. Foreign aid remains a vital resource flow for many developing countries. It can finance investment in infrastructure and services, supplement capabilities in health and education, and provide access to new ideas in the realm of policy. These characteristics make it possible for aid to have a significant impact on global poverty alleviation. The motivations of foreign aid donors have varied widely and include advancing geopolitical objectives, stimulating economic development, ameliorating poverty and suffering, promoting political outcomes, and ensuring civil stability and equitable governance. Given both these mixed objectives and the low quality of some developing country governance systems, aid has not always been effective.[25]

That said, with the end of the Cold War calculus of donors and a greater emphasis on governance in the developing world, evidence that aid is more effective now than ever before is continuing to emerge.[26] Sustaining the positive impact of aid requires *both* increasing aid flows *and* using them better. Some progress has been made in increasing the flows of aid. Foreign aid flows have increased significantly in nominal terms in recent years, from approximately US$50 billion in 2000 to approximately US$130 billion in 2010. In real (constant 2010 US dollars) per capita terms, these aid flows increased from US$15 per capita in 2000 to US$22 per capita in 2010. However, the 1990 value was US$20 per capita and the 1980 value US$21 per capita, so we need to keep the increase in some perspective. To put these flows in some perspective, it is also worth noting that developed countries spend approximately the same amount on agricultural subsidy payments

---

[25] As is evidenced in the disparate view of Sachs (2005), Easterly (2006), and Collier (2007), there is a great deal of disagreement among prominent economists on the role of aid in development.

[26] See, for example, Radelet, Clemens, and Bhavnani (2005).

(producer support) as on foreign aid and that developing countries spend about one third the amount of foreign aid on arms imports. Both of these expenditures are anti-development.

A persistent and important challenge for foreign aid is assisting weak or even failed states. These countries often vary widely in their problems, and approaches that work in a "typical" low-income country might not be effective in failed states. Large-scale financial transfers are unlikely to work well, and emphasis should be placed on capacity building to facilitate change, as well as on a limited reform agenda, stressing governance, basic health, educational services, infrastructure, and peacekeeping. This is one of the most difficult problems facing the aid process.

1.4.4 MIGRATION

We define migration as the temporary or permanent movement of persons between countries to pursue employment or education (or both) or to escape adverse political climates. In this book, we do not consider rural–urban and other sorts of migration *within* countries. Migrants can be categorized in a number of ways. For example, Beath, Goldin, and Reinert (2009) used the categories of permanent high-skilled migrants, temporary high-skilled migrants, temporary low-skilled migrants, family migrants, co-ethnic and national priority migrants, asylum seekers, refugees, and undocumented migrants. Migration has become politically sensitive in many countries, particularly for the case of undocumented migrants.

As Goldin, Cameron, and Balarajan (2011) show, migration has historically been the most important means for poor people to escape poverty. Indeed, by some estimates, 10 percent of the world's population permanently relocated between 1870 and 1910 during the first phase of modern globalization described above.[27] This historical pattern has been greatly reduced by the development of nation states. At the beginning of the twentieth century, it has been further reduced by the use of passports and a growing range of mechanisms to identify and control individual movement.[28] Consequently, migration is much less free but is no less important for poverty alleviation.

In addition to the direct "escape from poverty" function, migrants also provide significant remittance flows to their families in their home countries. Remittances to the developing (low- and middle-income) world in 2010 were

---

[27] See, World Bank (2002b).

[28] Dauvergne (2008) noted: "At the outset of the twentieth century, migration was in the process of being 'legalized.' It was not until early in that century that a robust system of passports and visas was fully established to regulate border crossing. The great waves of migration of earlier eras took place largely without the framework of migration laws . . . In contrast with the legalization of migration that took place at the outset of the previous century, we are currently witnessing the 'illegalization' of migration" (p. 2).

US$325 billion. This was more than double the amount official development assistance (ODA) in that year. These flows can have significant and positive impacts in developing countries by directly transferring income more efficiently than foreign aid. On the other hand, migration also causes what is known as "brain drain," the loss of educated and high-skilled citizens to other countries. This has detrimental impacts, particularly in the case of what is known as "medical brain drain," the loss of doctors and nurses.

There is one largely unexploited way for migration to positively affect global poverty. This is through the further development of the temporary movement of workers in services trade.[29] These labor-intensive exports of services through the temporary movement of persons have the potential to allow developing countries to benefit from global services trade in a manner similar to the developed countries in other modes of service delivery, namely FDI in financial services and the temporary movement of corporate personnel.[30]

Current migration restrictions give rise to criminal activity and the exploitation of unsuspecting illegal migrants, often with tragic consequences. As in the case of capital flows, migration flows need to be carefully managed, preferably but not exclusively through multilateral frameworks. The effective management of global migration flows is a difficult and controversial, but very important, challenge for the world community.

1.4.5 IDEAS

Ideas are the most powerful influence on development. Ideas are the generation and transmission of distinctive intellectual constructs in any field that can have an impact on production systems, organizational and management practices, governance practices, legal norms, and technological trends.[31] One well-known category of ideas is intellectual property, which can be thought of as an asset defined by legal rights conferred on a product of invention or creation.[32] Ideas are not just commercial, however. For example, the notion that human rights need to be respected and protected by governments is an

---

[29] In the parlance of trade policy, this is known as "Mode 4" service trade, one of the four modes of services trade identified in the World Trade Organization's General Agreement on Trade in Services (GATS).

[30] See, for example, Walmsley and Winters (2005).

[31] On the ideas dimension of economic globalization and development, see Goldin and Reinert (2010). Lin (2009) stated: "Ideas are the most vital determinants of whether a developing country will be able to achieve long term dynamic growth. With the guidance of right ideas, a developing country will be able to exploit the advantage of backwardness, achieve dynamic growth and converge with developed countries" (p. 92).

[32] As defined by the World Trade Organization, *intellectual property* includes copyrights, trademarks, geographical indications, industrial designs, patents, and layout designs of integrated circuits.

idea of paramount importance.[33] Additionally, flows of ideas across borders play an important role in shaping policies, as well as the perceptions and reality of poverty. In this book, we concentrate on ideas that shape economic activities rather than on those that have primarily cultural or political content, although we are mindful that these are distinctions mostly of convenience and need to be treated with care.

The evaluation and adaptation of ideas requires local capacity in the form of both skills and institutions, as well as a culture of learning. Developing countries can bridge existing gaps in knowledge by acquiring, absorbing, and communicating knowledge. Openness to ideas has historically been and continues to be an important way to alleviate poverty.[34] Ideas can affect poverty through a variety of mechanisms and can interact in important ways with all of the other dimensions of economic globalization. More effective policy regimes, better technological innovations, greater respect for human rights, and the improved social status of women can all help the lives of poor people. The challenge in harnessing ideas to alleviate poverty lies in adapting them to the many local socio-cultural contexts of the developing world. A full understanding of this challenge is still in progress, but it is clear that supporting the exchange of ideas and learning is vital to accelerating the beneficial impact of globalization. As emphasized by Goldin and Reinert (2010), it is important for developing countries to maintain a minimal degree of both *autonomy* and *agency* in the global idea environment.

The development community's understanding of the most effective way to achieve development objectives has evolved over time with the accumulation of evidence and experience. Approaches that appeared at the time to be both correct and obvious have been undermined by experience and closer analysis. This has seen the broadening and deepening of what is meant by "development," from income to include health, opportunity, and rights. Recent years have seen a greater recognition in the policy debate of the *complementarities* between markets and governments. Clearly, experience shows that the private market economy must be the engine of growth, but it shows also that a vibrant private sector depends on well-functioning state institutions to build a good investment climate and deliver basic services competently. Indeed, in many crucial areas—such as health, education, and infrastructure—public–private partnership is essential.

---

[33] This point was made in the case of international business by Ruggie (2008).

[34] This is the main argument of Landes (1998). Landes's work, however, has come under some criticism for overemphasizing the role of European ideas at the expense of ideas from other part of the world.

1.5 **Areas for action**

History and the recent experiences of many countries have taught us that global integration can indeed be a powerful force for reducing poverty and empowering poor people. Poor people are less likely to remain poor in a country that is exchanging its goods, services, and ideas with the rest of the world. Yet, although participation in the global economy has generally been a powerful force for reducing poverty, the reach and impact of globalization remains uneven. In addition, the accelerated pace of globalization has been associated with a rapid rise in global risks, which have outpaced the capacity of global and national institutions to respond. The financial crisis of 2007 to 2009 has been a dramatic reminder of this. Additionally, the increasing global impact of national policies, ranging from armaments and contributions to climate change, points to the need for more effective global governance. If the globalization train is to pull all citizens behind it, policies that ensure that the poor people of the world share in its benefits are required.

In Chapter 8, our concluding chapter, we draw together the many issues considered in this book and provide a policy agenda designed to make it more likely that increased globalization helps rather than hurts poor people. In the area of *trade*, we consider policies related to developing country market access, trade related capacity building, arms trade, and forced labor. In the *finance* dimension, we consider capital account reform, prudential policies to reduce systemic risk, and standards for multinational enterprises. With regard to *aid*, we focus on maintaining aid flow volumes, untying aid, harmonization and alignment, evaluation and knowledge sharing, and debt relief. In the *migration* realm, we consider the multilateral coordination of policy, the temporary movement of persons (labor intensive service provision), brain drain, brain waste and the diaspora, managing remittances, and research and data issues. For our last dimension of globalization, *ideas*, we consider knowledge management, the limits of intellectual property harmonization, access to medicines, and technology transfer.

It is becoming increasingly clear that a necessary condition for globalization to support development is the management of the global commons. Active issues in this area include climate change, fisheries, water resources, food security, pandemic threats, biodiversity, and human security. For this reason, Chapter 8 also considers some essential policies in this area. These include insurance for climate change related risks, combating anti-microbial resistance, agricultural development for food security, and human security.[35]

---

[35] The issue of human security was the subject of the 2011 *World Development Report*. See World Bank (2011c).

We hope that, through our analysis and prioritization of practical actions, we usefully contribute to ongoing discussions of globalization and poverty.

1.6 **The purpose of this book**

The purpose of this book is to provide an understanding of the main aspects of economic globalization and their impact on poverty and development. By examining these dimensions in some detail, we hope to resolve, at least in part, the confusion about globalization represented in public debate. In our view, globalization can be managed so that its benefits are more widely shared than they are today and so that its negative impacts are identified and mitigated. Achieving these outcomes is a global, national, and local responsibility. In the following chapters, we analyze the dimensions of this responsibility.

2 Globalization and poverty

As we suggested in Chapter 1, the relationship between globalization and global poverty is not straightforward. For example, we distinguished in that chapter among three stages of modern globalization: a first stage between 1870 and 1914, ending with World War I, a second stage following the end of World War II and continuing to the mid-1970s, and a the third stage from the mid-1970s to the present. Global poverty rose during the first stage of globalization, but it also rose during the retreat from globalization during World Wars I and II. During the third stage of globalization, there is some evidence that global poverty finally leveled off somewhat and that extreme global poverty began to fall.

Given these historical facts, it is difficult to make simple statements about globalization and poverty: accurate statements about this relationship are necessarily complex. In this chapter, we begin to unravel some of these complexities, setting the stage for our investigation into the relationship between globalization and poverty in the remainder of this book. We begin by considering the developing world, where global poverty is concentrated. We then take on particular aspects of global poverty itself. Next, we consider the five dimensions of globalization considered in this book: trade, finance, aid, migration, and ideas. Finally, we consider the issue of the global commons.

2.1 The developing world

Global poverty is concentrated in what is commonly referred to as the *developing world* consisting of low-income and middle-income countries. As shown in Figure 2.1, the countries of the developing world became distinct by the nineteenth century as their per capita incomes began to lag behind those of other parts of the world. Although by 1820 per capita income in Western Europe was approximately double that of the rest of the world, subsequently the increases in incomes in Western Europe and Japan were far more rapid than they were in Latin America, Eastern Europe, and the former USSR, Asia (excluding Japan), and Africa. The exact causes of these changes are still being debated among economic historians. Indeed, in considering the nexus of change in Western Europe—Great Britain in the late eighteenth century—Crafts (2001) noted:

This was still an economy which . . . had many limitations, including weak science and technology, small markets, and many attractive rentseeking opportunities for the

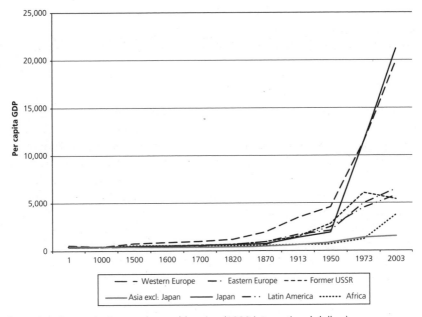

Figure 2.1. Per-capita income by world region (1990 international dollars)

Source: Maddison (2007).

talented. Indeed, a World Bank economist, given a basic description of the late 18th century British economy without knowing to which country it applied, might well conclude that here was a case of very poor development prospects.[1]

Maddison (2001) provided a contrasting perspective, noting Britain's improvements in "banking, financial and fiscal institutions and agriculture" as well as a "surge in industrial productivity."[2] Such varying interpretations of how Great Britain, the other countries of Western Europe, and Japan began their revolutionary economic changes leave the processes less than fully explained. That the changes were indeed revolutionary, however, is not in doubt. The absence of these changes in the developing world became one of the main characteristics defining it. The early nineteenth century featured as a transition between two waves of colonial expansion, the first beginning in 1400 and the second ending with World War I in 1914. The concurrent second phase of colonial expansion and the first phase of modern globalization were described by Szirmai (2005) as "the apex of... Western political, economic, military and cultural dominance" in which 80 percent of the surface of the

[1] Crafts (2001), p. 313.
[2] Maddison (2001), p. 21.

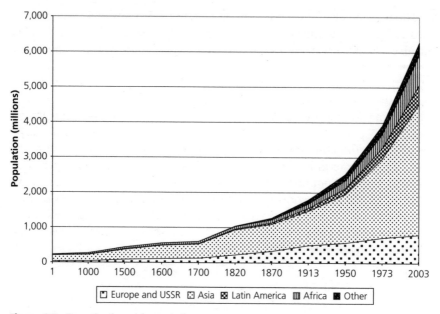

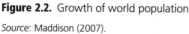

Figure 2.2. Growth of world population

Source: Maddison (2007).

earth came under various European powers.[3] This colonial history, too, began to define the developing world.[4]

Colonial institutions had a lasting impact on many developing countries. As emphasized by many social scientists, institutional development has a strong element of *path dependence*. In the words of North (1990), institutional change is "overwhelmingly incremental," so colonial histories matter. For example, the work of Bolt and Bezemer (2009) showed that variations in colonial education investments within sub-Saharan Africa help to explain human capital levels as far forward as 1995. They further showed that colonial educational investments help to explain current institutional quality in the form of measures of democracy and constraints on the executive. Similarly, Banerjee and Iyer (2005) demonstrated path dependent results for colonial land tenure systems in India. These legacies can impact patterns of global poverty.

[3] Szirmai (2005), p. 51.

[4] Lin (2009) noted that "before the Industrial Revolution in the eighteenth century, China was more industrialized than the West.... In the seventeenth century the Indian subcontinent was not significantly less developed than Britain and, before 1800, India was a major supplier of cotton and silk textiles in international markets, including to Europe" (pp. 20–1). Late colonialism changed this: "Like the citizens of China and India, people in most other parts of the developing world were unable to control their own fate; their economies were plundered and exploited by the colonizers" (p. 21).

The movement of the world economy through these historic changes was also reflected in dramatic increases in population levels (Figure 2.2). This involved an increase in the absolute size of the developing world's population. From 1000 to 2003, the developing world added nearly 5 billion persons, while the rest of the world added slightly over 1 billion. What is most apparent here is the rapid expansion of the Asian region in total population. This took place even with Asia's total *share* of world population declining from approximately 65 percent in the year 1000 to 60 percent in 2003. These large increases in the absolute numbers of people in the developing world are part of its long term history and can be forecasted forward as in Figure 2.3. In 2040, the total population of the developing world will be approximately three times the total world population in 1950. While populations of rich countries have become relatively older, those of the developing world have become relatively younger. Meeting the development and employment needs of these young people remains a great challenge.[5]

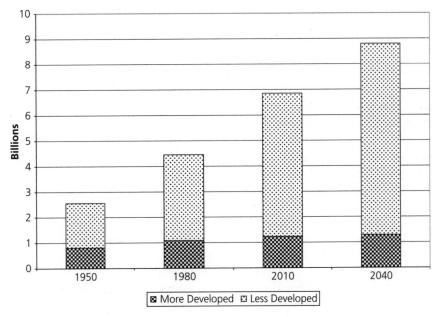

Figure 2.3. Total population by region

Source: United States Bureau of the Census, http://www.census.gov/ipc/www/idb/

---

[5] See United States Department of Commerce (2009). As we will discuss in Chapter 6, the "graying" of some high income countries (e.g. Japan) and the youthfulness of many developing countries provides incentives for migration in order to support social security systems in the former countries. On this and other migration issues, see Pritchett (2006) and Goldin, Cameron, and Balarajan (2011).

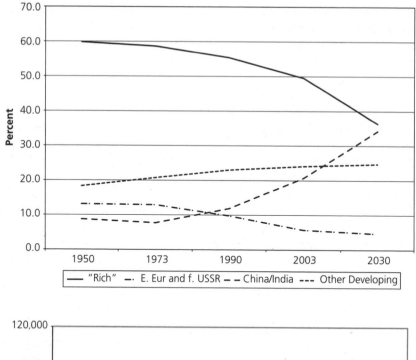

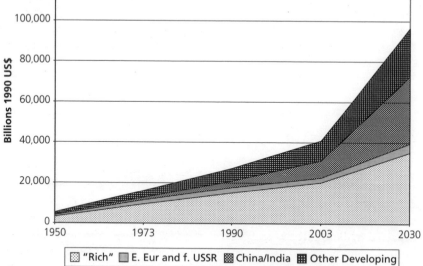

Figure 2.4. Relative economic size of developing countries (percent of world GDP in constant US dollars)

Note: "Rich" refers to Western Europe, United States, Japan, Australia, Canada, and New Zealand.
Source: Maddison (2007).

The increase in the size of the developing world is not confined to population. Large parts of the developing world are emerging in terms of gross domestic product (GDP) as well. Consider Figure 2.4. This figure plots GDP for four regions as a percentage of total world GDP, both historically back to 1950 and projected forward to 2030. The four groups of countries considered are the "rich" countries, Eastern Europe and the former Soviet Union, China, and India combined and other developing countries combined.

We see in Figure 2.4 that the combined size of China and India increased from less than 10 percent of the world total in 1950 to approximately 20 percent in 2003. It is projected to increase to over 30 percent by 2030. The share of other developing countries increased from slightly under 20 percent in 1950 to approximately 25 percent in 2003 and is not forecasted to increase significantly to 2030. The combined share of the developing world, however, more than doubles in Figure 2.4 from 1950 to 2030, ending the forecasted period at approximately 60 percent of total world output. Thus it is evident that at least some parts of the developing world are emerging as relatively economically significant. The fact that some developing countries (including India and China) are also emerging as centers of innovation makes these changes even more significant.[6]

Today the developing world is divided into two sets of countries for analytical and statistical convenience. These are the low-income countries and the middle-income countries. At the time of this writing and for data through 2009, low-income countries are those with a per capita income of less than US$996, and middle-income countries are those with a per capita income between US$996 and US$12,195.[7] The list of these two sets of countries is presented in the annex to this chapter.

2.2 **Poverty**

Recall from Chapter 1 that we can associate poverty with deprivations of income, health, education, and empowerment. Recall also that, although *relative* deprivations are important, we have chosen to focus in this book on the more crucial issue of *absolute* deprivations.[8] The longest record of world poverty was provided by Bourguignon and Morrisson (2002). These estimates covered the 1820 to 1992 period and include both the "poor" and the "extremely poor" (Figure 2.5). In this study, the *poor* were defined as those living on less than US$2

---

[6] See, for example, Yusuf, Nabeshima, and Perkins (2006).

[7] Income per capita is based on the World Bank's Atlas Method.

[8] As Streeten (1995) noted, "Some authors regard all poverty as relative, but this is surely confusing inequality—an evil, but a different evil—with poverty. Everyone in a society can be equally starving, and we would not want to say that they are not poor" (pp. 32–3).

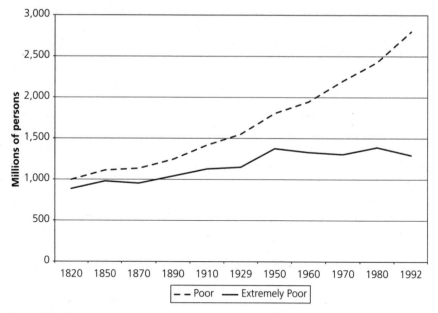

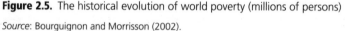

Figure 2.5. The historical evolution of world poverty (millions of persons)

Source: Bourguignon and Morrisson (2002).

BOX 2.1 THE EXPERIENCE OF BEING POOR

For approximately 45 years, until her recent retirement, Jayamma went every day to the brick kiln and spent eight hours a day carrying bricks on her head, 500 to 700 bricks a day... Jayamma balanced a plank on her head, stacked twenty bricks at a time on the plank, and then walked rapidly, balancing the bricks by the strength of her neck, to the kiln, where she then had to unload the bricks without twisting her neck, handing them two by two to the man who loads the kiln. Men in the brick industry typically do this sort of heavy labor for a while, and then graduate to the skilled (but less arduous) tasks of brick molding and kiln loading, which they can continue into middle and advanced ages. Those jobs pay up to twice as much, though they are less dangerous and lighter. Women are never considered for these promotions and are never permitted to learn the skills involved... Nonetheless, they cling to the work because it offers regular employment, unlike construction and agriculture; kilns also typically employ children workers, so Jayamma could take her children to work with her. She feels she has a bad deal, but she doesn't see any way of changing it.

Source: Nussbaum (2000), pp. 18–19.

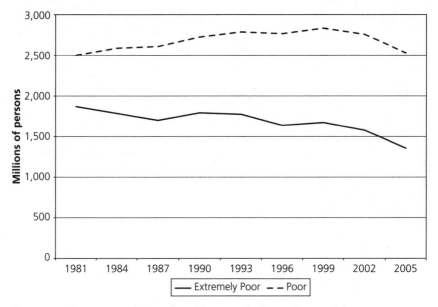

Figure 2.6. The recent evolution of world poverty (millions of persons)

Source: World Development Indicators (http://databank.worldbank.org), 2010.

per day (in 1985 purchasing power parity dollars), and their numbers increased steadily from just under 1 billion persons in 1820 to 2.8 billion persons in 1992. The *extremely poor* were defined as those living on less than US$1 per day (in 1985 purchasing power parity dollars), and their numbers increased and decreased over time, hovering over 1 billion persons for the entire twentieth century up to 1992.[9] An example of what poverty entails is given in Box 2.1.

According to Bourguinon and Morrisson, the persistence of world poverty over the long term was associated with an increase in global inequality, both within and among countries. They noted:

World economic growth since 1980 could have caused poverty to decline dramatically, despite population growth, had the world distribution of income remained unchanged. Had that been the case, the number of poor people would have been 650 million in 1992 rather than 2.8 billion and the number of extremely poor people 150 million instead of 1.3 billion. Likewise, the leveling off in the number of extremely poor people since 1970 can be attributed to the stabilization of their relative position since then.[10]

---

[9] Recall from Chapter 1 that purchasing power parity (PPP) dollars adjust for differences in the cost of living among the countries of the world, and that this adjustment is especially important because non-traded services tend to be less expensive at low levels of income.

[10] Bourguignon and Morrisson (2002), p. 733.

More recent data on world poverty are provided by the World Bank in its World Development Indicators. These estimates currently cover the 1981 to 2005 period and again include both the poor and the extremely poor.[11] In these data, the poor are defined as those individuals living on less that US$2 per day, and the extremely poor are defined as those living on less that US $1.25 per day in terms of purchasing power parity dollars. We can see in Figure 2.6 that here that there is both good and bad news. The good news is that the number of *extremely poor* individuals has been declining over time to a level below 1.5 billion. There is broad agreement in the field that most of this decline has been due to development processes in China and, to a lesser extent, in India.[12] The bad news is that the number of *poor* is more or less constant at approximately 2.5 billion. While this data series appears to be on a downward trend from 1999 to 2005, it is likely that the financial crisis that began in 2007 mitigated this to some extent. The poverty challenge is therefore immense.

With the movement of some large countries from low-income to middle-income status (India and Indonesia, for instance), the majority of the world's

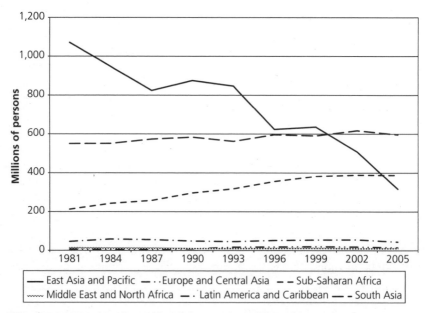

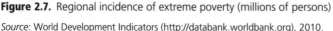

Figure 2.7. Regional incidence of extreme poverty (millions of persons)

Source: World Development Indicators (http://databank.worldbank.org), 2010.

---

[11] See, among others, Chen and Ravallion (2004) and Ravallion, Chen, and Sangraula (2009).
[12] This point was also made in Bardhan (2006) and Ravallion (2006).

extremely poor now reside in middle- rather than low-income countries.[13] Therefore, along with growth, it is often the distribution of income within middle-income countries that is important for alleviating income poverty. Consequently, social welfare programs such as conditional cash transfer schemes in middle-income countries matter a great deal.[14]

The picture of poverty painted by Figure 2.6 is improved somewhat when it is considered in terms of what development economists term the *headcount index* rather than the absolute number of poor people. The headcount index measures poverty as a percentage of population. For the poor, the headcount index fell from 69 percent of the developing world's population in 1981 to 47 percent in 2005. For the extremely poor, it fell from 52 percent of the developing world's population to 25 percent in 2005. Thus, relative to significantly expanding populations, poverty incidence as measured by the headcount index has fallen significantly.

The regional composition of global poverty is also relevant. This is plotted in Figure 2.7. An examination of the data in this figure reveals that extreme poverty is primarily a South Asian and African phenomenon. In East Asia, the number of extremely poor has been declining steadily and significantly since the early 1980s, primarily but not exclusively due to changes in China. In South Asia, the number of extremely poor has declined somewhat, with almost all of this smaller change being accounted for by India. In sub-Saharan Africa, extreme poverty has been *steadily increasing*, with the number of people in this group increasing by over 100 million since the early 1980s. These are the patterns of extreme poverty that need to be addressed.

2.2.1 HEALTH DEPRIVATIONS

As the various regions of the world diverged in per capita incomes, so they diverged in health outcomes.[15] One key measure is life expectancy, low levels of which reflect deprivations in health (see Figure 2.8). It is important to note that the historical evidence suggests that these changes in life expectancies were not driven entirely by the changes in per capita incomes. Changes in science and public health had significant impacts in their own right.[16] As with the gains in per capita incomes, the gains in life expectancies beginning in the early

---

[13] See Sumner (2010) who places the figure at three-fourths of the world's extremely poor living in middle-income countries.

[14] See, for example, Rudra (2008). Rudra notes that many social welfare systems in developing countries support the middle rather than the lower classes.

[15] For a discussion of globalization and health in general terms, see Deaton (2004).

[16] As Crafts (2001) noted, "any index of living standards that gives substantial weight to life expectancy will make the developing countries of the recent past look much better in welfare comparisons with the leading countries of 1870 than does a judgment based simply on real GDP per capita" (p. 325). See also Preston (1975).

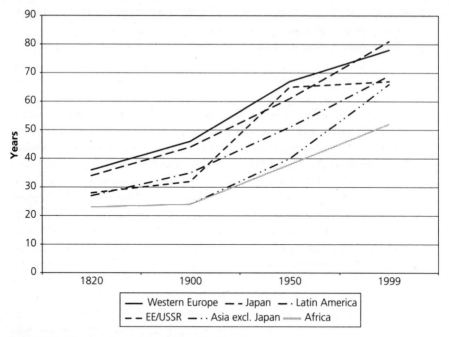

Figure 2.8. Life expectancy by world region (years)

Note: EE/USSR refers to Eastern Europe and the former USSR.

Source: Maddison (2001).

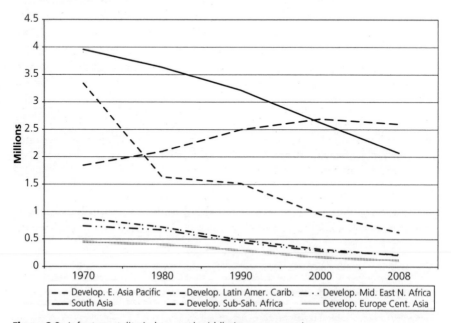

Figure 2.9. Infant mortality in low- and middle-income countries

Source: World Development Indicators (http://databank.worldbank.org), 2010.

nineteenth century were historically unprecedented. For example, Maddison's (2001) estimates of life expectancy in Roman Egypt at the dawn of the Common Era and fourteenth-century Great Britain are exactly the same: only 24 years. Even the slowest increases in life expectancy in Africa since 1820 have more than doubled that millennial norm. However, the substantial gap remaining between Africa and even the other developing regions is a cause for great concern. Another major cause for concern is the recent reversal in African life expectancy caused by HIV/AIDS and the accompanying problem of "AIDS orphans."

Perhaps the most important indicator of health poverty is infant mortality, a sad testament to the global failure to meet the most basic of needs. Total infant mortality in 2008 was just under 6 million, representing an enormous annual tragedy. Examining recent trends in infant mortality (Figure 2.9) leads to some important conclusions. First, as is evidenced by the case of South Asia where annual infant mortality has declined by nearly 2 million since 1970, it is possible to reduce infant mortality significantly even *without* significantly reducing extreme income poverty. Second, as is evidenced by the case of sub-Saharan Africa, where annual infant mortality has increased by approximately 750,000 since 1970, increases in extreme income poverty can exacerbate infant mortality. Third, as is evidenced by the Middle East and North Africa, it is possible to have significant infant mortality in the near absence of extreme income poverty. Taken together, these cases indicate that the relationship between income poverty and health poverty is not as direct as one might first assume. Factors other than income are at play as well.

Health deprivation is not by any means limited to infant mortality. For example, approximately 1 billion persons are malnourished, and over 150 million of these people are children. Annually, approximately 12 million infants are born underweight, a condition that can have lifetime deleterious consequences such as lower IQ, cognitive disabilities, and reduced immune function.[17] As noted by Streeten (1995):

Prolonged malnutrition among babies and young children leads to decreased brain size and cell number, as well as altered brain chemistry... Children who suffer from severe malnutrition show lags in motor activity, hearing, speech, social and personal behavior, problem solving ability, eye-hand coordination and categorization behavior, even after rehabilitation.[18]

Health poverty, then, is both serious and pervasive.[19]

Substantial evidence suggests that female education is positively associated with infants' and children's abilities to escape mortality and malnourishment.

---

[17] See Behrman, Alderman, and Hoddinott (2007).

[18] Streeten (1995), p. 57.

[19] There have been efforts over the years to combine income, health, and other aspects of poverty into a single, *multidimensional* measure of poverty. The most recent of these is that of Alkire and Santos (2010). For a critical review of these efforts, see Ravallion (2011).

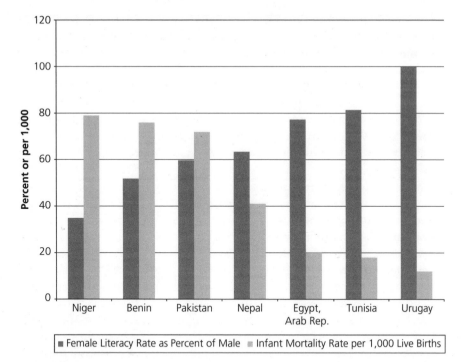

Figure 2.10. Female literacy as a percent of male and infant mortality, most recent year available, 2005 to 2008

Source: World Development Indicators (http://databank.worldbank.org), 2010.

The mediating factors include hygiene, nutrition, and child care practices. Further, the work of Osmani and Sen (2003) and others indicates that women's deprivation in nutrition and health contributes to the ill health of offspring *both as children and as adults* through the pathway of fetal health. So even the health of adults (and consequently their capacity to work) depends on the health of their mothers as health outcomes are transmitted from one generation to another. These are key reasons for focusing attention and policy measures on female education in developing countries.[20]

Consider the data shown in Figure 2.10. This figure plots female youth literacy as a percentage of male literacy using the dark bars. These range from

---

[20] For example, in their study of parental education and health in Brazil, Kassouf and Senauer (1996) concluded, "Some 25% of preschool children with mothers who had less than 4 years of schooling suffered from severe or moderate stunting (of growth). This figure would fall to only 15% if these mothers had a primary education of at least 4 but less than 8 years, and only 3% if these mothers had a secondary education of at least 11 years of schooling. Although not as strong as the effect of maternal education . . . improved paternal education would also lead to substantial reductions in child malnutrition" (p. 832). See also Schultz (2002) and Tembon and Fort (2008).

less than 40 percent in the case of Niger to approximately 100 percent in the case of Uruguay. There is thus a wide range of outcomes in developing countries with regard to female youth literacy. This is important in its own right as an issue in educational equity, but it also has implications for infant and child health poverty. Figure 2.10 also plots infant mortality for these seven countries using lighter bars, and we can see that infant mortality decreases significantly as female youth literacy increases, from nearly 80 per 1000 live births to less than 20 per 1000 live births. For reasons such as these, the gender aspects of health poverty matter a great deal.

2.2.2 A GLOBAL IMPERATIVE

Reducing extreme income poverty and extreme health poverty is a global imperative. It is also an economic imperative, because, according to the research of the World Health Organization, lower rates of infant mortality are associated with higher rates of economic growth (WHO, 2001b). Although the elements of globalization we consider in this book can have significant effects in reducing infant mortality, we do not want to claim too much for them, except perhaps to emphasize that accepted social roles of girls and women can be powerful in their effects in this area. As such, advances in gender equity are an important prerequisite to leverage globalization for development.

2.3 **Trade and foreign direct investment**

Increases in international trade and foreign direct investment (FDI) are potentially vital means to alleviate global poverty.[21] Examining this possibility requires an appreciation both of the kinds of trade and FDI the developing world engages in and of the way these activities have changed over time. FDI is distinct from other capital flows (portfolio equity investment, bond finance, and commercial bank lending, as well as aid and remittances) in that it primarily reflects managerial rather than portfolio behavior. Trade and FDI can also be related to one another through *global production networks* (GPNs) and *intra-firm trade*. Intra-firm trade takes place *within* multinational enterprises (MNEs) and accounts for approximately one-third of world trade.[22]

---

[21] The results of Wacziarg and Welch (2008), for example, suggest that openness to trade can increases investment and growth rates by over 1 percent. It is important to note that this overall result occurs within what Wacziarg and Welch describe as "considerable heterogeneity" in their country sample. For example, political instability can break the link between trade and growth.

[22] An introduction to GPNs and intra-firm trade is provided in chapter 10 of Reinert (2012).

As developing countries integrate into the world economy, they typically become increasingly involved with global GPNs and patterns of intra-firm trade. For example, some FDI can generate exports when the MNEs engage in foreign investment to build export capacity abroad.

For a sense of the magnitudes of trade and FDI consider Figure 2.11, which points out a number of important features of both exports and FDI inflows for the developing world:

- First, the exports and FDI inflows of the middle-income countries are much larger than those of the low-income countries.

- Second, exports are substantially higher than FDI inflows for both the middle-income countries and the low-income countries.

- Third, with the exception of investments in extractive industries, low-income countries as a group receive practically no FDI inflows at all.

- Fourth, the exports of the middle-income countries have increased dramatically faster than those of the low-income countries, particularly in recent years.

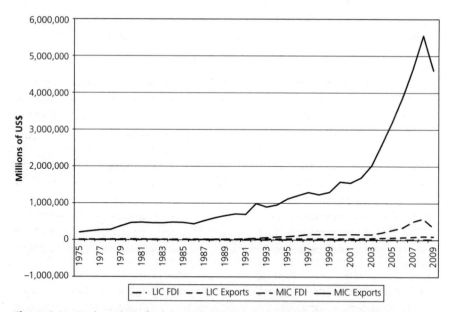

Figure 2.11. Trade and FDI for low- and middle-income countries (millions of current US dollars)

Source: World Development Indicators (http://databank.worldbank.org), 2010.

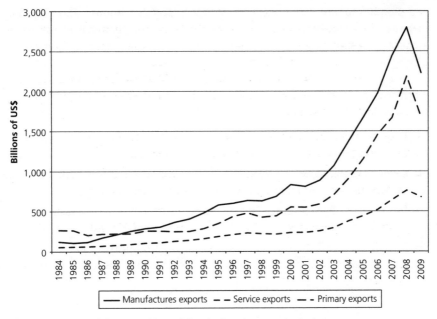

Figure 2.12. Sectoral composition of developing country nominal exports

Source: World Development Indicators (http://databank.worldbank.org), 2010.

The increase of exports from the middle-income countries is one of the recent success stories of the developing world and is not unrelated to the recent improvements in poverty measures discussed above. Because nearly all of sub-Saharan Africa is composed of low-income countries, there is a regional dimension to some of these trends: aside from petroleum and minerals, Africa has largely left out the growth of exports and FDI inflows, although a few African countries (e.g. South Africa) have been able to break this mold and have benefited from rapid growth in both investment and trade.[23]

The sectoral structure of developing world exports is presented in Figure 2.12. This figure differentiates manufactures exports, service exports, and primary exports (defined as a residual). By examining this figure, we learn three things:

- First, manufactured exports from the developing world have increased substantially. Indeed, despite a few temporary downturns (including in 2009), developing country manufactured exports have been steadily increasing since the mid-1980s when they were less than primary exports.

---

[23] For an examination of this, see Johnson, Ostry, and Subramanian (2010).

- Second, increases in primary exports (again defined as a residual) have also been substantial. This includes agriculture, minerals, petroleum, and other residual items.

- Third, despite a common perception of developing countries as being in "pre-service" stages of development, exports of commercial services have also increased substantially, if not as dramatically as the other two categories.

The increases in developing country manufacturing exports and FDI inflows reflect to some degree the increased integration of developing countries into the flexible manufacturing systems of the third stage of modern globalization, including evolving GPNs.[24] An increasing number of developing countries took this first step despite continued protectionism in areas such as textiles, clothing, and food products. Indeed, the increased involvement of some developing countries in GPNs is perhaps the most important characteristic of the third stage of globalization. It increasingly involved trade within narrowly defined sectors (intra-industry trade) and, as mentioned above, trade within multinational firms themselves (intra-firm trade).

There is a tradition in development economics that emphasizes the role of manufacturing in successful development trajectories. From this perspective, the upward trajectory in the manufacturing exports of developing economies is encouraging. However, there is a less well-known concern with the potential of agriculture (one part of primary exports) to contribute positively to development trajectories, and there is some evidence to support this view in the case of East Asia.[25] The expansion of developing country agricultural exports has taken place within a number of constraints. Among these are the bias against agriculture in most developing countries; the protection against developing country agricultural exports in both developed and other developing countries; and the extensive subsidization of agriculture in the developed countries, which undercuts successful agricultural production in the developing world.[26] The constraints on expansion of agricultural exports contribute to the continued stubbornness of rural poverty.

The extractive industries of mining and petroleum that are part of primary exports are a double-edged sword. While export revenues from these sources

---

[24] As described by Ocampo and Martin (2003): "This was the first step toward the development of internationally integrated production systems, in which production can be divided into various stages (a process known as 'the dismemberment of the value chain'). In such systems, the outsourcers in different countries can then specialize in the production of certain components, in particular phases of the production process, or in the assembly of specific models" (p. 4).

[25] See Brown and Goldin (1992), Park and Johnston (1995), Reinert (1998), and Martin and Mitra (2001). From different perspectives, each of these sources treats the agricultural sector as *potentially dynamic*, something that has not always been well appreciated.

[26] On agricultural subsidies in high-income countries, see Peterson (2009).

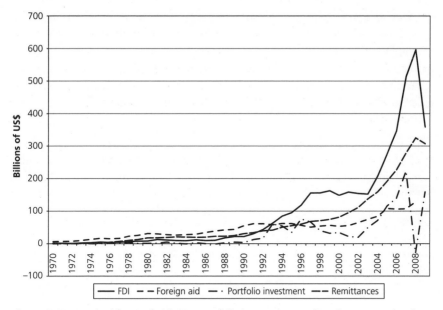

Figure 2.13. Nominal flows of aid, FDI, portfolio investment, and remittances to developing countries

Source: World Development Indicators (http://databank.worldbank.org), 2010.

are welcome, there are notorious problems of corruption in these sectors. Consequently, their development potential is often compromised. In these cases, difficult reforms are a prerequisite for primary exports contributing to development.[27]

Finally, the slow increase in commercial services represents the increased involvement of developing countries in transportation, tourism, and business services. Because the data on provision of these services are imperfectly collected, the actual increase in commercial services over time might be even larger than that illustrated in Figure 2.12. The potential role for service exports to transform economies is even less well appreciated than in the case of agriculture. Recent research suggests that this potential can be significant.[28] In light of this, it is important to recognize the fact that even the low-income countries are active in this area.

[27] See, for example, chapter 9 of Collier (2007).
[28] See Mattoo (2009) and Francois and Hoekman (2010).

2.4 **Capital, aid, and remittance flows**

Capital, aid, and remittance flows are important channels through which poorer countries can gain access to resources from abroad. Each of these activities is identified by international and development economists as an additional way to reduce global poverty, albeit with some disagreement.[29] We consider each of these globalization dimensions to gain a sense of their relative magnitudes.

If we consider recent trends in capital, aid, and remittance flows for developing countries, a number of important characteristics become visible (Figure 2.13). Since the early 1990s, FDI has emerged as the most important foreign resource flow for the developing world as a whole, surpassing foreign aid or *official development assistance* (ODA) by increasing amounts. Despite some volatility in the 2000 to 2003 period, the long-term growth and volume of these flows has been remarkable, inspiring much comment on the possibility of private capital replacing aid. Recent data demonstrates an enormous rise in FDI inflows since 2004, more than tripling to approximately $600

BOX 2.2 VOLATILE WIDGETS IN THE 1990s

Imagine landing on a planet that runs on widgets. You are told that international trade in widgets is highly unpredictable and volatile on this planet, for reasons that are poorly understood. A small number of nations have access to imported widgets, while many others are completely shut out even when they impose no apparent obstacles to trade. With some regularity, those countries that have access to widgets get too much of a good thing, and their markets are flooded with imported widgets. This allows them to go on a widget binge, which makes everyone pretty happy for while. However, such binges are often interrupted by a sudden cut-off in supply, unrelated to any change in circumstances. The turnaround causes the affected economies to experience painful economic adjustments. For reasons equally poorly understood, when one country is hit by a supply cutback in this fashion, many other countries experience similar shocks in quick succession. Some years thereafter, a widget boom starts anew.

Substitute "international capital flows" for "widgets" above and the description fits today's economy quite well. We (went) through a lending boom-and-bust cycle in Asia that is astounding in its magnitude. In 1996, five Asian countries (Indonesia, Malaysia, the Philippines, the Republic of Korea, and Thailand) received net private capital inflows amounting to US$93 billion. One year later (in 1997), they experienced an estimated outflow of US$12.1 billion, a turnaround in a single year of US$105 billion, amounting to more than 10 percent of the combined GDP of these economies.

Source: Rodrik (1998).

---

[29] For the case of capital flows, see Kose et al. (2009).

billion in 2008 and then falling significantly in 2009 in response to the financial crisis. In part, these new flows have been related to the increased manufacturing exports of the developing world, because FDI has been a vehicle for these countries to integrate into GPNs.

Along with FDI, portfolio flows such as equities and bonds began to increase significantly in the 1990s. In contrast to FDI, however, these flows have proved to be volatile, dropping significantly between 1996 and 2002 and again in 2008, having reached a peak of over US$200 billion in 2007. The volatile nature of portfolio flows gives rise to the cautionary approach we take toward portfolio capital in Chapter 4 and is reflected in Box 2.2 on "volatile widgets."[30] Also, as we discuss in Chapter 4, it is important to break up portfolio flows into its component parts to assess it potential development impacts.

In contrast to both FDI and portfolio flows, foreign aid or ODA is a historically recent flow. Aid increased slowly from the 1960s until around 1990. Between 1990 and 2001, aid flows stagnated, and as a share of rich countries incomes or per capita requirements of poor people, declined precipitously: from around 0.32 percent of *gross national income* (GNI) or US$35 per African in 1990, to 0.22 percent of GNI or US$17 per African in 2000. More recently and as evident in Figure 2.13, the downward trend in aid was reversed with a number of countries having committed themselves to doubling their aid budgets by 2010 and with aid flows reaching over US$100 billion. Like other capital flows, aid has been concentrated in a relatively small number of countries, although since the end of the Cold War donors increasingly have directed their aid to countries that are more effective at using the aid and those where most poor people live. The UN Millennium Declaration in 2000 marked the beginning of a renewed push for increased aid and for greater aid effectiveness. Recent years have seen considerable progress toward increasing the impact of aid on the part of both the recipients and donors. As we emphasize in Chapter 5, both the quality and the quantity of aid matter enormously for poor people. Further, the impact of aid is not limited to its monetary value—the associated flow of ideas and capacity building can also play a vital role.

The remittance flows of global migrants have been characterized by a long-term upward trajectory almost as significant as that of FDI. Remittance flows to developing countries increased to over US$300 billion in 2008 and 2009, more important than both aid and portfolio investments to the alleviation of poverty. Remittances are the financial manifestation of the international movement of persons. Their increase reflects the fact that the world's foreign-born population has more than doubled since 1965 and currently stands

---

[30] On the volatility of portfolio capital, see Obstfeld (1998), Eichengreen (1999, 2004), Reinhart and Rogoff (2009), Rodrik and Subramanian (2009), and Goldin and Vogel (2010).

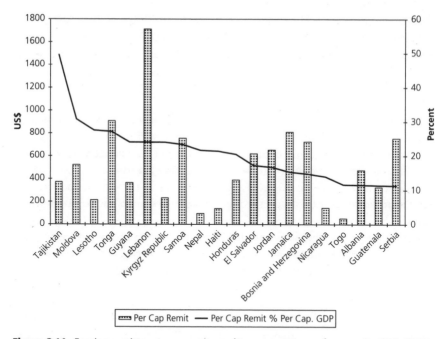

Figure 2.14. Foreign remittances per capita and as a percentage of per capita GDP, 2008

Source: World Development Indicators (http://databank.worldbank.org), 2010.

at approximately 200 million persons or 3 percent of the world's population.[31]

Remittance flows can have significant and positive impacts in developing countries by directly transferring income more efficiently than foreign aid. For example, Woodruff and Zenteno (2007) provided evidence that migrant networks between the United States and Mexico have helped channel remittance flows to microenterprise development in Mexico. Similar efforts have taken place in El Salvador. There is also evidence that remittances can act as a risk management strategy for poor households in developing countries through income source diversification and can contribute to human capital investments in some cases, offsetting to some extent brain drain effects. Further, Dadush and Falcau (2009) noted that "the availability of foreign exchange through remittances increases the food security of drought prone countries and enables countries to import medicines and other technologies."[32] We address these potentially significant effects further in Chapter 6.

The country-specific nature of remittances can be appreciated from Figure 2.14. This figure plots two measures of remittances. Data on 2008 per

---

[31] For a concise review, see Pozo (2009).
[32] Dadush and Falcau (2009), p. 2.

capita remittances in US dollars is measured on the left-hand side axis and indicated with vertical bars. The countries are ranked by per capita remittances as a percentage of per capita GDP, which is measured on the right-hand side axis and indicated with a line. Remittances can be significant from both perspectives. For example, per capita remittances are over US$600 in Tonga, Lebanon, Samoa, El Salvador, Jordan, Jamaica, Bosnia, and Serbia. Per capita remittances as a percentage of per capita GDP in this figure range from approximately 50 percent to 11 percent. This figure indicates that the money sent home by migrants from these countries is a significant source of income compared with domestic production, so it can have a significant impact on poverty.

Finally, each of the above flows (FDI, portfolio investment, foreign aid or ODA, and remittances) is of a lesser order of magnitude than trade (see also Figure 2.11). That does not make these flows unimportant; it makes the trade aspect of globalization especially important. Additionally, as we will discuss in subsequent chapters, leveraging capital and aid flows in creative ways for effective poverty alleviation becomes crucial given their lower orders of magnitude.

2.5 **Ideas**

Ideas are the generation and transmission of distinctive intellectual constructs in any field that can affect production systems, organizational and management practices, governance practices, legal norms, and technological trends.[33] By their very nature, it is difficult to accurately compare idea flows to the other kinds of flows considered here. Given our concern with poverty, perhaps the most important set of ideas connected to globalization is what Meier (2001) called "ideas for development." Meier noted that "ideas are fundamental to the future progress of development."[34] Idea formation and reformation have been and continue to be integral to development processes and policies since, as emphasized by Adelman (2001), development processes are significantly nonlinear and non-unique. Consequently, ideas play a key role in organizing and making sense of development experience and have gone through a number of paradigm shifts.

Despite these paradigm shifts, if one looks hard enough, there is an apparent middle ground among past ideological divisions in development thinking. For example, there is now a better appreciation than in the past of the roles of institutions, history, the public sector, and human welfare in development processes. One recent idea in this realm is that of *global public goods*, described

---

[33] See Goldin and Reinert (2010), for example.
[34] Meier (2001), p. 1.

in Box 2.3. This emerging middle ground does not offer any simple, one-size-fits-all prescriptions. In some ways, we have arrived at a stage in which "we know that we do not know" (Hoff and Stiglitz 2001), but there is no small measure of ironic comfort in this. As has been emphasized in Rodrik (2007), there is now intellectual room for multiple, successful routes to development that involve large measures of local learning and experimentation.

Another important idea relevant to reducing deprivations is that of *human rights*, which has influenced governance practices and legal norms in significant ways. This idea, which is coincident with the second and third stages of modern globalization, is a positive example of what Ocampo and Martin (2003) called the "globalization of values." With its roots in the Universal Declaration of Human Rights (adopted in 1948), it is perhaps the International Covenant on Civil and Political Rights (adopted in 1966) that has been the most influential. This covenant prohibited torture, slavery, forced labor, and arbitrary arrest. The notion of human rights has been essential in promoting the place of human security (as opposed to national security) as a modern concept.[35] Human rights are also relevant to issues of global

---

BOX 2.3 THE IDEA OF GLOBAL PUBLIC GOODS

One recent idea in international economic policy that is relevant to our investigation of globalization is that of global public goods. A public good is a desired object that has some particular features setting it apart from private goods. First, its consumption is "nonrival" in that more than one person can consume it at the same time. Second, its benefits are "non-excludable" in that people cannot be easily prevented from claiming them. For example, road safety is a well-known local public good, evident from the fact that we do not privately purchase traffic lights.

A global public good is a public good with benefits that accrue more or less globally, benefiting persons in most countries. Examples include the multilateral trading system, international peacekeeping, disarmament agreements, disease eradication, and measures to prevent global warming. As noted by Kaul, Grunberg, and Stern (1999), the "concept of global public goods is crucial to effective public policy under conditions of increasing economic openness and interdependence among countries" (p. 9).

Because the benefits of global public goods are spread around the world, no single nation has the incentive to provide them. Unlike local public goods, the absence of a global government leads to their under provision. Consequently, international cooperation is crucial. As these authors remark, "In today's rapidly globalizing world, peoples' well-being depends on striking a careful balance not only between private and public goods but also between domestic, regional and global public goods" (p. 16). Achieving the cooperation among countries to provide global public goods is a significant and ongoing challenge.

Source: Kaul, Grunberg, and Stern (1999).

---

[35] See, for example, Axworthy (2001). He noted, "The international discourse on human security is beginning to effect change on the institutions and practice of global governance... Globalization has made individual human suffering an irrevocable universal concern" (p. 20).

poverty in its focus on shortfalls in basic needs.[36] As stressed by Ruggie (2008), extending human rights into the realm of foreign direct investment is an important and ongoing project.

The flow of ideas can be closely related to other dimensions of globalization. For example, behind trade, finance, aid, and migration there can be important relationships that assist in learning, and in the transmitting and adapting ideas. As will be discussed at various junctures in the chapters that follow, long-term poverty alleviation involves learning of various kinds. For example, learning is involved in the positive transmission of technological change from exporting and FDI inflows. Without the learning relationships for transmitting ideas, these technological changes cannot easily take place. In the case of aid, for example, Pomerantz (2004) emphasizes that "the quality of the relationship may, in fact, be more important in influencing policy directions and ensuring successful outcomes, than the money itself."[37] This can sometimes be true for other dimensions of globalization as well.

Ideas can be imagined as a current flowing through channels created by trade, capital flows, aid, and migration. However, it is not easy to accurately measure idea flows as we do the other globalization flows considered here. Instead, we can assess the *capacity* for global idea flows. As we will see in Chapter 7, one measure of capacity is telecommunications connectedness (depicted in Figure 7.1). Whether measured in terms of telephone landlines, mobile phones, or internet usage, the low-income countries of the world are at a significant disadvantage compared with the middle-income countries, and at even more of a disadvantage compared with the high-income countries. For example, mobile phone usage in the low-income countries is less than half of that of the middle-income countries, albeit increasing in many instances. This lack of connectedness reflects a lack of infrastructure available to poor people that would enable them to share in the global exchange of ideas, methods, and technology.[38]

2.6 **The global commons**

As we welcome the projected 2 billion new global citizens between now and 2050 (the equivalent of two new Indias), it will become increasingly clear that a positive relationship between globalization and development depends on the effective

---

[36] See, for example, Pogge (1999) and Reinert (2011).

[37] Pomerantz (2004), p. 8.

[38] For example, the World Bank's *World Development Indicators* estimated a 2002 waiting list for telephone mainlines of over 4.5 million persons in the low-income countries, reflecting an unfilled demand for these services.

management of the *global commons*. By global commons, we mean fragile global resources that are important to large numbers of countries. The issue of global commons management is not necessarily or primarily economic, although the financial crisis demonstrated the extent to which global management of economic systems is vital and how the existing institutional framework is unfit for this purpose. Important emerging global commons issues include climate change, fisheries, water resources, food security, pandemic threats, biodiversity, and human security. Each poses a difficult public policy problem in its own right.

A first best approach to managing global commons issues is via multilateral agreements. These are not easy to reach, but successes in the area of multilateral environmental agreements (MEAs) suggest that difficulties can indeed be overcome.[39] As emphasized by Buchan et al. (2009), this is an issue of *global cooperation* in which "parochialism interacts with globalization."[40] If we are to overcome parochialism to achieve global cooperation, it is necessary that the threats of non-cooperation be made explicit, that any significant economic losses inherent in cooperation be addressed, and that successful models in one area (e.g. trade or the environment) be used in other areas.

In the area of climate change, for example, Schelling (2009) rightly pointed out that the developing world is likely to experience the most significant potential damage. Addressing this potential damage will require some form of international cooperation to both protect vulnerable people and help to restructure the emerging energy systems in the developing world itself. It is likely that solving emerging food security issues will be contingent on international cooperation on climate change, as well as reinvigorating the Consultative Group on International Agricultural Research (CGIAR), ignored for too long under the assumption that the food security issue had been "solved."

With regard to pandemic threats, the oft-forgotten case of the "Great Influenza" of 1918 stands as a cautionary tale. A similar outbreak in the modern era could result in the deaths of hundreds of millions, a health deprivation on a vast scale.[41] Responding to such a threat relies on the work of the World Health Organization with the budget of only that of a single, modern university hospital. This is insufficient preparation.

The global commons agenda is admittedly huge and perhaps overwhelming. The daunting nature of the task cannot be an excuse for inaction, however. If it is, history will not look kindly on the current generation.

---

[39] Some existing MEAs include the Convention on International Trade in Endangered Species (CITES), the Montreal Protocol on Substances that Deplete the Ozone Layer (Montreal Protocol), and the Convention of Biological Diversity (CBD). There are many others.

[40] Buchan et al. (2009), p. 4138.

[41] For such an assessment, as well as a medical history of the Great Influenza, see Barry (2005).

2.7 **Summary**

What do we learn from the information presented in this chapter? First and most important, global poverty is a widespread phenomenon (even in its extreme form) that has finally shown some recent trend toward leveling off and even declining somewhat. Second, a ranking of the various dimensions of globalization in terms of US dollar value flow volumes appears to be trade, foreign direct investment, remittances (reflecting migration), other capital flows, and aid. Third, the impact of globalization as measured through our economic dimensions are highly uneven—the low-income countries are much less involved in trade and FDI activities, for example, than middle-income countries. Fourth, ideas permeate all the other globalization activities, supporting to greater and lesser degrees crucial learning processes that are important to long run poverty reduction. In fact, poverty is, to an important extent, a poverty of learning, and any improvement in the way globalization benefits poor people will involve supporting poor peoples' learning in multiple realms. Finally, addressing a host of issues related to the global commons is an important prerequisite to leverage globalization for development.

We will begin to examine in detail each of our globalization dimensions and their links to global poverty in Chapters 3 through 7. These examinations, along with that of this and the previous chapter, will lead us to a set of policy recommendations we present in Chapter 8. This last chapter recognizes that global poverty in all its dimensions requires adequate policy responses from national and world communities.

Annex: Low- and middle-income countries, 2010

Table 2.1 Low-income countries (US$995 per capita or less)

Afghanistan	Guinea	Nepal
Bangladesh	Guinea-Bisau	Niger
Benin	Haiti	Rwanda
Burkina Faso	Kenya	Sierra Leone
Burundi	Korea, Dem. Rep.	Solomon Islands
Cambodia	Kyrgyz Republic	Somalia
Central African Rep.	Lao PDR	Tajikistan
Chad	Liberia	Tanzania
Comoros	Madagascar	Togo
Congo, Dem. Rep.	Malawi	Uganda
Eritrea	Mali	Zambia
Ethiopia	Mauritania	Zimbabwe
Gambia, The	Mozambique	
Ghana	Myanmar	

Source: World Bank, World Development Indicators (http://databank.worldbank.org).

Table 2.2 Lower middle-income countries (US$996 to 3,945 per capita)

Angola	India	São Tomé and Principe
Armenia	Iraq	Senegal
Belize	Jordan	Sri Lanka
Bhutan	Kiribati	Sudan
Bolivia	Kosovo	Swaziland
Cameroon	Lesotho	Syrian Arab Rep.
Cape Verde	Maldives	Thailand
China	Marshall Islands	Timor-Leste
Congo, Rep.	Micronesia, Fed. Sts.	Tonga
Côte d'Ivoire	Moldova	Tunisia
Djibouti	Mongolia	Turkmenistan
Ecuador	Morocco	Tuvalu
Egypt, Arab Rep.	Nicaragua	Ukraine
El Salvador	Nigeria	Uzbekistan
Georgia	Pakistan	Vanuatu
Guatemala	Papua New Guinea	Vietnam
Guyana	Paraguay	West Bank and Gaza
Honduras	Philippines	Yemen, Rep.
Indonesia	Samoa	

Source: World Bank, World Development Indicators (http://databank.worldbank.org).

Table 2.3 Upper middle-income countries (US$3,946 to 12,195 per capita)

Albania	Dominican Rep.	Namibia
Algeria	Fiji	Palau
American Samoa	Gabon	Panama
Antigua and Barbuda	Grenada	Peru
Argentina	Iran, Islamic Rep.	Romania
Azerbaijan	Jamaica	Russian Federation
Belarus	Kazakhstan	Serbia
Bosnia and Herzegovina	Lebanon	Seychelles
Botswana	Libya	South Africa
Brazil	Lithuania	St. Kitts and Nevis
Bulgaria	Macedonia, FYR	St. Lucia
Chile	Malaysia	St. Vincent and the Grenadines
Colombia	Mauritius	Suriname
Costa Rica	Mayotte	Turkey
Cuba	Mexico	Uruguay
Dominica	Montenegro	Venezuela, RB

Source: World Bank, World Development Indicators (http://databank.worldbank.org).

3   **Trade**

International trade is potentially a powerful force for poverty reduction. Trade can contribute to poverty alleviation by expanding markets, creating jobs, promoting competition, raising productivity, and providing new ideas and technologies. Each of these has the *potential* for increasing the real incomes of poor people. We emphasize the word "potential" here because the link between trade and poverty alleviation is *not automatic*. Indeed, as the recent histories of a number of developing countries demonstrate, it would be a mistake to rely on trade liberalization alone to reduce poverty. A more comprehensive approach is needed, one that addresses multiple economic and social challenges simultaneously and that emphasizes the expansion of poor people's capabilities, especially in the areas of health and education. Such an approach also needs to address the institutional climate, infrastructure, and other barriers that can prevent potential importers and exporters from benefiting from the opportunities afforded by more open markets.

As we emphasize below, improving market access for developing countries is a central priority embedded in the current Doha Round of multilateral trade negotiations. Improving market access would yield benefits that far exceed those of additional aid or debt relief. However, additional aid to enhance trade opportunities (aid for trade or trade-related capacity building) is a vital complement necessary to ensure that low- and middle-income countries can take advantage of increased access to markets. Increased market access and trade-related capacity building must work together for trade to play a positive role in development.

3.1 **International trade and poverty**

As has been long recognized by international economists, international trade is a means of expanding markets, and *market expansion* can generate employment and incomes for poor people. In many discussions of globalization, comparisons have been made between the wages of workers in poor country export industries and the wages of workers in developed countries. In these comparisons, the wages of workers in developing countries' export industries often appear to be very low. Consequently, globalization has often been identified as worsening poverty. However, a comparison between what poor people earn before and after trade opportunities become available is more relevant. From a poverty perspective, a relevant comparison is between the wages of export sector workers and agricultural day laborers, both in the same developing country. Often the alternative of agricultural day labor is much worse than the work of an export sector worker. It is precisely this type of income comparison that draws workers into export industries.[1]

It must also be kept in mind that not all export activity is equal from the point of view of raising the incomes of poor people. The export sector can best help to alleviate poverty when it supports labor-intensive production, human capital accumulation (both education and health), and technological learning. These characteristics were often present in the successful East Asian export expansions of recent decades. Their absence in other countries' export expansions helps to explain why these expansions have not always helped poor people. In addition, the incomes of poor individuals depend on buoyant and sustainable export incomes, which in turn depend on export prices and the degree of export diversification. Export activity with declining or volatile export prices in a narrow range of goods and services does not lend itself to sustained poverty alleviation.[2]

International trade is also a means of *promoting competition,* and in many instances, this can help poor people. Increased competition lowers the real costs of both consumption and production. For example, domestic monopolies charge monopoly prices that can be significantly higher than competitive prices. The competition introduced by imports erodes the market power of such firms. These "pro-competitive effects" of trade can make tight household budgets go farther and lower the costs of production. Lower production costs can have knock on employment effects advantageous to poor individuals by lowering non-wage costs in labor-intensive production activities. Pro-competitive effects can also arise in the case of monopsony (single buyer) power. In this case, sellers (small farmers, for example) to the previously monopsonistic buyer are able to obtain higher prices for their goods as the buying power of the single buyer is eroded.

For export activities to support poverty alleviation in a sustained manner, it helps if those activities lend themselves to technological upgrading and associated learning processes. There is some evidence that international trade can *promote productivity* in a country, and it is possible that productivity increases can in turn support the incomes of poor people. For example, the export process can place the exporting firms in direct contact with discerning

---

[1] To make this observation is not to downplay the exploitation that can often occur in export sectors, such as 14-hour days. Labor standards do matter. But it is decidedly *not* the case that exploitation is absent from agricultural day labor. We will discuss these issues in more detail below, especially health and safety concerns.

[2] See for example, Brenton et al. (2009).

international customers, thus facilitating upgrading processes. These process-es are not automatic, however. It is not the case that exports *of all types* or *in all countries* generate positive productivity effects, but there is evidence that this is the case in certain important instances. While there is no consensus among international economists on the extent of these upgrading effects, they nonetheless remain an important possibility.

Productivity increases can occur because of imports as well as exports. In this case, the process is typically related to the imports of new machinery that embody more advanced technologies than older machinery. Again the issue arises as to the extent to which this upgrading supports the incomes of poor people. For example, as developing countries liberalize their trading regimes, firms can import more physical capital (machines) to remain competitive. Embodied in these machines is a newer technology level that demands relatively more *skilled workers* than the old technology. Consequently, as trade is liberalized, the unskilled workers lose in terms of relative wages, while workers who are more highly skilled gain. Because poor people are almost always unskilled, these particular changes work against them.[3] As discussed by de Ferranti et al. (2002) in the context of Latin America, this is one of a number of reasons why skills upgrading is crucial for trade to have a positive impact on poverty.

For positive effects of trade to occur, developing countries need access to foreign markets. Unfortunately, for decades, the high-income countries of the world have maintained their greatest protective measures in exactly the same markets that are most important for the developing world: agriculture, food processing, and labor-intensive manufactures. In addition, there is substantial evidence of what trade economists call *tariff escalation*, where high-income countries increase the level of protection with the degree of processing of a product, preventing diversification along *value chains* that is so important to development processes.[4] In many cases, lack of market access hurts poor individuals both directly by reducing employment opportunities and indi-rectly by contributing to unstable export prices.[5]

International trade can have direct health and safety effects on poor individuals, which can be beneficial or detrimental. Improving the health

---

[3] See Cragg and Epelbaum (1996), Robbins and Gindling (1999), Gindling and Robbins (2001), chapter 5 of de Ferranti et al. (2002), and Edwards (2004). More generally, Winters, McCulloch, and McKay (2004) noted that "trade liberalization may be accompanied by skill biased technical change, which can mean the skilled labor may benefit relative to unskilled labor" (p. 75).

[4] A *value chain* is a series of value added processes involved in the production of a good or service. When value chains are linked across countries, they are known as *global production networks* or GPNs. See Chapter 10 of Reinert (2012).

[5] To be fair, there are also market access issues *among* developing countries that are becoming increasingly important as what international economists call "South–South trade" increases. See, for example, Hertel and Ivanic (2006).

outcomes of poor people usually involves imports of medicines and medical products. It is simply not possible for small developing countries to produce the entire range of even some of the more basic medical supplies, much less more advanced medical equipment and pharmaceuticals. However, it is also the case that many developing counties import (legally or illegally) large amounts of weaponry and export sexual services, both of which can have dramatically negative outcomes for the health and safety of poor individuals. In addition, the production processes of some export industries can adversely affect the health of workers in those industries, and a small but important amount of trade involves hazardous waste dumping.

Before we begin our analysis of the relationship between trade and poverty alleviation, let's recall a few relevant characteristics of developing country trade from Chapter 2. First, total trade flows (for example, total exports) of developing countries are substantially larger than inflows of FDI, portfolio investment, and foreign aid receipts. Even the largest of these (FDI) is only approximately one-fifth the size of exports. Trade is therefore of utmost importance for developing countries as a whole. Second, for low-income countries, we need to modify this first statement somewhat: aid sometimes reaches the value of a third of their exports. Relative to exports, aid is more important than FDI for these poorer countries. Third, manufactured exports are increasingly important for developing countries, both low- and middle-income, although primary exports are more important for low-income countries than for middle-income ones. Fourth, service exports are increasingly important for all developing countries.[6] These are a few important characteristics of trade that we will keep in mind as we investigate its role in global poverty alleviation.

3.2 Market expansion

It is possible for trade in the form of exports to help poor people by expanding markets. This possibility is illustrated in evidence presented by Dasgupta et al. (2007) who noted that "in a number of countries that successfully integrated into global markets, export-led growth has eventually brought large employment dividends."[7] Because these processes are not automatic, however, there are a number of factors that must be aligned to facilitate the connections from increases in exports, to increased employment and finally to reductions in poverty.[8]

---

[6] See, for example, Mattoo (2009).

[7] Dasgupta et al. (2007), p. 330.

[8] See both Dasgupta et al. (2007) and Brenton et al. (2009). Hallaert and Munro (2009) stated: "The ability of poor women and men to participate in the gains from trade depends on several factors,

In discussions of the more high-tech aspects of globalization, it is often forgotten that 70 percent of the world's extremely poor individuals reside in rural areas. For this reason, poverty alleviation cannot ignore rural development, and the potential role that trade can play in poverty alleviation depends in large measure on the possibility of supporting rural incomes, either through farm or nonfarm activities. One such example can be found in Vietnam's rice sector.

3.2.1 VIETNAM'S RICE SECTOR

The support of rural areas via trade expansion has occurred in the case of Vietnam. As a result of a package of reforms initiated in the late 1980s that included gradual trade liberalization, Vietnam turned from a rice importer to a rice exporter despite the role of this crop as the country's main staple food. Vietnam is now one of the largest rice exporters in the world. This trade-based market expansion in Vietnam supported household incomes because of the widespread participation of small farms in Vietnam's rice sector. Indeed, rice is grown by two-thirds of Vietnam's households. Rice exports increased the incomes of these small farms and, because rice production is labor intensive in Vietnam, increased demand for rural labor.[9] Thus, Vietnam's rice exports have indeed supported rural incomes, helped to alleviate poverty, and even improved nutrition and reduced child labor.[10] The key here is the involvement of labor-intensive, smallholder farmers. Where export expansion supports large-scale, capital-intensive agriculture and where land ownership is highly concentrated, these poverty alleviation effects are weaker.

Empirical evidence of the link between export expansion and poverty reduction in Vietnam was provided by Heo and Doanh (2009). These authors noted that "trade liberalization in Vietnam has arguably made a vital contribution to the outstanding performance of the economy in recent decades."[11] They explicitly attribute this to the labor-intensive nature of Vietnam's exports, including rice, coffee, and light manufacturing. The analysis of

---

including: i) how much of the trade induced growth occurs in sectors where a large number of the poor are economically active; ii) how much of that growth translates into job creation and wage increase; iii) how much growth trickles down to other sectors that can absorb excess labor; and, iv) how well the poor are equipped (in terms of human, economic and financial assets) to take advantage of the new job opportunities resulting from trade" (p. 14).

[9] Minot and Goletti (2000) reported that "Rice production in Vietnam is characterized by small irrigated farms, multiple cropping, labor intensive practices, and growing use of inorganic fertilizer, though there are substantial regional differences" (p. xi).

[10] See Jenkins (2004). On the impact on child labor, see Edmonds and Pavcnik (2005).

[11] Heo and Doanh (2009), p. 942. They reported high-growth elasticities of poverty, indicating pro-poor growth.

Klump (2007) supported the same conclusions but emphasized the important role of land reform (de-collectivization) as an important initial condition.

Finally, it is important to note that Vietnam's trade liberalization has not been orthodox. For example, it has employed an export quota (maximum exports) to ensure that domestic rice prices do not rise too much to the detriment of consumption. This has been important for the rural poor for whom the bulk of caloric intake is from rice. Similarly, Vietnam was careful to promote human capital accumulation in both education and health forms. As always, the successful leveraging of trade for poverty reduction took place in a broader supportive environment.

3.2.2 BANGLADESH'S CLOTHING INDUSTRY

Although rural incomes are most often central to large scale poverty allevia-tion, supporting the goal of poverty alleviation is not confined to agriculture. Indeed, labor-intensive manufacturing has been an important part of poverty alleviating trade expansions in much of the developing world. This was the case in the famed export expansion of East Asian countries and Mauritius, but it has also been seen in more recent cases such as Bangladesh's clothing exports. The Bangladeshi clothing sector has emerged as a multi-billion US dollar export earner accounting for approximately two-thirds of the country's total exports. There are more than 2 million Bangladeshis working in approx-imately 4000 firms. As it has turned out, the clothing sector has contributed significantly to poverty reduction through labor-intensive production.[12]

Although it is true that the wages in the Bangladesh garment sector are appallingly low, they are increasing over time and consequently have provided an opportunity to leave worse conditions in rural and urban poverty.[13] To be blunt, it has been a difference between poverty and *extreme* poverty. Indeed, using survey data, Zohir (2001), Kabeer (2004), and Kabeer and Mahmud (2004) provided evidence that work in the garment sector has had a number of beneficial effects on women workers in Bangladesh. These include first-time access to cash income, support of families in rural areas through remittances, support of siblings' education, and increased household status.

---

[12] For a review of the emergence of the Bangladeshi clothing sector, see Haider (2007). Oxfam's (2002) description of this sector illustrated the point that wage comparisons in this sector must be relevant to the workers themselves to be truly useful: "Most of the (clothing) workforce consists of young women, many of whom have migrated from desperately poor rural areas. The wages earned by these women are exceptionally low by international standards, and barely above the national poverty line. Yet their daily wage rates are around twice as high as those paid for agricultural labourers, and higher than could be earned on construction sites. Employment conditions in the export zones are scandalously poor, with women denied even the most basic rights. Yet for most women working in the garments sector, their employment offers a higher quality of life than might otherwise be possible" (p. 56).

[13] Haider (2007) reports wages more than doubling from US$0.16 per hour in 1993 to US$0.39 in 2002.

Similar evidence of the way exports can support women's incomes was provided by Nordas (2003), who concluded that export industries in Mauritius, Mexico, Peru, the Philippines, and Sri Lanka are more likely to employ women than men and that they also tend to increase women's wages relative to men's.

Having established a successful and poverty alleviating export sector, Bangladesh is in a position to now consider responding to concerns about working conditions within the sector. Zohir (2001) had raised concerns about the effect of garment sector work on women's health and the increased risk of harassment. Haider (2007) went further and suggested that working conditions are beginning to impede the competiveness of the sector given increasing use of compliance codes by international buyers. He noted that, despite successfully addressing the child labor issue, "informal recruitment, low literacy levels, wage discrimination, irregular payment and short contracts of service are very common practices."[14] Addressing these work condition issues is the next step for poverty alleviating exports in Bangladesh.

Clothing sector exports in Bangladesh thus stand as an important example of the potential poverty alleviating effects of trade. But, as emphasized by Sen, Mujeri, and Shahabuddin (2007), it must be recognized that this success took place in a larger environment of significant improvements in human development indicators (in both health and education) and certain pockets of institutional improvement. It was also accompanied by increases in inequality that will require continued scrutiny.

3.2.3 TRADE LIBERALIZATION AND POVERTY

Along with the possibility of labor-intensive export expansions contributing to poverty alleviation, there is also the possibility of trade *liberalization* (the removal of quotas and reduction of tariffs) worsening poverty.[15] There are many technical issues that vex the analysis of the links between trade liberalization and poverty, including properties of household surveys (rural vs. urban) and the measurement of import barrier declines.[16] In principle, trade liberalization can affect poor people both by changing prices of consumption goods (expenditure side effects) and changing labor market conditions (earnings side effects). Evidence seems to suggest that earnings side effects are more important (e.g. Porto, 2006) but that these could both harm or benefit the poor depending on the initial patterns of protection.

---

[14] Haider (2007), p. 16.

[15] Goldberg and Pavcnik (2004) noted that "while the literature on trade and inequality is voluminous, there is virtually no work to date on the relationship between trade liberalization and poverty" (p. 231).

[16] See, for example, Hertel and Reimer (2005).

Therefore, there does not seem to be an overall pattern of trade liberalization worsening or ameliorating initial poverty levels. Rather, the effects of trade liberalization on poverty need to be analyzed on a case-by-case basis.[17]

3.3 **Competition**

International economists have begun to understand the ways that international trade can promote competition in developing countries. In many instances, increased competition can help poor people by lowering the real costs of household consumption and production. As mentioned above, a domestic firm with market power can raise prices above competitive levels, and import competition can erode this market power. Pro-competitive effects can also occur in the case of monopsony (single buyer) power. What trade economists call the "pro-competitive effects of trade" has the potential to help the poor in some instances.[18]

For some time, pro-competitive effects of trade were somewhat of a theoretical curiosity. But there has been accumulating evidence that they do exist, including in developing countries. This evidence comes from the examination of price cost or profit margins of firms in countries where trade liberalization has taken place. In the case of India, for example, Kambhampati and Parikh (2003) and Goldar and Aggarwal (2005) have found that the trade liberalization experience has indeed resulted in reduced margins of domestic firms. The same appears to have been the case in Mexico as examined by Grether (1997). These results are important because they suggest that poor people had to pay less for products in these cases.

3.3.1 GRAMEEN PHONE

An interesting example of pro-competitive effects that intersects with technological issues is the Grameen Bank's Village Phone Program. This program demonstrates how imported technologies, when introduced in the context of a well thought out and targeted policy framework, can make a dramatic

---

[17] In a review of this issue, Goldberg and Pavcnik (2004) concluded: "most of the existing evidence on the link between trade policy and poverty has focused on how trade policy affects household poverty through labor market outcomes. The existing work has not provided a *clear* message as to whether trade liberalization has contributed to phenomena that are typically associated with a higher probability of poverty, such as unemployment, informal employment, unskilled labor wages, and child labor. A direct connection to an increase—or reduction—in poverty is naturally even more tenuous" (p. 257).

[18] On the pro-competitive effects of trade, see Markusen (1981).

difference in the lives of the poor people. Before this program, Bangladesh had one of the lowest telephone penetration rates in the world: only 1.5 percent of households had access to a telephone. Although the lack of a functioning telecommunications service posed serious frustrations for all Bangladeshis, it was particularly costly for the country's farmers and local producers. For these individuals, the lack of telecommunication service imposed serious costs by denying them critical access to the price information necessary to make efficient production decisions and to negotiate with middlemen and marketers on a fair basis.

In 1997, the Grameen Bank, Bangladesh's renowned village-based micro-credit organization, launched the Village Phone Program. The program provided select female members of Grameen Bank's peer-based microcredit networks with loans of taka 12,000 (US$200) to purchase an imported cellular handset, solar recharger, and mobile service subscription. The women were then trained on the use and marketing of mobile phone technology, enabling them to earn money while helping their fellow villagers gain access to information at a fraction of what it had previously cost them.

Recent estimates suggest that there are now over 200,000 "phone ladies" taking part in this program, each earning more than three times the average per capita income of Bangladesh.[19] Grameen Phone provides 50 million people living in remote rural areas with access to telecommunications facilities. The advent of village phones has dramatically improved the profitability of small farmers, helping to facilitate the regular delivery of inputs at low cost, reducing the risk of new diseases infecting poultry or livestock, and offering assistance in averting the adverse effects of natural calamities. Thus, the combination of imported technology with an anti-poverty policy framework has improved competition in a manner that has been quite beneficial for poor individuals. By vesting control of this new technology in the hands of poor female villagers, the Grameen Bank program represented a dramatic change in economic tradition for Bangladesh, where local elites had ordinarily introduced new innovations and reaped large profits as a consequence.

Under certain circumstances, then, poor people can take advantage of increased competition that can result from international trade. Assessing such effects is an emerging area of inquiry. Nevertheless, we are convinced that such effects matter for poor people. It also must be recognized, however, that there are circumstances where certain kinds of liberalization that accompany trade liberalization episodes can actually be anti-competitive (for example, some kinds of privatization where new monopolies are created) and hurt the poor. It is necessary to keep an eye on competitiveness issues to fully assess the impact of trade on poverty.

---

[19] See Simanis and Hart (2006) and Lehr (2008).

3.4 **Productivity**

There is an insight from the field of the microeconomics of labor markets that has important implications for poverty alleviation. This insight is that long-term increases in real (price adjusted) wages require long-term increases in productivity. As noted by UNCTAD (2004), "sustained poverty reduction occurs through the efficient development and utilization of productive capacities in a manner in which the working age population becomes more and more fully *and productively* employed."[20] There is some evidence that international trade can promote productivity, and that productivity increases can in turn support the incomes of poor people. The link between trade and productivity improvements is a *potential* one and is not automatic. It can be related to both imports and exports.[21]

On the import side, trade allows countries to import ideas and capital goods (such as machinery) embodying the new technologies that make productivity increases possible. New technologies, however, require a learning process both to master them and to adapt them to local conditions. As described by Rodrigo (2001), "Learning takes place when unit variable cost in production declines with cumulative output as workers, supervisors and managers build up skills around a specific production process."[22] Without learning, technological improvements are usually impossible.

On the export side, foreign market access supports the learning process. Again, as described by Rodrigo (2001), "By opening up a channel to the world market, trade...serves to promote specialization and sustain production tempos of goods in which learning effects are embodied; if constrained by domestic market size alone along with associated domestic business cycle uncertainty of demand, firms would be less willing to make the investments needed to capture gains from learning."[23] Thus, openness to trade, both import and export, can support technological upgrading via learning.[24] Evidence of learning from exporting, for example, was provided by Bigsten et al. (2004) for four African countries and Hossain and Karunaratne (2004) for Bangladesh.[25] For this process to occur, trade needs to support human capital accumulation upon which learning depends.

---

[20] UNCTAD (2004), p. 90 (emphasis added).

[21] For a review of the evidence on trade liberalization and productivity, see Winters, McCulloch, and McKay (2004).

[22] Rodrigo (2001), p. 88.

[23] Ibid., p. 90.

[24] As emphasized by Bruton (1998), "For the development objective, the main role of exports is its possible contribution to the acquisition of new technical knowledge and consequent increase in productivity through contact with foreign importers combined with the pressures of strong competition" (p. 924). The same can be said of imports.

[25] Importantly, Bigsten et al. (2004) distinguished between the efficiency gains from exporting and the self-selecting of efficient firms into exporting. The four African countries were Cameroon, Ghana, Kenya, and Zimbabwe.

3.4.1 THE IMPORTANCE OF LEARNING

Productivity increases can occur in agriculture, manufacturing, and services. They are not, as often supposed, limited to manufacturing alone.[26] As discussed in Chapter 2, trade in agriculture, manufacturing, and services are all important for the low- and middle-income countries of the world, and trade-induced learning processes can operate across all three of these sectors in the developing world. Evidence on learning and technological upgrading is more readily available for the manufacturing sector, so it is worth considering this sector as an example of the way that trade-induced learning can support real incomes over the long term. However, there is emerging evidence that productivity increases in services are necessary for the export success of the agricultural and manufacturing sectors.[27]

In the realm of manufacturing, the importance of learning was reflected in the observation of Lall and Teubal (1998) that, for developing countries, mastering existing technologies is more important than innovating new technologies. The learning process in manufacturing is characterized by these authors as "constant, intensive and purposive" and requires the external support of education and training that is technology-specific. This indicates that complementary education policies of the public sector are important for trade-supported productivity gains. Trade alone is not sufficient. One example of this is the initiative of the Costa Rican government to supply schools with computer technologies in support of a hoped for emergence of an export-oriented computer products sector. This effort proved to be successful.

The empirical evidence on the manufacturing sector suggests that successful learning is not as widespread as one would hope. Note the evidence presented in Figure 3.1. This figure considers the sophistication of manufactured exports for a set of low- and middle-income countries for the year 2008. The evidence presented here suggests that high-technology manufactured exports (HTME) are quite concentrated in the developing world. Very few countries have HTME exports that exceed one-fifth of their total manufacturing exports. As emphasized some time ago by Lall (1998):

The nature of learning varies greatly by country, depending on initial capabilities, the efficacy of markets and institutions, and the policies undertaken to improve them. Some countries lack the skill and technical base to engage in modern manufactured exports, except for the simplest ones (low quality garments or toys) where foreign

---

[26] On the presence of productivity increases in agriculture, see Martin and Mitra (2001). On the role of services in supporting productivity increases in manufacturing, see Francois and Reinert (1996) and Francois and Woerz (2008).

[27] See Brenton et al. (2009). These authors note that "firms that have to pay more than their competitors for energy, telecommunications, transport and logistics, finance, and security will find it hard to compete in domestic and overseas markets" (p. 27).

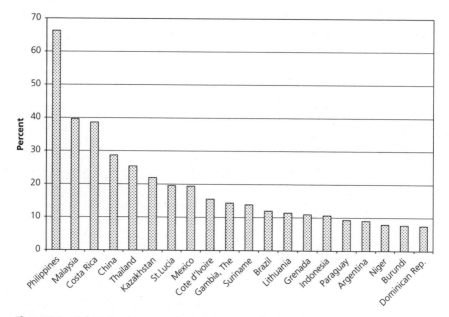

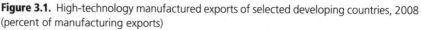

Figure 3.1. High-technology manufactured exports of selected developing countries, 2008 (percent of manufacturing exports)

Source: World Development Indicators (http://databank.worldbank.org), 2010.

investors bring in the technology and provide the (minimal) training needed; some can tackle the manufacture of complex products (automobiles); and some can manage the design and development of new technologies in advanced products. Their capability differences determine the nature and dynamism of comparative advantage.[28]

Indeed, one can distinguish (as Lall 1998 did) between the *basic learning* that is required to export low-technology manufactured exports and the *deep learning* that is required to export high-technology manufactured exports. The required complementary education and training policies differ in these two instances. As Lall pointed out, "In early stages of industrialization, when skill needs are fairly low and general, the correct policy is functional support for schooling and basic vocational training. In later stages, with more complex activities and functions, skill needs grow more demanding, diverse, and specific to particular technologies" (p. 68). Beginning the process of basic learning, supported by functional educational advances, and then transitioning into deep learning, supported by more specific educational advances, are both important but not easy to achieve, especially when educational resources

[28] Lall (1998), p. 66.

are scarce. But it is essential, as the long-run support of real incomes depends on countries' abilities to do this.[29]

3.4.2 THE MAQUILADORA EXPORT SECTOR

The deep learning process that supports high-technology manufacture exports is important because there is some evidence that low-technology manufacturing exports can fail to deliver long-term real wage increases. It is becoming clear that not all manufacturing activity supports productivity increases from technological learning over the long term. For example, the country in Figure 3.1 with the eighth highest level of high-technology manufacturing exports as a percent of total manufacturing exports is Mexico. However, the bulk of its manufacturing exports are low-technology in nature. In the case of the assembly or maquiladora export sector of Mexico, there are limits to productivity increases despite the generation of over 1 million jobs.

For example, Figure 3.2 plots imported inputs, value added, and wages as a percentage of gross production value for a quarter of a century in Mexico. As can be seen in this figure, imported intermediate products as a percentage of production value has been on a steady rise, while value added and wages as a percent of production value have been on a steady decline. Why does this matter? There is a great deal of evidence that long-term productivity in exporting activities in support of long-term increases in real wages relies on manufacturing export activities being integrated into the local economy via sourcing of local inputs and local value added. Just the opposite appears to have occurred in the Mexican *maquila* sector. As a consequence of this, export multipliers are lower in Mexico than in Brazil or the United States.[30]

The manufacturing exports of developing countries are often the result of inward FDI. This is an important link between two realms of globalization we examine in this book: trade and capital flows. From the point of view of poverty alleviation, the question becomes: how can the FDI-export process support domestic learning and upgrading, leading to productivity and real wage gains? One way of maximizing the benefits of FDI in the areas of employment and technology is by facilitating the use of local suppliers on the part of the foreign multinational enterprises (MNE) by developing *backward linkages.* The increased role of MNEs in an economy without significant backward links results in "enclaves," which have little connection to the rest of the economy and little contribution beyond direct employment effects.

---

[29] It is important to emphasize that basic education is only a necessary but not a sufficient condition for learning. Indeed, measures of human capital such as average years of schooling explain very little of the variation among developing countries in either low-technology manufacturing exports or high-technology manufacturing exports.

[30] See *The Economist* (2010b).

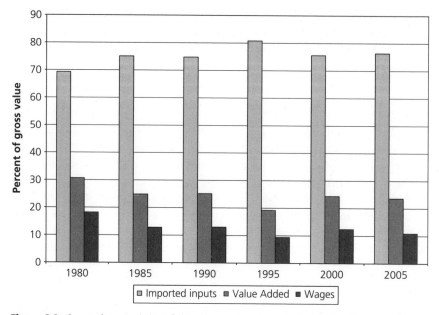

Figure 3.2. Some characteristics of the Maquiladora industry in Mexico (percent of gross value of output)

Source: Economic Commission for Latin America (http://www.census.gov/ipc/www/idb/), 2010.

Traditionally, the way to avoid enclave FDI was through local content requirements, but with the advent of the WTO in 1995, such requirements for local inputs became illegal.

The important policy question for developing countries is how to foster backward links between foreign MNEs and potential local suppliers. The link promotion process involves many players, including the government, the foreign MNEs, the local suppliers, professional organizations, commercial organizations, and academic institutions. The key role of the government is one of *coordination,* attempting to bridge the "information gaps" among the players. We will address this issue in more detail in Chapter 4 on capital flows.

3.4.3 MAURITIUS

The most well-known group of countries that have pursued trade-supported productivity increases for long-term poverty reduction is East Asia.[31] However, another notable example is the African country of Mauritius. As described by Subramanian and Roy (2003), Mauritius pursued a trade strategy that supported productivity and income gains throughout the 1980s and

---

[31] See, for just one example, Rodrigo (2001).

1990s. Indeed, a very high openness ratio (the sum of imports and exports as a percentage of GDP) helps explain the fact that productivity gains of Mauritius in the 1990s nearly reached those of East Asia in the late 1980s to early 1990s. Export-processing zones (EPZ) helped in this endeavor (Box 3.1). However, as these authors note, this process of trade-supported productivity gains "would probably not have been a success, or at least not to the same extent, without the policies of Mauritius's trading partners, which played an important role in ensuring the profitability of the export sector."[32] Indeed, at least 90 percent of Mauritian exports were accounted for by *preferential market access* for sugar, textiles, and clothing in the European Union and the United States.

Trade in the form of export expansion does not alone explain the Mauritian success, however. As emphasized by Sobhee (2009), equally important were advances in human development (education and health), institutional quality, gender equity, and responsible macroeconomic policy. These efforts came together in what Sobhee termed the "consolidation of physical, human and social capital."[33]

BOX 3.1 EXPORT-PROCESSING ZONES

One means by which developing countries have tried to promote the upgrading of their exports is through the use of export-processing zones (EPZs). EPZs are areas of the host country in which multinational enterprises (MNEs) can locate and in which they enjoy, in return for exporting most or the whole of their output, favorable treatment in the areas of infrastructure, taxation, tariffs on imported intermediate goods, and labor costs. EPZs have been used in many countries around the world with 3,000 of them in existence in 2006. In most cases, EPZs involve relatively labor-intensive, "light" manufacturing such at textiles, clothing, footwear, and electronics.

A number of studies have tried to assess EPZs from a benefit and cost framework. These studies show that in many (but not all) cases, the benefits do outweigh the costs. For example, Jayanthakumaran (2003) assessed EPZs in China, Indonesia, Malaysia, the Philippines, South Korea, and Sri Lanka. He concluded that the EPZs were an important source of employment in all six of these countries. Also, in all but the Philippines, the benefits outweighed the costs. In the case of the Philippines, the infrastructure costs of setting up the EPZ were too high for a net positive benefit. In the case of Costa Rica, Jenkins (2006) found that EPZs were very helpful in diversifying the industrial structure of the country and attracting FDI, but that there were limitations in the extent to which firms formed linkages to local firms.

More generally, a review by Aggarwal, Hoppe, and Walkenhorst (2009) suggests that EPZ location, infrastructure quality, and governance structures can affect the success of EPZs. Therefore, we cannot make general statements about the success of EPZs. Instead, they need to be examined on a case-by-case basis.

Sources: Johansson and Nilsson (1997), Schrank (2001), Jayanthakumaran (2003), Jenkins (2006), Singa Boyenge (2007), and Aggarwal, Hoppe, and Walkenhorst (2009).

---

[32] Subramanian and Roy (2003), p. 223.
[33] Sobhee (2009), p. 39.

3.5 **Trade and growth**

Many trade and development economists and have suggested that countries' openness to international trade has a positive impact on growth in per capita GDP and, therefore, on poverty alleviation.[34] Although explanations vary, we can consider this possibility as the potential result of the market expansion, productivity improvement, and pro-competitive effects of trade discussed above but acting over time. The historical experience of East Asia is a key reference point in establishing this possibility. Early studies such as Sachs and Warner (1995) and Edwards (1998) appeared to show that the more open countries are to international trade, the faster their growth in per capita GDP. However, another studies by Fosu (1996) and Levin and Raut (1997) showed that these externalities are notably *absent* in the case of *primary product exports*, which characterize many developing countries.[35]

Subsequent work has shown that the early studies did possess some weaknesses (e.g. Rodríguez and Rodrik 2001 and Wacziarg and Welch 2008). However, statistical analysis based on extended and improved indicators does seem to support the trade and growth link. The results of Wacziarg and Welch (2008), for example, suggest that openness to trade can increases investment and growth rates by over 1 percent. That said, this overall result occurs within what Wacziarg and Welch (2008) describe as "considerable heterogeneity" in their country sample. For example, political instability can break the link between trade and growth.[36]

The establishment of a link between trade expansion and growth is only one step in establishing a link between trade and poverty. As the evidence presented in Bardhan (2006) and Ravallion (2006) suggests, however, the link between trade expansions and poverty can be somewhat fragile, with other factors playing a more important role. For this reason, as with the issue of trade liberalization and poverty discussed above, we are often forced to consider country cases one at a time as we did with Bangladesh and Vietnam.

3.6 **Market access**

Poverty alleviating trade requires market access for developing country products, whether in agriculture, manufacturing, or services. Unfortunately, poor people face substantially more trade protection than the non-poor.

---

[34] See Dollar and Kraay (2004), for example. An alternative view is given in Rodríguez and Rodrik (2001).
[35] Greenaway, Morgan, and Wright (1999) showed positive results for fuels and metals (but not other primary exports).
[36] In particular, institutions matter a great deal. See Rodrik, Subramanian, and Trebbi (2004).

Products from developing countries face at least six hurdles in gaining access to foreign markets: tariffs, subsidies, quotas, standards and regulations, rules of origin, and security checks. Let's consider each in turn.

3.6.1 TARIFFS

Tariffs are taxes on imports, imposed to various degrees by all countries of the world. They have the effect of reducing import levels and raising the price of the imported good within the importing country. Poor people face higher tariffs than the non-poor. For example, the World Bank (2002a) compared the effective tariffs faced by poor people and by the non-poor.[37] The results were that poor people faced effective tariffs that are more than twice as high as those faced by the non-poor. Poor people also face significant tariff peaks in products of export interest to them, where the tariffs are several times the average rate and can range to over 100 percent. There is thus a significant bias in the world trading system against poor people. These are the people who should be supported, not undermined, by trade policies.

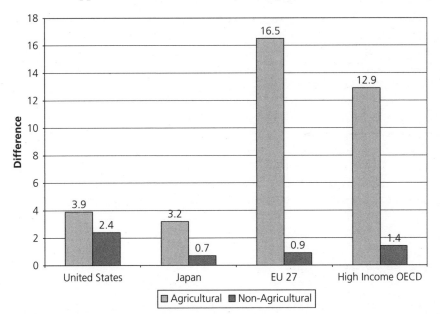

Figure 3.3. Tariff escalation, 2006–2009 (difference from raw to finished)

Note: EU 27 and High Income OECD are trade weighted averages.

Source: World Bank, World Trade Indicators (http://go.worldbank.org/7F01C2NTP0), 2010.

[37] The assumption here was that poor people earn their incomes from labor-intensive merchandise production, while the non-poor earn their incomes across the full array of economic activities. The "poor" are defined as those living on less than US$2 per day. See Chapter 2.

Tariff levels faced by poor people are only one part of tariff protection. The rich countries of the world also engage in policies known to trade policy experts as *tariff escalation*. This means that the rich countries increase their protection with the level of processing or value added in a product. This type of protection, depicted as overall averages in Figure 3.3, occurs in food, textiles and clothing, footwear, and wood products—all sectors in which the developing world has the most interest in exporting labor-intensive goods. The problem with tariff escalation is that it prevents developing countries from capturing more value added domestically and from vertically diversifying their exports. It also inhibits basic and deep learning processes required for long-term productivity gains, as discussed in the previous section.

3.6.2 SUBSIDIES

Unequal tariff protection is only one component of limited market access for developing countries. There are subsidies that developing countries need to compete against. Data on this type of support comes from the Organisation for Economic Cooperation and Development (OECD) and is presented in Figure 3.4. This chart plots two categories of support. The first is direct

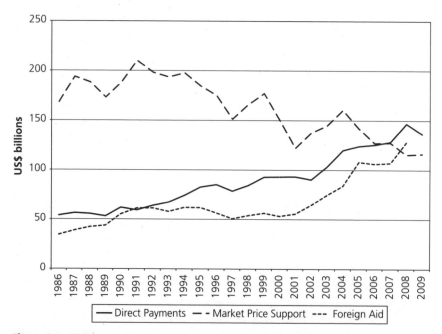

Figure 3.4. OECD agricultural subsidies compared to foreign aid

Source: OECD STAT (http://stats.oecd.org/) and World Development Indicators (http://databank.world bank.org), 2010.

payments to farmers, and the second is market price support.[38] These two types of support are compared with foreign aid in Figure 3.4 for the years 1986 to 2009, although at the time of this writing, foreign aid is not yet available for that final year. As this figure makes clear, direct payments to farmers have increased steadily over time from approximately US$50 billion in 1986 to approximately US$150 billion in 2008 and 2009.[39] These payments have tracked foreign aid closely, typically exceeding it by some tens of billions of dollars each year. Market price support has been on a gentle downward trend over time, but is currently the same order of magnitude as foreign aid.

As Peterson (2009, chapter 5) makes clear, whether measured in terms of total agricultural trade or the GDP of regions such as sub-Saharan Africa, these subsidy flows are very large. Consequently, in the overall "subsidy war" of global agricultural trade, *most developing countries simply do not have anywhere near enough resources to compete.* The notion that one could somehow create a level playing field by equally applying distortions is misguided. The only solution to the subsidy problem is that *they be significantly reduced.* It makes no sense from a development standpoint to have what foreign aid flows do occur being offset by development-unfriendly agricultural subsidies.[40]

This is not to suggest that rich OECD countries do not have the right to look after their own rural areas, but when this is done, it should be in a non-distortionary manner.[41] Such policies could be in the form of income subsidies and conservation specific support. Indeed, from the point of view of either environmental or small farmer considerations, most agricultural subsidies are harmful. For example, 70 percent of the nitrogen oxide pollution in the European Union is due to agriculture. And although people imagine that EU agricultural subsidies support the goat farmers and other small farmers of Provence, all but a small fraction of the subsidies in the European Union and the United States are captured by large farmers. This is why Peterson (2009) noted that these subsidies "seem to have more to do with pork-barrel politics than saving family farms" (p. 11).

3.6.3 QUOTAS

Throughout the period following the end of World War II and the liberalization of (some kinds) of trade under the auspices of GATT and WTO, developing countries have faced extensive quota protection in developed

---

[38] The issue of how to appropriately measure agricultural subsidies in the OECD is discussed in chapter 5 of Peterson (2009). Here we subtract market price support from the overall producer support estimate (PSE) to calculate direct payments.

[39] This trend is discussed further in Chapter 5. See also Figures 5.6 and 5.7.

[40] There is an important *asymmetry* here. If developing countries subsidize their manufacturing sectors, they are subject to countervailing duties under the Subsidies and Countervailing Measures (SCM) Agreement of the World Trade Organization. But no such measures apply to the developed world's agricultural subsidies. On the specific case of cotton subsidies' impact on poverty in Mali, see Boccanfuso and Savard (2007).

[41] In the language of agricultural trade negotiations, rural support should not include export subsidies or domestic support in the "amber box" where trade distortions occur.

country markets for their agricultural, textile, and clothing exports. These quota systems evolved beginning in the early 1960s and continued in full force through the end of the Uruguay Round in 1994. In the case of agriculture, these quotas were finally replaced by (equally protective) tariffs. In the case of textiles and clothing, the quotas were only fully phased out by 2005. The developing world suffered through 40 years of extensive quota protection in the very sectors where their comparative advantage tends to be strongest.

3.6.4 STANDARDS AND REGULATIONS

Increasing evidence suggests that developing countries face challenges in gaining market access due to standards and technical regulations (STRs). It is important to recognize that, whereas tariffs and quotas are in almost all cases welfare-worsening for the country imposing them, this is not the case with standards and regulations, which have important public goods characteristics. As such, they should not be condemned in general. However, there is growing evidence that, in some cases at least, standards and regulations constitute important non-tariff measures.

Consider the case of EU food standards. Otsuki, Wilson, and Sewadeh (2001) examined EU standards for aflatoxin (toxic compounds produced by molds) in food exports from Africa. These authors estimated that these standards, which would reduce EU health risks by less than 2 deaths per billion per year, would decrease African exports of cereals, dried fruits, and nuts by 64 percent (US$670 million). EU food standards are currently being tightened to include stringent reporting requirements of developing country farmers. For example, Jaffee and Masakure (2005) highlighted a *vast array* of both official and private standards affecting developing country exporters of fresh produce (primarily in Africa).

EU assistance to help farmers meet these stringent but still evolving standards is not adequate. An additional problem is that the standards are applied in a discriminatory fashion and require specialized skills and equipment beyond the capability of most of the low-income countries. If developing countries are to face increases in standards and regulations in rich country markets, they need to be assisted with capacity building in the areas where standards are applied.[42] (The Integrated Framework trade building initiative is briefly considered in Box 3.2.) Jaffee and Masakure (2005) presented evidence that some Kenyan fresh produce firms have been able to respond positively to increased standards and that these "gains have included an improvement in industry reputation, enhanced sales margins, and an

---

[42] For empirical evidence on the role of capacity building in standards, see Kim and Reinert (2009).

BOX 3.2 THE INTEGRATED FRAMEWORK

One example of trade-related capacity building that focuses on the least developed countries (LDCs) is the Integrated Framework or IF. The roots of the IF lie in the 1996 Singapore Ministerial Meeting of the WTO, which adopted a plan of action for the least developed countries. This plan of action called for "closer cooperation between the WTO and other multilateral agencies assisting least developed countries" in trade-related matters. Subsequently, a consensus emerged that the WTO should work with the International Monetary Fund (IMF), the World Bank, the United Nations Conference on Trade and Development (UNCTAD), the International Trade Centre (ITC), and the United Nations Development Programme (UNDP) in the Integrated Framework.

The precipitating event in this consensus was a high-level meeting on least developed countries, convened by the WTO in 1997. Originally, the IF planned to address trade-related capacity building needs through a twofold process of needs assessment and round table discussion. Despite early enthusiasm and 40 completed needs assessments, by the end of 1999, only five roundtables had been held (Bangladesh, The Gambia, Haiti, Tanzania, and Uganda), only one of which had been considered to be successful (Uganda).

Representatives of the six IF agencies met in 2001, presenting a joint communiqué on the redesign of the IF. The "new IF" involved LDCs in "mainstreaming" trade into their development policies through a "trade integration chapter" that was to be included in their Poverty Reduction Strategy Papers (PRSPs) submitted to the World Bank and IMF. Additionally, three of the six IF agencies agreed to take lead roles: the World Bank as lead agency for "mainstreaming," the WTO as secretariat, and the UNDP as manager of an IF Trust Fund (IFTF).

LDCs chosen to participate in the IF engage in a process known as "diagnostic trade integration studies" or DTIS. This process consists of five components: a review and analysis of the country's economic and export performance; an assessment of the country's macroeconomic and investment climate; an assessment of the international policy environment and specific constraints that exports from each country face in world markets; an analysis of key labor-intensive sectors where there is a potential for output and export expansion; and a "pro-poor trade integration strategy," with proposed policy reforms and action plans.

Support of the IF process by the IFSC was reaffirmed in 2003. Diagnostic studies were undertaken in 21 countries with a further 16 in the pipeline. Financial commitments to the process continued to grow to reach US$13 million by 2005. The IF donors summed up some of the most important goals of trade-related capacity building as follows: "We stand ready to help developing countries and LDCs engage in the multilateral trading system. Removing supply side constraints to trade is important in generating a response to market access opportunities. We will step up assistance on trade-related infrastructure, private sector development, and institution building to help countries to expand their export base." To achieve this end, it was estimated that a further US$200 to US$400 million would be required in IF grants.

A 2005–2006 taskforce resulted in yet another phase of the IF, namely what became known as the "Enhanced IF" or EIF. Hoekman and Kostecki (2009) described progress under the EIF as "slow," but in 2008 the institutional features of it were put in place and US$200 million had indeed been pledged. After over a decade of effort, the IF is still trying to find its feet.

Sources: www.integratedframework.org and Hoekman and Kostecki (2009).

improved capacity to chart future investment and marketing plans."[43] Maertens and Swinnen (2009) presented similar evidence for Senegal. However, due to management constraints and lack of access to credit, not all Kenyan fresh produce firms have been able to successfully upgrade. Consequently, EU food standards remain a difficult issue.

3.6.5 RULES OF ORIGIN

OECD countries have offered preferential access to developing country exports through schemes such as the European Union's Everything But Arms (EBA) arrangement, the United States' African Growth and Opportunities Act (AGOA), or a host of preferential (regional) trade agreements. Leveraging these opportunities, however, can be more difficult than it first might appear due to rules of origin (ROOs).[44] Evidence presented by Anson et al. (2005) and Collier and Venables (2007) suggests that ROOs do pose a problem for developing counties gaining market access to OECD markets. This is particularly true for narrowly defined manufacturing tasks that often make up modern global production networks. The presence of ROOs, and their strictness in some instances, helps to explain why some preferential access arrangements do not bring the benefits one might expect.

3.6.6 SECURITY CHECKS

Since the attacks in the United States in September 2001, the exports of some developing countries have been subject to increased surveillance and security checks. This has been true of the US–Canadian border, no less between the United States and developing countries. For some particular developing countries, such as Pakistan, this has had a negative impact on sustained market access because imports into developed countries have been sourced from other countries seen as more secure. Because countries perceived to be insecure tend to be low-income, these increases in security measures have had negative impacts on poverty.

---

[43] Jaffee and Masakure (2005), p. 331.

[44] As outlined by Krishna (2009), ROOs can be defined using four criteria. The first of these is the amount of *domestic content* of the good, measured either in terms of value added or in direct, physical terms. The second is in terms of a *change in tariff heading* (CTH) where the good must move from one tariff category to another during a production process in a FTA member country. The third is in terms of *specified processes* (or tasks) which outline the actual production processes that must take place within the FTA. The fourth approach is in terms of *substantial transformation*, a loosely defined term that can vary from one instance to another.

3.6.7 COSTS FOR DEVELOPING COUNTRIES

What are the costs of trade protectionism for the developing world? A number of studies have tried to assess this. To take one example, van der Mensbrugghe (2006) considered the impact of a Doha Bound trade liberalization scenario. The welfare gains to developing countries of this liberalization scenario are estimated to be over US$86 billion.[45] This is on the same order of magnitude as the annual value of foreign aid. The number of individuals moved out of poverty due to this trade liberalization exceeds 65 million. Anderson, Martin, and van der Mensbrugghe (2006) went a step farther to estimate the effect of removing all merchandise trade distortions, including agricultural subsidies. They found that developing country exports of agricultural goods would rise by US$200 billion annually, and that exports of non-agricultural goods would rise by US$400 billion annually. These researchers noted that this amounts to more than six times the 2003 burden of foreign debt service and eight times the official development assistance in 2003. Both of these studies suggest that the effects of trade protectionism on developing countries are very detrimental.

3.7 **Primary products**

If the exports of developing countries are to support the incomes of their poor residents, the incomes generated by those exports must increase over time. Export incomes can increase in three ways: increases in export quality, increases in export quantities, and increases in export prices. Many developing countries depend on the exports of a small number of natural resource-based goods known as *primary commodities*. Examples are aluminum, coffee, leather, rubber, and sugar. By their very nature, primary commodities are characterized by low levels of value added and limited room for quality improvement. Unfortunately, for some time, they were also characterized by a long-term, downward trend in export prices.

Ocampo and Parra (2003) analyzed commodity prices from 1900 to 2000, noting declines in 24 of 31 commodities considered. In addition, these researchers also reported that an overall index of food products fell by 50 percent, an index of non-food products fell by 15 percent, an index of metals fell by 7 percent, and the well known *Economist* commodity price index fell by 60 percent. Evidence suggests that the period from 1990 to 2000 was characterized by particularly steep price declines.

---

[45] This figure includes "static" gains only; "dynamic" gains that reflect growth effects are much higher. These dynamic gains reflect alleged productivity gains that are the result of increased exports. However, the magnitude of these dynamic gains is uncertain.

Taking a more recent and decadal approach, however, provides a more positive picture of commodity prices. Consider Table 3.1. This table presents the 1960 to 1990, 1991 to 2000 and 2001 to 2009 periods separately. The period from 1960 to 1990 was characterized by large increases in commodity prices, while the period from 1991 to 2000 was one of falling commodity prices. However, with increases in global demand returning beginning in 2001, commodity prices increased substantially, providing significant benefits in export revenues for many developing countries.

Table 3.1 Commodity price changes during the last half century (percent change)

Commodity	1960–1990	1991–2000	2001–2009
Lead	300.9	−18.6	261.0
Gold[a]	992.9	−22.9	259.0
Cacao	96.2	0.6	242.6
Coal[b]	368.0	−33.3	238.7
Silver	427.3	23.8	235.0
Rubber	10.8	−19.1	234.2
Copper	292.7	−22.4	226.9
Tin	190.9	−34.0	220.7
Palm Oil	29.2	−6.8	170.2
Cocoa Beans	115.3	−24.2	166.0
Nickel	443.3	5.7	145.8
Petroleum	725.5	40.9	138.5
Soybean Oil	161.1	−21.2	126.8
Coffee	129.1	9.5	120.5
Zinc	516.6	0.6	87.0
Maize	120.5	−17.9	84.7
Timber	402.4	5.8	78.8
Wheat	133.7	−11.4	76.2
Jute	42.6	−23.7	70.0
Sugar	383.6	−34.9	68.9
Tea	42.0	34.7	58.5
Oranges[c]	132.9	−30.3	52.6
Bananas[c]	119.9	−24.5	45.0
Tobacco[d]	181.6	−14.6	41.8
Cotton	193.0	−23.2	30.7
Wool	232.9	9.6	24.9
Beef	248.0	−27.3	23.9
Aluminum	220.5	19.0	15.4
Lamb	301.3	7.6	12.8

[a] Series starts in 1963. [b] Series starts in 1967. [c] Series starts in 1975. [d] Series starts in 1968.
Source: http://www.imfstatistics.org/imf/ and authors' calculations.

The 2007 to 2009 crisis did cause reductions in commodity prices beginning in 2008 in some instances. For example, drops in aluminum prices had a detrimental impact on the economy of Mozambique, and drops in copper prices had a detrimental impact on Mongolia.[46] Such declines in commodity prices can be disastrous for the very poor. As noted by UNCTAD (2004), "the major sin of omission in the current international approach to poverty reduction is the failure to tackle the link between commodity dependence and extreme poverty."[47] For example, declines in coffee prices have caused deaths from malnutrition in Guatemala where such tragedies had been thought to have been a thing of the past. For these reasons, the overall good news of Table 3.1 can mask some specific and severe challenges.

Protectionist policies in the developed world exacerbate commodity prices problems when they occur. First, the agricultural subsidies discussed above can contribute to commodity price declines. Second, tariff escalation makes it difficult for developing counties to escape primary product traps by vertically diversifying their exports along value chains toward greater value added to commodities (for example, from cacao to chocolate). Third, manufactures protection of the type described above (for example, in textiles and clothing) tends to concentrate developing countries in primary commodities, limiting horizontal diversification out of primary commodity exports, thereby exacerbating commodity price declines and contributing to the instability of export revenues. Finally, limited market access increases the uncertainty developing countries face with regard to future protection levels as does the unpredictable management of phytosanitary and other non-tariff barriers. This reduces investor confidence in both primary and non-traditional productive sectors.[48]

It is also necessary for foreign aid to take into account the limitations of specialization in primary commodities. Hard thinking about realistic alternatives within rural development must yield alternative routes to support incomes of the poor over the long term. This will in most instances require a strategy of export diversification.[49] This is no easy task. Until such alternatives are found, the promotion of "fair trade" commodities that ensure the maximum value for developing country producers and help develop niche markets can play a useful role in mitigating the negative effects of price declines in some important cases.[50]

[46] See Hallaert and Munro (2009).
[47] UNCTAD (2004), p. xii.
[48] Some time ago, Francois and Martin (2002) noted that foreign market access security "serves to reduce uncertainty for foreign investors about the ability of an economy to link itself with the global economy and hence to generate returns that can ultimately be repatriated" (p. 545).
[49] The results of Lederman and Maloney (2009) suggest that it is the lack of diversification that makes primary exports problematic rather than the exports themselves.
[50] See Raynolds (2000) and Bacon et al. (2008). The "fair trade" designation is the responsibility of the Fairtrade Labelling Organizations International (FLO). While we support the goals of this effort

3.8 **Trade-related capacity building**

Market access for developing country exports is an important step in allowing for poverty-reducing international trade. However, market access must be combined with efforts to promote export *capacity* in low- and middle-income countries. Most discussions of aid and trade view them as substitutes for one another, with trade being the favored of the two. It is indeed true that, from a poverty alleviation standpoint, trade can play a much larger and sustained role than aid. However, it is important to appreciate the potential complementary relationship between aid and trade, what is sometimes called "aid for trade." Indeed, trade policy experts now recognize that, without such assistance, developing countries will not be able to exploit the market access that is available to them.[51]

In the past, efforts to relax trade capacity constraints occurred under what was known as *trade-related technical assistance.* However, more recent appreciation of capacity constraints has motivated a change of focus to what is now known as *trade-related capacity building.* There is also a recognition that trade-related capacity building relies, at least to some extent, on outside assistance, making this an issue of foreign aid. Hallaert and Munro (2009) identified four areas where trade-related capacity building (or aid for trade) can help support a positive relationship between trade and development: increasing trade, diversifying exports, maximizing export sector linkages with the rest of the economy, and increasing adjustment capacities. The specific areas that trade-related capacity building can address include: human capital, access to information, infrastructure, institutions, WTO representation, standards, and exchange rates. We consider each in turn.

3.8.1 HUMAN CAPITAL

Trade can make new opportunities available to poor people, but if these individuals do not have the requisite levels of human capital in terms of

---

with respect to maximizing the incomes of poor people, we do not embrace some of its general, anti-market statements. Collier (2007) casts doubt on fair trade effectiveness, suggesting that it traps countries in unproductive (e.g. primary) activities. But given market access limitations and the potential for some degree of forward movement along value chains (e.g. into preliminary processing), as well as the fact that fair trade can provide alternatives in the craft sector, it does seem to have a role to play.

[51] One example is the generalized system of preferences (GSP) granted the least developed countries (LDCs) by the developed world. As was observed by Inama (2002), "Almost 30 years of experience with trade preferences, and particularly with the GSP schemes, have largely demonstrated that the mere granting of duty free market access to a wide range of LDCs' products does not automatically ensure that the trade preferences will be effectively utilized by beneficiary countries" (p. 114).

both education and health, they will not be able to take advantage of these opportunities. Despite the role of human capital in the analysis of growth, it has not played a central role in trade-related capacity building. In our view, that is a mistake. As discussed in Chapter 4, minimal levels of human capital play a role in attracting and benefiting from foreign direct investment (FDI), and this investment can be important in locating export-oriented FDI. Indeed, Brenton et al. (2009) describe education and training as a "critical service" for export growth.

3.8.2 ACCESS TO INFORMATION

It is not often appreciated that basic information is a crucial component of export development. In point of fact, however, even basic knowledge of export possibilities is often lacking in developing countries. Supplying this information to potential exporters is a basic public good, and consequently, developing information systems regarding potential export markets can be very helpful. Many successful East Asian exporters had a government agency playing this trade facilitation role. This can even involve the simple function of identifying *new* markets for *existing* products. As noted by Brenton et al. (2009), this path can be even more important than moving into new products. That said, however, efforts to promote diversification of exports via new products can help developing countries to escape the primary product limitations described above.

3.8.3 INFRASTRUCTURE

Infrastructure bottlenecks hamper export growth, and improving infrastructure can be an important activity for trade-related capacity building. This can involve traditional infrastructure elements such as roads, ports, and airports, but that is not the only relevant area. As emphasized by Brenton et al. (2009) and Hoekman and Kostecki (2009), infrastructure elements also include service inputs such as telecommunications, transport and logistics, finance, and security. We therefore need to think of trade-related infrastructure in both its traditional and business service components.

3.8.4 INSTITUTIONS

In the research literatures on growth and FDI, institutions rise to the service as a relevant explanatory factor. Institutions involve many dimensions of economies and can include the rule of law, property rights, contract enforcement, regulation, and social insurance.[52] Institutions are important generally

---

[52] See, for example, chapter 5 of Rodrik (2007).

for growth, but can have a particular impact on trade-related capacity. For example, Johnson, Ostry, and Subramanian (2010) have identified regulatory costs and other "micro-institutions" as constraining African export growth. These authors also note that these sorts of micro-institutions can vary independently of the macro-institutional variables mentioned above.[53] Therefore, reducing the cost of doing business generally and the cost of exporting in particular needs separate attention.

3.8.5 WTO REPRESENTATION

International trade operates within the rules set by the World Trade Organization (WTO), but many developing WTO members are underrepresented there. Better representation in the WTO and other international organizations related to trade is important. For example, the promotion of representative capacity can assist "an Algerian diplomat to negotiate his country's WTO accession, and an Indonesian civil servant to prepare a legislative proposal on copyrights, or a Mali exporter to understand business implications of the WTO Agreement on Textiles."[54] Further, upgrading negotiating capacities of trade ministries, including training in WTO legal matters and accession processes can boost developing countries prospects in these arenas. The review of Kostecki (2001) suggested that emphasis needs to be placed on genuine needs assessment and beneficiary orientation, sufficient funding, escaping bureaucratic restrictions through arm's length delivery organizations, and a re-evaluation of the professional qualifications of capacity-building staff.

Some initiatives have been ongoing, including the Advisory Centre on WTO Law, the Swiss funded Agency for International Trade Information and Cooperation, and the Canadian funded Centre for Trade Policy and Law, and the International Trade Centre's World Tr@de Net. In the case of the Advisory Centre on WTO Law (ACWL), efforts have been made to provide assistance to developing countries on WTO legal matters, particularly dispute settlement. Evidence presented in Brown (2009) suggests that it has made a difference, although not for all developing countries. As such, its efforts should be supported and expanded if possible.

---

[53] Johnson, Ostry, and Subramanian (2010) state: "While there is a presumption that macro and micro institutions should broadly co-move, there can clearly be exceptions. One possibility is that macro and micro institutions could be measuring distinct functions that institutions perform. For example, while broad institutions such as the judiciary will determine the protection of property rights and enforcement of contracts, the costs of doing business measured at the micro level could relate to ease of acquiring specific licenses, which could be the domain of other institutions/authorities" (p. 141). See also Redding and Venables (2004).

[54] Kostecki (2001), p. 4.

3.8.6 STANDARDS

As we discussed above, standards and technical regulations (STRs) pose a constraint on developing country export expansions. As noted by Kim and Reinert (2009), upgrading systems to meet the increasing number and strength of evolving STRs is a trade-related capacity requirement. For example, Brenton et al. (2009) stressed the importance of metrology, testing, and conformity assessment facilities in helping potential exporters meet STR. Chen, Wilson, and Otsuki (2008) showed that certification procedures pose particular challenges to developing country export expansions and recommend the negotiation of Mutual Recognition Agreements (MRAs) to overcome this hurdle. Since standards are increasingly important in exports markets of interest to developing countries, this is a key area for trade-related capacity building efforts.

3.8.7 EXCHANGE RATES

Export development can be held back by inappropriate exchange rate policies as well as by limited capacity. There is emerging evidence that overvalued currencies can suppress export-led growth and that perhaps undervalued currencies can contribute to export-led growth. These arguments have been made most recently by Gala (2008) and Rodrik (2008), for example. In its simplest form, the argument is that the production of traded goods involves positive growth externalities. Rodrik (2008) argued that "there is something 'special' about tradable goods in countries with low to medium incomes" and that a production switching process towards tradable goods can "foster desirable structural change and spur growth."[55] Rodrik provided evidence of this sort of process for a number of countries such as China, India, South Korea, Taiwan, Uganda, Tanzania, and Mexico. There have been criticisms of his methodology, but the study at least alerts us to the possibility of these sorts of effects. It also clearly cautions against pursuing overvalued currencies in developing countries, perhaps as a result of capital and foreign aid inflows, or as a result of deliberate government policy.[56]

3.8.8 THE ROLE OF BINDING CONSTRAINTS

Recent analysis of trade-related capacity building suggests that it is important to identify which of the above factors is the most *binding constraint* on trade

---

[55] Rodrik (2008), p. 370.
[56] On the exchange rate effects of foreign aid, see Rajan and Subramanian (2011). Some time ago, Lipumba (1994) warned against overvalued currencies in African countries. See also Dasgupta et al. (2007) and Johnson, Ostry, and Subramanian (2010).

expansion and diversification. For example, this has been suggested by Hallaert and Munro (2009) as part of the OECD's involvement in trade-related capacity building efforts. The idea is to include all of the above factors into a hierarchical decision tree to indentify which factors are most pressing. This allows for better sequencing of reforms and directs efforts and resources to where they are most needed. Evidence presented in Johnson, Ostry, and Subramanian (2010) suggests that the notion of binding constraints has some relevance. For these reasons, the binding constraint idea should inform trade-related capacity building efforts.

3.9 **Health and safety**

As noted by Deaton (2004), many treatments of globalization ignore health issues altogether. In our view, that is a mistake. In particular, we mentioned in Chapter 1 that, to help poor people, trade activities need to support the development of human capital in the forms of education, training, and health. There are cases in which trade activities (both imports and exports) can actually undermine human capital by compromising the health and safety of the poor. In the case of imports, a notable example is arms, which can have disastrous impacts on the safety of citizens in the importing country. Another example is imports of toxic waste. In the case of exports, some production processes can compromise the health of the workers producing the exported products.

3.9.1 TRADE IN ARMS

Despite the pressing human development needs of poor countries, arms can compose a large part of low- and middle-income country imports. It is not unusual for arms imports to constitute up to 10 percent of developing country imports. As is evident in Figure 3.5, the top 25 developing country arms importers on a per capita basis include some of the poorest countries in the world such as Eritrea and Namibia. During an era in which there is increasing concern about missing many Millennium Development Goals, this in unfortunate. Even more seriously, civil conflicts and other forms of violence in poor countries have been estimated to result in an annual loss of at least a half million lives, putting development into reverse.[57] Approaches to

---

[57] Former World Bank president James Wolfensohn (2002), for example, highlighted that "the world's leading industrial nations provide nearly 90 percent of the multibillion dollar arms trade—arms that are contributing to the very conflicts that all of us profess to deplore, and that we must spend additional monies to suppress" (p. 12).

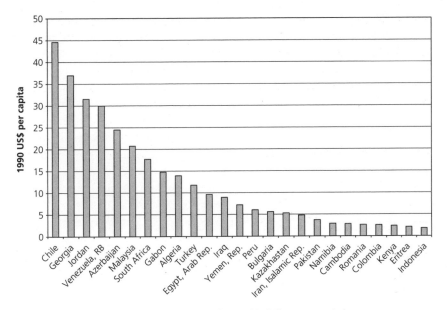

Figure 3.5. Arms imports per capita, 2007 (1990 US dollars per capita)

Source: World Development Indicators (http://databank.worldbank.org), 2010.

regulate the global arms trade to conflict zones therefore require serious consideration.[58]

3.9.2 TRADE IN HAZARDOUS WASTE

Similar health and safety issues can arise through the imports of hazardous waste, which can cause serious environmental effects as well.[59] These harmful effects can be long term as well as immediate and can impose economic costs. Importing hazardous waste into poor countries is motivated by lower disposal costs in those countries, as well as by growing opposition to disposal in rich countries. In contrast to the case of arms trade, however, there is already a multilateral agreement governing hazardous waste trade—the Basel Convention on the Control of Trans-Boundary Movements in Hazardous Wastes and their Disposal. This was signed in 1989 and entered into force in 1992. It

---

[58] The Commission for Africa (2005) and the United Kingdom Foreign Secretary have recently highlighted the need for further progress in this area, as have organizations such as Oxfam, Amnesty International, and the International Action Network on Small Arms. See, for example, www.iansa.org

[59] Krueger (2001) wrote that "Hazardous waste can range from materials contaminated with dioxins and heavy metals, such as mercury, cadmium, or lead, to organic wastes. The waste may take many forms, from barrels of liquid waste to sludge, old computer parts, used batteries, or incinerator ash" (p. 43). See also Clapp (2001).

operates through a system of notification and consent, and was strengthened in 1995. Although the Basel Convention has not been without controversies and disagreements, with some NGOs being critical of it, it has nevertheless been important in controlling hazardous waste trade, and is in the process of improving compliance efforts with a central office and staff.[60]

3.9.3 EXPORT PRODUCTION PROCESSES AND HEALTH

There are cases in which the export production processes compromise the health of workers. The export of Nemagon, an insecticide used in banana production, is a case in point.[61] This insecticide was banned in 1979 in the United States because it causes skin diseases, sterility, and birth defects. Despite this, it was used in Central American banana production through the 1980s and, in some cases, through the mid-1990s. Banana workers in Central America began to report many severe symptoms, including anencephaly, a malformation in which conceived fetuses fail to develop brains. In 2004, over 1,000 affected Nicaraguan workers marched to their capital city, Managua, to demand compensation, and similar concerns were voiced in Honduras and in some cut flower export industries of Colombia and Ecuador, again involving the use of insecticides. In Ecuador, for example, Thomson (2003) reported that "studies that the International Labour Organization published in 1999 and the Catholic University issued here last year showed that women in the industry had more miscarriages than average and that more than 60 percent of all workers suffered headaches, nausea, blurred vision or fatigue."[62]

The health threat of pesticides that do not meet international standards in both export and domestic industries is an issue that has gained the attention of the World Health Organization. According to its estimates (WHO 2001a), nearly one-third of the pesticides marketed in developing countries do not meet international standards. These "frequently contain hazardous substances and impurities that have already been banned or severely restricted elsewhere" or "the active ingredient concentrations are outside internationally accepted tolerance limits."[63] The WHO calls upon all governments and international and regional organizations to adopt the World Health Organization / Food and Agricultural Organization pesticide specifications to help alleviate these health threats. Again, greater multilateral efforts are needed.

---

[60] For a concise but detailed review of the Basel Convention, see Krueger (2001) and Clapp (2009).

[61] Nemagon is derived from debromochloropropane (DBCP) and kills a nematode that damages banana production.

[62] Thomson (2003).

[63] WHO (2001a).

3.9.4 HEALTH AND SAFETY COMPROMISED

In all these cases, a similar issue arises. Although trade activities typically generate incomes and other potential benefits for poor people, health and safety may be compromised, sometimes seriously. From a development perspective, this is a trade-off to be avoided if at all possible. The alleviation of income deprivation by increasing health deprivation is not an escape from income poverty but an exacerbation of health deprivation. In these instances, trade cannot be claimed to be fully alleviating poverty. Further, because the affected poor people are usually not fully aware of risks, we can in no sense assume they have fully accounted for them in their choices.

3.9.5 ILLICIT TRADE

As Naím (2005) highlighted, increased globalization has been associated with an escalation of illicit trade. Increased trade and movement of people, together with technological advances in financial markets, communication, and transport, have been exploited by criminals to what Naím warns are unprecedented levels. He estimated that money laundering exceeds US$1 billion per year; the illegal drug trade US$800 billion; counterfeiting US$400 billion; illegal arms sales US$10 billion; cross-border human trafficking US$10 billion; and cross-border sales of art US$3 billion. These figures suggest that illegal flows account for as much as 20 percent of world trade. Naím emphasized the interconnected nature of illegal flows (for example, the money laundering of drug sales), and of legal and illegal flows (for example, drugs concealed in shipping containers). Illicit trade also has detrimental impacts on endangered species and the cultural patrimony of many countries. The challenge is to control illicit flows while preserving the underlying benefits of increased trade and globalization. The need for enhanced security and regulation carries the risk of adding considerable friction to the movement, not only of goods and services, but also of financial flows and migration.

3.10 **Conclusions**

The link between trade expansion and poverty alleviation is not automatic. However, trade has been a powerful force for poverty alleviation in a number of ways. Exports can expand markets, helping to generate incomes for the poor. Both imports and exports can promote competition, lowering consumption and production costs in the face of monopoly (single seller) power, and raising prices for suppliers in the case of monopsony (single buyer) power. Both imports and exports can support productivity improvements through access to new machinery and contact with discerning international customers. Imports are also important for health aspects of human development, because many medical supplies need to be imported to combat health deprivations. In each of these areas, empirical evidence suggests that trade can play a positive role in helping poor people to better their lives.

The possibility of exports helping to alleviate poverty is significantly curtailed by trade protectionism in rich countries. This occurs in the form of tariffs, subsidies, quotas, standards and regulations, rules of origin, and security checks. Even conservative estimates of the potential gains from reducing protectionism in rich countries are many times the size of annual foreign aid flows. Rich country protectionism poses a significant barrier to poverty alleviation, not to mention the overall participation of the developing world in the global economy. Lack of progress in (and even attention to) the Doha Round of multilateral trade negotiations should not obscure this important point.[64]

Developing countries relying on the export of primary commodities initially suffered from a century-long decline in primary commodity prices. This decline reversed itself beginning in 2001, and this had substantial benefits for many primary commodity exporters. Instability in commodity prices brought about by the 2007 to 2009 crisis, however, demonstrated continued vulnerabilities in many developing countries. This instability seems to have passed as of 2010, but concerns remain.

For trade to benefit poor people, increases in market access for developing countries must be combined with trade-related capacity building. These capacity-building efforts are often *prerequisites* for developing countries to overcome supply constraints, and this is an area where trade and aid act as positive complements. As new thinking in development policy stresses, capacity building should be beneficiary-driven and partnership-based, strive to develop local capacities and skills, and place trade issues in a broader development perspective. This process needs to identify binding constraints on a case-by-case basis among human capital, access to information, infrastructure, institutions, WTO representation, standards, and exchange rates. This is not an easy task, and experience to date with the Integrated Framework suggests we have a great deal of distance to go in this endeavor.

In some cases, trade can have a direct, negative impact on the health and safety of the poor. This occurs with imports of arms and toxic waste and also with export-production processes that compromise the health of workers. In each of these cases, concrete, multilateral steps need to be taken to ensure that trade does not compromise poverty reduction and human development but

---

[64] See Hoekman, Martin, and Mattoo (2010) on the potential gains from a concluded Doha Round and a call for its conclusion.

supports it. Multilateral agreements such as the Basel Convention on Hazardous Wastes provide one model for moving forward in these areas of concern. As noted by Deaton (2004), the primary means through which globalization affects health outcomes is via the flow of *ideas* (discussed in Chapter 7), but that does not suggest inattention to areas where trade impinges on health outcomes.

We have shown in this chapter that trade reforms in both rich and developing countries have a vital role to play in ensuring that globalization benefits the poor. The movement of economies toward more trade-oriented profiles typically involves processes of trade liberalization, often under the auspices of the WTO, the World Bank, the IMF, or preferential trade agreements. The transition costs associated with these reforms can be significant and may actually worsen poverty for some classes of households. For this reason, as developing countries consider the role that increased trade can play in poverty alleviation, they need to guard against the real possibility of increasing the poverty of some groups in the trade liberalization process. Safety nets (social protection), complementary anti-poverty programs, and direct compensation might be necessary to achieve poverty alleviating transitions. Trade reform is vital but should be placed within a comprehensive approach to overcoming poverty in all its dimensions.

4 Finance

Global financial flows are an important resource for developing countries. These capital flows augment domestic savings and can contribute to investment, growth, financial sector development, technology transfer, and poverty reduction. These possibilities are reflected in the standard view of international economics that capital flows are beneficial in almost all circumstances. However, this view is backed only by *ambiguous* evidence regarding the growth gains from capital flows.[1]

Further, the experience of developing countries during the 1997 Asian crisis and the 2007–2009 global financial crisis suggests that capital flows may entail potential costs that are both larger than in the case of trade and tend to be disproportionately carried by poor people. Of all the dimensions of globalization considered in this book, capital flows are the most implicated in systemic risk and global financial fragility. Additionally, not all capital flows are the same in their benefit and cost characteristics. For all these reasons, a careful assessment of the impact of capital flows on global poverty does not lend itself to across-the-board statements. Rather, the cost and benefit characteristics of distinct types of capital flows must be considered in some detail.

4.1 Capital flows and balance of payments

Capital flows are recorded in the capital and financial accounts of countries' balance of payments. The assets exchanged on the capital and financial accounts of the balance of payments consist of various financial objects with monetary values that can change over time in the portfolios of both individuals and firms. There are a number of legitimate ways to classify capital

---

[1] Prasad et al. (2005) noted that "if financial integration has a positive effect on growth, there is as yet no clear and robust empirical proof that the effect is quantitatively significant" (p. 5). Kose et al. (2009) were more positive. They suggested that the benefits of financial globalization are "indirect" and "catalytic," but noted the presence of threshold effects as well as potential problems of capital account opening under fixed exchange rate regimes. Prasad, Rajan, and Subramanian (2007) conducted a thorough empirical investigation and concluded that "developing countries that have relied more on foreign finance have not grown faster in the long run, and have typically grown more slowly" (p. 162). Obstfeld (2009) concluded that "it is hard to find unambiguous evidence that financial opening yields a net improvement in economic performance for emerging countries" (p. 103).

flows and various subcomponents of the capital account. In this chapter, we will distinguish among four types: foreign direct investment, equity portfolio investment, bond finance, and commercial bank lending.

Foreign direct investment (FDI) is the acquisition of shares by a firm in a foreign-based enterprise that exceeds a threshold of 10 percent, implying managerial participation in the foreign enterprise. FDI is important for the global production and trade of both goods and services. Under the right conditions, FDI can generate direct and indirect increases in employment, and increase productivity by promoting competition, improving the training of host country workers, and facilitating technology transfer to developing countries. It may also subject workers to unsafe working conditions, compromise the natural environment, and increase the dominance of foreign cultures over host country cultures.

Equity portfolio investment is similar to FDI in that it involves the ownership of shares in foreign countries. It differs from FDI in that the share holdings are too small to imply managerial participation over the foreign enterprise. It is thus *indirect* investment, rather than direct investment. Because equity portfolio investment is undertaken for portfolio reasons rather than managerial reasons, the behavior of investors can be quite different than with FDI. To generalize, equity portfolio investment tends to be motivated by shorter time horizons than FDI's horizon and is subject to the portfolio considerations of investors.

Bond finance or *debt issuance* is a second kind of portfolio activity. In a bond finance transaction, the government or firms in developing countries issue bonds to foreign investors. These bonds can be issued in either the domestic currency or in foreign currencies, and can involve different kinds of default risks. Bond portfolio investment has in common with equity portfolio investment that both are held in international portfolios. Portfolio considerations and their relatively short-term characteristics are therefore important to both. Indeed, they are often combined in simple balance of payments accounts under the heading of "portfolio investment."

Commercial bank lending is another form of debt. Unlike bond finance, it does not involve a tradable asset. Commercial bank loans can be short-term or long-term loans, can be made with fixed or flexible interest rates, and can take the form of inter-bank loans. A single bank or a syndicate of banks can be involved in any particular loan package. Commercial bank lending has played a role in a number of financial crises.

Although FDI can affect poor people directly by generating employment and transferring technology, much of the potential impact of other capital flows on poverty is indirect, taking place through the broad process of financial development. For this reason, before taking up the individual categories of capital flows and their potential impacts on poor people in the

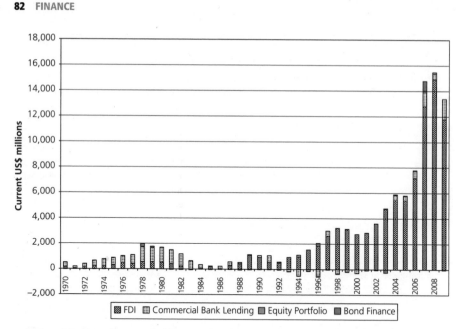

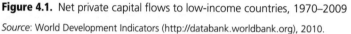

Figure 4.1. Net private capital flows to low-income countries, 1970–2009

Source: World Development Indicators (http://databank.worldbank.org), 2010.

rest of this chapter, we consider both the recent trends in capital flows to the developing world and the overall process of financial development.[2]

4.1.1 CAPITAL FLOWS TO LOW-INCOME COUNTRIES

Figure 4.1 presents net capital flows for the low-income countries of the developing world. Examining this figure, a number of important observations can be made. First, until the 1990s, commercial bank lending was the primary source of foreign capital for the low-income countries, although it declined significantly after the 1982 debt crisis. On a net basis, bank lending remained positive for most years during the 1990s but then became negative in 1998 after the Asian financial crisis (Box 4.1). This reflected the drastic decline in access to commercial bank funds suffered by the low-income countries and their continued payments of old commercial bank debt. This net outflow continued through 2003, and then commercial bank lending began to regain some significance, reaching US$1.6 billion in 2009.

Second, although FDI comprised a significant portion of total capital inflows to the low-income countries in the 1970s, it became even more

---

[2] We focus on the actual flows rather than on various measures of capital control policies because, as pointed out by Kose et al. (2009), actual flows provide a better measure of financial integration than *de jure* (or even *de facto*) capital control policies.

BOX 4.1 CRISES

Financial crises of various kinds have plagued the developing world with detrimental impacts for poor people. Although there are a number of ways of categorizing these crises, that of Reinhart and Rogoff (2009) is very useful and captures the possible variety of financial difficulties. These authors' list is as follows: inflation crises, currency crashes, the bursting of asset price bubbles, banking crises, external debt crises, and domestic debt crises.

One notable crisis of the 1980s was that of Mexico. The decade of the 1980s began with a significant increase in real interest rates and a significant decline in non-oil commodity prices. These increased borrowing costs and reduced export revenues for many developing countries, including Mexico. In 1982, in the face of capital flight, the Mexican government announced that it would stop servicing its foreign currency debt. Subsequently, both Argentina and Brazil entered into similar debt and balance of payments crises.

Despite the efforts of the International Monetary Fund to effectively address these crises, international commercial banks began to withdraw credit from many of the developing countries of the world, and the debt crisis became global. Within a few years of the outbreak of these crises, the phenomenon of net capital outflows appeared in which the capital account payments of debtor countries exceeded their capital account receipts. Poverty increased substantially, and much of the developing world, particularly Latin America and Africa, entered what came to be known as the lost decade.

Mexico underwent a second crisis in late 1994 and early 1995 in which it had to abandon its pegged exchange rate, and this was soon followed by the "Asian crisis." Beginning in 1997, crises struck Thailand, Indonesia, the Republic of Korea, and Malaysia, and in 1998, a crisis also hit Russia. In each of these cases, sharp depreciations of the currencies resulted. Subsequent crises hit Brazil in 1999 and Argentina in 2001, bringing the crisis process back to Latin America again.

Eichengreen (1999) made a distinction between "low tech" debt and balance of payments crises such as those of the 1980s and "high tech" financial crises of the 1990s. According to Eichengreen, the following features distinguish the latter, more recent crises: 1. Financial firms had significant exposures in real estate and equities; 2. Capital accounts were liberalized to allow firms (including banks) to take on short-term foreign debt, including debt denominated in foreign currencies; 3. Banks were less than fully regulated and supervised as the countries involved liberalize financial markets and capital accounts; and 4. Firms (including banks) did not adequately hedge their foreign exchange exposures, resulting in vulnerable financial positions. Policy makers need to be aware of each of these potential causes to better mitigate the risks poor people suffer when hit by the effects of crises.

But not all crises originate in developing countries. The world economy, including its developing countries, is now trying to manage a crisis with origins in the developed world. This crisis emerged in the summer of 2007 but hit hard in the fall of 2008. The causes of this crisis were located in the United States and included an unprecedented housing price bubble (nearly doubling in real terms in the decade up to 2007), huge inflows of capital (financing a current account deficit of over 6 percent of GDP), and a lack of prudential financial regulation (including overly-sanguine Chairmen of the US Federal Reserve Alan Greenspan and Ben Bernanke).

In their analysis of this current crisis, Reinhart and Rogoff (2009) stated that "The U.S. conceit that its financial and regulatory system could withstand massive capital inflows on a sustained basis without any problems arguably laid the foundations for the global financial crisis of the late 2000s . . . Outsized financial market return were in fact greatly exaggerated by capital inflows, just as would be the case in emerging markets" (p. 212). Goldin and Vogel (2010) pointed to the rise of systemic risk as increasingly globalized finance outpaces institutional structures to manage it. They warned that "A fundamental regulator shift is nowhere in sight and no international supervisory body has done more than make vague recommendations about the radical structural . . . changes needed" (p. 10). These considerations suggest that crises will be with us for some time to come.

Sources: Eichengreen (1999), Reinhart and Rogoff (2009), and Goldin and Vogel (2010).

significant in the 1990s and 2000s, far exceeding commercial bank lending. FDI flows stagnated from 1998 to 2001 after the 1997 Asian crisis, but recovered in 2002, grew strongly through 2008 but decreased in 2009 due to the financial crisis. FDI now stands as by far the most important capital flow to the low income countries, having reached US$15 billion in 2008. However, these FDI flows are both small relative to the total population of the low-income countries and very unevenly distributed among them.

Third, portfolio investment in the form of bonds and equities has been an occasionally significant but fickle source of resources for the low-income countries. These investments provided substantial positive net flows in some years, but also substantial negative net flows in other years. For example, equity investment was approximately US$140 million in 2007 and 2008 but turned negative in 2009. Bond finance has been negligible since 2000. This sort of volatility is part and parcel of portfolio investment flows.

4.1.2 CAPITAL FLOWS TO MIDDLE-INCOME COUNTRIES

Figure 4.2 presents net capital flows to the middle-income countries of the developing world. These are an order of magnitude larger than those to the low-income countries (Figure 4.1 is in millions of US dollars whereas Figure 4.2 is in billions of US dollars). Capital flows to the middle-income countries have also behaved somewhat differently than those to low-income countries. Again, in the early years, commercial bank lending was the most important source of foreign capital. This type of lending was reduced after the 1982 Mexican crisis, and FDI began to replace it in the late 1980s. As with the low-income countries, despite some stagnation after the 1997 Asian crisis, FDI currently dwarfs all other sources of capital flows to the middle-income countries.

Commercial bank lending and portfolio bond and equity flows were important during the 1990s. Portfolio bond flows held up better after the Asian crisis than they did in the low-income countries, and these flows recovered substantially beginning in 2004. Indeed, commercial bank lending, equity investment, and bond finance were all important even relative to FDI

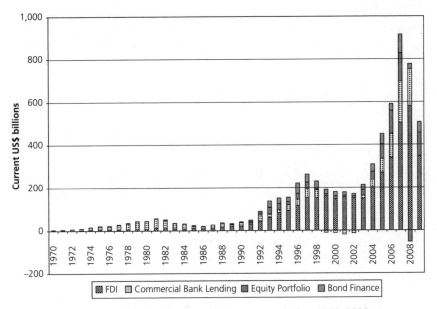

Figure 4.2. Net private capital flows to middle-income countries, 1970–2009

Source: World Development Indicators (http://databank.worldbank.org), 2010.

from 2005 through 2007. In 2008, however, bond finance collapsed and net equity investment turned negative, again pointing to the volatile nature of these portfolio flows.[3]

4.1.3 CAPITAL FLOWS IN PERSPECTIVE

What explains the significant increase in capital flows to the developing world beginning in the 1990s? Analysts typically divide explanations into internal or "pull" factors and external or "push" factors.[4] Internal factors included improved relationships between developing countries and their creditors, the pursuit of more sound fiscal and monetary policies, capital account liberalization, and the privatization of state-owned assets. External factors included the decline in world interest rates that made assets in developing countries relatively more attractive for portfolio investments, recessions in major developed countries, and a growing integration of world capital markets. This last

[3] One potential point of confusion can arise in interpreting Figures 4.1 and 4.2. As we will see in the next section on financial development, beginning in 2000, the developing world became an *exporter* of capital to the developed world rather than an importer. How then can the positive inflows of capital into the low- and middle-income countries take place? The answer is that the *private* capital inflows of Figures 4.1 and 4.2 are offset by *official* capital outflows that take place through the actions of central banks, especially in the case of the middle-income countries.

[4] See, for example, Calvo, Leiderman, and Reinhart (1996) and de la Torre and Schmukler (2007).

external factor involved the increased participation of global financial firms in developing country markets and the increased role of institutional investors. As such, trade in financial services supported expansions in capital flows, with the trade and capital flow dimensions of globalization interacting to support the expansion in private capital flows. All of these factors changed the global capital flows regime in significant ways.

It is useful to consider the recent history of total capital flows to the developing countries as a percentage of GDP for both low- and middle-income countries (Figure 4.3). Until the 1990s, these ranged between 1 and 2 percent of GDP. During the 1990s, these values began to increase, reaching nearly 4 percent in the case of middle-income countries and over 2 percent for low-income countries. After the Asian crisis, the values fell again, but recovered significantly though 2007 at nearly 6 percent for middle-income countries and at 4 percent for low-income countries. The crisis beginning in 2007 (see Box 4.1) reduced these values in 2008, but it is relevant that beginning in 2008, for the first time since 1970, private capital flows as a percent of GDP are equal for the low- and middle-income countries, reaching only 3 percent of GDP in 2009. Private capital flows are still relatively small as a percentage of developing country GDP and are somewhat volatile.

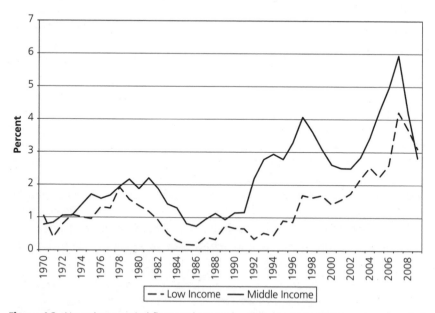

Figure 4.3. Net private capital flows to low- and middle-income countries as a percent of GDP, 1970–2009

Source: World Development Indicators (http://databank.worldbank.org), 2010.

4.2 **Financial development**

A basic, theoretical insight in the field of international finance suggests that flows of capital from developed to developing countries can potentially improve welfare in developing countries.[5] Developing countries can receive net inflows of capital and invest it at relatively high rates of return, the capital being supplied from developed countries where rates of return are relatively low. This reflects the fact that, at early stages of development, the need for capital is high, while domestic saving is low. As development proceeds, the need for capital slowly declines and domestic saving slowly increases. This theoretical framework is highly idealized, however, and a number of intervening factors inhibit capital flows from developed to developing countries. These include political risk, default risk, differences in levels of human capital and technology, and differences in institutional quality.[6] In addition, as first pointed out by Hymer (1976) many years ago, rate of return analysis is *wholly insufficient* even at a theoretical level to explain FDI flows.[7]

Since 2000, the idealized flow of funds has been turned on its head. Due in large part to current account deficits in the United States that has exceeded 5 percent of its GDP, and reflecting the high level of savings on the part of central banks in developing countries, the developing world is now an *exporter* of capital to the developed world rather than an importer. This has come to be known as the "Lucas paradox" after Lucas (1990). At the time of this writing, Chinese official reserves alone are approximately US$2.5 trillion. For rich countries as a whole, for example, global capital *imports* exceeded US$500 billion in 2008. The United States actually imported approximately US$700 billion in 2008, with capital exports of Japan, the European Union, and other high-income countries making up the $200 billion difference. Most of these developing country capital exporters are in East Asia and the Middle East. While this imbalance appears to have been partially corrected by the most recent recession, the IMF predicts that US capital imports will still exceed US$300 billion in 2010, the opposite of what we would desire from a development or poverty alleviation standpoint. Addressing fiscal imbalances in the United States is, therefore, of key importance to poverty alleviating capital flows.

These sorts of global imbalances are only one side of the explanation of why the developing world fails to attract more capital. As just mentioned, the relevant factors include political risk, default risk, differences in levels of human capital and technology, and differences in institutional quality. While

---

[5] See, for example, Taylor and Williamson (1994).

[6] See, for example, Lucas (1990) and Alfaro, Kalemli-Ozcan, and Volosovych (2008).

[7] See also chapters 1 and 2 of Caves (2007) on the role of firm-specific assets in the modern theory of multinational enterprises and patterns of FDI.

not wanting to downplay any of these factors in particular cases, the empirical evidence of Alfaro, Kalemli-Ozcan, and Volosovych (2008) suggest that institutional factors loom large in the failure of developing countries to attract more capital. So along with fiscal adjustment in the United States, institutional development in low- and middle-income countries remains a priority.

4.2.1 FINANCIAL MARKETS AND FINANCIAL SECTOR DEVELOPMENT

Financial markets, both global and domestic, are an important component of economic development and poverty alleviation. Capital flows can support savings mobilization and deployment, financial sector development, and technology transfer. They also have the potential to manage various types of risk and to monitor the performance of firms' managers. Empirically, there is some (admittedly ambiguous) evidence that financial sector development helps to explain economic growth.[8] It appears that this growth effect occurs primarily through increasing productivity and reducing external finance costs rather than through increases in savings.[9] The potential growth effects of financial sector development appear to be important for both banking and equity markets.[10]

Global capital flows are only one aspect of financial sector development, and the flows themselves are not always taken into account in growth investigations. This weakness was strenuously studied by Prasad, Rajan, and Subramanian (2007). Their results suggest that one key institutional weakness in developing countries is financial sector development itself. In particular, financial sector underdevelopment is what prevents foreign capital from contributing positively to growth. In the view of these researchers, "if poor countries are seeking to improve financing for industry, instead of just hankering after additional financing in the form of foreign capital, they can reap substantial benefits from focusing on domestic financial development."[11]

There is also evidence that not all types of capital flows have the same impact on growth and development. For example, capital inflows in the form of FDI and equity portfolio investment appear in some studies to be more beneficial than both bond finance and commercial bank lending.[12] More generally, there

---

[8] This possibility was discussed in Pagano (1993). Evidence was provided by King and Levine (1993). See also Prasad, Rajan, and Subramanian (2007).

[9] On productivity effects, see Beck, Levine, and Loayza (2000). This research supports what is known as the "Schumpeterian view" of the role of finance in development (after Schumpeter 1934/ 1949) in which the primary effects of financial development are on the productivity of firms. On external finance effects, see Rajan and Zingales (1998).

[10] See Levine and Zervos (1998).

[11] Prasad, Rajan, and Subramanian (2007), p. 195.

[12] See Reisen and Soto (2001) and Kose et al. (2009). The overall growth effects of FDI had been called into question by Caves (2007), who wrote: "No overall theoretical prediction connects the stock

is widespread agreement that financial globalization via capital flows can make effective financial development more challenging by increasing *both* benefits *and* risks. In particular, Goldin and Vogel (2010) drew attention to increases systemic risk inherent in global capital flows. For these reasons, general, across-the-board statements about the role of capital flows in financial development are thus difficult to support.

It is also important to view capital flows in the context of domestic capital mobilization. As we saw in Figures 4.1 and 4.2, the most important type of capital inflow into developing countries is FDI. However, on average, FDI is but a relatively small portion of total domestic investment (and savings) in low- and middle-income countries. For example, for these two groups of countries in 2008, FDI was 18 percent and 15 percent of total domestic investment, respectively. Therefore, increases in the capital flow dimension of economic globalization have in no way lessened the importance of domestic investment, domestic savings, and the domestic environments influencing them. This point is particularly important in light of the evidence presented in Prasad, Rajan, and Subramanian (2007) that in most developing countries domestic investment translates more quickly into growth than foreign investment and by Rodrik and Subramanian (2009) that many developing countries are investment constrained.[13]

Residents of low- and middle-income countries hold a great deal of their wealth in the form of *flight capital,* which are assets held abroad because of poor domestic investment opportunities and high domestic risks. Estimates of the magnitude of flight capital vary and, because such flows are not always officially recorded, must be regarded with some caution. They suggest, however, that capital flight represents a substantial portion of private wealth and a multiple of foreign debt for sub-Saharan Africa.[14] Consequently, any significant improvement in the investment and financial climates of these developing regions could result in a substantial repatriation of resources. Not all resources for development and poverty alleviation need to come from foreign sources. It would be possible for repatriated wealth to provide a substantial portion of a country's resources.[15]

The financial markets involved in equity portfolio investment, bond finance, and commercial bank lending are characterized by a number of imperfections, which economists call *market failures.* In normal circumstances, these imperfections contribute to a certain amount of market

---

of foreign investment to the rate at which national income grows" (p. 278). This ambiguity is reiterated in the case of Africa by Bhinda et al. (1999). Alfaro et al. (2004, 2009), however, have pointed to the role of financial development in the effect of FDI on growth.

[13] See also Nunnenkamp (2004).

[14] See Collier, Hoeffler, and Pattillo (2001) and Ndikumana and Boyce (2010).

[15] This point has been forcibly made by Fofack and Ndikumana (2010).

volatility. Under certain circumstances, they can lead to full-blown financial crises of the kind experienced in Mexico (1994–1995), Asia (1997), Russia (1998), Brazil (1999), and Argentina (2001) and the United States (2007–2009).[16] It is important to understand these market imperfections to appreciate the effects of these three types of capital flows on poor people.

Financial markets do not operate with full information. By their very nature (which involves the exchange of assets), financial markets have an important inter-temporal component, and no market participant possesses perfect information about the future. Consequently, financial markets inherently involve an inter-temporal "leap in the dark" of one sort or another. There is often an *asymmetry* in the information available to borrowers and lenders in which borrowers have more information about their creditworthiness than lenders.[17]

In situations where monitoring borrowers' behavior is costly and where weak property rights mean enforcing collateral obligations is problematic, repayment of loans is likely to be low, making financial institutions reluctant to lend. Such asymmetries in information can lead to market failure in which changes in expectations cause swift changes in behavior, despite the lack of change in fundamental economic conditions. This can be pernicious because lender confidence consequently tends to be "pro-cyclical," remaining strong in business upturns but suddenly evaporating during downturns of various sorts.

For example, financial market failure in the form of asymmetric information has been shown by Yuan (2005) to contribute in certain circumstances to generate a behavior known as *contagion* (see Box 4.2) Contagion exists where problems with regard to one financial instrument or country spread to other financial instruments or countries. The key contributing factor is attempts by market participants to maintain liquidity. Further, there is a feedback in that Mishkin (1999) has shown that financial crises can worsen asymmetric information problems.

Credit rating agencies provide information to potential investors in capital markets. Their ratings are closely scrutinized by investors, and achieving "investment grade" status is an important milestone for governments, public utilities, and corporate entities seeking to raise money in international markets. Extending the reach of credit rating agencies to include a growing number of developing countries has helped to widen information about these markets. Credit rating agencies play a vital role in overcoming information asymmetries in financial markets, but the fact that they only partially extend across middle-income countries and are virtually absent from low-income countries means

---

[16] Reviews of the economic literature on crises can be found in Eichengreen (1999) and Reinhart and Rogoff (2009).

[17] See, for example, Stiglitz and Weiss (1981) and Williamson (1987). For the role of asymmetric information in influencing institutional investors, see Frenkel and Menkhoff (2004).

BOX 4.2 CONTAGION

The idea of contagion in international finance refers to the spread of a financial crisis from one country to another. As expressed by Kaminsky, Reinhart, and Végh (2003), "some financial events . . . trigger an immediate and startling adverse chain reaction among countries within a region and in some cases across regions" (p. 51). At times, contagion episodes take on more colorful language. For example, the spread of the 1994–1995 Mexican crisis to other countries in Latin America became known as the "tequila effect," and the spread of the 1997 crisis in Thailand to other countries in Asia became known as the "Asian flu." Contagion can make economic management even more difficult than it normally is.

The notion of a crisis "spreading" from one country to another is informal. More formally, we need to consider what exactly is transmitted across national boundaries. Unfortunately, there are a wide variety of possibilities here and differing opinions among specialists in international finance. Some common identifiers include shifts in expectations and confidence ("herding" or "informational cascades"), asset prices ("financial linkage"), and capital flight ("sudden stops"). Historically, commercial bank lending is often an important component of sudden stops, but equity and bond finance flows can also be involved.

Contagion does not always take place in cases where we might otherwise expect it. For example, Kaminsky, Reinhart, and Végh (2003) noted the lack of contagion accompanying the 1999 devaluation of the Brazilian real, the 2001 demise of the Argentine currency board, and the 2001 devaluation of the Turkish lira. These are indeed very large emerging markets, so the lack of contagion in these cases was notable. These authors identify three causal factors that contribute to episodes of contagion: sudden stops in capital inflows, surprise announcements to financial markets, and highly leveraged financial institutions. Joyce and Nabar (2009) showed that sudden stops interact with banking sectors to cause banking crises. It therefore appears that sudden stops, banking crises, and contagion can all be related to one another.

Sources: Kaminsky, Reinhart, and Végh (2003) and Joyce and Nabar (2009).

---

that their limitations need to be recognized. Their ratings also are not predictive in nature: countries and companies that have performed well in ratings have succumbed to crises and failure. Credit rating agencies enhance information flows, and this may even at times exacerbate herding in markets. They perform a vital function, but are no panacea for asymmetry of information in the markets.

Financial market imperfections are compounded by government failure in at least two ways. Firstly, excessive government debt can precipitate full scale financial crisis, as occurred in the Latin American debt crises of the 1980s. Secondly, necessary attempts to regulate financial markets can at times make matters worse. Like other financial market participants, governments also suffer from imperfect information, and their attempts to offer support in times of crisis can provide an incentive for excessively risky behavior in financial markets, something that economists call "moral hazard." Both market failure and government failure characterize markets in equities, bonds, and bank lending, and they can complicate hoped for effects of poverty alleviation.

Imperfections in financial markets appear to be particularly problematic when commercial banks in developing countries are given access to short-term, foreign-lending sources.[18] The resulting problems have three causes:

- First, systems of financial intermediation in developing countries tend to rely heavily on the banking sector, because other types of financial intermediation are typically underdeveloped.

- Second, developing countries have been encouraged to liberalize domestic financial markets, sometimes before systems of prudential bank regulation and management are put in place.

- Third, developing countries have sometimes prematurely liberalized their capital accounts, on which most of the private capital flows take place.[19]

Consequently, and as will be discussed below, care must be taken in managing evolving banking systems and their access to international capital flows.

Financial crises are devastating to poor people and therefore should be avoided if at all possible. Poor people are particularly vulnerable to crises because they do not have the savings or safety nets to protect themselves from the income losses that are an inherent part of these events. It is common to consider the costs of crises in terms of the percentage of GDP lost in a particular country or region. For example, Eichengreen (2004) estimated the cost of an average crisis to be approximately 9 percent of GDP for the country in question. In the case of the Asian crisis, Dobson and Hufbauer (2001) estimated the cost to the *region* at up to 1.5 percent of GDP, but World Bank estimated that it involved 20 million persons falling back into poverty and 1 million children being withdrawn from school. Even this estimate may understate the impact. Suryahadi, Sumarto, and Pritchett (2003), suggested that, in Indonesia alone and at the peak of the increase in poverty, approximately 35 million persons were pushed into absolute poverty. During the Argentine crises of 2001, close to one-fourth of the population became extremely poor, while one-half of the population fell below the national poverty line.

The global nature of the 2007–2009 crisis may mean its costs to the developing world are even higher than for the Asian crisis: the World Bank

---

[18] Kose et al. (2009) state that "The procyclical and highly volatile nature of...short-term bank loans...can magnify the adverse impact of negative shocks on economic growth" (p. 38).

[19] As the World Bank (2001) noted, "Poor sequencing of financial liberalization in a poor country environment has undoubtedly contributed to bank insolvency" (p. 89). Hanson, Honohan, and Majnoni (2003) also noted that "the riskiness of capital account liberalization without fiscal adjustment...and without reasonably strong financial regulation and supervision and a sound domestic financial system, is well recognized" (p. 10). Rodrik and Subramanian (2009) cautioned that "Even advanced economies have a hard time putting in place the kind of finely tuned and calibrated prudential regulations that would rein in excessive risk taking by financial intermediaries that have been set free" (p. 125).

estimated that low- and middle-income countries lost 3–8 percent of potential output compared with the pre-crisis path, with 64 million more people in absolute poverty than if the crisis had not occurred.[20] The United Nations Food and Agriculture Organization estimated that the crisis increased the number of undernourished people by tens of millions.[21] Changes in poverty of these magnitudes matter a great deal.[22]

Given these potentially severe poverty effects, caution is warranted. Although there is not complete agreement among those who have examined these issues, there is evidence that the sequence and timing of financial sector reforms can mitigate financial turmoil and, thereby, prevent negative effects on poor people. As mentioned above, the liberalization of financial markets can strengthen the development process in the long run. However, financial liberalization without the proper surveillance capability may destabilize local financial sectors, real economies, and domestic political environments.[23] There are many examples where excessive liquidity associated with booms and market overconfidence were followed by excessive pessimism and capital flow reversals. In all of these outcomes, poor people suffer the most. Careful financial sector development should therefore be combined with carefully targeted safety nets to protect poor people.

The difficulty here is that, as pointed out by Rodrik and Subramanian (2009), implementing the prudential regulation to shelter developing countries from the vicissitudes of global finance is not easy. As is now clear in the current crisis, even the developed countries with the allegedly most advanced financial systems (e.g. the United States and United Kingdom) have not been able to effectively take on this important task. We therefore need to be cautious about asking developing countries to take on too much in the area of building systems of prudential regulation before they are in a position to do so. We return to this important issue at the end of the chapter.

---

[20] See World Bank (2010).

[21] See United Nations Food and Agriculture Organization (2009). They estimate that the number of undernourished people has now risen over 1 billion, the highest number since 1970.

[22] Even short of actual crises, there is some reason for concern about the potentially negative impact of capital flows on poor people. For people at or near poverty lines, any volatility in consumption can be quite detrimental or even disastrous. From a theoretical point of view, capital flows can reduce the volatility of consumption by de-linking it from national output volatility. Unfortunately, there is empirical evidence that increased financial integration through expanding capital flows can increase rather than decrease consumption volatility in developing countries. See Kose, Prasad, and Terrones (2003), Prasad et al. (2005), and Kose et al. (2009).

[23] These risks are all the more significant when countries are characterized by "currency mismatches" in which assets are denominated in the local currency and liabilities in foreign currencies. Consequently, net worth is directly tied to the value of the local currency. On this issue, see Goldstein and Turner (2004).

4.3 **Foreign direct investment**

Foreign direct investment can have positive effects on poverty alleviation by creating employment, improving technology and human capital, and promoting competition. While FDI can and does often contribute in these ways, at times it may adversely affect certain dimensions of poverty through unsafe working conditions, environmental destruction, and increased corruption. Nevertheless, if we were to identify the most promising category of capital flows from the point of view of poverty alleviation, FDI would be it.

As shown in Figure 4.4, global flows of FDI are highly concentrated, with low-income countries being dramatically uninvolved as FDI recipients. In 2009, for example, the low-income countries accounted for 12 percent of global population, only 1 percent of global GDP, and only 1 percent of global FDI. The middle-income countries are much more active as FDI recipients. In 2009, these countries accounted for 71 percent of global population, 43 percent of global GDP, and 32 percent of global FDI. As is also clear from Figure 4.4, the bulk of global FDI flows in 2009 (67 percent) went to the high-income countries of the world.

The lack of involvement on the part of low-income countries as FDI hosts is a major impediment to poverty alleviation. Even the fact that the low-income countries received only 1 percent of FDI in 2009 vastly understates the problem, because this 1 percent of the total flows is highly concentrated

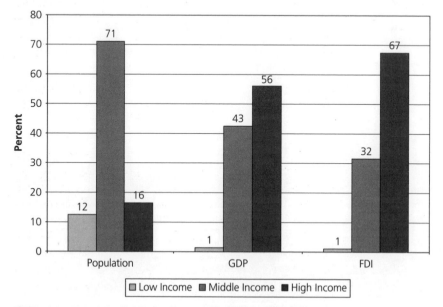

Figure 4.4. Global shares of population, PPP GDP, and FDI, 2009

Source: World Development Indicators (http://databank.worldbank.org), 2010.

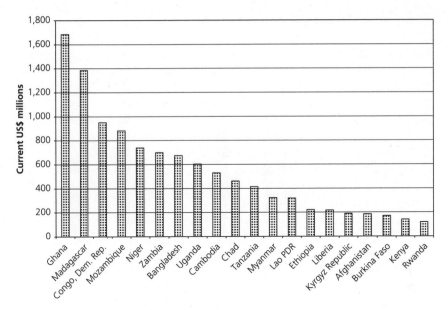

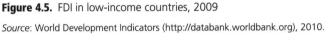

Figure 4.5. FDI in low-income countries, 2009

Source: World Development Indicators (http://databank.worldbank.org), 2010.

among these poor countries. As is shown in Figure 4.5, the top five low-income countries accounted for more than half of the FDI flows into all low-income countries. For most low-income countries, access to FDI has remains elusive with growth driven by low levels of domestic rather than foreign investment. Consequently, foreign aid in support of growth continues to be important to the low-income countries.

Might it be possible to overcome the lack of FDI in low-income countries? Noting that investment climate rankings (particularly that of *Institutional Investor*) tend to lag real reform efforts in low-income countries, Collier (2007) was unhopeful. He stated, "don't count on global capital mobility to develop the bottom billion."[24] But this conclusion begs the question of what reforms might help in promoting FDI inflows. Bénassy-Quéré, Coupet, and Mayer (2007) rightly drew attention to the concept of "institutional distance" in inhibiting FDI inflows (or promoting outflows), and such distance is not easily overcome. While difficulties in attracting FDI are notable, successes are also evident. A comparison of net FDI inflows between 1990 and 2008 for low-income countries shows dramatic increases in FDI for some of these countries.

For example, Figure 4.6 reports FDI flows for Bangladesh, Ethiopia, the Gambia, Ghana, Guinea, Mozambique, Rwanda, and Uganda as a percent of

[24] Collier (2007), p. 93.

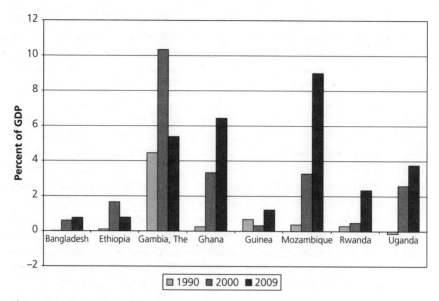

Figure 4.6. FDI in selected low-income countries as a percent of GDP

Source: World Development Indicators (http://databank.worldbank.org), 2010.

GDP for 1990, 2000, and 2009. While it is true that most of these increases are from extraordinary low levels, it does seem that change is possible over time. Institutional change can occur, but ensuring that the resulting flows are development friendly will always be a key issue.

4.3.1 LEVERAGING FDI

Many developing countries lack access to the technologies available in developed countries. Since multinational enterprises (MNEs) account for approximately three-fourths of worldwide civilian research and development, hosting MNEs from developed countries is potentially one important way to gain access to that technology. There are two problems with this idealized scenario, however. First, MNEs will employ the technology that most suits *their* strategic needs, not necessarily the development needs of host countries. For example, MNEs can employ processes that are much more capital intensive than host country employment considerations may want. For example, Caves' (2007, chapter 9) relatively extensive review suggested that, although some MNEs adapt their technologies to local environments, this adaptation is not widespread or more than minimal.

Second, there has been a tendency for MNEs to conduct their research and development (R&D) in their home bases rather than in host countries. For example, UNCTAD (2005) reported that "R&D is among the least internationalized segments of the (MNE's) value chain; production, marketing and other functions have moved abroad much more quickly."[25] This historical pattern of R&D on the part of MNEs is now undergoing a change. Part of the reason is due to increased expansion of information and communication technologies (ICT). A second reason is the increased prominence of key emerging markets and the need to better tailor products to these markets. A third reason, is the fact that scientific and engineering talent is no longer confined to the traditional home bases of MNEs, namely Western Europe, the United States, and Japan. To name just two countries, China and India have emerged as sources of scientific and engineering talent.[26] MNEs that want to tap into this talent can either recruit this talent by bringing it to their home bases and other R&D sites via high-skilled migration. Alternatively, they can begin to relocate their R&D. Many MNEs have begun to relocate more applied research (the D in R&D).[27]

Despite these limitations, there is evidence that, in some important cases, MNEs do transfer technology and establish significant relationships with host country suppliers through what economists call *backward linkages*.[28] For example, Moran (2001) reviewed the evidence in the automotive, computer, and electronics sectors and summarized his conclusion as follows:[29]

Foreign investors whose local operations comprise an integral part of the parent's global or regional sourcing network introduce state-of-the-art technology and business practices into the host economy both via the investment that the parent makes in the performance of its own subsidiary and via the supervision that the parent and subsidiary exercise over the performance of local suppliers.[30]

If the foreign MNE begins to source inputs locally rather than importing them, the host country can gain a number of important benefits:

- Employment can increase because the sourced inputs represent new production.
- Production technologies can be better adapted to local conditions because suppliers are more likely to employ labor-intensive processes.
- The MNE can transfer state-of-the-art business practices and technologies to the local suppliers.
- It is possible that the local suppliers can coalesce into a spatial cluster that supports innovation and upgrading.

The policies required to support such links are considered in Box 4.3.

Taking Japanese MNEs in Thailand as an example of creating links, Moran (2001) reported:

---

[25] UNCTAD (2005), p. 121.
[26] See, for example, Yusuf, Nabeshima, and Perkins (2006).
[27] See, for example, chapter 7 of Caves (2007) and the many references therein.
[28] See Javorcik (2004), for example.
[29] See also Moran (1998).
[30] Moran (2001), p. 24.

BOX 4.3 CREATING LINKAGES

The World Trade Organization includes an Agreement on Trade Related Investment Measures (TRIMs) that prohibits local content requirements that developing countries used to deploy to ensure backward linkages from MNEs to domestic suppliers. As a result of this changed policy context, new thinking has suggested that local content requirements should be replaced by efforts to support local suppliers in their attempts to secure contracts with foreign MNEs. This backward linkage promotion process involves many players, including the government, foreign MNEs, local suppliers, professional organizations, commercial organizations, and academic institutions. The key role of the government is that of coordinator, attempting to bridge the "information gaps" among the players. The government can do this in a number of different ways:

- First, in the realm of information, attempts can be made to provide a matching service between MNEs and local suppliers. This can be done by inviting the relevant players to link promotion forums.

- Second, in the realm of technology, efforts can be made to provide support in standards formation, materials testing, and patent registration. In addition, foreign MNEs can be invited to be involved in programs designed to upgrade local suppliers' technological capabilities.

- Third, in human resources development, efforts can be made to provide technical training and managerial training.

- Finally, in the area of finance, obstacles to access on the part of small firms can be removed.

Efforts in these and other areas typically must be coordinated by a lead agency. In the cases of Costa Rica, Ireland, and Singapore, the Costa Rican Investment Board, an Irish National Linkage Program, and the Singapore Economic Development Board have played this role. Other developing countries can learn from these experiences.

Sources: Battat, Frank, and Shen (1996) and UNCTAD (2001).

As for the impact of foreign investors on local Thai firms, the Japanese assemblers took an active role in organizing 'cooperation clubs' of the kind that were characteristic of supplier relations in the home country to assist with quality control, cost reduction, scheduling and delivery, and product improvement. Within the first 10 years after the turn toward offshore sourcing by the Japanese parents, some 150 local firms qualified for original equipment manufacturer (OEM) status.... An additional 200 to 250 Thai firms received replacement equipments manufacturer (REM) certification. These suppliers, like the foreign affiliates themselves, were able to capture economies of scale, and to use different and more sophisticated production techniques, than local firms elsewhere in Asia.[31]

4.3.2 SPILLOVER EFFECTS

Another avenue through which MNEs can positively affect host economies is through "spillovers" to other firms operating in the same industry and to

---

[31] Moran (2001), pp. 17–18.

other sectors of these economies. For example, FDI in the automotive sector might benefit production technology in domestic auto part firms or in domestic machine tool firms. Indeed, there is a presumption in much of the literature on FDI that MNEs provide positive spillovers in the form of upgrading technology to domestic firms in the host country. This line of thinking goes back to Caves (1974) who empirically tested this possibility for Canada and Australia. The evidence to date suggests that such spillovers do occur in some circumstances and can be significant, but overall the evidence is somewhat mixed and nuanced.

A sample of studies in this area is given in Table 4.1. As can be seen here, most studies do find evidence of positive spillovers. However, in the words of Blomström and Sjöholm (1999), they are not "guaranteed, automatic, or free." Further, as noted by Caves (2007), "demonstrated spillovers occur so as to suggest domestic firms must possess *substantial competence* before they can sup up spilled technology."[32] This has led to an exploration of domestic preconditions that can contribute to or suppress positive spillovers.

What determines whether positive technology spillovers will occur? One key factor is the capacity of local firms to absorb foreign technologies. Blomström and Kokko (2003) suggested that *learning* is a key capacity that is responsive to various host country policies, and evidence presented in Tsang, Nguyen, and Erramilli (2004) in the case of Vietnam supported this view. Because learning is so important, a lack of human capital in the form of skills and education tends to prevent the generation of positive spillovers. For example, Kokko (1994) found evidence of learning barriers in Mexico in that spillovers were negatively related to the productivity gaps between MNEs and domestic firms. Additionally, Kokko and Blomström (1995) found evidence that the technology transfers of US MNEs have been positively affected by levels of education in host countries. Consequently, basic education and skills development have a major role in making the most of FDI for poverty alleviation.

Relatedly, there is strong evidence that MNEs offer higher *wages* than domestic firms. This is the conclusion of te Velde and Morrissey (2003) based on evidence from five African countries.[33] This effect is more predominant for skilled than unskilled workers. In the long run, wages depend on education and training levels, and there is some evidence that MNEs will engage in important training activities. This appears to be more likely when MNEs are large, operate in competitive environments, and are export oriented.[34] As with the wage effects, however, training is more likely to be directed toward skilled than toward unskilled workers. In a way similar to that of international trade (discussed in Chapter 3), then, FDI can have differential effects that are positive

---

[32] Caves (2007), p. 221 (emphasis added).
[33] See also Arnold and Javorcik (2009).
[34] See te Velde (2001) and references therein.

Table 4.1 A sample of research on the spillover effects of FDI

Study	Countries	Findings
Aitken and Harrison (1999)	Venezuela	Found two effects of FDI on local firms. First, a positive relationship between foreign equity and performance in plants with less than 50 workers. Second, negative spillovers from market-stealing effects. On net, evidence of only a small impact of FDI on plant productivity.
Arnold and Javorcik (2009)	Indonesia	Evidence of positive spillovers due to acquisition and restructuring of domestic firms. Foreign ownership leads to higher productivity and share of skilled workers.
Blalock and Gertler (2008)	Indonesia	Evidence of positive spillovers due to technology transfer to local suppliers and positive externality from these suppliers to other downstream buyers.
Blomström (1986)	Mexico	Evidence of positive spillovers due to increased competition.
Blomström and Sjöholm (1999)	Indonesia	Evidence of positive spillovers due to increased competition restricted to non-exporting, local firms.
Blomström and Persson (1983)	Mexico	Evidence of positive spillovers associated with increased technological efficiency.
Chuang and Lin (1999)	Taiwan	Evidence of positive technology spillovers.
Chudnovsky and López (2007)	Argentina, Brazil, and Uruguay	No evidence of spillovers (Argentina). Negative spillovers for local firms from competition (Brazil and Uruguay). In all countries, spillover effects depend on the capacity of absorption of domestic firms.
Haddad and Harrison (1993)	Morocco	Although the dispersion of productivity levels is narrower in sectors with more foreign firms, no evidence of positive spillovers.
Javocik (2004)	Lithuania	Evidence of positive spillovers to local suppliers through backward linkages. These effects come from joint ventures rather than wholly-owned foreign firms.
Kohpaiboon (2006)	Thailand	Foreign firms can either positively or negatively affect the productivity of local firms depending on the trade regime.
Kokko (1994)	Mexico	Potential positive spillovers were negatively related to productivity gaps between MNEs and domestic firm and differ among industries.
Kokko, Tansini, and Zehan (1996)	Uruguay	Little evidence of positive spillovers with only a small effect when the technology gap between local and foreign firms is small.
Kugler (2006)	Colombia	Evidence of spillovers to local upstream suppliers through diffusion of generic upstream suppliers.
Liu (2002)	China	Evidence of positive spillover effect on domestic sectors through technology transfers.
Marin and Bell (2006)	Argentina	Evidence of positive spillovers conditional on activity of MNE subsidiaries. Spillover effects depend on the local knowledge creation of subsidiaries.
Tsou and Liu (1994)	Taiwan	Evidence of positive spillovers for firms with technological capabilities.
Wei and Liu (2006)	China	Evidence of positive spillovers.

for skilled workers but that exclude unskilled workers. This can result in what te Velde (2001) referred to as the "low-income low-skill trap."

Emerging evidence (e.g. Alfaro et al. 2004 and Alfaro, Kalemli-Ozcan, and Sayek 2009) suggests that *financial development* itself is one precondition for positive technology spillovers. This is simply due to the fact that, in order to take advantage of new technological possibilities, domestic firms will most likely need to make some additional investments via domestic borrowing. Without adequately developed domestic financial markets, this is not possible. Consequently, issues of financial development discussed above are relevant to possible spillover effects.

4.3.3 COSTS OF HOSTING FDI

Hosting FDI is not without its potential costs. For example, concern has been raised about the practice of *transfer pricing*. Transfer pricing involves the manipulation intra-firm trade prices by MNEs to reduce their global tax payments. In the case of the United States, with more resources to martial against this practice than any other country, it has been estimated that annual losses in tax revenue are on the order of US$50 billion.[35] The solution to the transfer pricing problem is multifaceted and not straightforward, but it is clear that a multilateral approach is the preferred solution. Such options include forming international guidelines and codes of conduct, using international standards of invoicing and customs procedures, harmonizing global tax systems, negotiating and concluding international conventions, and establishing international arbitration procedures. However, to make these options work, resources must be provided to low-income countries for them to effectively combat transfer pricing abuses.

Further costs of FDI can be encountered in the petroleum and mining sectors, sometimes referred to as "extractive industries." These costs include environmental degradation, social dislocation, social and ethnic conflict, and corruption in revenue streams. There is no evidence that FDI in the aggregate contributes to conflict (e.g. Blanton and Apodaca 2007), but in some circumstances FDI in extractive industries can do so (e.g. conflict minerals in the Democratic Republic of the Congo). As we will discuss further in Chapter 8, these costs can potentially be mitigated through the Extractive Industries Transparency Initiative.

4.3.4 AN ASSESSMENT

FDI is potentially the most important capital flow from the point of view of poverty alleviation. FDI can be a means of employment generation, especially

---

[35] See Plender (2004).

when it takes place in labor-intensive sectors. It can also be a means of technology and management transfer, especially where effective backward linkages have been established. Technology transfer and spillover effects involve learning processes, and these in turn require that minimal thresholds of human capital be met. Without advances in education, training, and health, few long-term gains from FDI take place. Advances in the investment climate and the environment for doing business, both for foreign and domestic investors, are also vital. Policy makers have a role to play in facilitating investment by combating corruption, streamlining procedures, and investing in the physical and human capacities that are the foundation for not only foreign but more importantly for domestic investment.

For FDI to have a greater role in poverty reduction, it is also necessary to address the following issues. First, FDI is highly concentrated among middle-income countries and just a handful of low-income countries. Second, for extractive industries (such as mining and petroleum), steps must be taken to ensure that the FDI does indeed contribute to poverty alleviation, especially in the context of weak governance mechanisms. Third, transfer pricing abuses may rob developing countries of the tax revenues they desperately need to make the very investments required for FDI to contribute positively to poverty alleviation. We return to some of these issues in Chapter 8.

4.4 Equity portfolio investment

Evidence suggests that financial development can have a positive impact on growth, but not all types of financial activity and capital inflows have the same effects. In particular, capital inflows in the form of equity portfolio investment might be more beneficial than either bond finance or commercial bank lending. For example, Reisen and Soto (2001) examined the impact of all four capital inflows considered in this chapter on growth for a sample of 44 countries. They found that FDI and equity portfolio flows did have a positive impact on economic growth. Bond finance, considered below, did not have any impact on growth. Commercial bank lending, also considered below, had a negative impact. These results suggest that equity inflows, along with FDI, could play an especially positive role in growth, development, and poverty alleviation.

Why can equity portfolio investment play a positive role in growth and development, at least under some circumstances? Rousseau and Wachtel (2000) addressed this question with four possibilities:

- Equity portfolio inflows are an important source of funds for developing countries.

- The development of equity markets helps to provide an exit mechanism for venture capitalists, and this increases entrepreneurial activity.
- Equity portfolio inflows assist developing countries to move from short-term finance to longer-term finance. They also help to finance investment in projects that have economies of scale.
- The development of equity markets provides an informational mechanism evaluating the performance of domestic firms and can help provide incentives to managers to perform well.

Some evidence suggests that institutional investors managing equity flows are less likely than banks to engage in herd and contagion behavior, thus making volatility less of an issue. However, under some circumstances, these herd and contagion behaviors appear strongly, especially for non-resident, foreign investors who are at an informational disadvantage. Figure 4.7 shows that, after a period of volatility in the 1990s and early 2000s encompassing the Asian crisis and the 2001–2002 recession, 2002–2007 saw strong growth in equity flows to the developing world, supporting significant gains in emerging market stock indices.

After peaking at US$133 billion dollars in 2007, however, equity flows in the developing world collapsed and reversed themselves to a US$53 billion outflow in 2008 following the US sub-prime crisis. This recent history (a classic "sudden stop") calls into question the common characterization of equity flows as non-volatile. Although equity flows have subsequently recovered since 2008, the dangers of excessive volatility even in this type of capital flow are

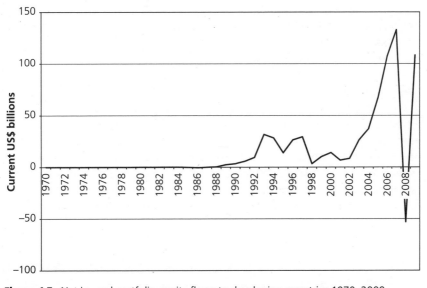

Figure 4.7. Net inward portfolio equity flows to developing countries 1970–2009

Source: World Development Indicators (http://databank.worldbank.org), 2010.

now clear. According to the World Bank (2010), long-term prospects for equity finance are positive, although risks remain.

The evidence on the role of global integration on equity market prices, as opposed to flows, is more mixed. For example, Asian equity markets recovered values fairly quickly after the 1997 crisis. Emerging economy equity prices were strongly and adversely affected in 2007–2008 by the global financial crisis, which originated in the developed world. However, by 2009 emerging market stock indices had recovered more than half the value lost during the crisis, rebounding much more strongly than developed economy equity prices. As noted some time ago by the World Bank (2001):

There is no clear theoretical presumption as to whether local stock prices will be more or less volatile after integration into the world market. Integration should insulate the prices from shocks that affect the nonmarket wealth or savings behavior of local investors, but could expose them more to fluctuations in world asset prices and to shifts in external investor preferences.[36]

4.4.1 DEVELOPING COUNTRY EQUITY MARKETS

In general, equity markets are underdeveloped in much of the developing world. For example, nearly the entire net portfolio equity inflows into sub-Saharan Africa are accounted for by one country alone: South Africa. Between 2000 and 2007 stock market capitalization in developing countries increased by 79 percent of GDP in developing countries. Nonetheless, market capitalization in low-income countries is still low compared with that in high-income countries. Furthermore, the World Bank (2004b) summarized the features of developing country equity markets as follows:

Stock exchanges in developing countries . . . tend to lag technologically behind developed markets. Technology plays a major role in the trading, clearance, and settlement processes; problems in those areas can discourage sophisticated investors. Institutions that supervise and support the operation of the stock exchange also tend to be weaker in developing countries.[37]

The example of the Nairobi Stock Exchange is taken up in Box 4.4. Elsewhere in Africa, the Johannesburg stock market has a capitalization that far exceeds that of the rest of Africa (US$690 billion in August 2009). In many respects, it has become a model for emerging markets, but it too has suffered from the migration of some of the most global listings to London and New York.

---

[36] World Bank (2001), p. 173. See also Hanson, Honohan, and Majnoni (2003).
[37] World Bank (2004b), p 95.

BOX 4.4 THE NAIROBI STOCK EXCHANGE

Although equity exchange in Kenya has a history going back to the 1920s under British colonial rule, the Nairobi Stock Exchange (NSE) came into being only in 1954. From its inception until 1991, it was a voluntary association registered under the Kenyan Societies Act. At about the same time, the NSE came under the regulation of the Capital Markets Authority (CMA). In 1995, exchange controls that limited foreign participation in the NSE were removed. As with most other African stock exchanges, the NSE has some characteristics of a frontier market. Its market capitalization was approximately US$10 billion in December 2009 (compared with the US$11 trillion market capitalization of the New York Stock Exchange). The number of companies listed in 2010 was only 48, down from 57 in 1992. That said, there are institutional changes that have strengthened the exchange, such as the implementation of an electronic central depository system and in 2006 an automated trading system, the adoption of international accounting standards, and the establishment of a Capital Markets Appeals Tribunal. All of these are valuable changes, but the exchange has some distance to travel in fulfilling development promises.

Sources: Ngugi, Murinde, and Green (2002) and Market Intelligence (n.d.).

The development of equity markets in low- and middle-income countries is more complex than it might first appear. This is because of the recent trends in the globalization of financial services. Observers have pointed to a set of domestic factors as particularly important in equity market development. These factors include sound macroeconomic policies, minimal required degrees of technology, legal systems that protect shareholders, and open financial markets. However, as was pointed out by Claessens, Klingebiel, and Schmukler (2002), these are precisely the factors that tend to promote the "migration" of equity exchange out of developing countries to the major exchanges in financial capitals of developed countries. This migration process complicates standard notions of equity market development. Steil (2001) argued that the way forward is to link local markets with global markets. However, medium size firms with local information needs might still benefit from some kind of domestic equity market. This is an area that urgently requires the development of novel approaches.

4.4.2 ASSESSMENT

Capital flows in the form of portfolio equity hold out some promise for poverty alleviation. Along with FDI, these indirect equity investments appear to have a positive impact on growth through a variety of mechanisms. Contagion and herd behavior are generally less prevalent than they are with commercial bank lending, and flows are expected to hold relatively steady in the near future. However, the underdeveloped nature of equity markets in most developing countries and some degree of market volatility are two obstacles associated with global equity flows. Developing equity financing to ameliorate these obstacles is a long-term priority for poor people, as these indirect investments can help to offset some of the problems with other sources of flows. This development needs to proceed in an open fashion that does not favor a narrow, investing elite with inside knowledge, but rather offers an open system for all medium size and large firms.

4.5 **Debt: Bond finance and commercial bank lending**

In the financial world, there are significant differences between portfolio equity investment and debt. This shows up in the fact that, in bankruptcy, debt is given priority over equity. This tends to support the preference for debt over equity in markets, a preference that might well be misplaced from the perspective of development and poverty alleviation. Debt contracts prove to be particularly problematic for developing countries during crises because they tend to be denominated in foreign currency, meaning that currency devaluation during the crisis makes servicing the debt considerably more burdensome. In this section, we consider two types of debt: bond finance and commercial bank lending. The main difference between these two forms of debt is that bonds are in the form of tradable assets. This provides more flexibility to lenders than bank lending.

4.5.1 BOND FINANCE

As shown in Figure 4.8, net debt flows to the developing world have evolved somewhat in recent years. Bond finance fell gradually between 1998 and 2001, and the 2003 to 2007 period showed substantial recovery in net flows to a level above the 1997 to 1998 period. The heightened appetite for emerging markets during the 2000s saw a growing number of developing countries accessing significant volumes of finance from the bond markets. Traditional issuers, such as Mexico, were able to extend the term of their bond issuance up to 30 years. Longer-dated sovereign bonds better match the assets and liabilities of governments and build the benchmark yield curve (which plot the yields of different maturities). Increased issuance in local currencies—such as Panda (Chinese Renminbi), Peso (Mexico), Real (Brazil), and Rand (South Africa) bonds—reduced currency mismatch, which was a major cause of financial instability in the 1980s and 1990s. At the same time, corporate borrowing grew significantly, accounting for about half of total emerging market bond issuance in 2004

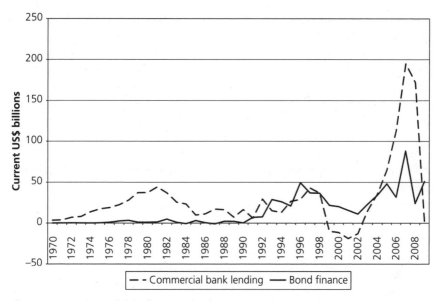

Figure 4.8. Net inward debt flows to developing countries 1970–2009

Source: World Development Indicators (http://databank.worldbank.org), 2010.

and giving emerging businesses access to a new and often lower cost of finance.

That said, the 2007–2009 financial crisis highlighted the risks associated with bond investment. Between September 2007 and January 2009 the spread on emerging market sovereign bonds grew from 200 to 750 basis points, reflecting a lack of liquidity in financial markets and a decrease in risk appetite of investors, making it considerably more difficult for developing country governments and corporations to service and roll over debt.[38] While the spread returned to 300 basis points by January 2010, recent experience illustrates that prudence and a balanced portfolio approach remain necessary.

4.5.2 COMMERCIAL BANK LENDING

As can be seen in Figure 4.8, net commercial bank lending to developing countries has been relatively volatile over the past two decades. It began to fall significantly in 1999 and did not begin to recover until 2004, after which it increased at an extraordinary pace to nearly US$200 billion in 2007–2008 before plummeting in 2009. Figure 4.8 shows that, despite declines in net lending in the early 2000s, commercial bank lending was still used by a wide

---

[38] See World Bank (2010).

variety of developing countries, with flows substantially above that for bond finance.

Above, we considered some features of financial markets that give them some important, "imperfect" characteristics. As mentioned, commercial bank lending appears to be particularly prone to these imperfections. For example, Dobson and Hufbauer (2001) noted that "Bank lending may be more prone to run than portfolio capital, because banks themselves are highly leveraged, and they are relying on the borrower's balance sheet to ensure repayment."[39] The World Bank (2001) also noted that "Incentives are key to limiting undue risk taking and fraudulent behavior in the management and supervision of financial intermediaries—especially banks that are prone to costly failure."[40] The reason for this fragility is the temporal aspect of the banking sector, namely the maturity transformation involved in its short-term borrowing and long-term lending structures.[41]

Before the Asian crisis, such an assessment might have been seen as exaggerated. Indeed, the pre-crisis data examined by Sarno and Taylor (1999) provided a relatively sanguine conclusion about commercial bank lending. Subsequent events, however, showed otherwise. Much of the debt involved in the Asian crisis was composed of short-term, inter-bank loans, and, as we saw in Figures 4.1 and 4.2, net commercial bank lending flows quickly became negative for both the low- and middle-income countries after 1997. Indeed, Goldstein, Kaminsky, and Reinhart (2000) included short term capital flows (most of which are inter-bank commercial lending) as a significant predictor of future financial crises based on a broad sample of countries. These points have recently been amplified by Reinhart and Rogoff (2009).

The picture that emerges from research on the banking sector is that the combination of capital inflows, asset price increases, and spotty banking regulation is a combustible mixture. Further, banking crises are particularly difficult in their contribution to prolonged recessions and fiscal costs. They can also contribute significantly to the systemic risk issues discussed by Goldin and Vogel (2010). Consequently, caution is warranted in relying on inflows of commercial bank lending for development purposes.

What can be done to support the safe development of banking sectors in developing countries? Some of the necessary steps can be thought of in terms of information, institutions, and incentives. For information, it is important for banks to embrace internationally sanctioned accounting and auditing procedures and to make the results of these assessments available to the

---

[39] Dobson and Hufbauer (2001), p. 47.
[40] World Bank (2001), p. 3.
[41] See Diamond and Dybvig (1983) and chapter 10 of Reinhart and Rogoff (2009).

public. For institutions or the rules of the "banking game," risk management practices (both credit and currency) must be sufficiently stringent and prudential regulation systems must be well developed. For currency risk, the World Bank (2004b) noted that "particular care should be taken to ensure that foreign currency liabilities are appropriately hedged."[42] These information and institutional safeguards are no small task, and they inevitably cannot be achieved in the short term.[43] Consequently, these safeguards should be buttressed with incentive measures in the form of market-friendly taxes on banking capital inflows. For example, Eichengreen (1999) argued that "banks borrowing abroad should be required to put up additional noninterest-bearing reserves with the central bank."[44] Such taxes on short-term capital inflows have been applied by Chile and others to prevent destabilizing episodes of over-borrowing.[45]

4.5.3 ASSESSMENT

Debt flows in the form of bond finance and commercial bank lending appear to have different properties than equity flows in the form of FDI. They are more prone to the imperfect behaviors that characterize financial markets and their positive growth effects do not seem to be as large as those associated with equity flows. Consequently, debt finance must be used cautiously and should be hedged against exchange rate risks. When it comes to debt flows, country governments are advised to *proceed with caution* to avoid substantial downside risks.

4.6 **Summary**

The capital flows with the greatest potential contribution to poverty alleviation are FDI and equity investment. Equity-related finance brings with it the

[42] World Bank (2004b), p. 30. Mistakes made in these areas have proved to be too costly to poor people for countries to relax their vigilance. Prasad et al. (2003) concluded that "The relative importance of different sources of financing for domestic investment, as proxied by the following three variables, has been shown to be positively associated with the incidence and the severity of currency and financial crises: the ratio of bank borrowing or other debt relative to foreign direct investment; the shortness of the term structure of external debt; and the share of external debt denominated in foreign currencies" (p. 49).

[43] Eichengreen (1999) noted that "the sad truth in all too many countries is that banks have a limited capacity to manage risk and that regulators have limited capacity to supervise their actions" (pp. 11–12).

[44] Eichengreen (1999), p. 117.

[45] This over-borrowing was described by McKinnon and Pill (1997).

natural benefits of risk sharing, and is far less subject to the sudden stops and reversals of debt flows. In the case of FDI, this is because investors have a tendency to reinvest a portion of retained earnings. Also, FDI capital stock depreciates, and new inflows are needed to sustain the existing capital stock. Finally, the benefits of FDI go beyond those relating to narrow financial issues: new ideas, technologies, and improvements in skills and training are all potential and important spillovers.[46]

That said, the *long term* trend of financial development is probably toward a mix of all four capital flows described in this chapter. The positions of developing countries with regard to capital flows can be generalized as in Figure 4.9. Here, for simplicity, our four types of capital flows are represented as the four corners of a diamond, with the relative strength of any particular flow indicated by proximity to a corner of the diamond. In the short term, most developing countries have no choice about their position in the diamond because they are constrained by the availability and cost of different capital flows. In the medium term, however, their actions can yield some influence over the availability and cost of capital flows: their choices can expand.

For example, there is a group of low-income countries who find themselves at approximately point "1" in the diagram, relying primarily on the commer-

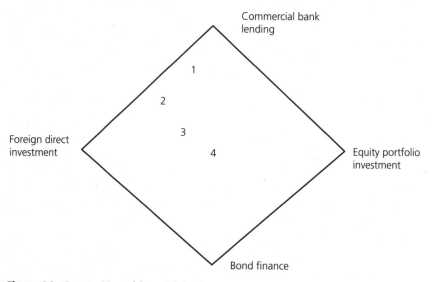

Figure 4.9. Composition of financial development

---

[46] China, for example, has focused on equity rather than debt, and inroads into poverty reduction have been significant.

cial bank lending form of capital flows.[47] Another set of low-income countries find themselves at approximately point "2," with a mix of commercial bank lending and FDI, the latter probably concentrated in petroleum or minerals. Many middle-income countries find themselves at approximately point "3," with the addition of some bond finance and equity portfolio investment. As financial development proceeds, there will be a move to somewhere in the vicinity of point "4" in which there is a broad mix of all four capital flows. Maintaining this position in a stable way would require that the financial development of the country be designed to mitigate the financial market imperfections discussed in this chapter. Capital inflows have a vital role to play. As noted by Fernandez-Arias and Montiel (1996), "the possibility that capital inflows may be welfare reducing does not mean that they are *invariably* harmful."[48]

If there is any convergence in the emerging literature on capital flows in the developing world, it concerns *absorptive capacity*, which acts as a set of necessary conditions for potential poverty alleviating effects. That is, for capital flows to positively help poor people, a number of things must be true:

- First, human capital must be developed. Without it, the hoped for positive spillovers from FDI will not emerge.
- Second, the domestic financial markets must be "deep" enough to support liquidity. Without liquidity, volatility will be a problem.
- Third, systems of oversight and regulation of domestic financial markets must be developed enough to prevent excessive volatility and crises.
- Fourth, levels of corruption should be low and strenuously combated.[49]

Each of these conditions takes some time to fulfill. Until they are achieved, caution is warranted. Thus, we sound a note of warning in providing an overall assessment of global capital flows and their relationship to poverty. As Hanson, Honohan, and Majnoni (2003) concluded, "the globalization of finance is not an unmixed blessing, but it appears to be inexorable."[50] Capital flows are an "inexorable" aspect of financial globalization, which have potential benefits *and* costs that are significant. Because poor people are particularly vulnerable to the potential costs, any errors in managing capital flows should be on the side of caution.

Capital flows in the form of FDI can contribute to positive development outcomes if accompanied by a commitment to investments in human capital.

---

[47] This group of countries, as well as those at point "2," would no doubt also be relying on foreign aid, but we leave this discussion to Chapter 5.

[48] Fernandez-Arias and Montiel (1996), p. 57 (emphasis added).

[49] According to the results of Wei (2000), corruption has a tendency to bias capital flows away from FDI and toward commercial bank lending.

[50] Hanson, Honohan, and Majnoni (2003), p. 25.

While there has been some evidence of positive development outcomes from equity investment, the volatility of this type of flow evident in Figure 4.7 lends a note of caution here. Bond finance and commercial bank lending have been implicated in a number of significant financial crises with adverse development impacts. For these reasons, with the exception of FDI, it is difficult to disagree with Rodrik and Subramanian's (2009) assessment that for capital flows "more is not necessarily better." It is certainly the case that financial sector development matters over the long run and that this needs to be accompanied by the construction of domestic systems of prudential regulation and counter-cyclical fiscal policy. But this is not easily achieved in the short term. For these reasons, in the realm of financial globalization considered in this chapter, positive development outcomes will be largely found in the realm of foreign direct investment.

Even in the realm of FDI, there will be no quick fixes or immediate results. As noted by Nunnenkamp (2004) and as discussed above, the relationship between FDI and development outcomes is indirect, depending on the ability to attract flows, the host country environment (particularly the level of human capital), and the qualities of the FDI itself. The cases in which these three factors are aligned properly are few, but they do exist and need to be appreciated for their potential.

5   Aid

This chapter examines foreign aid flows, historically the most recent of the global flows we consider in this book.[1] Although ideas, goods, investments, and people have crossed great distances for millennia in response to a host of economic opportunities, it is only relatively recently that governments began to provide financial and technical assistance to foreign countries. The purpose of this assistance has varied and has included geopolitical purposes as well as stimulating economic development, ameliorating poverty and suffering, promoting political outcomes, and ensuring civil stability and equitable governance. Although foreign aid is often visualized by citizens in rich countries in terms of financial "handouts" by rich countries to the world's poorest inhabitants, the truth is much more complex. Indeed, contrary to popular perception, low-income countries generally receive less than half of total aid.[2] Much of the remainder is made up by flows to middle-income countries such as Colombia and the Arab Republic of Egypt, and some countries of particular interest—Israel, and most recently, Afghanistan and Iraq—have received significant amounts of assistance.[3] The good news is that recent years have seen sharp improvements in both the quality and quantity of aid. Foreign aid from non-traditional donors including developing countries, private organizations, charities, and individual philanthropists has also increased.

Aid, or official development assistance (ODA) as it is technically known, covers a wide range of both financial and non-financial components.[4] Cash transfers to developing countries can be vital, but currently they account for less than half of the aid that goes to those countries. Non-financial forms of assistance include grants of machinery or equipment as well as less tangible contributions such as providing technical analysis, advice, and capacity building. Many donors also count their own administrative costs in their aid budgets as well as contributions to debt reduction and other financial

---

[1] This chapter draws on joint work with Halsey Rogers and Nicholas Stern. See Goldin, Rogers, and Stern (2002).

[2] In 2008 net official development assistance and official aid to low-income countries was US$37.54 billion. The figures for middle-income and high-income countries were US$53.93 billion and US$0.49 billion respectively (World Bank 2011b).

[3] For example, in 2009, the leading recipients of official aid among high-income countries (for which data is currently available) were Oman ($212 million), Croatia ($169 million), Equatorial Guinea ($32 million), and Barbados ($12 million) (World Bank 2011b).

[4] For an overview, see chapter 14 of Szirmai (2005).

allocations that never reach developing countries.[5] Just as there is consider-able heterogeneity in the types of aid disbursed, there is also a surprising amount of diversity in the countries that receive ODA. For some countries— such as those in early post-conflict situations or where institutions are particularly weak and corruption is prevalent—technical assistance may have a more positive impact than cash transfers, but in the majority of countries, cash transfers in support of government programs are most effec-tive in contributing to growth and reducing poverty.

An analysis of aid flows cannot be separated from an analysis of the development of the international development finance system and the role of institutions such as the World Bank as conduits for financial and other flows. This chapter therefore focuses on both bilateral and multilateral flows as well as on related issues such as the role of official debt and its cancellation.

5.1 A brief history of aid flows

In many ways, the histories of modern aid and colonialism are intertwined. In so far as colonialism was an exercise driven by a desire to stimulate and then exploit economic activity abroad, providing investment capital, technology, and technical assistance to colonies was integral to the process. This included constructing a railroad network in the Congo by Belgium to facilitate the extraction of ore deposits, establishing foreign legions of civil service employ-ees, and constructing the Suez and Panama Canals.

It was not until the early twentieth century, however, that colonial powers considered providing assistance to support general aspects of economic development that were not exclusively tied to extraction and exploitation. Even here, as noted by Little and Clifford (1965), in the case of the United Kingdom's 1929 Colonial Development Act, infrastructure rather than, say, education, played a central role. As stressed by Kanbur (2006), it was not until the 1940 and 1945 Colonial Development and Welfare Acts that the United Kingdom began to support education in its nascent foreign aid efforts, although its 1948 Overseas Development Act established the Colonial Devel-opment Corporation.

Even after countries gained independence, the colonial nature of foreign aid persisted. Szirmai (2005, chapter 14) stresses the role of aid in decoloni-zation processes, as well as in post-independence assimilation policies, par-ticularly in the cases of the United Kingdom and France. The Netherlands was

---

[5] Recall that we discussed trade-related capacity building in Chapter 3, for example.

not exempt in this process either. As Szirmai states, in an example not atypical of the early years of other aid programs,

In the case of the Netherlands, there was a sudden rift with Indonesia in 1949 after the so-called police actions of 1947–49. The Netherlands attempted to restore its damaged international prestige by participating on a large scale in multilateral technical assistance which was beginning at that time. The Netherlands had a reservoir of experience in the form of colonial training programmes, unemployed colonial civil servants and technical experts. It was quite successful in finding employment for its experts in multilateral aid programmes.[6]

A key feature of these early forms of development assistance was its "tied" nature, in which aid was restricted to importing from the donor country. This was true of the Colonial Development Act in the United Kingdom and the "Good Neighbor Policy" of the United States toward Latin America. The practice of tied assistance dominated bilateral aid flows during much of the Cold War and, although there has been considerable progress in untying aid, it remains a feature of a number of aid programs today. To the extent that aid is tied, receiving countries have struggled to extract the full potential benefit, as the assistance provided does not necessarily fit with local choices and priorities. At times, ostensibly magnanimous donations of assistance have in fact had a discernibly detrimental impact on local producers, to the advantage of exporters in the donating country. Concerns are often raised about the efficacy of foreign food aid, for instance, which may ultimately serve to undermine the markets of domestic growers while at the same time providing a captive source of demand for producers in the donor country.[7]

5.1.1 FOREIGN AID IN TTHE POST-WAR ERA

The advent of modern foreign aid may be traced back to the Marshall Plan for bilateral assistance between the United States and Europe in the wake of World War II, as well as to the Bretton Woods Conference and the creation of durable multilateral institutions to facilitate increased international assistance and cooperation, such as the United Nations, the World Bank, and the International Monetary Fund.[8] These efforts were informed by the adverse experiences of past conflicts, whereby the vanquished often had been compelled to pay reparations to the victors. As had been the case with Germany after World War I, such reparations often exacerbated and prolonged the impact of the conflict, leading to financial crises and a lasting sense of resentment. The succession of European wars and failed armistices that

---

[6] Szirmai (2005), p. 586.
[7] See, for example, Curtis (2001).
[8] See Hjertholm and White (2000) and Sorel and Padoan (2008).

resulted had, by 1945, provided a compelling lesson in the need to invest in peace and economic integration. Thus, it was in the shadow of World War II that the international aid architecture was first articulated. Together with much smaller but increasingly significant assistance from other developing countries and private foundations, the combination of bilateral assistance and multilateral institutions has remained the dominant paradigm of international aid flows to the present day. The amount of aid provided and the expansion of aid programs are traced in Table 5.1 and Figure 5.1.[9]

Figure 5.1 and Table 5.2 highlight the changing nature of the aid agencies over time, from agencies that focused almost exclusively on promoting exports to a broader multilateral agenda and then, more recently, to underpinning private sector investment. The European Bank for Reconstruction

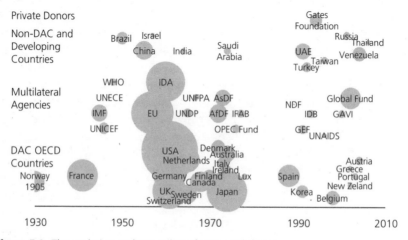

Figure 5.1. The evolution and expansion of major aid donors

Notes: Agencies are shown in year of creation. Most countries are shown in the year their first government department or agency for international development was formed (although many countries have a longer history of disbursing aid). In cases where countries do not have a separate ministry for development (such as Italy or Greece), the year for which they first reported aid statistics to the OECD is used. The year for Venezuela corresponds to the formation of ALBA and the year for Russia is the mid-point between the foundation of the Russian Federation in 1991 and the present day.

The size of the circle is proportional to the most recent annual aid commitment in US dollar. For multilateral agencies and developed countries the source data is OECD (2011) for the year 2009. The source data for Israel, Thailand, Turkey, and Taiwan are gross ODA disbursement statistics. The source data for Brazil, Russia, India, and China are rough estimates derived from Table 5.6. The source data for Venezuela and the Gates Foundation are long-term averages of foreign aid dispensed derived from the Gates Foundation website www.gatesfoundation.org) and Reality of Aid Network (2010). The source data for Saudi Arabia is the 2009 figure for the Saudi Fund in Saudi Riyal http://www.sfd.gov.sa) converted to US dollars.

The aid agency acronyms can be found on the OECD Stat website, http://stats.oecd.org

Sources: OECD STAT (http://stats.oecd.org) 2011 unless otherwise stated.

---

[9] With regard to the ideology column of Table 5.2, see also Lindauer and Pritchett (2002).

Table 5.1 Average annual aid flows per person in real 2007 US dollars, 1960–2008

Categories of recipients	1960–1969	1970–1979	1980–1989	1990–1999	2008–2009
Low-income countries	22.11	29.97	38.41	31.23	34.06
Middle-income countries	11.14	10.58	10.42	9.13	9.27
High-income countries	4.26	4.91	5.26	4.43	2.09

Source: World Development Indicators (http://databank.worldbank.org), 2010.

and Development (EBRD), established in 1991 after the collapse of the Berlin Wall to support the transition to a market economy in Eastern Europe, is the most modern of the multilateral development banks, and combines lending to both public and private sectors with and without government guarantees.

From 1944, upon their incorporation in Bretton Woods, New Hampshire, the initial focus of the World Bank and the International Monetary Fund (IMF) was on helping to rebuild and reinvigorate war-torn Europe and on ensuring the stability of the world financial system.[10] Of the World Bank's first six loans, five went to countries in Western Europe; the first four were explicitly for post-war reconstruction. The poor countries of the world were not the first priority, and the focus was on raising production and income rather than on broader notions of development. However, with rapid reconstruction progress and the increasing demands of the Cold War, this slowly began to change, and many low- and middle-income countries received increasing flows of international assistance. In 1949, US President Harry Truman set in motion the "Point Four" program for technical assistance in developing countries.[11] In 1961, the United States established the Agency for International Development (USAID), and this was followed by similar actions by Sweden in 1962 and Britain in 1964.[12] These agencies, along with the African, Asian, and Latin American regional development banks that were established around the same time, complemented the work of the World Bank and provided channels for increased aid flows to the world's poorest countries. The resulting flows of aid are plotted in Figure 5.2. They are given in per capita terms in Table 5.1.

For many European countries, the national aid agencies at first mainly concentrated on supporting their former colonies, leaving the broader global

---

[10] In the case of the IMF, it is worth noting that its resources were not sufficient to significantly support post-war reconstruction in Europe. Its Articles of Agreement set total drawing rights at $8.8 billion. By the time the IMF opened for business in 1947, post-war Europe's combined trade deficit was $7.5 billion. Given the size of this deficit in relationship to the IMF's resources, the United States had to step in to fill the gap. Through 1951, it provided $13 billion in Marshall Plan aid to Europe, thus significantly supplementing IMF resources. See Eichengreen (1996).

[11] "Point Four" refers to the fourth point in Truman's inaugural address.

[12] The Commonwealth members the United Kingdom, Australia, Canada, and New Zealand had signed the Colombo Plan for aid giving in 1950.

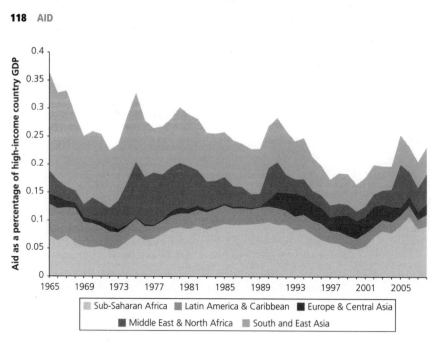

Figure 5.2. Inflow of official development assistance by region, 1965 to 2008

Source: World Development Indicators (http://databank.worldbank.org), March 2011.

challenges of reconstruction and development to global and regional institutions such as the World Bank and the African Development Bank. Increasingly over time, however, there has been a convergence of objectives and strategy, and a global professional cadre of development specialists has been built up. With rapid progress in post-war reconstruction, development assistance began to focus on raising incomes in what came to be called the developing world. At first, the goal was largely confined to raising *aggregate* national incomes. Then, with the growing recognition that population growth rates vary sharply (so aggregate income did not necessarily give a clear picture of changes in living standards), attention turned to *per capita* incomes. Soon, with increased understanding of the importance of income distribution, simply raising average per capita incomes also was recognized to be too limited a goal.

By the 1970s, the attention of international aid agencies focused on the twin problems of growth and income distribution and also, increasingly, on the basic needs of poor people.[13] Reducing income poverty became a greater priority for the international financial institutions as well as for governments. Some of the major deployments of aid relative to the size of the recipients' economies are summarized in Table 5.3. The table illustrates that, for very small economies, aid can even exceed the size of the national domestic

---

[13] See Seers (1972), Chenery et al. (1974), or Streeten (1979).

Table 5.2 Developments in the history of foreign aid

Decade	Dominant or rising institution	Donor ideology	Donor focus	Types of aid
1940s	Marshall Plan, Bretton Woods, and UN system	Planning	Reconstruction	Program assistance
1950s	United States, with USSR	Anti or pro-Communist, building regime capacity	Community development	Food aid and project-based financing
1960s	Bilateral programs	Anti or pro-Communist, building regime capacity	Productive sectors (e.g. Green Revolution), infrastructure	Technical assistance, budgetary support
1970s	Expansion of multilaterals (World Bank and IMF)	Building state capacity, fulfilling basic needs	Poverty and basic needs	Import support
1980s	Non-governmental organizations	Structural adjustment	Macroeconomic reform	Program-based, debt relief
1990s	Eastern European and ex-USSR as recipients	Structural adjustment, then state capacity	Macroeconomic reform and institutions	Human development and sector-focused assistance
2000s	Security and G-8 agenda, MDGs	Aid effectiveness, partnership, coherence	Result measurement, governance, post-conflict	Budget support, global programs (e.g. HIV/AIDS)
2000s	Developing countries and private donors	Strategic interests, mutual development, and philanthropy	Industrialization and market expansion, project support, humanitarian	Economic and technical cooperation, health programs, disaster relief

Source: Adapted by authors from Hjertholm and White (2000).

economy. On average, for low- and middle-income countries, aid contributes around 1 percent of national income, and in sub-Saharan Africa the average contribution is around 5 percent. However, as the table shows, some countries—such as Mozambique and Zambia in recent years—have seen aid levels well in excess of half of their domestic economy. Very small economies, with total national incomes of less than US$250 million and populations of fewer than 1 million people, and those emerging from conflict are most prone to very high levels of aid dependence, as Table 5.3 illustrates.

Although the motivation for providing aid in the immediate post-World War II period was driven at the Bretton Woods Conference by reconstruction and broader considerations, this soon was coupled by a growing preoccupation with the politics of the Cold War. From the mid-1950s to the fall of the Berlin Wall in 1990, aid was increasingly used as a means to support friendly states. Also, originating in the foreign policy of the United States during the

Table 5.3 Major deployments of foreign assistance

Country	Year	ODA received as percentage of Gross National Income
Palau	1994	242
Liberia	2008	186
Sao Tome and Principe*	1995	185
Congo, Dem. Rep.	2003	99
Rwanda	1994	95
Mozambique	1992	81
Guinea-Bissau	1994	79
Timor-Leste	2002	75
Nicaragua	1991	72
Somalia	1980	72
Gambia, The	1986	65
Zambia	1995	63
Guyana	1990	61
Albania	1992	59
Micronesia, Fed. Sts.	2001	58
Bosnia and Herzegovina	1995	57
Equatorial Guinea	1989	54
Marshall Islands	2001	54
Tonga*	1979	53
Cambodia	1974	52
West Bank and Gaza	2002	51
Kiribati	1987	50
Cape Verde	1986	50

* Figures for these countries relate to ODA as a percentage of GDP and are based on calculations derived from World Bank 2004c.

Source: World Development Indicators (http://databank.worldbank.org), March 23, 2011.

early years of the Cold War, economic and military aid were closely interconnected, and aid's strategic purpose was seen to be at least as much geopolitical as it was humanitarian. It was in this context that Hawkins (1970), in *The Principles of Development Aid*, suggested that foreign aid belonged to the field of political economy rather than economic analysis. Hayter's (1971) title, *Aid as Imperialism*, was even more direct. And Milton Friedman (1958, p. 63, cited in Kanbur 2006, p. 1565) from the other end of the ideological spectrum similarly observed, "Foreign economic aid is widely recognized as a weapon in the ideological war in which the United States is now engaged. Its assigned role is to help win over to our side those uncommitted nations that are also underdeveloped and poor."

When aid is disbursed for political or military reasons, with an eye to supporting donor country exports, or for transition or disaster relief in post-conflict stabilization, any positive effects for poor people generally occur with a long lag time. The end of the Cold War and progress in transition countries have made possible a more direct targeting of aid to poverty reduction efforts. As stated by Goldin, Rogers, and Stern (2002),

Donor financial assistance is targeted far more effectively at poverty reduction than it was a decade ago. At that time, Cold War geopolitics was still exercising a heavy influence on aid allocation, and too many recipient economies were poorly run, often suffering from excessive state intervention in economic activity and poor governance...As a result, the poverty-reduction effectiveness per dollar of overall ODA has grown rapidly.[14]

Unfortunately, the increase in the effectiveness of aid until 2001 was not accompanied by an increase in its availability. After rising rapidly from 1945 to the early 1960s, flows of aid declined in subsequent decades. Expressed as a percentage of high-income country income (Figure 5.2), aid trended down from slightly over 0.35 percent to approximately 0.2 percent of the GDP of high-income countries in 2000. The good news, however, is that in the last ten years this decline appears to have been partially reversed, with developed countries exhibiting a renewed commitment to increasing aid flows, which have so far remained relatively buoyant despite the detrimental impact of the 2007–2010 financial crisis on the economies of the developed world and trade and investment flows, discussed earlier in this book. For most countries aid falls far short of the target of 0.7 percent of GDP reaffirmed in the United Nations 2002 Monterrey Consensus, although the proportion of income devoted to aid has steadily increased since 2002 despite the global financial crisis. Table 5.4 presents the latest available data.

On the recipient side, when expressed as a percentage of the recipient country's GDP or Gross National Income (GNI), aid to low-income countries increased from the 1970s and then experienced a steep decline in the late 1990s, which has largely been reversed since 2000 despite a recent dip (Figure 5.3). Aid to middle-income countries as a percentage of recipients' GNI has been relatively constant over the entire period since 1965. The average amount of aid received by low-income and middle-income countries over the period 1965–2008 was 6.7 and 0.7 percent of GDP, respectively. That said, however, there have been significant declines since the early 1990s, especially for low-income countries. Thus, from the point of view of helping poor people, foreign aid as an aspect of economic globalization can be characterized as a significant, missed opportunity.

These numbers reflect the upper limit of what countries actually receive, because we know that most bilateral aid does not in fact end up as a cash transfer in the hands of the recipient country. Figure 5.4 illustrates that a great

---

[14] Goldin, Rogers, and Stern (2002), pp. 42–3.

Table 5.4 ODA as a share of GNI, 2009 and preliminary results for 2010

	2009		2010 Preliminary	
	Net ODA	ODA % GNI	Net ODA	ODA % GNI
Austria	1142	0.30	1199	0.32
Belgium	2610	0.55	3000	0.64
Czech Republic	215	0.12	224	0.12
Denmark	2810	0.88	2867	0.90
Finland	1290	0.54	1335	0.55
France	12600	0.47	12916	0.50
Germany	12079	0.35	12723	0.38
Greece	607	0.19	500	0.17
Hungary	117	0.10	113	0.09
Ireland	1006	0.54	895	0.53
Italy	3297	0.16	3111	0.15
Luxembourg	415	1.04	399	1.09
Netherlands	6426	0.82	6351	0.81
Poland	375	0.09	378	0.08
Portugal	513	0.23	648	0.29
Slovak Republic	75	0.09	74	0.09
Slovenia	71	0.15	63	0.13
Spain	6584	0.46	5917	0.43
Sweden	4548	1.12	4527	0.97
United Kingdom	11283	0.51	13763	0.56
EU Members, Total	67210	0.44	70150	0.46
Australia	2762	0.29	3849	0.32
Canada	4000	0.30	5132	0.33
Iceland	35	0.35	29	0.28
Japan	9457	0.18	11045	0.20
Korea	816	0.10	1168	0.12
New Zealand	309	0.28	353	0.26
Norway	4086	1.06	4582	1.10
Switzerland	2310	0.45	2295	0.41
United States	28831	0.21	30154	0.21
DAC Members, Total	119781	0.31	128728	0.32
Chinese Taipei	411	0.13		
Israel	124	0.06	141	0.07
Thailand	40	0.02		
Turkey	707	0.11	967	0.13
United Arab Emirates	834			
Other Donor Countries, Total	313		18	

Source: OECD Stat (http://stats.oecd.org/), April 24, 2011.

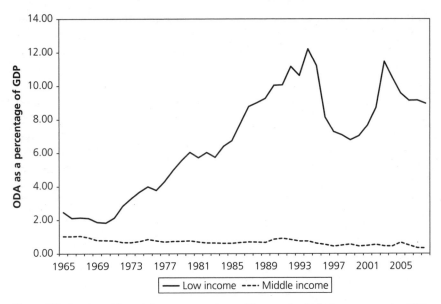

Figure 5.3. Foreign aid receipts as a percentage of low- and middle-income country GDP, 1965–2008

Source: World Development Indicators (http://databank.worldbank.org), March 24, 2011.

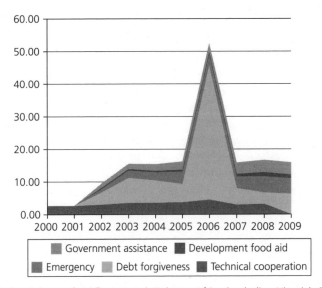

Figure 5.4. Breakdown of aid flows to sub-Saharan Africa (excluding Nigeria), 2000–2009

Source: OECD STAT (http://stats.oecd.org/) and World Development Indicators (http://databank.world bank.org), April 1, 2011.

deal of aid is not provided in the form of transfers of financial resources, but rather as food aid, emergency relief, technical cooperation, and debt relief. Although these non-discretionary forms of aid may make an important contribution, they too often are driven by the priorities of the donors rather than the recipients. One noteworthy achievement on this front is the decision to write off two-thirds of the debt owed by some of the poorest nations following the 2005 Make Poverty History campaign and the G-8 Summit at Gleneagles (hence the dramatic spike in Figure 5.4, amounting to more than US$41 billion of debt forgiveness in 2006).[15] There is, however, no substitute for predictable, multi-year flows of aid that are mobilized behind government budgets in national programs that are agreed to across the donor community. Improvements in the quality of aid are necessary as are increases in the volume of aid. For many countries, only a small part—on average around one-fifth—of the aid is provided in the form of direct support to budgeted government programs. This is one of the reasons that the transaction costs of aid are very high and in many cases divert scarce personnel from their ordinary activities of managing public resources.

Harmonization and coordination is vital to reduce the transaction costs of aid and to ensure that the national priorities of recipient countries are supported, particularly if these are not the same as the pet projects and programs of individual donors and recipient ministries. The transaction costs of aid transfers are also important in determining what portion of total aid flows is spent productively. When ministers have to spend their time hosting visiting dignitaries, and their officials are engaged in satisfying a wide range of donor reporting requirements, the administrative and other burdens imposed by the donors may not only undermine the benefits of the project but also distract officials and scarce skilled staff from more vital priorities. It is for this reason that the recent evolution of donor consultative forums, mobilized behind national strategies and reinforcing existing budget mechanisms and harmonized reporting standards, are so essential. Consider-able progress has been made in recent years in harmonizing approaches. A growing number of national and multilateral agencies are reflected in the 2005 Paris Declaration on Aid Effectiveness (which emphasized "ownership, harmonization, alignment, results and mutual accountability") and the 2008 Accra Agenda for Action (which reaffirmed the importance of "strength-ening country ownership," "building effective partnerships," and "delivering development").[16]

One shortcoming of such donor consultative systems, however, is that, because they weaken the direct link between an individual donor and an

---

[15] See http://go.worldbank.org/KNZR2IIQG0 and http://en.wikipedia.org/wiki/Developing_countries'_debt
[16] See OECD (2008b).

individual project, they render attributions of individual ODA efforts with country or project outcomes more complex. While harmonization and common platforms almost invariably enhance the effectiveness of ODA, it may be more difficult to demonstrate to skeptical voters in rich countries where their tax payments have gone. For this reason, care may need to be taken in the design of such systems to ensure that donors can still point to concrete examples of where their funding has made a difference.

5.1.2 MODERN GOALS OF DEVELOPMENT ASSISTANCE

In recent years, the goals of development have come to embrace the elimination of poverty in all its dimensions—income poverty, illiteracy, poor health, insecurity of income, and powerlessness. A consensus is emerging around the view that development means increasing the control that poor people have over their lives—through education, health, and greater participation, as well as through income gains. This view comes not only from the testimony of poor people themselves, but also from advances in conceptual thinking about development.[17] It is clear that the various dimensions of poverty are related, and that income growth generally leads to strong progress in the non-income dimensions of poverty as well. It is also clear, however, that direct action taken to reduce poverty in these other dimensions can accelerate the reduction of both income and non-income poverty. Aid policy is beginning to reflect these new understandings.

Levels of development assistance are small compared with both other financial flows and the scale of the challenge at hand. Aid to developing countries totaled about US$89 billion in 2009, for example. This was only one quarter as much as net foreign direct investment inflows in low- and middle-income countries (US$359 billion), which itself was only a small fraction of net FDI inflows (US$1.2 trillion). Similarly, although the World Bank is the world's largest external provider of assistance in the education sector, it typically provides less than US$2 billion in direct assistance for education each year.[18] By comparison, annual public spending on education in the developing world totals more than US$250 billion. Given this discrepancy in scale, even if the World Bank were to greatly increase its lending in the sector from around 1 percent to 2 percent, its effectiveness would have to come primarily through catalyzing institutional development and policy change in education rather than through resource transfer alone.

Since, in comparison with domestic investment and government expenditures, aid flows are typically small and should not be viewed as a permanent

---

[17] See Sen (1999), Chambers (2008), or UNDP (2010), for example.

[18] The resources that organizations such as the World Bank can possibly provide in support of education are dwarfed by the needs of developing countries.

source of finance, the key challenge is to ensure that they support systemic change, introducing ideas and improving practices that increase the overall size of the resources available for growth and poverty reduction. These indirect effects of aid are difficult to measure, however, and seeking attribution may undermine government leadership and harmonization with other donors. Measuring aid effectiveness is thus necessarily focused on its direct effects. However, because aid flows are relatively small, their direct effects in terms of income increases or reductions in mortality will often be swamped by other factors. For this and the reasons outlined in the next section, evaluating the impact of aid is extremely complex, although vital in order to enhance its effectiveness and create a virtuous cycle of greater willingness to provide aid.

5.2 **The multifaceted impact of aid**

The complexity of social and economic change means that the impact of foreign aid cannot be easily separated from other factors. Countries themselves bear most of the burdens of development, and they rightly claim credit when development succeeds. Assistance works best and can be sustained only when the recipients are strongly committed to development and in charge of the process.[19] In addition, successful projects that draw on foreign assistance in their early stages may later become self-sustaining and serve as sources for lessons that can be applied elsewhere without any foreign involvement at all. For these and other reasons, the positive impact of ODA can be very large. Nevertheless, identifying cause and effect and attributing outcomes to particular actions is often difficult.[20] Furthermore, any excessive attempt to claim credit for the successes of foreign aid can devalue the idea and practice of partnership and local leadership. Successful development strategies and actions generally depend on strong country ownership as well as good partnership among donors. This makes it difficult, even counterproductive, for any external actor to claim full credit for a reform or project.

When all aid is lumped together, some analyses have found no clear relationship between aid and growth or poverty reduction.[21] But not all aid is aimed directly at poverty reduction, nor has aid always been provided in

---

[19] See Kaufmann (2009).

[20] See Hansen and Tarp (2000).

[21] See, for example, Boone (1996), Bourguignon and Sundberg (2007), and Rajan and Subramanian (2008). Note, however, that Hansen and Tarp (2000 and 2001) find the contrary. For recent reviews of the effectiveness of aid, see Clemens, Radelet, and Bhavnani (2004) or Doucouliagos and Paldham (2009).

ways that will maximize growth. Moreover, because aid is often provided to help countries cope with external shocks, even if aid is reasonably well designed and allocated—and thus effective in helping the poor—the positive impact of such aid may be obscured by the magnitude of the shocks.

5.2.1 KINDS OF AID: DISASTER RELIEF, TRANSITION, AND ADJUSTMENT PROGRAMS

Disaster relief, for example, is not aimed directly at long-term poverty reduction and, thus, it is no surprise that such aid is not correlated with that result.[22] However, it does achieve its goal of helping to avert famine or assisting countries to recover from natural disasters. Similarly, large amounts of aid were directed at supporting the transition in Eastern Europe and Central Asia for both political and economic reasons. There, the mandate in the early 1990s was explicitly to help transform these countries into market economies, rather than to focus directly on reducing poverty.

In addition to these concerns with transition, donors initially placed too much emphasis on the role of what were often isolated projects, neglecting the quality of the overall country environment for growth—a mistake that adjustment (or policy-based) aid was intended to overcome. Finally, as mentioned above, aid was sometimes allocated for pure strategic reasons, with growth and poverty reduction in these cases being distinct secondary concerns, if indeed they were concerns at all. Given this diversity of motives, it is not surprising that aid did not always have the direct effects of spurring growth and reducing poverty.[23]

The *adjustment programs* that came into their own in part in response to the severe macroeconomic imbalances of the 1970s, including those that were the result of oil shocks, had their own problems. Donors incorrectly believed that conditionality on loans and grants could substitute for country ownership of reforms. Too often, governments receiving aid were not truly committed to reforms. Moreover, neither donors nor governments focused sufficiently on alleviating poverty in designing adjustment programs.[24] In the late 1970s and

---

[22] See Owens and Hoddinott (1998). As Clemens, Radelet, and Bhavnani (2004) note, "This kind of [disaster] assistance should have a negative simple correlation with growth, as the disaster simultaneously causes both low growth and large aid flows. While it is possible that aid might mitigate that fall in growth, any additional pathway of causation from humanitarian aid to growth is extremely difficult to detect" (p. 2).

[23] Alesina and Dollar (2000) analyzed the pattern of aid flows from the 1970s through the early 1990s. They concluded that "Factors such as colonial past and voting patterns in the United Nations explain more of the distribution of aid than the political institutions or economic policy of recipients" (p. 55).

[24] Stewart (1995) provides a useful overview of links between structural adjustment and poverty. For an introduction to structural adjustment itself, see chapter 24 of Reinert (2012).

early 1980s, the pendulum in leading donor countries swung to the new policies of Ronald Reagan in the United States, Margaret Thatcher in the United Kingdom, and Helmut Kohl in the Federal Republic of Germany. This was reflected in the World Bank by a new emphasis on "getting the prices right" and the articulation of the *Washington Consensus,* and the aid community focused on macroeconomic reform in developing countries.[25] While it was necessary to achieve macroeconomic stability as a prerequisite for sustainable growth and poverty reduction, both donor and recipient countries underestimated the importance of governance, of institutional reforms, and of social investments as a complement to macroeconomic and trade reforms. Prescriptions for reform were too often formulaic, ignoring the central need for country specificity in the design, sequencing, and implementation of reforms.[26]

As a result, weak governance and institutions reduced the amount of productivity growth and poverty reduction that could result from the macroeconomic reforms. Many of these factors came together in Africa, contributing to the lack of progress in the region. There are many causes to slow development in Africa, including poor domestic policies and institutions and weak commitment to reform, but too often aid did little to improve the situation and in some cases even worsened it. The notable case of Zaire is discussed in Box 5.1.

5.2.2 RETHINKING DEVELOPMENT MODELS AND THE ROLE OF AID

During the 1990s, a rethinking of development models and the role of aid began. This was facilitated by a combination of four developments.

- First, the end of the Cold War reduced the geopolitical pressures on aid agencies.

- Second, there was an increasing recognition of the successes of India, China, and other developing countries that had achieved macro balance and sustained growth while adopting their own particular development models.[27]

- Third, mounting evidence suggested an apparent failure of orthodox adjustment models adopted, albeit reluctantly, by African and other highly indebted countries, as seen by the lack of positive growth and poverty outcomes.

- Finally, as discussed in Chapter 7, a growing body of analytic literature highlighted the importance of the need for a more comprehensive approach to development and wider understanding of poverty, focusing

---

[25] Williamson (2000, 2009) provides a very useful overview and assessment of the Washington Consensus. A more critical assessment can be found in Weekes and Stein (2006).

[26] Taylor (1993) and Stiglitz (2002) offer forceful critiques along these lines.

[27] Some of these successes have been reviewed in the chapters contained in Rodrik (2003a).

BOX 5.1 AID IN ZAIRE

If there is a worst case of geopolitical aims undermining the effectiveness of foreign aid, it may be Zaire (now the Democratic Republic of Congo) under President Mobutu Sese Seko, who ruled from 1965 to 1997. Mobutu was primarily motivated by amassing his own personal fortune, which peaked in the mid-1980s at US$4 billion, even as GNP per capita fell from US$460 in 1975 to US$100 in 1996. Domestic policies were either nonexistent or bad, and private sources of credit consequently disappeared by the mid-1980s. However, with its huge size and strategic location, Zaire was seen as a buffer against the spread of communism in southern and central Africa. Consequently, both bilateral and multilateral aid began to fill the gap as private credit dried up. Between 1960 and 2000, donors disbursed more than US$10 billion in aid to Zaire, with the bulk of this beginning in the 1980s.

Failure to pay adequate attention to corruption and wasteful use of funds severely undermined the effectiveness of this foreign aid. Indeed, total capital flight from the country has been estimated by Ndikumana and Boyce (1998) to be US$12 billion in real 1990 dollars, and Transparency International estimates that US$5 billion was stolen by Mobutu himself. It would be hard to argue much was achieved in Zaire, either in economic or social terms, as a result of the aid.

The result has been increasing skepticism in the donor countries that aid is effective. Well over half of respondents in successive polls believe that aid is wasted, as indeed it often was when it was not aimed at poverty reduction. For aid to lead to poverty reduction, three things are necessary:

- It must aim for poverty reduction rather than geopolitical or other objectives.
- It must go to countries where poor people live.
- It must go to countries whose governments are committed to the eradication of poverty.

Sources: Burns, Holman, and Huband (1997), Ndikumana and Boyce (1998), *Financial Times* (2004), and Goldin, Rogers, and Stern (2002), and Transparency International (2004).

---

on human capital (education, health) and physical capital (infrastructure) as well as institutions, governance, and participation.[28]

As discussed in Chapters 1 and 2, the understanding that poverty is about more than income leads to the recognition that growth is not the only determinant of poverty reduction. Social indicators—health and education—improved far faster in all developing countries during the twentieth century than would have been expected, given the rate of income growth these countries experienced. Most countries have made major progress in increasing educational attainment and health outcomes by targeting these goals directly and by applying new knowledge and technologies to them specifically, rather than just waiting for the effects of income growth to improve these indicators. At every level of income, infant mortality fell sharply during the

---

[28] In the realm of foreign aid, some (but not all) of this new thinking was reflected in World Bank (1998).

twentieth century. For example, a typical country with per capita income of $8,000 in 1950 (measured in 1995 US dollars) would have had, on average, an infant mortality rate of 45 per 1,000 live births. By 1970, a country at the same real income level would typically have had an infant mortality rate of only 30 per 1,000, and by 1995, only 15 per 1,000. Similar reductions occurred all along the income spectrum, including in the poorest countries.

The improvements in social indicators have been remarkable by historical standards. Life expectancy in developing countries increased by 20 years over a period of only 40 years, as it increased from the mid-40s to the mid-60s.[29] By comparison, it probably took millennia to improve life expectancy from the mid-20s to the mid-40s. Literacy improvements have also been remarkable: whereas in 1970 nearly two out of every four adults were illiterate, now it is only one out of every five.

These advances in education and health have greatly improved the welfare of individuals and families. Not only are education and health valuable in themselves, but they also increase income earning capacity. Where macroeconomic analyses of the growth effects of education have been somewhat ambiguous, the microeconomic evidence of the returns to education is overwhelming and robust.[30] Research suggests that each additional year of education increases the average individual worker's wages by at least 5 to 10 percent.[31] Educating girls and women is a particularly effective way to raise the human development levels of children. Mothers who are more educated have healthier children, even at a given level of income. They are also more productive in the labor force, which raises household incomes and thereby increases child survival rates—in part because, compared with men, women tend to spend additional income in ways that benefit children more.[32]

5.2.3 THE IMPORTANCE OF PUBLIC POLICY

These trends make it clear that *public policy matters*. As we discuss in Chapter 7, government has a role not only in ensuring delivery of good basic services in health and education, but also in ensuring that technology and knowledge is

---

[29] The only exception is sub-Saharan Africa, where initially gains in life expectancy have been halted by the HIV/AIDS health pandemic. Over the last three decades life expectancy in the region as a whole has remained around 50 years with some countries experiencing drastic declines (World Bank 2011b).

[30] See, for example, Psacharopoulos (1985, 1994) and Psacharopoulos and Patrinos (2004).

[31] Krueger and Lindahl (1999) summarize the evidence.

[32] See Schultz (2002), who notes: "The conclusion of many empirical studies of child development is that increased schooling of the mother is associated with larger improvements in child quality outcomes than is the increased schooling of the father. This has been studied with birth outcomes (e.g., birth weight), child survival, good nutrition, earlier entry into school, increases in school enrolment adjusted for age, and more years of schooling completed on reaching adulthood" (p. 212). See also Tembon and Fort (2008).

spread widely through the economy. The dramatic improvement in life expectancy at a given income level is attributable to environmental changes and is the result of public health actions. The control of diarrhea-related diseases, including the development of oral rehydration therapy to reduce child mortality, is one example; the education of women was an important component of these efforts. Smallpox eradication, made possible through a combination of advances in public health research and effective program management, is another example of a successful twentieth-century public health effort.[33]

The statistical evidence shows that large-scale financial aid can generally be used effectively to reduce poverty when reasonably good policies are in place.[34] Donors have increasingly acted on these findings by tailoring support to local needs and circumstances. Thus, the balance of support has moved toward providing large-scale aid to those who can use it well and focusing on knowledge and capacity-building support in other countries. This has been reflected in greater selectivity and coordination in lending on the part of aid agencies, shifting resources toward governance and institutions, emphasizing ownership, and making room for diverse responses to local needs. These new approaches and procedures have begun to pay off. However, it is clear that there is still much to learn: for example, more work is needed on the question of how best to catalyze and support reforms and institution building in countries with very weak policies, institutions, and governance.

The importance of strong domestic policies is most apparent in times of economic and financial crisis. Some developing countries such as China, Korea, and South Africa have learned vital lessons from countries that have previously failed to maintain responsible policies. For example, Jeon Hyo-Chan (2010) shows how sound fundamentals in the public and private sector of Korea's economy (including fiscal balance, low debt, and the availability of credit) has enabled the country to escape the worst of the current global financial crisis and recover faster than most experts have predicted. In the Korean case many of the improved policies and macroeconomic fundamentals owe much to the lessons learned from the 1997 East Asian currency crisis. Such examples show that better and more responsible policies can pay huge dividends to poor countries and boost poverty reduction.

---

[33] These significant health achievements do hide regional and country divergences. Like income growth, improvements in health status and life expectancy have not been equally distributed. The health status and life expectancy of the poorest nations lag behind the rest of the world, and within countries, the health of the poor is worse than that of the rest of the population. Poverty is the most important underlying cause of preventable death, disease, and disability; and there is growing recognition that poor health, malnutrition, and large family size are key determinants of poverty.

[34] See Burnside and Dollar (2000), Collier and Dollar (2002), Brautigam and Knack (2004), Bourguignon and Sundberg (2007), Rajan and Subramanian (2008), Baliamoune-Lutz (2009), Baliamoune-Lutz and Mavrotas (2009). The Burnside and Dollar (2000) results were questioned by Easterly, Levine, and Roodman (2004).

Collier, Devarajan, and Dollar (2001) and Collier and Dollar (2004) sought to quantify the extent to which policies matter for aid effectiveness. Their analysis claims that in 1990, countries with worse policies and institutions received US$44 per capita in ODA from all sources (multilateral and bilateral), while those with better policies received less: only US$39 per capita. By the late 1990s, the situation was reversed: better policy countries received US$28 per capita, or almost twice as much as the worse policy countries (US$16 per capita). As a result, the poverty reduction effectiveness per dollar of overall ODA has grown rapidly. In 1990, a one-time aid increase of US$1 billion allocated across countries in proportion to existing ODA would have permanently lifted an estimated 105,000 people out of poverty; but by 1997–1998, that number had improved to 284,000 people lifted out of poverty.[35] In other words, the estimated poverty reduction productivity of ODA nearly tripled during the 1990s. Similar lines of inquiry (for example, Collier and Dollar 2002) suggest that reallocating existing levels of aid more effectively could double the numbers of people lifted out of poverty by these flows. The Collier and Dollar analysis has been subject to a number of critiques and as Bourguignon and Sundberg (2007) concluded, the empirical literature on aid effectiveness has yielded unclear and ambiguous results. They highlighted the heterogeneity of aid motives, the limitations of the tools of analysis, and the difficulties associated with attributing outcomes to any one specific policy event or budgetary contribution. Despite these reservations, the consensus among development practitioners is that the policy and governance environment matters a great deal to the effectiveness of aid.

Why would the overall environment matter so much in determining the effectiveness of ODA? The first reason is very straightforward: policies and institutions affect project quality. For example, a major reason for the dramatic decline in measured World Bank project outcomes in the 1970s and 1980s was the deterioration in policy quality and governance in many borrowing countries. No matter how well designed, a project can easily be undermined by high levels of macroeconomic volatility or government corruption.

The second reason is more subtle. Even if a project does seem to succeed—based on narrow measures of economic returns and successfully attaining project objectives—the actual marginal contribution of aid funneled through that project may be small or even negative. This is because government resources are often largely fungible: money can be moved relatively easily from one intended use to another. Thus if donors choose to finance a primary

---

[35] Poverty is defined here as living on less than US$1 per person per day, adjusted for cross-country differences in living costs. It must be emphasized that moving people above the poverty line represents just one effect of the aid, which also helped increase income and other dimensions of development throughout the economy.

education project, displacing local money that would have been used for education, that local money could then be shifted to less productive purposes, such as military spending. In a country with poor public expenditure management, the displaced money could even be diverted to the personal uses of corrupt officials. In this case, the indirect but very real effect of aid could be to promote corruption.[36]

Should we then use only policy and institutional quality as measures in determining aid flows? Should countries with poor policy and poor institutional quality receive no aid at all? This would probably be too rash a conclusion. Research by Clemens, Radelet, and Bhavnani (2004) takes an entirely different approach. Instead of focusing on the different policy and institutional characteristics of recipient countries, they focus on the characteristics of different types of aid flows. Importantly, they consider only what they term "short impact" aid, which includes budget and balance of payments support, infrastructure investments, and aid for productive sectors such as agriculture and industry. In contrast to previous studies, they find a strong impact of aid on growth (and thus on poverty reduction, at least to some extent) regardless of institutions and policies.[37] Similarly, Ouattara and Strobl (2008) found that project aid is far more likely to spur economic growth than financial program aid, technical assistance, or food aid. In light of such evidence, it is necessary to be cautious and avoid a new faddism or herd behavior in the reallocation of aid flows to a small group of countries that meet the criteria. Timely interventions to support reform efforts and to avert famines and other crises remain a vital function of aid.

The above considerations suggest that aid can indeed be very productive. Evidence also suggests that developing countries have never as a group been better able to absorb distributed aid. Additionally, aid agencies have never been better able to disburse aid more effectively. Remarkably, however, as discussed above, although there is virtual unanimity that aid effectiveness has improved, the amount of aid given by rich countries as a share of their income has declined. Since 2001, this trend has reversed, but even by 2009, aid only accounted for 0.31 percent of OECD donors' income, down from 0.33 percent in 1992 but up from the trough of 0.22 percent.

---

[36] The issue of fungibility is taken up in chapter 3 of World Bank (1998). Pettersson's (2007) study of 57 aid-receiving countries found no evidence to suggest that "non-fungible aid would work better than fungible aid" (p. 1091).

[37] Clemens, Radelet, and Bhavnani note that "The result is robust over a wide variety of specifications...It holds over various time periods, stands up whether we include or exclude influential observations, and remains robust when controlling for possible endogeneity of several independent variables" (p. 40).

5.3 **Improving the effectiveness of aid**

As we have seen, the development community's understanding of both development and poverty has evolved in some significant ways. Most importantly, it is now widely accepted that poverty reduction efforts should address poverty in all its dimensions—not only lack of income, but also the lack of health and education, vulnerability to shocks, and poor peoples' lack of control over their lives.[38] This conception of poverty can call for different approaches than those used in the past. Examples of these different approaches include an increased focus on public service delivery to vulnerable groups and greater attention to early disclosure of information that poor people can use.

Another way of improving aid effectiveness has been through the increased use of randomized control trials (RCTs)—pioneered by economists at MIT and Harvard—to identify cleanly the effects of particular programs. These are now used extensively by the World Bank in its Development Impact Evaluation Initiative (DIME) and have been particularly valuable in the areas where an experimental design can most readily be applied, such as health, education, and income support.[39] However, as Goldin, Rogers, and Stern (2006) argue, it is important to recognize the limitations of RCTs. Firstly, in cases such as exchange rate policy or central bank independence, they are simply not feasible. Secondly, even in cases in which they are feasible they may not be efficient or ethical if the need for assistance is urgent and there is good reason to believe a program will be effective. Thirdly, the results they yield may be heavily dependent on cultural and social contexts and may be difficult to scale up to an economy-wide level or to transfer to different countries. Perhaps most importantly, a combination of economic theory and the demands of developing world policy makers must still inform which permutations of the many potential interventions to experiment with.

As we discuss in Chapter 7, experience has shown that neither the central planning approach followed by many countries in the 1950s and 1960s nor the minimal government, free market approach advocated by many aid agencies in the late 1970s and the 1980s will achieve these development and poverty alleviation goals. Most effective approaches to development will be led by the private sector, but they need to have effective government to provide the governance framework, to assist with or provide physical infrastructure, to invest in education and health, and to ensure the social cohesion

---

[38] This multidimensionality of poverty is embodied in the Millennium Development Goals (MDGs) adopted by heads of state at a United Nations summit in 2000. See also Sen (1999) and Kakwani and Silber (2008).

[39] See http://go.worldbank.org/9R255TPZQ0 Banerjee and He (2008) and Banerjee and Duflo (2011) are among the few economists who have pioneered this approach.

necessary for growth and poverty reduction.[40] Institutional development has too often been neglected in past policy discussions, but it is now recognized to be essential to sustained poverty reduction. Although a number of key principles for effective development are clear, there is no single road to follow. Countries must devise their own strategies and approaches, appropriate for their own country circumstances and goals.

The most successful development assistance will have effects that reverberate far beyond the confines of the project itself, either because the ideas in the project are replicated elsewhere or because the intervention has helped institutionalize new approaches. As noted above, levels of aid are small relative to the private capital and public resources that it can leverage. Therefore, aid's largest impact will come through the effects of such demonstration and institution building. These wider or deeper effects of aid are far harder to measure than its direct effects.

China, India, Mozambique, Poland, Uganda, and Vietnam are all examples of countries where, within the past two decades, policy and institutional reforms have sparked an acceleration of development. In each of these cases, the country and its government have been the prime movers for reform, and each country mapped out its own development strategy and approach. Their experiences do have some common features—most notably an increase in market orientation and macroeconomic stability—and all have seen their growth powered by private sectors (both farms and firms) that have begun to thrive. Although these countries did act along those broad guidelines on development, none of them closely followed any external blueprint for development offered by international institutions and foreign donors.

Yet in all of these cases, development assistance from many sources has supported the transformation. In some cases, advice was more important than lending. In China, for example, aid flows have been dwarfed by inflows of private capital. But development assistance helped pave the way for private sector growth and international integration. For example, external analysis and advice was provided to help China open its economy to investment, unify its exchange rate, and improve its ports early in its transition period.

The converse is also clearly true. There are many examples of countries that have received very large volumes of aid over time, with little result in terms of poverty reduction. A case in point, discussed in Box 5.1, is the Democratic Republic of Congo (formerly Zaire). Also, donor-supported progress on

[40] Social cohesion or "social capital," as pointed out by Woolcock and Narayan (2000) and Fukuyama (2002), is an underappreciated element of development. It brings together the realms of culture, governance, and institutions. Baliamoune-Lutz and Mavrotas (2009) examine the aid-social capital-growth nexus. See Woolcock (2010) for a recent review of the rise and impact of social capital as an analytical concept over the last twenty years.

human development indicators in some countries has been largely reversed by the AIDS epidemic or by conflict. In Botswana, which otherwise has a highly successful economy, AIDS reduced life expectancy from 64 years in the early 1990s to 49 years in the early 2000s before partially recovering to 54 years in 2008. In Sierra Leone, an eleven-year conflict and its aftermath reduced male life expectancy to around 37 years in the 1990s.[41] We take up the issues of both HIV/AIDS and conflict in Chapter 8 when we present our policy agenda.

Commitment of the leadership is one of the most critical conditions for ensuring the success of reforms, whether they are in the area of the macro-economy or in combating epidemics such as HIV/AIDS. Evidence has shown that policy change is driven by the country's own initiative, capacity, and political readiness rather than by foreign assistance and associated loan conditionality.[42] Relying heavily on conditionality is ineffective for several reasons:

- It can be difficult to monitor whether a government has in fact fulfilled the conditions, particularly when external shocks muddy the picture.
- Governments may revert to old practices as soon as the money has been disbursed.
- When assessments are subjective, donors may have an incentive to empha-size progress to keep programs moving.

Without country ownership, adjustment lending has not only failed to support reforms, but may have contributed to their delay. For example, case studies of Côte d'Ivoire, the Democratic Republic of Congo, Kenya, Nigeria, and Tanzania all concluded that the availability of aid money in the 1980s postponed much needed reforms.[43]

In practice, country commitment has often proved difficult to assess. For example, a government may be seriously committed to a reform program but subsequently find it impossible to implement key measures, sometimes for reasons not fully under the government's control. In other cases, the government may be interested primarily in the funds, not in the reforms on which the funding is conditional. For this reason, the government's track record, as measured by the quality of the policies and institutions it has already put in place, is often a good indicator of its commitment to reform. That said, as discussed in the previous section, some types of aid might be effective even

---

[41] The decline in female life expectancy in the 1990s was less pronounced and remained in the early 40s. Life expectancy (male and female) in Sierra Leone increased by a decade (from 38 years in 1995 to 48 years in 2008) following the aftermath of the civil war. Persistent conflict in Afghanistan has kept life expectancy in the early 40s since 1980. Life expectancy in Iraq declined from 71 years in 2001 to 68 years in 2009 (World Bank 2011b).

[42] See World Bank (1998) and IMF (1998).

[43] See Devarajan, Dollar, and Holmgren (2001).

with a limited degree of reform. For example, the delivery of aid to eliminate school fees or through providing an incentive to attend school has the potential, already in progress, to educate millions more African children than are educated today.[44]

5.4 **Assisting weak states**

If the conclusion of the past 50 years of aid is that aid (and debt relief) should be allocated to countries with a policy and institutional environment that is conducive to effective use, what should be done in countries where this does not happen? Or to put it another way, how can the international community assist countries where states can be characterized as "weak" or "failed"? Approaches that work in the typical low-income country may not be appropriate in post-conflict and weak states, as such states usually lack the governance, institutions, and necessary leadership for reform. In these circumstances, traditional lending conditionality has not worked well to induce and support reform.

Countries with weak or failed states vary widely in their problems and opportunities. As for the better performing countries, no single strategy will be appropriate for all of them. Each has its specific challenges and must look for unique solutions. Nevertheless, it is useful to distinguish approaches in post-conflict and weak states from those that will work in countries with better policies, institutions, and governance.

Large-scale financial transfers are unlikely to work well in post-conflict and weak states because the absorptive capacity in these environments is quite limited. Instead, donors should focus on knowledge transfer and capacity building to facilitate change. Because of constraints on government capacity, such efforts should concentrate on a limited reform agenda that is both sensible in economic terms (that is, mindful of sequencing issues—what is possible to achieve and what should be prioritized) and feasible from a socio-political standpoint. Only when they develop greater capacity will these countries generally be able to make good use of large-scale aid. There will often be a case for using aid to improve basic health and education services. To be effective, however, funding should probably be directed through channels other than the central government. This suggests wholesale retail structures in which a donor-monitored wholesaling organization contracts with multiple channels of retail provision, such as the private sector, NGOs, and local governments. The role of the United Nations and its agencies in emergency relief and coordination

---

[44] See Dugger (2004) and chapter 1 of Oxfam (2005). Ethiopia, Kenya, Lesotho, Malawi, Tanzania, Uganda, and Zambia have all recorded large increases in enrolments with the reduction or abolition of school fees. In many cases, aid has supported these achievements.

with donors on refugees for funding and provision of basic services is important and not always sufficiently recognized. The very least that poor people in dire emergencies should be able to expect is that the international community demonstrates that it is able to coordinate and act effectively.

Improvements in policies and institutions in many sub-Saharan African countries, combined with examples of successful poverty reduction in a few countries, now provide grounds for hope.[45] As policies in many sub-Saharan African countries improved, so did economic performance: GDP growth rates rose to an average of 4 percent in 1994–2009, or nearly 2 percentage points higher than it was in the 1980s A few countries, such as Mozambique and Uganda, have seen especially strong returns to reform. These developments have important implications for aid allocation: although not every country in Africa could absorb an increase in large-scale aid (for reasons described in the previous section), as the effectiveness of aid rises, so too should the amount of aid allocated to the region. Instead, African countries with good policy saw a substantial decline in aid flows in the 1990s, with aid per capita falling by roughly a third, even as prices for export commodities also fell sharply. Annual per capita aid in Africa is currently well below the levels of 25 years ago, while policies are greatly improved, both in the recipient and in the donor countries. For these reasons, much more aid than is currently given to well-performing countries can be effectively utilized.

Although aid effectiveness requires that large-scale financial assistance be allocated to poor countries that have demonstrated the capacity to use aid well, the international community cannot simply abandon people who live in countries that lack the policies, institutions, and governance necessary for sustained growth and for effective use of aid. Poor people in these countries are among the poorest in the world and face the greatest hurdles in improving their lives. Experience suggests that current technical assistance for capacity-building efforts, as well as the promise of greater financial assistance if policies, institutions, and governance improve, is often insufficient to enable these countries to initiate and sustain reform.

Of the two or three dozen countries with the poorest institutions and policies, only a few have made major improvements in their environments for growth and poverty reduction over the past decade, in contrast to the broad improvements in policies in other developing countries. Ethiopia, Mozambique, Rwanda, and Uganda are unusual among former post-conflict countries in having achieved significant progress. Other post-conflict countries have

---

[45] Additionally, arguments that foreign aid given to weak African states tends to *exacerbate* problems appear to be untrue. For example, Goldsmith (2001), based on a statistical analysis, concluded, "Foreign aid provides the wherewithal for African states to pay for and carry out many basic public functions. Yet being reliant on aid does not necessarily mean that these states would have evolved in a dramatically more favorable direction had they received less aid. Something closer to the opposite seems more likely" (p. 144). See also Schwalbenberg (1998) and World Bank (2011c).

seen little development progress, and the performance of the development agencies lending portfolio in this group has been relatively poor. Projects have failed there at double the rate for other countries.

5.5 **Innovative aid programs**

Despite huge advances in science and in the understanding of the aid and development processes, there is much that we still do not know. Perhaps most important, we do not understand fully how to help improve institutions and governance, especially in the poorest countries where the needs are greatest.[46] And we are still learning how best to deal with pressing cross border issues—such as disease, environmental problems, and political instability—that threaten development.

Global development challenges such as conflict, loss of biodiversity, deforestation, climate change, and the spread of infectious diseases cannot be handled solely by individual countries acting at the national level. They require sustained, multilateral action. As the number and scope of global challenges have grown, so too have the number of actors involved, creating a need for new partnerships and networks among stakeholders. Private charities have become a force in the areas of environment and health. Pharmaceutical companies have become donors to global health initiatives. As discussed in Chapter 4, private capital flows to developing countries (especially in the form of FDI) now dwarf official development assistance. The search for international common ground, together with a variety of formal and informal international agreements, have led to new alliances and revised roles for a range of institutions that include the Global Environment Facility, the World Trade Organization, and the various UN bodies. No single actor can speak to all of these challenges, but efforts to address them have been growing rapidly.

According to the UN Secretary General's office, hundreds of new programs to address issues of global scope are being created each year. Although multi-national initiatives are required, they often must be linked to country actions. Many global initiatives address problems that have both important domestic effects and major cross border spillovers, such as financial contagion, the spread of AIDS, ozone depletion, and toxic pollution. Other global problems call for increasing the efficiency of resources spent at the country level through the use of science and technology available only in the richer countries or globally supported research centers. In most cases, complementary national efforts in developing countries are central to either achieving objectives of the global

---

[46] For an assessment, see Fukuyama (2004) and Collier (2007).

programs (such as biodiversity conservation, which often builds on local programs) or ensuring developing countries' access to their benefits (such as agricultural productivity, where new crop varieties must be matched to locally adapted cultivation practices). Here, we take up just three examples of effective global programs, which highlight the benefits of global action on aid.

5.5.1 ONCHOCERCIASIS CONTROL PROGRAM

The first program addresses river-blindness or onchocerciasis, a disease widespread in Africa. It causes blindness, disfigurement, and unbearable itching in its victims, and has rendered large tracts of farmland in Africa uninhabitable. The Onchocerciasis Control Programme (OCP) was created in 1974 with two primary objectives. The first was to eliminate onchocerciasis as a public health problem and as an obstacle to socio-economic development throughout an 11-country area of West Africa (Benin, Burkina Faso, Côte d'Ivoire, Ghana, Guinea, Guinea-Bissau, Mali, Niger, Senegal, Sierra Leone, and Togo). The second objective was to leave participating countries with the capacity to maintain this achievement. OCP was sponsored by four agencies: the United Nations Development Programme (UNDP), the Food and Agriculture Organization (FAO), the World Bank, and the World Health Organization (WHO).

OCP has now halted transmission and virtually eliminated prevalence of onchocerciasis throughout the 11-country subregion containing 35 million people. About 600,000 cases of blindness have been prevented, 5 million years of productive labor added to the economies of 11 countries, and 16 million children born within the OCP area have been spared any risk of contracting onchocerciasis. In addition, control operations have freed up an estimated 25 million hectares of arable land that is now experiencing spontaneous settlement. OCP has been hailed as one of the most successful partnerships in the history of development assistance.[47] As summarized by Benton et al. (2002), "Through a combination of persistence, dedication, and happenstance, the Onchocerciasis Control Programme evolved from an ambitious plan to a sterling example of disease control."[48]

Given this success, the program has extended operations to what is now called the African Program for Onchocerciasis Control (APOC). This program, begun in 1995, extends the OCP to the remaining 19 Onchocerciasis-infested African countries and has been equally successful. It has been estimated that in 2007 almost 1 million disability adjusted life years (DALYS)[49] were saved through

---

[47] The OCP involved the pharmaceutical company Merck's drug ivermectin or Mectizan®. The partnership thus extended across public–private boundaries.

[48] Benton et al. (2002), pp. 8–9.

[49] A disability adjusted life year (DALY) is a measure of disease burden that captures the number of years lost due to ill health, disability, and death.

APOC and this figure is projected to exceed 15 million DALYs in 2015—the year the project is scheduled to end.[50] This incredible achievement involves establishing networks of community directed drug distributors (CDD) that can potentially be used to combat other health problems in the region. Again, as summarized by Benton et al. (2002), "What began as a top-down, vertical, disease-control programme has evolved into a bottom up, integrated approach that couples strong regional co-ordination with the empowerment of local communities to address not only onchocerciasis but, potentially, many other health problems."[51] The potential of the CDD to help combat HIV/AIDS is particularly of interest here.

5.5.2 THE GREEN REVOLUTION

Sometimes building on success involves helping to diffuse ideas across countries and regions through partnership with other development actors.[52] The *Green Revolution*, which began in South Asia in the 1970s and spread to Africa and Latin America, has led to impressive gains in production of basic food crops across the developing world, as shown in Table 5.5. Between 1970 and 2009 yields of cereals and coarse grains more than doubled in Asia and South America. While the benefits of the green revolution have been unevenly distributed, substantial gains have been made across the board and Africa as a whole has done particularly well in terms of increasing the yield of roots and tubers. International aid agencies supported this sweeping change through its lending for irrigation, rural infrastructure, and agriculture, and by mobilizing support with other donors through the Consultative Group for International Agricultural Research, better known by its acronym, the CGIAR. This is a second example of an effective aid program.

The CGIAR, created in 1971, now includes 15 international agricultural research centers. More than 8,500 CGIAR scientific staff members currently work to produce higher-yield food crops, more productive livestock, fish and forestry, improved farming systems, better policy options, and enhanced scientific capacity in developing countries.[53] The knowledge generated by CGIAR—and the public and private sector organizations that work with it as partners, researchers, and advisors—has paid poor consumers handsome dividends in terms of increased output and lower food prices. More than 300 varieties of wheat and rice and more than 200 varieties of maize

---

[50] WHO (2007), p. 11.

[51] Benton et al. (2002), p. 12. WHO (2007) attributes the relative success of APOC—in contrast to other less successful health care initiatives—to the bottom-up "community direct approach" that underpins treatment.

[52] We take up the role of ideas in earnest in Chapter 7.

[53] For reviews of the CGIAR system, see Greenland (1997) and Sagasti and Timmer (2008).

Table 5.5 Yields of major crops (Hg/Ha) in Africa, Asia, and South America, 1970–2009

	AFRICA			ASIA			SOUTH AMERICA		
	Cereals and coarse Grain	Roots and Tubers	Pulses	Cereals and coarse Grain	Roots and Tubers	Pulses, Total	Cereals and coarse Grain	Roots and Tubers	Pulses
1970–1974	9038.8	59569	4768.4	11208.2	115098.4	6182.8	16210.4	115320	6262.4
1975–1979	9967.8	65663	5434.4	13731	123089	6410.6	17786.6	108390.8	5446.4
1980–1984	10359.6	67346	5595	15996.4	135211.2	6498.6	20427	108611.8	5067.4
1985–1989	10602.4	73046	5392.6	17519.4	140636.4	6893.6	21132.2	117462.6	4971
1990–1994	10124	80279.2	5100	21177.8	145819.2	6886.2	23421.4	118932.4	6109
1995–1999	10598	82015.2	4838.8	24297.8	158323	7374	28937	124220.4	6924.4
2000–2004	11316.2	84310.2	5550.8	25619.2	169353	7680.6	33831.2	132065.2	7950.8
2005–2009	12107.2	90665.6	5763.6	30339.6	174905	7880.6	37402.2	137465.4	9067.4
Change*	33.95%	52.20%	20.87%	170.69%	51.96%	27.46%	130.73%	19.20%	44.79%

Note: Cereals and coarse grains consist of Barley, Buckwheat, Canary seed, Cereals nes, Fonio, Maize, Millet, Mixed grain, Oats, Popcorn, Quinoa, Rice paddy, Rye, Sorghum, and Triticale and Wheat

Roots and Tubers consist of Cassava, Potatoes, Roots and Tubers nes, Sweet potatoes, Taro (cocoyam), Yams, and Yautia (cocoyam)

Pulses consist of Bambara beans, Beans dry, Broad beans, Horse beans dry, Chick peas, Cow peas dry, Lentils, Lupins, Peas dry, Pigeon peas, Pulses nes, and Vetches

* Percentage change from 1970–1974 to 2005–2009

Source: Calculated from FAOSTAT (www.fao.org), March 30, 2011.

developed through CGIAR-supported research are being grown by farmers in developing countries. Food production has doubled, improving health and nutrition for millions. New, more environment-friendly technologies developed by CGIAR have released between 230 and 340 million hectares of land for cultivation worldwide, helping to conserve land and water resources and biodiversity. CGIAR's efforts have helped to reduce pesticide use in developing countries. For example, control of cassava pests alone has increased the value of annual production in sub-Saharan Africa by US$400 million.

Yet the CGIAR must now meet new challenges. Agriculture research technology has changed, giving prominence to molecular biology and genetic approaches. More robust intellectual property rights have produced an explosion in private investment for agricultural research. These changes pose new challenges to the CGIAR size, organization, and approach as does the urgent need to lift agricultural productivity in Africa. The Commission for Africa (2005) notes that US$340 million a year is required by the CGIAR to help offset Africa's agricultural productivity deficit.

5.5.3 AFRICAN ECONOMIC RESEARCH CONSORTIUM

A third example of a successful global program is the African Economic Research Consortium (AERC), which is less well known than the first two. Like the river-blindness control program, the AERC is a regional program focused on addressing one of Africa's greatest needs: strong domestic capacity for policy analysis and formulation. Recent development experience shows clearly that development strategy must be "owned" by the countries that implement them, not dictated by outside donors. But the ability to participate in design and decision making that is necessary for ownership depends on local capacity for policy analysis. For this reason, capacity building is an essential element of development assistance.

The international nature of the AERC has made it stronger by supporting a critical mass of researchers and academic institutions, and by encouraging the sharing of experiences across countries. Its mission statement has as its principle objective "to strengthen local capacity for conducting independent, rigorous inquiry into problems pertinent to the management of economies in Sub-Saharan Africa." Established in 1988, this initiative now covers 22 countries.

Established by 6 international and bilateral agencies and private foundations, AERC is now funded by 17 donors, including foundations, governments, and multilateral organizations.[54] It has a budget of approximately US$15 million a year. The AERC conducts research in-house and administers a small grants program for researchers in academia and policy-making institutions.[55] In

---

[54] See www.aercafrica.org
[55] A number of publications that are a result of this research are available at www.aercafrica.org

addition to its research program, the AERC began in 1992 to administer a two year collaborative Masters of Arts (MA) program in economics with students and faculty from 23 universities in 19 sub-Saharan African countries. As of 2010, the program has produced about 1800 MA graduates and 300 PhD graduates in economics to date. Many graduates of the AERC have gone on to research and teaching posts throughout the region, and others to high-level positions in African central banks and finance ministries.

5.6 **Easing the burden of debt**

As we reported in Chapter 4, debt financing has been an important part of financing in developing countries for centuries and no reading of economic history is complete without reference to the debt crises of previous eras. The first recent major debt crisis to take place, and in which aid policies included significant debt components, occurred when an oil price shock and global recession hit in the late 1970s and early 1980s. Commodity prices turned sharply against the non-oil commodity exporters, making it difficult for them to pay for both imports and debt service. While interest rates were rising, official lending increased to help cushion the effects of the shock, and to substitute for finance from commercial sources, which for most borrowing countries evaporated.

For all countries, including developing countries, any deficit on the current account (such as through trade deficits) that is not made up for by net factor receipts, transfers such as foreign aid, FDI, or a reduction in foreign reserves necessarily translates into foreign debt as the country sells financial assets of various kinds to generate an offsetting surplus on the capital account.[56] It sometimes makes sense for developing countries to engage in short-term borrowing of this kind to cover short-term current account deficits.

Increasingly from the 1950s, developing countries had access to more long-term borrowing, which in most instances is better suited to their needs. However, where such borrowing is not used to make productive investments that increase output of the tradable sectors of the economy (which increase exports relative to imports), current account deficits will persist indefinitely, and debt will build up to unsustainable levels.

In many of the highly indebted countries, the expected improvements in policy performance did not materialize, whether because of insufficient commitment by borrowers or because the design of the adjustment had not paid enough attention to the political economy of reform, governance, and

---

[56] See chapter 12 of Reinert (2005).

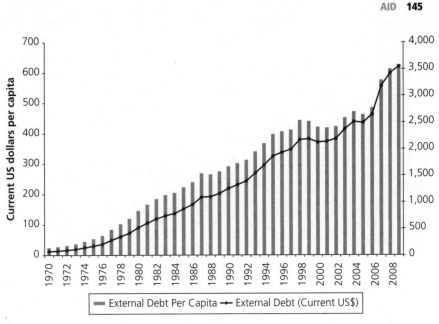

Figure 5.5. External debts of developing countries

Source: World Development Indicators (http://databank.worldbank.org), March 2011.

corruption, or to social concerns. In other cases, reforms were implemented but did not lead to the expected supply and growth response. As a result, the GDP average growth rate between 1980 and 1987 of the 33 countries that were characterized in the mid-1990s as the most severely indebted low-income countries was just 1.9 percent—which translated into an income decline in per capita terms. The cumulative effect of the shock and economic decline was that a debt burden that had been reasonable became unsustainable. Between 1982 and 1992, the debt to export ratio of the 33 most highly indebted countries rose from 266 to 620 percent.[57]

5.6.1 THE DEBT CRISIS AND DEBT-RELIEF INITIATIVES

The recent history of external debt is traced in Figure 5.5, both in total terms (solid line and right-hand axis) and in per capita terms (vertical bars, left-hand axis). Significant increases in both measures began in the mid-1970s. Beginning in 1976, the IMF began to sound warnings about the sustainability of developing country borrowing from the commercial banking system. The banking system reacted with hostility to these warnings, arguing that the Fund had no place interfering with private transactions.

[57] See World Bank (1994b).

The IMF's warnings became clear when the "debt crisis" began in 1982. The initiating event was Mexico's announcement that it would stop servicing its foreign currency debt. Within months, the debt crisis had spread to Brazil and Argentina. In 1982, the total external debt of developing countries was approximately US$680 billion and per capita external debt was approximately US$185. As can be seen in Figure 5.5, both total and per capita external debt continued to increase significantly through 1999 to approximately US$2,185 billion and US$440 per capita. Indeed, between 1990 and 2009, the total external debt for developing countries increased by approximately US$2.3 trillion, the bulk of which was for middle-income countries. These continued debt burdens in the developing world negatively affect both growth prospects and the financing of basic public services. Both of these, in turn, negatively affect poverty in all its dimensions.

Since the late 1980s, the international development community has attempted to address the problem through a variety of debt reduction mechanisms. In 1996 it went a step further, creating the Heavily Indebted Poor Countries (HIPC) debt relief initiative to deepen debt relief for poor countries suffering from unsustainable debt burdens. The initiative aims to *increase the effectiveness of aid* by helping poor countries achieve sustainable levels of debt while strengthening the link between debt relief and strong policy performance. Forty countries, primarily from the sub-Saharan Africa region, are identified as eligible (or potentially eligible) to receive debt relief under this initiative. As of December 2010, 36 countries had met the required governance and other standards and are receiving debt relief under the HIPC initiative amounting to US$75 billion.[58] *Debt service to export ratios* have been reduced for this set of countries to an average of 8.9 percent.[59]

Not only does HIPC reduce *debt overhang*, it also supports positive change toward better poverty reduction. Debt relief under the HIPC initiative is intended for countries that are pursuing effective poverty reduction strategies as ascertained by the World Bank and the IMF; both better public expenditure management and increased social expenditures are critical elements of this affirmation of effectiveness. For the countries that have received HIPC relief, the ratio of social expenditures to GDP has increased

[58] See IMF (2010). Cohen (2001) notes that, measured at market rather than at face value, the committed debt relief would be substantially smaller than this announced value. The World Bank estimated the net present value of the debt relief involved to be US$62 billion (World Bank 2004a).

[59] This is the average for the period 2001 to 2008. The average is projected to fall to 3.9 percent between 2009 and 2013 (see IMF 2010, table 1). The relevant countries are Afghanistan, Benin, Bolivia, Burkina Faso, Burundi, Cameroon, Central African Republic, Chad, Republic of Congo, Democratic Republic of Congo, Côte d'Ivoire, Ethiopia, The Gambia, Ghana, Guinea, Guinea-Bissau, Guyana, Honduras, Liberia, Madagascar, Malawi, Mali, Mauritania, Mozambique, Nicaragua, Niger, Rwanda, São Tomé and Principe, Senegal, Sierra Leone, Tanzania, Togo, Uganda, and Zambia.

significantly.[60] The challenges are to ensure that these expenditures translate into better outcomes in the social sector; that vital infrastructure improvements also increase; and, more important, that the broader policy environment continues to improve and support growth and poverty reduction.

The HIPC experience has demonstrated that debt relief can work. It is clear, however, that the amounts allocated within HIPC—the debts that are written off—are insufficient to put all low-income countries on a sustainable debt repayment path and to ease the pressure on their debt servicing sufficiently to allow an accelerated reallocation of funds toward required investments in infrastructure, education, health, and other poverty reduction expenditures. A new framework for debt sustainability was therefore needed to match the need for funds in low-income countries with their ability to service debt. This requires substantial increases in the funds available. The July 2005 commitment at the Gleneagles, Scotland, summit of the Group of Eight leaders to allocate US$40 billion for additional debt relief was a significant step forward. The Group of Eight confirmed that these funds will be "additional" to previous commitments to increase aid (including to the International Development Association) and that finance that would go to the better performers who had paid their debts would not be cannibalized to write off the debts of the eligible HIPC countries. Moreover, in 2005 the HIPC initiative was supplemented with the Multilateral Debt Relief Initiative (MDRI) in an effort to boost poverty reduction in the poorest heavily indebted countries. The MDRI allows for 100 percent relief of eligible debts to the IMF, World Bank, and African Development Fund. Since 2007 the Inter-American Development Bank has provided additional debt relief to the HIPCs in the Western Hemisphere.[61]

While the accelerated cancellation of debt has been widely welcomed, there are concerns regarding the moral hazard and incentive effect of debt write-offs. For those countries that have diligently repaid their debts or carefully constrained their debt burden, the prospect of additional aid flows being given to reduce the obligations of those who have been less prudent may seem unfair. To add to this complexity is the question of the inter-temporal nature of debt—the debts being repaid today typically were incurred by previous generations of leaders. Many individuals and some current governments in countries where dictators incurred debts argue that these debts are illegitimate. There are moves that do not necessarily have government support in a wide range of countries, including Indonesia, Nigeria, and South Africa to write off what may be termed illegitimate or "odious" debts, and this precedent has been established for Iraq.[62]

---

[60] See IMF (2009).

[61] See IMF (2010).

[62] Interestingly, the government of South Africa does not support the writing off of apartheid-era debts. See www.worldbank.org/hipc

Without debating the virtues of this position, the key issue is the source of these additional funds. Global flows, like national flows, need to be sourced and paid for with additional commitments. In honoring their commitments to increasing aid, the rich countries need to ensure that funding to meet debt forgiveness is additional and does not represent a claim on existing or future commitments to other forms of aid. They also need to ensure that all countries that are able to use aid effectively benefit from additional flows, so that easing the burden of debt does not come at the expense of poor people in other countries.

5.7 The Millennium Development Goals and donor coordination

A key driver of the effectiveness of aid flows is that they become more predictable and that there is harmonization behind country-owned pro-grams. Too many ministers and civil servants in poor countries spend their time servicing the needs of donors—from taking visiting dignitaries to visit their pet projects to meeting the unique audit and reporting needs of the different aid and donor agencies. In Tanzania, for example, it was estimated that well over a thousand quarterly reports needed to be completed for donors in the 1990s. Aid agencies have a responsibility to ensure that their requirements are harmonized in a set of common standards and that their demands on countries are focused on ensuring that the money goes to projects and programs prioritized in national budgets, rather than to indi-vidual projects in localities favored by foreign or domestic politicians. In addition, donors have a responsibility to ensure that their flows are predict-able, that they agree to multi-year commitments, and that they are not restrict-ed to contracts or goods and services procured from the donor country. A visit to virtually any low-income country reveals the carcasses of projects and programs initiated through donor pressure and promises and that have failed through lack of follow-through in funding and maintenance. The 2005 Paris Declaration signified a commitment of the part of developed nations to donor coordination and harmonization and greater predictability of aid flows. This commitment was reaffirmed in the 2008 Accra Agenda for Action, although unfortunately donor performance falls far short of the pledges made in 2005 and 2008.

The commitment in 2002 by heads of state of both rich and poor countries to achieving the Millennium Development Goals (MDGs) requires the following, as set out in more detail in Box 5.2:

- halving poverty and hunger by 2015
- achieving universal primary education

BOX 5.2 MILLENNIUM DEVELOPMENT GOALS

The Millennium Development Goals are an ambitious agenda for reducing poverty and improving lives that world leaders agreed on at the Millennium Summit in September 2000. For each goal one or more targets have been set, most for 2015, using 1990 as a benchmark:

1. **Eradicate extreme poverty and hunger**

Target for 2015: Halve the proportion of people living on less than a dollar a day and those who suffer from hunger.

2. **Achieve universal primary education**

Target for 2015: Ensure that all boys and girls complete primary school.

3. **Promote gender equality and empower women**

Targets for 2005 and 2015: Eliminate gender disparities in primary and secondary education preferably by 2005, and at all levels by 2015.

4. **Reduce child mortality**

Target for 2015: Reduce by two-thirds the mortality rate among children under five.

5. **Improve maternal health**

Target for 2015: Reduce by three-quarters the ratio of women dying in childbirth.

6. **Combat HIV/AIDS, malaria, and other diseases**

Target for 2015: Halt and begin to reverse the spread of HIV/AIDS and the incidence of malaria and other major diseases.

7. **Ensure environmental sustainability**

Targets:

- Integrate the principles of sustainable development into country policies and programs and reverse the loss of environmental resources
- By 2015, reduce by half the proportion of people without access to safe drinking water
- By 2020 achieve significant improvement in the lives of at least 100 million slum dwellers.

8. **Develop a global partnership for development**

Targets:

- Develop further an open trading and financial system that includes a commitment to good governance, development, and poverty reduction—nationally and internationally
- Address the least developed countries' special needs, and the special needs of landlocked and small island developing states
- Deal comprehensively with developing countries' debt problems
- Develop decent and productive work for youth
- In cooperation with pharmaceutical companies, provide access to affordable essential drugs in developing countries
- In cooperation with the private sector, make available the benefits of new technologies—especially information and communications technologies.

Sources: White (2006) and http://www.undp.org/mdg/

- eliminating gender disparity in education
- reducing by three-quarters maternal mortality
- combating HIV/AIDS and other diseases
- halving the proportion of people without access to potable water
- a global partnership for development.

This agreement reflected a unique coming together in terms of defining the problem and the role of different actors. It has given clear common goals to the international community, and not least to donor agencies and the multilateral institutions, as well as a set of agreed measurable targets and results.

Unfortunately, it is now becoming clear that many or most of these goals will be missed. Indeed, there is a consensus that perhaps only one goal, that of halving income poverty, will be met at the aggregate global level. To help meet this and other goals, in 2005 a set of high-income countries committed themselves to increasing their aid donations to 0.7 percent of GDP. Nearly every rich country, however, has failed so far to meet this target, although Sweden, Denmark, Luxembourg, Norway, and the Netherlands allocate over 0.7 percent of their income to aid (Table 5.4). The latest available aid statistics suggest "the world's biggest aid donors have collectively missed their [2005] targets by $19bn." Only around US$1 billion of this shortfall is

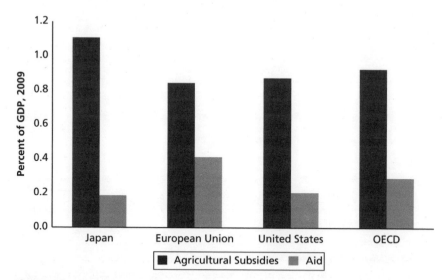

Figure 5.6. Aid and support for agriculture as a share of GDP, 2009

Source: OECD STAT (http://stats.oecd.org/), World Development Indicators (http://databank.worldbank.org), and authors' calculations, March 2011.

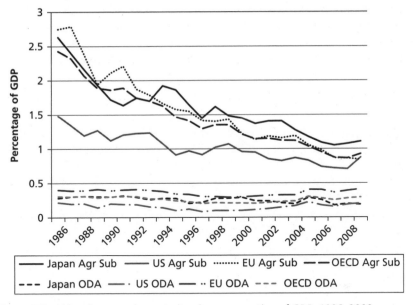

Figure 5.7. Aid and support for agricultural as a proportion of GDP, 1986–2009

Source: OECD STAT (http://stats.oecd.org/), World Development Indicators (http://databank.world-bank.org), and authors' calculations, March 2011.

due to the current financial crisis.[63] It is worth noting that the funds represented by this 0.7 percent of GDP target have remained less than half of what the rich world spends of agricultural subsidies (Figure 5.6)—despite the renewed commitment to aid over the last decade and the long-term decline in support for agriculture since the mid-1980s (Figure 5.7). It follows that meeting the 0.7 percent of GDP target is more a question of will than a question of feasibility (although a marginal improvement shows up in Figure 5.7 from 2004).[64]

5.8 **Non-traditional donors: New challenges and opportunities**

Non-traditional donors including developing countries, private sectors organizations, and individual philanthropists have become increasingly important

---

[63] See *The Guardian* (2011).

[64] Taking the combined GDP of the *entire* set of high-income countries, the 0.7 percent target translates into approximately US$309 billion in 2008, for example. This is about US$65 billion less than the OECD countries spent on agricultural protection in the same year.

sources of aid over the last twenty years. These donors have the potential to make a significant contribution to reducing global poverty and are likely to become increasingly important players in the medium to long term. The rise of non-traditional donors, however, implies new challenges and opportunities.

5.8.1 AID FROM DEVELOPING COUNTRIES

In particular, economic cooperation between low- and middle-income countries including aid flows and technical assistance between developing countries has become a prominent issue.[65] Aid flows between developing countries is not a new phenomenon (as Figure 5.1 implies). For example, Saudi Arabia gave US$48 billion to developing countries between 1975 and 1987, with annual aid flows averaging a massive 4.2 percent of national income.[66] Moreover, China has a long history of involvement with Africa that predates the 1955 Bandung conference[67] and monumental achievements such as the Tanzam railway in the early 1970s. What is relatively new, however, is the increasing magnitude of aid flows between developing countries. For donors reporting to the OECD, non-DAC aid flows rose from 1.5 percent of total aid in 1998 to 6.6 percent in 2008. These figures vastly understate the true extent of aid flows from developing countries as key donors such as the "BRIC" countries (Brazil, Russia, India, and China) do not report to the OECD. The problem is compounded by the fact that comparable estimates of aid donations from emerging economies are not readily available. Some rough-and-ready estimates of aid flows from the BRIC countries are summarized in Table 5.6.

Table 5.6 Rough estimates of aid flows from the BRIC countries

Brazil [a]	2010 estimate	US$1.2 billion
Russia [b]	2007 pledge as part of an expanding aid program	US$400–500 million per annum
India [c]	2007 estimate	Likely to exceed US$150–200 million per annum
China [d]	2007 estimate	US$3.0 billion

[a] Economist (2010a).
[b] http://go.worldbank.org/8CYJJ1N2Y0
[c] http://www.planetd.org/2007/02/05/indias-foreign-aid-program/
[d] Brautigam (2009), p. 169.

---

[65] In some cases, low- and middle-income countries have sent humanitarian aid to developed countries following natural disasters. For example, in 2005 India pledged $5 million to the United State Red Cross following the New Orleans floods (Wikipedia 2011). Moreover, in the wake of the recent catastrophe in Japan (March 2011), China has set old rivalries aside by providing $4.5 million in emergency relief to the survivors of the earthquake and tsunami (Bergman 2011).

[66] See SAMIRAD (2011).

[67] The 1955 Bandung conference brought 29 developing countries together including China, Ethiopia, Sudan, and Liberia. (Many other African countries were not yet independent.) It produced

While high-growth, middle-income economies can afford to spend the most on foreign aid, even some relatively poor countries and transition economies such as India, Russia, Poland, and the Czech Republic have managed to spend significant sums of money on overseas assistance and humanitarian aid (see Tables 5.4 and 5.6). Other middle-income countries that fund overseas development projects include Chile, Colombia, Lithuania, South Africa, and Thailand.[68]

In the case of the largest and most successful non-traditional donor, the People's Republic of China, the story of aid is more complex and nuanced than often implied. The lion's share of Chinese aid is allocated to Africa (an estimated US$2.1 billion in 2009) with the remainder going to Asia and Latin America.[69] Wang (2007) and Johnston (2011), like many other writers, emphasize the importance of China's strategic integration into the world economy and the expansion of domestic and overseas markets as the driving force behind economic and technical cooperation with Africa. Chinese aid, however, is not simply driven by mutual demand for exports or infrastructure requirements. As previously mentioned, China has a long history in Africa which predates her relatively recent reforms and "Going Out" strategy by several decades. Although a large part of Chinese assistance is aimed at key industries (especially natural resources and energy) and construction (infrastructure projects), direct aid flows have been made available over the medium and long term to support African health, education, and training projects (see Looy 2006). Moreover, Christensen (2010) notes that while the bulk of Chinese aid takes the form of grants and concessional loans from the Ministry of Commerce, humanitarian and other types of aid dispensed by other ministries may not be adequately captured in statistics.[70]

China's 2010 White Paper on China–Africa economic trade and cooperation helps explain the general philosophy behind Chinese assistance in terms of mutual cooperation and co-development:

During their years of development, China and Africa give full play to the complementary advantages in each other's resources and economic structures, abiding by the principles of equality, effectiveness, mutual benefit and reciprocity, and mutual development, and keep enhancing economic and trade cooperation to achieve mutual benefit and progress. Practice proves that China-Africa economic and trade

the five principles of peaceful coexistence that remain central to Chinese policy and cooperation (Johnston 2011).

[68] The Aid Data website (www.aiddata.org) includes information on aid projects funded by many developing countries and Arab nations, although there are no aggregate aid disbursement statistics.

[69] It is estimated that Chinese aid to Africa has increased dramatically from US$0.3 billion in 2001 to the present level. In 2006 the creation of a China–Africa Development Fund was announced with an initial fund of US$1 billion intended to grow to US$5 billion within a few years (see Christensen 2010).

[70] Christensen (2010), p. 6.

cooperation serves the common interests of the two sides, helps Africa to reach the UN Millennium Development Goals, and boosts common prosperity and progress for China and Africa.[71]

In practice, aid from China, like aid from many other donors, is shaped by a combination of factors including commercial interests, mutual cooperation, and altruism.

In other cases, the phenomena of South–South Aid raises different issues. In Latin America, for example, the upturn in Cuban–Venezuelan relations and the establishment of the Bolivian Alternative for the Americas (ALBA) has generated significant amounts of aid and cooperation. In 2008 Venezuela is reported to have provided between US$1.2 billion and U$2.5 billion in aid, which is equivalent to the annual aid budget of some OECD countries. However, this relationship goes well beyond economic cooperation and embraces cultural, social, and political factors relating to oil, and the establishment of an independent foreign policy and trade area.[72] Such initiatives have been criticized in some circles as examples of "rogue aid" that seek "to reshape the world into a place very different from where the rest of us want to live."[73]

As the remarks imply, the composition of aid between developing countries often differs from that of DAC donors: there is more emphasis on mutual benefit for donor and recipient, with a greater proportion of aid given in the form of concessional loans for infrastructure projects, often tied to purchases from donor firms.[74] While aid between developing countries remains a modest fraction of total aid, and while it is understandable that low- and middle-income donors are concerned with ensuring aid is beneficial to them, the increasing significance of aid between developing countries means it is important to ensure its effectiveness is maximized for recipient countries.

5.8.2 PRIVATE DONORS AND CHARITIES

In addition to the increases in aid between developing countries, private donors and charities have played an increasingly important role since the 1980s (Figure 5.8). Since 2002 ODA reported to the OECD has increased rapidly reaching more than US$32 billion in 2007 before falling back to just under US$23 billion in 2009 (Figure 5.9). The official data reported in these graphs is probably only a fraction of real donations. In 2007 alone, the Hudson Institute (2009, p. 3) managed to identify US$49.1 billion in private

---

[71] *China Daily* 2010.
[72] See the Reality of Aid Network (2010) report for a discussion.
[73] Naím (2007), p. 95.
[74] Kharas (2007).

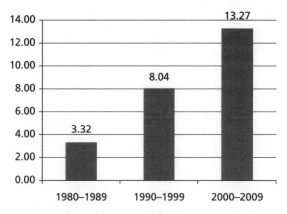

Figure 5.8. Average private flows of ODA in US$ billions, 1980–2009

Source: OECD STAT (http://stats.oecd.org/), March 31, 2011.

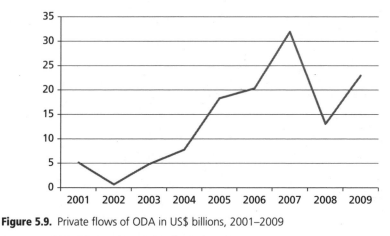

Figure 5.9. Private flows of ODA in US$ billions, 2001–2009

Source: OECD STAT (http://stats.oecd.org/), March 31, 2011.

philanthropy to developing countries from leading developed countries.[75] The Bill and Melinda Gates foundation is the largest single private donor, spending US$24.5 billion on overseas aid between 1994 and 2010 (an average of US$1.5 billion per annum).[76] The Gates Foundation's Global Health

---

[75] See also www.global-prosperity.org The 2010 Hudson Report acknowledges the global downturn in private sector giving (Hudson Institute 2010).

[76] These figures refer to the amount spent outside the USA on global health and global development. The foundation spent a further US$5.9 billion on programs in the USA between 1994 and 2010. Total grant payments in 2010 were US$2.6 billion. See http://www.gatesfoundation.org/about/Pages/foundation-fact-sheet.aspx

Program has an annual budget of approximately US$800 million, about 15 percent of the budget of the World Health Organization.

The expansion of private aid flows poses new opportunities and challenges for development. Most obviously, the rapid growth of private sector philanthropy (much of which remains unrecorded) offers welcome new sources of funding for many development projects. In the case of the USA, private sector giving dwarfs official development assistances[77] encouraging some commentators to refer to the privatization of foreign aid.[78] Others are pragmatic enough to recognize that private philanthropy cannot replace or "offset" government aid, although it may be able—in the words of Bill Gates—"to contribute more than its proportional share."[79] Indeed, the Gates Foundation in its relatively short life has already achieved tangible results in terms of public health (through vaccination, water, and sanitation programs) and is working toward enhancing nutrition (through more controversial large-scale farming and GM technologies).[80]

One possibility is that private sector resource flows can be mobilized to help maintain aid flows during times of economic crisis. In 2008, for example, the IMF actively called for private donors to help fill any gaps left in aid flows by either the impending global financial crisis or the food and fuel crisis in low-income countries. Specifically, it was hoped that private aid flows would help the international community sustain momentum toward the MDGs.[81] The growth of private sector donations may also improve the efficiency and accountability of aid flows. Private sector donors are more likely to be subject to market forces, more likely to produce innovative results, and are more likely to respond quickly to inefficiency.[82] As one critic of government aid argues "[b]ad news travels fast, and private charities are unlikely to send their resources where they are likely to be wasted, because their contributions would soon dry up."[83] There is also evidence to suggest that effective private aid can "crowd in" public sector spending on development and encourage governments to provide better services through "demonstration effects," "competition effects," and "intrinsic pressure" that empowers and gives voice to the poor.[84]

Of course, many of the positive attributes of private sector aid mentioned above have corresponding downsides that raise new challenges. While the generosity of private individuals, organizations, and corporations should not

[77] See Evans (2005) and Adelman (2009).
[78] A notable example is Carol Adelman (2003).
[79] Vidal (2011).
[80] For details, see http://www.gatesfoundation.org/
[81] See IMF (2008).
[82] See also Marten and Witte (2008).
[83] Paul (2006).
[84] Kapur and Whittle (2010).

be underestimated, private development assistance can be subject to fads, fashions, and swings that influence the overall effectiveness of aid. In this respect, support might quickly switch from providing malaria nets one year to measles vaccination or water standpipes the following year with little long-term continuity of planning. Private sector aid is also results-orientated and favors projects and outcomes that can be easily measured and quantified in order to satisfy the demands of funders and marketing programs. Consumers are frequently told that regular donations of relatively small amounts (one or two dollars, Euros, or pounds) can produce no end of worthwhile outcomes. Private aid also discriminates against long-term projects and hardware such as infrastructure, which are relatively hard to finance. It also favors development projects in appealing and pleasant environments over those in failed states. For these reasons philanthropy is often regarded as a complement rather than a substitute for government aid.

One of the central challenges facing private sector aid is the coordination of more effective development projects. In some cases the conflicting objectives and priorities of private donors may serve to undermine the effectiveness of aid. The effectiveness of private sector aid may also be hampered by information asymmetries and collective action problems. Even when private donors' objectives are aligned, funds at times may be better used elsewhere and not reflect government priorities. A report by the Tsunami Evaluation Coalition concluded that the outpouring of private donations in the wake of the 2004 Indian Ocean Tsunami exceeded the "absorptive capacity" of the humanitarian organizations involved.[85] Like aid between developing countries, the effectiveness of private aid flows is maximized when they are integrated into large-scale multilateral programs. A good example of this is the role of pharmaceutical firm Merck in the Onchocerciasis control program described earlier in this chapter.

A closely related challenge is to fully integrate private sector aid with government funded programs to improve the effectiveness of international aid. Writing for the Brookings Institute, Desai and Hermias (2008) observes that "while international and domestic philanthropies and NGOs now deliver a larger and larger share of total development aid, they are rarely included in development policy planning meetings that are usually reserved for ministers and official aid agency representatives." They go on to argue that "recipient countries and international organizations alike must develop formal mechanisms to include private sector actors in the development policy making process. In turn, a seat at the policymaking table could help private players become more accountable."

---

[85] See Tsunami Evaluation Coalition (2007).

5.9 **A new way forward**

What does this analysis imply about aid flows and poverty? One lesson is that external resources alone will not be sufficient to ensure that poverty goals are met. The recipient country's level of commitment and the quality of its policies and institutions are the primary determinants of progress. Experience and analysis have taught us that outside aid cannot substitute effectively for these factors. It can, however, be an effective complement, supporting national efforts to reduce poverty. A second lesson is that, when a country is committed to reform and poverty reduction, external support has substantial pay-offs. External support can take several forms including, but not limited to, aid.

As we show elsewhere in this book, an important area in which rich countries can provide support is through reforms of their own trade policies. The external environment has a strong influence on the returns to reform in developing countries. Robust global growth is important, but so is reform of the protectionist policies of rich countries, which target such areas as agriculture and textiles and clothing and are thus particularly damaging to poor countries. As we reported in Chapter 3, the empirical evidence shows that open market access for poor countries, combined with other trade reforms, has a significant impact on poverty elimination.

Coherence between aid policies and other policies is vital to enhance aid effectiveness. For example, giving support to small farmers or entrepreneurs is undermined by shutting them out of the donors' markets or by applying tariffs that discriminate against processed goods. Similarly, aid donors' support for health and educational systems is undermined by the recruitment of teachers, doctors, and nurses to work in the rich countries. Donors' support for governance reforms and combating corruption is not always matched by donors' pursuit of their citizens or firms who are complicit in corruption or siphoning aid funds into donor country bank accounts. Ensuring greater coherence between aid and other potentially complementary government policies and actions is important to increase the quality of aid.

Many global development challenges—such as stopping the spread of infectious diseases; building an international trade and financial architecture that is fair to all countries; and halting deforestation, climate change, and loss of biodiversity—cannot be handled solely by individual countries. These challenges require multilateral action: unilateral aid flows and arrangements cannot deal with some of the most pressing global issues. Aid for multilateral institutions and objectives, be it aid targeted toward the environment, diseases, agricultural development, or trade reform, is an essential complement to national bilateral aid efforts.

The decline in aid flows over the 1990s came precisely at a time when the returns on aid increased sharply. We have summarized the evidence on returns—if countries are willing to take the steps necessary to reform, then assistance in the form of capacity building, financial assistance, and analytical support typically has large returns. With continued reform momentum and steady external support, past experience suggests strongly that developing countries can extend and deepen the progress of the last half century.

Despite the progress made in the past 50 years, an immense poverty challenge remains. The latest estimates are that there are still some 1.25 billion people living on less than US$1.25 per day (in 2005 prices). This will remain a critical challenge as the population of the developing world increases by an estimated 2 billion people over the next 30 years. To address a challenge of these dimensions, aid will need to have effects far beyond the value of the money alone. This means that aid must support the frameworks for private economic activity and social improvements, ensuring that its effects go far beyond any individual project, and it must contribute to greater capacity and greater knowledge. Continued learning on the part of both developed countries and other parties in the development community is essential to these aims. Aid is a complement to the other flows we have identified—trade, capital, ideas, and migration—not a substitute.

Aid has never been more effective in supporting growth and poverty reduction. Much more aid and higher quality aid is needed. At a minimum, doubling the actual amount of aid—along with untying it to ensure it reflects real needs rather than disguised efforts to support domestic enterprises in rich countries—and coordinating its flows to ensure that predictable flows of highly concessional finance and other resources are mobilized in support of the many governments that can use it effectively are priorities for a more inclusive globalization.

6 **Migration**[1]

Since the 1970s the flow of migrants has increased in scale and diversity, prompting a new age of international migration. Globalization and the falling costs of travel and communication are making migration attractive for more people. In contemporary times, however, the primary destination countries of migrants have imposed new controls and limits on the movement of people across borders.[2] These controls have typically been used to select migrants who are useful to the economy, have relevant family or ancestral relations, or are fleeing persecution.

Nonetheless, globalization sets in motion economic and social forces that are shaping the structures and networks that impact upon the migration decision. Convergence, deregulation, the growth of transnational corporations, the competition for skilled labor, growing income inequality, and the opening of emerging economies are introducing new risks, opportunities, and networks, as well as political and social change. Together, these transformations have helped to turn this period into another "age of migration."[3]

Migration does not usually begin and end with one choice. It involves a sequence of decisions that are influenced by the changing values and goals of the migrant in response to his or her conditions. Insofar as potential migrants are free to move, their decision is a cost/benefit calculation that takes stock of both the promises of migration and its psychological and financial risks.[4] Networks and social capital inform the decision to migrate, lower barriers, and facilitate cross-border mobility for certain individuals and groups. Individual choices and social networks are created within the context of macro-level structures, demographic, economic, and political conditions that exert "push" and "pull" forces.

The impact of international migration is perhaps the most widely researched topic in the field of migration studies, but it is also the most

---

[1] This chapter is derived from the introduction and chapters 4, 5, and 6 of Ian Goldin, Geoffrey Cameron, and Meera Balarajan, *Exceptional People: How Migration Shaped our Past and Will Define our Future* (Princeton: Princeton University Press, 2011). We are grateful to Andrew Beath who provided extensive research assistance on an earlier version of this chapter, and to Princeton University Press for providing the necessary permissions for the inclusion of this chapter and the associated figures and tables. Readers are referred to *Exceptional People* for the full acknowledgements and further analysis of the issues raised in this chapter.

[2] This is a notable departure from the period before 1914, when controls were minimal and often ineffective (Massey and Taylor 2004).

[3] Castles and Miller (2009).

[4] Haug (2008).

commonly misunderstood in public discourse. News broadcasts refer to an "invasion of illegal aliens," fear of a "flood of migrants," and the "threat" of "brain drain." Around 50 percent of respondents in both Europe and the United States perceive immigration as more of a problem than an opportunity, citing concerns about immigration leading to a rise in crime, increasing tax rates, and taking jobs away from natives.[5] Although the views of politicians at times may be more favorable to immigration, governments respond to negative public perceptions by introducing populist regulations and policies intended to restrict the flow of migrants. To the extent that they are effective, such policies could suffocate national economies, deepen poverty, and starve societies of diversity.

Even modest increases in the rate of migration would produce significant gains for the global economy. Both rich and poor countries would benefit from increased migration, with developing countries benefiting the most. As increased migration has a more dramatic impact on the incomes of the poor countries, it serves to reduce inequality between countries. The World Bank estimates that increasing migration equal to 3 percent of the workforce in developed countries between 2005 and 2025 would generate global gains of US$356 billion.[6] Other models suggest that with a 5 percent increase in migration, 80 percent of the gains would accrue to developing countries.[7] Completely opening borders, some economists predict, would produce gains as high as US$39 trillion for the world economy over 25 years.[8] These numbers compare with the US$70 billion that is currently spent every year in overseas development assistance and the estimated gains of US$104 billion from fully liberalizing international trade.[9] A small increase in migration would produce a much greater boon to the global economy and developing countries than free trade and development assistance combined.

While most of the benefits of migration are dispersed and generalized, the burden of bearing the costs falls narrowly and unevenly on particular people, sectors, and localities. The costs of migration are often short run, while the full benefits of increased mobility appear only in the medium or long run. In this respect, the issues raised by increasing migration resemble the long standing debate over free trade: the economic benefits are distributed and not necessarily tangible, whereas the costs are highly visible and localized. This pattern is evident in both developed and developing countries. Reaping the full benefits of migration requires governments to relieve its short-run

---

[5] Transatlantic Trends (2008).

[6] World Bank (2005), p. 31.

[7] See van der Mensbrugghe and Roland-Holst (2009), cited in UNDP (2009), p. 84.

[8] Anderson and Bjorn (2008).

[9] Pritchett (2006). See Chapter 3 for the gains from trade liberalization and van der Mensbrugghe (2006).

costs and mitigate negative impacts on localities and groups that are shouldering a heavier share of the costs.

6.1 A brief history of migration

Throughout history, as remains the case today, people have moved under conditions that are not typically of their own choosing. Even those under the most restrained and difficult circumstances have navigated new social and cultural settings with determination and ingenuity. By adapting, innovating, and combining knowledge across cultural barriers, migrants have advanced the frontier of development since humans departed from Africa, some 50,000–60,000 years ago. The emergence of early civilizations around 4,000 BCE drew people from scattered settlements into dense patterns of complex social life. The first civilizations, like social magnets, brought people from the hinterlands into the life of the cities—as labor, merchants, traders, and administrators—and propelled city dwellers into the frontiers to find resources and trading partners.

The growth of civilizations quickened the pace of exchange and the commerce of ideas and technologies. As increasingly complex societies developed in Eurasia, traders, adventurers, missionaries, and conquering armies broke down the frontiers separating distant empires. Valuable technologies and commercial and other practices, which at times took many centuries to develop, were shared over ever-increasing distances. Migrants carried with them religious teachings, agricultural techniques, and commercial practices. The scourge of war and the lure of commerce propelled people across old frontiers, reconnecting communities from eastern China to West Africa, which had developed distinct cultures over tens of thousands of years.

The expansion of seafaring trade during the second millennium brought new levels of prosperity to China and Europe, which both saw the launch of ambitious voyages into uncharted waters to find new markets for their goods. As China suddenly terminated its explorations near the turn of the fifteenth century, Portugal was beginning to fund open-ended expeditions across the Atlantic Ocean; the coincidence of these two developments would precipitate European contact with the Americas and a seismic shift in global power. The European "Age of Discovery" (also termed the "Age of Gunpowder Empires")[10] between the fifteenth and seventeenth centuries completed the process of reconnecting humanity. European ships were now dominating trade within the Indian Ocean and extracting resources in New World plantations. Regional

---

[10] Harzig, Hoerder, and Gabaccia (2009), p. 26.

mercantile trading networks became knitted into a global power structure with force and control projected across vast distances.

With the emergence of global networks and the development of a world economy, the pace of economic development began to drive migratory flows, most significantly in the form of chattel slavery. International trade and the industrial revolution fueled competition, promoting innovation and expanding production in Europe. Many people traveled across oceans of continents, some in search of a better life. Millions more, particularly from Africa, were forced to move under the tyranny of slavery or indentured labor. In this new era of globalization, free and forced migrants were the causes and consequences of economic growth.

The twentieth century has witnessed the proliferation of states and the extension of government bureaucracies into the management of migration. The introduction of passports, strict border controls, immigration quotas, guest worker programs, and the distribution of rights on the basis of nationality are all features of the new era of highly managed migration. Passports and border controls are relatively new innovations, and their increasingly strict enforcement in the twentieth century dramatically changed the dynamics of migration. International migration became regulated at the level of the nation state. Apart from measures to protect refugees, international cooperation has largely neglected the vital dimension of migration.

6.2 **Contemporary migration**

There are now more than 200 million migrants in the world, making up almost 3 percent of the world's population. Migration between developing countries is almost equal to migration from these countries to developed countries. About a third of the world's international migrants have moved from one developing country to another. Migration is not a phenomenon experienced exclusively by richer countries (see Figure 6.1). Nevertheless, the increasing scale of migration over the past two decades has led to a relative concentration of migrants living in the developed regions of the world. Seventy-five percent of all international migrants live in 12 percent of all countries, and one in five migrants live in the United States.[11] While the number of migrants in developing countries grew by only 2.8 million between 1990 and 2005, those living in the more developed regions increased by 33 million (see Table 6.1).

---

[11] United Nations (2006), p. 12.

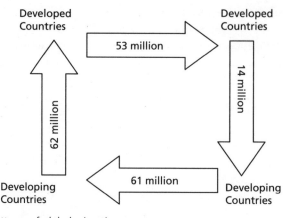

Figure 6.1. Patterns of global migration

Notes: The numbers reflect UN calculations of total migrant stocks.

Source: United Nations (2006).

Table 6.1 Estimated number of international migrants, 1990–2005

	Number of international migrants (millions)		
World region	1990	2005	Increment (millions)
More developed regions	82.4	115.4	33.0
Less developed regions	72.5	75.2	2.8
Least developed regions	11.0	10.5	−0.5

Source: United Nations (2006), p. 29.

The increasing number of migrants living in developed countries is not simply a consequence of movement *out* of developing regions. Citizens of wealthy countries are also more mobile than ever before, especially within the European Union (EU). Governments in recipient states have responded to these accelerating flows of people by structuring legal channels to regulate their entry and access to labor markets. Some of these channels, such as those for refugees and asylum seekers, are defined by international law. Others, such as high-skill, low-skill, student, and family classes, are the result of national policies that reflect emerging international norms in immigration law.

Table 6.2 provides a summary overview of the magnitude and direction of modern international migration flows. The "channels" of migration are grouped into a broad typology, which is meant to be indicative rather than exhaustive: economic migration (high-skilled, low-skilled, student, visa-free); social migration (family, ancestral); and refugee migration (refugee, asylum seeker). Because of the limitations of migration data, in terms of its availability, accuracy, and comparability, this table should be read as simply indicative of current migration trends. Migrants may move from one channel to another

Table 6.2 Major channels of international migration[a]

Regulatory Channel	Leading Source Countries	Leading Recipient Countries	Estimated Annual Flow (Millions)
Economic			
High-Skilled[b]	India	US	0.6
	US	UK	
	China	Canada	
	Philippines	Australia	
	UK	Germany	
Low-Skilled[c]	Philippines	Saudi Arabia	3.5
	India	Thailand	
	Poland	UAE	
	Indonesia	Malaysia	
	Bangladesh	Kuwait	
Visa-Free[d]	Poland	Germany	1.0
	Romania	Spain	
	Germany	UK	
	Italy	Ireland	
	UK	Italy	
Students[e]	China	US	2.9
	Korea, Rep of	UK	
	India	Germany	
	Japan	France	
	Greece	Australia	
Social			
Family[f]	Mexico	US	1.7
	Philippines	Canada	
	China	UK	
	India	Australia	
	Vietnam	France	
Refugee			
Asylum Seekers[g]	Iraq	US	0.4
	Somalia	Canada	
	Russia	France	
	Afghanistan	Italy	
	China	UK	
Refugees[h]	Afghanistan	Pakistan	1.5
	Iraq	Syria	
	Colombia	Iran	
	Sudan	Germany	
	Somalia	Jordan	
Undocumented[i]	Mexico	US	2.5
	El Salvador	Germany	

(*Continued*)

Table 6.2 Continued

Regulatory Channel	Leading Source Countries	Leading Recipient Countries	Estimated Annual Flow (Millions)
	Guatemala	Spain	
	Philippines	Italy	
	Honduras	UK	
TOTAL[j]	Mexico	US	14.1
	India	Germany	
	Bangladesh	France	
	China	India	
	UK	Canada	

Notes: [a] The leading rank-ordered source and recipient countries are primarily presented in terms of recent annual flows, but where this data has been difficult to identify or verify we use measures of recent migrant stocks. Sources for the table are listed in the endnotes corresponding to each category.

[b] **Source countries** based on flows from Goldin and Reinert (2007), table 6.3, p. 258. **Recipient countries** based on the stock of migrants with tertiary education in OECD countries in 2000 (see Docquier and Marfouk 2006). **Annual flow** based on calculations in Goldin and Reinert (2007), table 6.3, p. 258.

[c] **Source countries** calculated based on flows from Goldin and Reinert (2007), table 6.3, p. 258. **Recipient countries** based on the stock estimates of temporary foreign workers in Martin (2008). **Annual flow** based on calculations in Goldin and Reinert, (2007), table 6.3, p. 258.

[d] **Source countries, recipient countries,** and **annual flows** all derived 2006 flows in OECD (2008a), Part VI (country notes), pp. 226–89.

[e] **Source countries** based on 2004 flows available through the *Institute for International Education* Atlas of Student Mobility http://www.atlas.iienetwork.org/?p=48028 **Recipient countries** drawn from the number of foreign students in OECD countries in 2005 (see OECD 2008a, table I.6, p. 52). **Annual flow** based on calculations from *Project Atlas 2007*, which draws data from partner organizations, UNESCO/OECD. See http://www.atlas.iienetwork.org/?p=48027

[f] **Source countries** are derived from 2001 US flows because the US accepts several times more family migrants than any other country. In 2005, the US accepted 782,100 family migrants, more than the next nine highest recipient countries combined (see Kofman and Meetoo 2008. p. 165). **Recipient countries** and **annual flows** are derived from 2006 flows in OECD (2008a), Part VI (country notes), pp. 226–89.

[g] **Source countries** are determined based on asylum applications lodged in 2008 in 44 industrialized countries (UNHCR 2008b, Appendix table 2, p. 15). **Receiving countries** are determined based on the total number of accepted asylum seekers in 2007 (ibid., table 2, p .7). **Annual flow** is rounded up from total numbers provided in the same report (ibid., Appendix table 2, p. 15).

[h] **Source countries** and **receiving countries** reflect refugee stocks at the end of 2007 (see UNHCR 2008c, p. 8). **Annual flow** calculated based on increase of 9.9 million refugees at the end of 2006 to 11.4 million refugees at the end of 2007 (ibid., p. 6).

[i] **Source countries** are based on US-estimated stocks because the United States attracts by far the highest number of undocumented migrants, and while undocumented migration is also high in Europe the source countries differ widely from country to country. The American numbers are from the US Department of Homeland Security (Hoefer, Rytina, and Campbell 2007). **Recipient countries** are based on estimated stocks of undocumented migrants in the United States and in Europe, drawn from the Database on Irregular Migration developed by the Clandestino Project, based at the Hamburg Institute of International Economics. See http://irregular-migration.hwwi.net/Database_on_irregula.estimates.0.html?&no_cache=1 **Annual flow** is based on calculations made by the Global Commission on International Migration (2005), p. 85.

[j] **Source countries** and **recipient countries** are based on the total share of the migrant population in Parsons, et al. (2007), table 7. **Annual flow** is the total of the values above.

and be double counted—for example, a student may graduate and be admitted as a high-skilled worker in the same country without ever leaving. In some categories, the estimated annual flows are based on crude estimates, especially in the case of undocumented workers, where the Global Commission on International Migration estimated the annual flow between 2.5 and 4 million. The conceptual distinction between channels can also be fuzzy, such as between asylum seekers and refugees, or between low-skilled and undocumented workers. Despite the hazards of presenting this table using imperfect migration data, it still serves as a helpful illustration and approximation of current trends.

Several patterns emerge from the overview of international migration flows in Table 6.2. We look first at the economic and social channels. In the high-skilled category, the leading source countries include both more developed and less developed countries. The United States is both a leading source and recipient country, illustrating the fact that migration is both a cause and consequence of a dynamic economy. Low-skilled migration emerges as the single largest channel, with most migrants working in the Gulf Cooperation Council states, dominated by Saudi Arabia, and Southeast Asia, notably Thailand and Malaysia. The sources of labor are relatively nearby, and this proximity contributes toward the development of regional migration systems. Student migration is dominated by advanced or advancing Asian economies, which are sending increasing numbers of their young people to study in Western universities. In the visa-free channel, two of the poorest and most recent EU member states—Poland and Romania—are the leading source countries, although Italy, Germany, and the UK are leading source *and* recipient countries. As in the case of skilled migration flows, intra-EU mobility illustrates how migration (both outward and inward) fuels dynamism. Last, family migration emerges as a leading legal channel for permanent migration to developed countries. The leading recipient countries are the "traditional countries of immigration," the United States, Canada, Australia, and France and the UK, former colonial powers.

Public discourse around immigration in many developed countries is infused with fears of mass entry by refugees, asylum seekers, and undocumented migrants, but the fact is that these movements, while significant, constitute less than a third of total flows. The estimated annual flow of asylum seekers is the smallest of all channels. Far more people fall into the refugee category, and most of the leading hosts are low-income countries that absorb the outflows of people fleeing conflict in neighboring countries. Last, undocumented migrants constitute one of the largest flows, primarily because of movement into the United States. While unauthorized entry is a leading pathway for these migrants into the United States, most undocumented migrants in Europe simply overstay visitor visas.[12]

It is notable that African countries are neither the leading source nor leading destination countries in most categories. This reflects the fact that migration is not simply driven by poverty, contrary to public perceptions (particularly in Europe) that Africa is a leading source of migrants. It also reflects the paucity of reliable data on migration within and from Africa. As a continent, Africa receives only US$9.3 billion in recorded remittances a year,

---

[12] Duvell (2009).

compared with US$53.3 billion in South America, US$47.5 billion in East Asia, and US$39.9 billion in South Asia.[13] Many of the leading source countries of migrants are emerging economies that are undergoing development and integration into the world economy. Increasing mobility is a corollary of national development and global interdependence. The nature, magnitude, and composition of each of the major channels of migration identified in Table 6.2 are now considered in turn.

6.2.1 ECONOMIC CHANNELS OF MIGRATION

Economic channels of migration involve recruiting increasing numbers of highly skilled workers into key sectors of the economy as well as large numbers of low-skilled temporary workers in response to labor shortages. Many migrant workers are visa-free or originally arrived as foreign students.

The basic definition of a *highly skilled* migrant is one who has completed a formal two-year college education or more. Highly skilled migrants "are mainly in high value-added and high productivity activities that are essential in the global knowledge society."[14] In the early 1990s, traditional countries of immigration redoubled their efforts to attract high-skilled migrants to work and settle permanently.[15] McLaughlan and Salt note, "the mainspring for policy has been the perceived benefit to national economic growth derived from the permanent acquisition of high level human expertise."[16] Global economic competitiveness has driven a contest for skilled migrants to work in growing service sectors and the "knowledge economy."

In skilled migration programs, admission is often linked to employment conditions. In most countries, government agencies identify particular sectors with shortages of local workers through "labor market testing." Some countries measure talent by awarding "points" on the basis of education, experience, language ability, and past earnings. Commonly, permanent residence is only extended to temporary migrants after their potential value to the economy has been demonstrated.[17] Many of the workers moving through high-skilled migration channels have come from less developed countries with respected higher education institutions. India, for instance, has dominated the international market for computer skills, accounting for over 60 percent of migrants heading to the United States to work in the field. The Philippines, to take another example, exports up to 85 percent of the

---

[13] IOM (2008), p. 515.
[14] See Lowell (2008), pp. 52–3.
[15] Zlotnik (2005), p. 24.
[16] McLaughlan and Salt (2002), p. 4.
[17] Papademetriou (2003).

nurses it trains.[18] And in the UK, the majority of newly registered nurses in 2002 reported foreign qualifications.[19]

There is no standard definition of *low-skilled* migrants, aside from their exclusion from most work permit schemes or points systems designed to attract skilled labor. Low-skilled migration can refer to the characteristics of either the worker or the job performed. Many countries' low-skilled migrant programs focus on low wage non-tradable sectors: construction, services (such as home and garden care), and seasonal agricultural labor. Low-skill migrants are diverse in origin, destination, and function, but they typically arrive under a short-term, low-cost service contract (or illegally) and are expected to return home at the end of it.

As the workforces of developed countries have become more highly educated, the unmet demands of agricultural, manufacturing, and service sectors have led states to open migration channels for foreign low-skilled workers. Recruiting low-skilled workers on short-term or seasonal contracts carries the risk of unintentionally generating a stream of permanent migrants (such as that which resulted from post-World War II "temporary" guest worker programs in Europe).[20] Managing temporary programs, therefore, involves extensive state intervention, cooperation with employers, and the use of incentives and penalties to induce the return of low-skilled migrants. As a result of new programs, temporary low-skilled migration is "significant and growing," according to the OECD.[21]

In Middle Eastern oil exporting countries, low-skill migrants make up significant portions of the population and workforce. Labor markets have gradually segmented: top managers are resident nationals; other Arabs and nationals from other countries (not least the United Kingdom, Australia, South Africa, and Pakistan) fill the other professional positions; and low-wage jobs go to migrants from South and Southeast Asia. Generally speaking, Indians and Pakistanis serve as laborers and construction workers (although many are also engineers and managers). Maids, nurses, and other service workers primarily come from Sri Lanka, the Philippines, and Thailand. With high unemployment among young adults, some Gulf States are capping migrant labor in the public service and selected sectors.

East Asian economies have also grown rapidly in recent decades, and many have turned to neighboring countries to fill low-skill manufacturing and service positions. Hong Kong, Japan, Malaysia, Singapore, South Korea, and Thailand all receive low-skilled migrants from less developed neighbors such

---

[18] Aiken et al. (2004).

[19] The respective numbers were 16,155 (with foreign qualifications) versus 14,538 (with domestic qualifications). See Aiken et al. (2004).

[20] Castles (2006).

[21] OECD (2008a), p. 133.

as China, Indonesia, and the Philippines, sometimes through official programs. Korea and Japan have historically resisted implementing official programs; instead they have filled many low-skill jobs with part-time foreign trainees, students, or overstaying visitors. Japan has also "repatriated" citizens of Latin American countries with ancestral connections to Japan (Nikkeijin). Middle-income countries of Southeast Asia often both receive and send low-skilled expatriate laborers: Thailand receives laborers from Cambodia, Laos, and Myanmar, and it sends them to Middle Eastern construction and home care industries. Malaysia has long served Singapore with inexpensive labor, while hosting some 1.4 million foreign workers of its own (approximately 15 percent of its labor force).[22]

Countries in Europe and North America, as well as Australia and New Zealand, are also reintroducing temporary low-skill migration programs. New temporary worker programs involve stringent admission procedures, employer incentives and sanctions, and high levels of government regulation. Entry is usually contingent on a job offer, and there are limits on access to public services. The implementation of programs designed to attract temporary low-skill workers has been slow in many developed countries because of the expectation that migrants arriving through other channels will take on less desirable jobs. The number of temporary low-skill workers admitted into OECD countries rose every year between 2000 and 2008. In 2005 to 2006, Australia, Canada, the United States, and New Zealand accepted 1.24 million temporary migrant workers.[23] The 2008–2009 recession undercut the demand for the low-skill workers and prompted discussion of new protectionist measures and limits on migration in many countries, including the United States, Italy, the United Kingdom, and Spain.

Regions of *visa-free migration* are social and economic experiments in opening up labor market access to non-nationals. While some regional trading blocs have visa-free travel provisions, the European Union and Australia and New Zealand have each established unique systems that allow citizens of one member country to reside, work, and access social benefits in the other(s). Movement within the European Economic Area now makes up a significant proportion of all permanent type and temporary migration in many European countries.[24]

All EU nationals have the right to free movement between countries, although some countries continue to apply transitional restrictions to workers from the newest states. Before the 2004 expansion, fewer Europeans were taking advantage of their right to free movement than many predicted. Most intra-EU flow was a legacy of guest worker programs and informal labor

---

[22] IOM (2005).
[23] See Martin (2008), pp. 82, 85.
[24] OECD (2008a), p. 35.

migration during the 1950s and 1960s, when sizable income differentials were prevalent. Convergence in wage and unemployment rates and cultural and linguistic preferences decreased incentives for many Europeans to migrate. In 2000, less than 0.1 percent of the EU's population moved to another EU country.[25] The incorporation of the relatively lower income eight countries from Eastern Europe into the European Union (known by the acronym "A8"), however, has led to a significant increase in intra-EU migration. These flows are highly variable and not necessarily permanent. There is mounting evidence to suggest that some Eastern European migrants have returned home, particularly in the wake of the current economic downturn. In 2008, net migration to Britain (the number of people arriving minus those leaving) fell by more than a third.[26]

By looking at the relationship between a country's migration propensity to the UK and its GDP per capita, one can see that economic prosperity in the source country is a strong influence on intra-EU migration flows.[27] Citizens of Lithuania and Latvia, the poorest of the A8 countries, exhibit the highest propensity to move, whereas those from the Czech Republic and Slovenia, the wealthiest A8 countries, have markedly lower rates of migration to the UK.[28]

Student migration has emerged as a significant migration channel since the 1990s, as economic considerations have increased the opportunities and incentives for student mobility. Student migration has followed advances in travel and communications, the growth of networks with previous student migrants, and university marketing campaigns. Policy makers recognize that in addition to providing much needed income for educational establishments and foreign exchange, foreign students are potentially useful as future skilled workers and thereby provide a flexible source to address skill backlogs in national labor markets. Students see overseas study as increasing their employability at home and/or their chances at future emigration. Foreign students tend to be concentrated in programs for graduate study or advanced research, where they can make up a quarter of the total student population at a university.[29] The leading destinations for foreign students are universities in the more developed countries.[30]

---

[25] See Recchi et al. (2003), p. 17.

[26] The net migration figures for the EU and A8 countries fell by one half and three quarters respectively. Net migration to the UK increased in 2009, although figures for the EU and A8 countries declined slightly. See ONS (2010), table 1.

[27] Chappell, Sriskandarajah, and Swinburn (2008), p. 14.

[28] As shown in Goldin, Cameron, and Balarajan (2011), figure 5.4.

[29] OECD (2008a), p. 117.

[30] The majority of foreign students are concentrated in the United States (20 percent), United Kingdom (13 percent), France (8 percent), Germany (8 percent), Australia (7 percent), Canada (5 percent), and Japan (4 percent) with other countries accounting for the remainder (Institute for International Education 2009).

Almost three million students study overseas each year. EU countries provide around half the foreign students in France, Germany, and the United Kingdom.[31] Overall, however, about two-thirds of foreign students in OECD member countries are from developing countries, and Asia is the largest and fastest growing source of foreign students.[32] China, India, and South Korea send large numbers, particularly to Australia, the United Kingdom, and the United States.[33] China, which sent barely any students abroad under 30 years ago, is now the world's largest source of foreign students thanks to the country's "open door policy" and modernization program.[34]

Foreign students who want to stay in their host country to work are not automatically granted work permits, but governments increasingly recognize the value of foreign graduates for their workforce. The US Competitiveness in the Twenty-First Century Act of 2000 effectively exempted foreign graduate students from highly skilled H-1B visa quotas. In Canada, Australia, and New Zealand foreign graduates receive extra points in their work visa application for local qualifications. France and the UK have also streamlined the visa application process in order to make it easier to retain highly skilled graduates from outside the EU.

In consequence, stay rates of foreign graduates are high, and a significant proportion of migrants admitted through high-skilled channels come from the ranks of the foreign student population. For example, 68 percent of foreign students who received doctorates from American universities in 2000 were still in the United States in 2005.[35] Such trends raise concerns relating to the "brain drain" in so far as they do not return to their countries of origin.

6.2.2 SOCIAL CHANNELS OF MIGRATION

While immigration policy is primarily determined by economic priorities, most states provide channels for social migration. Social migration channels allow for movement to join members of the same family, household, or ancestral group. This channel often leads to permanent residency in the destination country and can produce unanticipated and variable flows of migrants.

Family migration is the largest single category for permanent entry into developed countries, and it is dominated by women. While there is widespread support for family migration channels, the definition of "family" differs across legal contexts, shaping the character and volume of flows. There is limited consensus in policy across countries beyond the common

---

[31] IOM (2005), p. 483.   [32] Vincent-Lancrin (2008).   [33] IOM (2005), p. 120.
[34] Tremblay (2005).   [35] Finn (2007).

practice of allowing spouses and unmarried dependent minors to obtain permanent residence. In some countries, siblings, adult children, husbands, or parents of citizens are denied access to permanent residence. Policy makers who want to apply restrictive definitions are sometimes constrained by human rights and other constitutional obligations.[36] In France and Germany, the judiciary blocked policy changes by governments to restrict family migration. Belgium, Italy, the Netherlands, and Spain have also amended their legislation to recognize family reunification through migration as a human right.

The United States extends entry rights to "immediate relatives" of United States citizens (spouses, parents, and unmarried children), subject to financial support from the "sponsoring citizen."[37] In EU countries, only those who are dependent on the primary migrant are generally permitted to enter as family members. In 2003, EU members (excluding Denmark, Ireland, and the UK) established "minimum standards" for family migration, entailing the reunification of "nuclear families" where one member is an EU resident. Family migration policies were initially designed with the assumption that future immigration would replicate previous patterns. However, some groups of migrants have been more likely than others to be followed by relatives.

Family channels mostly facilitate the flow of migrants from low- and middle-income countries to high-income countries. Two-thirds of migration to the United States and more than a quarter of migration to Canada and Australia occur through family channels.[38] The majority of female migrants to Australia, New Zealand, Europe, and North America move for family reunification (although the proportion moving as primary migrants is increasing). In contrast, countries in the Middle East and Southeast and East Asia, which tend to discourage long-term settlement, have negligible flows of family migrants.

While the volume of family migrants to a country tends to be determined by the strength of migrant networks and their ability to leverage opportunities in immigration policy, *ancestral migration* is usually demand led. States use these channels to encourage those with ancestral ties to their country to "return home." Globally, ancestral channels for migration involve relatively smaller flows of migrants, although they are significant for particular countries. The most prominent forms arise from "ethnic reunification" policies that promote permanent settlement by non-residents who have an ancestral connection to the primary national group. Underlying ancestral migration is the judicial norm of *jus sanguinis*, meaning "the right of blood": citizenship is determined by ancestry, not residence. Germany, Israel, and Russia are classic cases of providing legal avenues for co-ethnics to

---

[36] Article 16 (3) of the Universal Declaration of Human Rights affirms that families are entitled to protection by society and the state.

[37] National Foundation for American Policy (2006).

[38] Kofman and Meetoo (2008), p. 151.

"return home," but many other states have adopted policies granting partial or full citizenship rights to foreigners with ancestral connections.

Whether such preferential treatment accords with liberal democratic values (by allowing members of the same national group to overcome "accidental" geographic separation) or constitutes unfair discrimination (by favoring those with certain racial characteristics) is a subject of debate. While ancestral migration channels continue to be available in many countries, particularly in Europe, flows have been decreasing since the end of the Cold War.

6.2.3 REFUGEE CHANNELS OF MIGRATION

While the channels thus far discussed have primarily been shaped by the immigration policies of states, the refugee migration channel has emerged through the development of international law. A *refugee* is one who seeks protection in a non-native country because of fear of persecution in his or her country of nationality.[39] The status of refugees is protected under the 1951 United Nations Convention Relating to the Status of Refugees, which has been signed by 147 UN member states. Countries that have signed the Convention or its 1967 Protocol agree to offer protection to refugees and not to return them to countries where they may face persecution.

In the 1980s and early 1990s, the number of refugees increased sharply as a result of conflicts in Latin America, Africa, and Asia, and later the collapse of the Soviet bloc and civil war in former Yugoslavia (see Figure 6.2). Following the end of the Cold War, the number of refugees seeking asylum in Europe and North America increased, and many destination countries introduced new policies to manage and restrict their entry. Consultations on a common asylum policy for Europe continue to emphasize migration management and border control over broader humanitarian issues. These increasingly restrictive policies are partially responsible for the decline in the number of refugees over the past decade.

In early 2011, the UNHCR counted about 10.4 million refugees in the world. The greatest share of refugees moves from one developing country to another, seeking safety or protection. While developed countries provide most of the funding to support refugee agencies, developing countries host the majority of the world's refugees (see Table 6.3). Asia and Africa host 75

---

[39] The United Nations Convention Relating to the Status of Refugees, chapter 1, article A (A.2.) formally defines a refugee as "Any person ... who owing to a well founded fear of being persecuted for reasons of race, religion, nationality, membership of a particular social group or political opinion, is outside the country of his nationality and is unable or, owing to such fear, is unwilling to avail himself of the protection of that country; or who, not having a nationality and being outside the country of his former habitual residence as a result of such events, is unable or, owing to such fear, is unwilling to return to it."

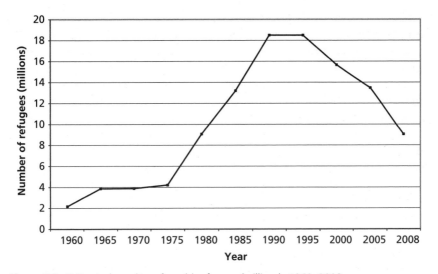

Figure 6.2. Estimated number of world refugees (millions), 1960–2008

Notes: 1960–2005 values are taken from mid-year totals. The 2008 number is taken from the end of the year.

Sources: United Nations Population Division (2006) and UNHCR (2009).

Table 6.3 Total refugees by countries of origin and destination, end-2008

Source Country	Refugees	Destination Country	Refugees
Iraq	1,873,519	Pakistan[a]	1,780,900
Afghanistan	1,817,913	Syria	1,105,698
Somalia	559,153	Islamic Rep. of Iran	980,109
Sudan	397,013	Germany	582,735
Dem. Rep. of Congo	367,995	Jordan	500,413
Occupied Palestinian Territory[b]	333,990	Tanzania	321,909
Viet Nam	328,183	Kenya	320,605
Burundi	281,592	Chad	302,687
Turkey	214,376	China	300,967
Serbia	185,432	UK	292,097

[a] Includes Afghans in refugee-like situations.
[b] Refers to Palestinian refugees under the UNHCR mandate only. Most Palestinian refugees fall under the mandate of the UNWRA.

Source: UNHCR (2009), appendix.

percent of the world's refugees. The West Bank/Gaza, Jordan, Syria, Lebanon, Chad, and Ecuador host the largest number of refugees in proportion to the size of their national populations, and all six of these countries have annual per capita incomes below US$10,000. Of the six countries that host the largest numbers of refugees, five are developing countries: Pakistan, Syria, Iran, Jordan, and Tanzania.

Over 12 million refugees have returned home over the last decade, and around two-thirds had UNHCR support. Repatriations and a declining number of violent conflicts worldwide have contributed to falling worldwide refugees stocks since 2000. However, some conflicts drag on, leaving large numbers of refugees unable to return home. The UNHCR estimates that the average duration of major refugee situations in developing countries increased from 9 years in 1993 to 17 years in 2003.[40]

To manage the dilemma between prematurely repatriating refugees and maintaining long-term border refugee camps, resettlement in a third country may be preferable. In 2008, the UNHCR submitted about 121,000 refugees to member states for resettlement.[41] This number is, however, greatly exceeded by the number of refugees that have been trapped in "protracted situations," living semi-permanently in refugee camps.[42] Accordingly, a process of rationing resettlement slots has evolved, under the guidance of the UNHCR. Priority cases include those at immediate risk of persecution, *refoulement*,[43] or violence; those who are injured or traumatized; as well as those who have other compelling reasons for resettlement due to legal, humanitarian, or medical concerns. Nevertheless, political concerns in receiving countries frequently influence resettlement priorities. Furthermore, political interest groups may arise to exert pressure on governments to accept or reject particular flows.

Refugees may also apply directly for humanitarian protection as *asylum seekers*, in which case they may obtain recognition through asylum channels that differ from one country to the next. Asylum seekers are in the minority of refugees; most refugees live temporarily in countries close to the one they have fled with the intention of returning home. Asylum seekers, on the other hand, are more likely to apply, often individually or in small groups, for protection in more distant countries. A successful application for asylum is likely to bring access to assistance, benefits, and permanent residence in a host country.

The vast majority of asylum applicants are turned down. While refugee migration channels are derived from international law, asylum processes are still heavily determined by the policies adopted by governments to determine the validity of claims. These policies may be influenced by popular pressure to "crack down" on asylum claims or define the criteria for refugee status very

---

[40] United Nations Population Division (2004).

[41] UNHCR (2008a), p. 38.

[42] Protracted situations occur when populations of 25,000 or more have been in exile for five or more years in developing countries.

[43] The 1951 Convention Relating to the Status of Refugees states in article 33(1): "No Contracting State shall expel or return ('refouler') a refugee in any manner whatsoever to the frontiers of territories where his life or freedom would be threatened on account of his race, religion, nationality, membership of a particular social group, or political opinion."

narrowly, at the expense of humanitarian considerations. As a result of different asylum policies, destination countries show wide discrepancies in the rates at which asylum applications are accepted.[44] While only 15 percent of Iraqi asylum seekers in the UK were granted refugee status, more than two-thirds were recognized in Germany, and none were recognized in Greece.[45]

6.3 **The drivers of migration**

The decision to move is made at the individual or household level, when the risk and uncertainty of migration is weighed against the opportunities and benefits it promises. Social networks and institutions facilitate the migration process overtime and shape the cost/benefit calculus of individual migrants and their families. At the global level, macro factors including demographic and economic conditions in the source and destination countries exert powerful effects on the propensity of people to move. Political conflict and persecution also influence migration decisions and flows. Over time environmental pressures and climate change are likely to become increasing sources of migration between countries.

6.3.1 WAGE DIFFERENTIALS

At the individual level, economic theory explains the migration decision through basic utility maximization. It assumes that, all else remaining unchanged (economists' heroic "ceteris paribus" assumption), individuals want to seek their highest utility, or well-being, and typically this involves pursuing higher wages. Migration is a way to invest one's "human capital": people will assume the financial and psychological costs of migration in order to achieve the greatest return on their skills. According to this approach, migration flows between two countries are the product of aggregated individual moves undertaken in response to individual cost/benefit calculations of this sort.[46]

On the surface, the neoclassical approach appears to offer an explanation. After all, most migration is from developing countries to developed countries, where wages are much higher. Unadjusted for purchasing power parity (PPP), wages in Japan are about US$13.32 an hour, whereas in Vietnam, they are

---

[44] UNHCR (2005) records the following recognition rates of asylum applications for industrialized countries: Australia (14.6 percent), Austria (9.1 percent), Belgium (24.8 percent), Canada (52.1 percent), Denmark (72.4 percent), France (20 percent), Germany (7.6 percent), Italy (13.4 percent), Netherlands (27.3 percent), United Kingdom (34.9 percent), and United States (17.9 percent).

[45] UNHCR (2008b), p. 17.

[46] Massey et al. (1993), p. 435.

13 cents an hour. A low-skilled construction laborer in the United States will work less than 4 minutes to make enough to buy a kilogram (2.2 pounds) of flour, whereas a Mexican laborer at home will have to work for more than an hour.[47] A worker moving to the United States could increase his or her earnings (adjusted for PPP) from US$17,000 to US$37,989 per year through migration, with no extra training.[48] Wage differentials offer powerful incentives for cross-border migration to better paying labor markets.

Historically, wage gaps between Asian and European countries and the New World were influential in driving the movement of migrants during the nineteenth century.[49] Migration rates to America fell sharply leading up to World War I as real wages in Europe began to catch up to those in the New World, keeping more migrants at home. A similar phenomenon has been identified in Morocco, Turkey, Malaysia, Taiwan, and South Korea which have all undergone a "migration transition" from source country to destination country as wages rise.[50] When wages are too low, however, chronic poverty can inhibit potential migrants from investing in migration.

At a general level, then, the migration transition from sending country to receiving country takes on the form of a "migration hump" that follows rising wage levels.[51] As real wages increase, more people can assume the costs and risks of migration, but as the wage gap closes, migration rates proceed to fall again. The phenomenon of the migration hump is supported by other demographic and social changes related to socio-economic development, but changes in wage ratios remain central to explaining why developing countries gradually transform from labor exporters to labor importers over time (see Figure 6.3).[52]

While the neoclassical approach is appealing in its simplicity, it does not offer a comprehensive explanation for why people migrate. Sometimes people stop emigrating in large numbers long before wages equalize.[53] In other cases some people from the same localities choose to migrate while others with similar socio-economic characteristics do not. Often people choose to move (or not) to fulfill additional goals, values, or desires: status, comfort, autonomy, and being close to family, their community, and friends.[54] While migrants often move in response to economic incentives, many will have a "target accumulation" motivation: moving to a high-wage labor market just

---

[47] See Pritchett (2006).

[48] Jasso et al. (2004).

[49] Hatton and Williamson (1994).

[50] de Haas (2007a).

[51] The "migration hump" concept was developed by Martin (1993).

[52] de Haas (2008a), p. 16.

[53] Notable examples include the end of mass migration from Puerto Rico in the 1970s (see Levitt 2001) and falling migration patterns from Spain and Germany (Massey et al. 2002, p. 9).

[54] Haug (2008), p. 587.

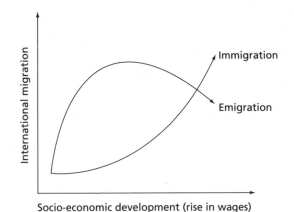

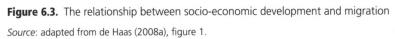

Figure 6.3. The relationship between socio-economic development and migration

Source: adapted from de Haas (2008a), figure 1.

long enough to save enough money to invest back home, to pay for a dowry, a house, or a business, for example.

The first people to migrate are often single and young, have fewer family obligations at home, and are thus more prone to take risks in response to wage differentials between countries. For many people it is difficult to know with any degree of certainty whether migration will improve their lives. Migration often takes place in the context of social and economic change in which the potential migrant's values, status, and goals are augmented. Douglas Massey et al. (2002) note that people have "a propensity to stay at home that is overcome only during certain exceptional periods when usual circumstances coincide to alter the socio-economic context for decision-making in ways that make migration appear to be a good and reasonable investment of time and resources."[55]

6.3.2 FAMILY AND SOCIAL NETWORKS

The new economics of labor migration (NELM) approach proposes that the family, not the individual, is the primary unit of migration decision making. Migration is still treated as a rational response to wage disparities, but this approach accounts for relationships and duties, such as sending remittances, that characterize many migrant experiences. The migration of one family member is a group response to risk in the absence of a welfare state. "Migration decisions are often made jointly by the migrant and by some group of non-migrants."[56] Some members of a family may work in the local economy,

---

[55] Massey et al. (2002), p. 10.   [56] Stark and Bloom (1985), p. 174.

while others are sent to work overseas, often with higher wages, with the agreement that they will share their earnings.

Rates of migration tend to be highest from lower-income developing countries undergoing rapid economic growth. When people are displaced from their traditional livelihoods, they are economically vulnerable, and the migration of family members to work abroad and send money home can help to keep the family out of poverty during periods of unemployment. Women are generally regarded as a more reliable source of remittances than men, so their migration is often encouraged and financially supported to draw more income into the family or community.

While migration may be risky for an individual, it can be an effective strategy for a family to diversify its sources of income. A family can collectively save to finance the migration of one member and support him or her during the initial search for work in the destination country. In the future, if one source of the family's income (such as local farming) should fail, another remains available. Regular remittances from overseas can allow a family to finance capitalist production, invest in new technologies, and purchase consumer durable goods such as cars and electrical appliances (especially in cases where credit is not readily available).[57]

These factors only alter the decision making calculus at the micro-level. The translation of *potential* migration into *actual* migration draws attention to the social capital, relationships, and intermediaries that connect potential migrants with opportunities in destination countries. Networks serve to transmit knowledge, information, and social norms from migrants to family and friends at home, and they can be channels for cross-border mobility. Migration both relies on networks and creates and reinforces them.

In the first phase in the migration process, micro-level determinants may be particularly important; those willing to shoulder more risk ("pioneer" or "bridgehead" migrants) will seek out opportunities to migrate overseas.[58] The movement of the first groups of migrants produces a "herd effect": a stream of migrants emerges between a source country, undergoing economic development, and a destination country with higher wages. This migration stream eventually becomes self-sustaining, and as migrants maintain contact with family and friends at home, they create a "network effect" that increases the rate of migration even further. Networks relay information and resources that lower the risks for others to migrate, and a migration channel is opened up between source and destination locations through these networks. The continued movement of people through this channel strengthens the network and expands the number of people and locations it connects together. Over time and as migrant communities grow, networks can diminish in their

---

[57] See Massey et al. (1993, p. 436), Martin and Taylor (2001), and Massey et al. (2002, pp. 257–68).
[58] Castles (1989), p. 106. See also Borjas and Bronars (1991).

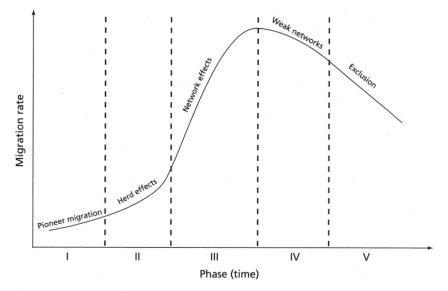

Figure 6.4. Network effects of migration to a particular country

Source: Adapted from de Haas (2008b), figure 5.

significance as the connection between settled migrants and new arrivals from "home" weakens. Networks may eventually be used to discourage further migration if competition for migrant jobs in the destination country becomes more severe (see Figure 6.4).[59]

Within this stylized description of the migration process, networks play critical roles at two stages. The first stage involves institutional networks, which assist migration in areas where social networks are not sufficiently well developed to facilitate cross-border movement.[60] State-supported or private labor recruiters help to initiate migrant flows by spreading (often limited) information about the destination country and offering jobs, accommodation, and support for potential migrants. Private intermediaries are prominent in Asian countries. China grants licenses to state-owned contractors and local cooperatives to recruit and place workers overseas. In Mexico, Morocco, the Philippines, and Turkey, the state cooperated with authorities in receiving states to promote early migration flows. Cross-border job brokering creates labor flows between states that have few prior political or economic linkages.

At the second stage, social networks connect family and friends between source and destination countries. They continue to channel the movement of people long after the economic justification for migration has diminished.[61] Networks turn cross-border family and friendship ties into social capital for

---

[59] Epstein (2008).   [60] See Abella (2004).   [61] Portes and DeWind (2004), p. 831.

potential migrants at home to use to access a higher-wage economy. Social networks provide information that lowers the risks and uncertainty of migrating, resources that diminish the financial burden of moving, and contacts that provide job opportunities. Furthermore, many destination countries have family reunification policies that provide legal channels for the social migration of relatives.

The availability of social networks in a destination country can also influence the migration decision. Moving to an area with a high density of migrants lowers the costs associated with leaving home, such as financial uncertainty and feelings of alienation and loneliness. The relationship between past and future migration from particular regions is characterized by "chain migration": for every migrant who moves for economic reasons, others (such as family members) are "pulled" along for other reasons. Chain migration is a result of the lowered risks associated with moving, the creation of new incentives for moving (to be close to family and friends), and policy channels that facilitate family migration.

Areas with high populations of migrants are also more likely to have specialized services that help new arrivals find accommodation and employment. The type of networks used by migrants can depend on their skills and education. Those of higher educational background tend to rely more on such expatriate or hometown networks than on kin networks to initiate migration. A migrant can also use more than one network which is often the case with students. The development of migrant networks and expanding connectivity supports transnational relationships and enterprises based on ties of family, kin, or village. It has also shaped government policies toward migrants.

Networks can also have a downside. Globalization and the international migration of criminals have facilitated the growth of transnational criminal organizations that profit from smuggling people. As borders become tighter, smuggling operations become more expensive, but they continue to provide a network of last resort for desperate migrants. Others end up as unwitting migrants, as they are deceived and entrapped by criminal networks that illicitly move people around the world to work as sex workers or cheap laborers.

6.3.3 DEMOGRAPHIC AND ECONOMIC CONDITIONS

Macro-level factors also regulate the flow of people across borders. A country's distribution of age groups in the population, its demographic profile, can influence both its supply and its demand of migrants. Many developed countries have demographic profiles in which the number of working-age people is gradually being exceeded by the elderly and retired. This is a result of several decades of falling fertility rates, which is correlated with levels of economic development, urbanization, and female education and employment, and population aging as a result of healthier lifestyles and medical innovations. The least developed countries, on the other hand, typically have lower life expectancies and higher fertility, giving their demographic profile a "pyramid" shape.

The example of South Korea in 1960 and in 2000 illustrates the changing demographic structure of a country as it undergoes transformation into an industrial modern economy.[62] In 1960, it has a pyramid shape, with most of its population concentrated among the younger age groups, and by 2000, it has a rugby ball shape. Projections for 2040 are that it will look more like a coffin, with a larger elderly population. The demographic transition correlated with economic development mirrors the migration transition discussed earlier, where a country undergoing rapid economic transformation evolves from a migrant source country to a destination country.

Often it is those who are young and without children of their own that bear the uncertainty of migration. When a large share of the population is concentrated in the 18 to 35 age groups, emigration rates tend to be higher. As fertility levels decline, rates of emigration fall.[63] Population growth does not in and of itself fuel emigration, but when combined with other economic and political conditions, it can reinforce a tendency toward emigration.

Today, European countries are concerned about population decline because of falling fertility rates. Most countries' fertility rates are below 2.1 children per woman, which is the "replacement fertility rate" for population levels to stay constant in developed countries. Declining fertility rates require governments to raise taxes, cut social benefits, keep more native born people in the labor force (women, unemployed, older people), and/or attract migrant workers. The need to sustain the size of the workforce is leading authorities to argue for more liberal immigration policies to fill short-term labor gaps.

The demographic differences between rich countries and their neighbors create incentives for both migrants and policy makers to increase labor flows. Generally speaking, people move away from areas of economic contraction toward areas of growth. The centers of innovation and growth in a dynamic economy are always changing, and new industries develop as old ones fall away, creating the need for labor to be reallocated. The movement of people is expected to follow the movement of capital. This equilibrium model of migration relies on assumptions that are not consistently displayed in practice: rational behavior, perfect information, complete markets, little risk, and open borders are theoretical constructs that seldom exist in reality.[64] As we

---

[62] As shown in Goldin, Cameron, and Balarajan (2011), figure 4.3.
[63] See Hatton and Williamson (1998), p. 40.
[64] See Massey et al. (2002), pp. 15–16.

have discussed, migration processes are more complex and dynamic than the perfect mobility equilibrium theory might suggest.

6.3.4 CONFLICT AND DISPLACEMENT

Since the end of the Cold War, civil wars have increased in frequency as interstate conflict has declined.[65] These internal conflicts have been connected to ethnic divisions, problems of state formation, and competition for natural resources. Political conflict destroys livelihoods, threatens lives, spreads disease, and leads to refugee flows. The scale of the problem is borne out by figures from the UNHCR (2010), which identifies seven categories of "people of concern" as a result of political distress: asylum seekers; internally displaced persons (IDPs) assisted by the UNHCR; stateless persons; returned refugees; returned IDPs; and a broad category of "others of concern." By 2009, the total population of concern was estimated at 42 million persons, including 15.2 million refugees. The political, economic, and social elements of instability and conflict are closely interrelated. Repressive totalitarian regimes frequently divert resources away from economic development and toward the military. During times of war, land, labor, and capital are not used to foster economic growth and development, which in turn gives rise to poverty, which becomes part of the conflict itself.

The root causes of civil conflict need not in themselves cause population displacement. They include historical events and conditions that have existed over many years, such as long-standing territorial disputes or important historic events. Proximate causes are the more immediate sources of conflict that arise from political mobilization around a long-standing root cause.[66] For example, while a border dispute may lie at the heart of a conflict, a series of escalating struggles to resolve the issue may eventually produce civil conflict. A large population of IDPs can act as a proximate cause in that it provides a reservoir of people seeking to escape misery at home. Eight of the top ten source countries of asylum seekers going to the EU also have large populations of IDPs.

Existing migration routes and migration networks abroad facilitate the flow of refugees. The majority of refugees, however, remain within their region of origin. UNHCR estimates that more than a third of recognized refugees originate from Africa, virtually all of whom are hosted within the continent.[67] Asylum seekers looking for third country settlement are attracted to particular countries based on historical ties between origin and destination countries (colonial linkages, political and economic relations, preexisting

---

[65] Human Security Centre (2005), figure 1.1.
[66] Lindley (2008).   [67] Lucas (2005), p. 67.

migration networks); perceptions of a country's economy, society, and asylum policies; physical and legal accessibility; and chance events during the journey.

6.3.5 ENVIRONMENTAL PRESSURES

The Intergovernmental Panel on Climate Change has noted that shoreline erosion, coastal flooding, and agricultural disruption can promote human migration as an adaptive response. Over the coming decades, climate change is expected to make many parts of the world less viable places to live, threatening the security and livelihoods of millions of people.[68] As with the other factors influencing the supply of migrants in the future, it is impossible to arrive at a reliable estimate of the number of people who will migrate in response to environmental changes. While there is widespread agreement that humanity will face unprecedented and systemic environmental disruption in the medium and long term, how people respond to these challenges will be heavily influenced by local conditions and the political response of states.

It is also vital to be clear about the time horizons being considered. While in the coming few decades the impact of climate change may not lead to a highly significant change in local weather conditions, in the medium and long term it is likely to lead to dramatic changes in many parts of the world. By the end of this century, unless there is an urgent and global response to the challenge of climate change and greenhouse gas emissions are dramatically slowed and arrested, we may expect that climate change will have led to fundamental changes in climate around the world. When considering this longer-term horizon, climate change and environmental pressures may contribute to mass migration. However, in the period up to around 2050 it is likely to remain a significant, albeit growing, contributory factor in accounting for migration. In certain specific countries we are likely to find, as in the past, that environmental factors may be identified exceptionally as the primary cause of migration, but for the most part for the coming few decades we should continue to see environmental pressures as compounding other dimensions which explain migration, rather than a separate cause.[69]

The International Organization for Migration refers to "environmental migrants" as "persons or groups of persons who, for reasons of sudden or progressive changes in the environment that adversely affect their lives or

---

[68] Constant and extreme drought are anticipated to become more frequent and severe; storms and floods are expected to intensify with more rain falling in South Asia and less falling in interior sub-Saharan Africa by 2015. Agricultural yields in sub-Saharan Africa and Central and South Asia could, as a consequence, fall dramatically. As a result of melting glaciers in South Asia, China, and the Andes, flooding is expected to increase during the wet season and water supplies would diminish during the dry season—potentially affecting more than a billion people. Sea-level rise could lead to the significant loss of coastal lowlands by 2050 (among other things). See Brown (2007).

[69] See Goldin (2011).

living conditions, are obliged to leave their habitual homes, or choose to do so, either temporarily or permanently, and who move either within their territory or abroad" (IOM 2011).[70] International migration is contemplated when the socio-economic basis of peoples' livelihoods is severely and permanently threatened and domestic alternatives are exhausted. Families may send a member overseas to diversify their sources of income if farming is less productive or if traditional sources of employment are less lucrative. However, historical examples suggest that people prefer to move only short distances (often not crossing borders) in response to environmental change. In the case of encroaching desertification in the Sahel, for example, the response of many residents appears to be temporary internal movement and/or the diversification of income opportunities. As many have identified in Sudan and elsewhere in the Sahel, environmental stress may also lead to tensions and conflict over land and resource use, and political refugees may cross over borders. The environmental effects of climate change will also be accompanied and compounded by population growth and urbanization over the coming half-century.

6.4 **The impacts of migration**

The impacts of migration are felt by receiving countries, sending countries, and individual migrants. In receiving countries, we examine how migration affects the economy through growth, wages, and innovation. We also review the fiscal impacts of migration and how increasing diversity impacts societies. For sending countries, particularly developing countries, debate over the benefits of migration often revolves around remittances, the "brain drain," and the role of "diasporas" in development. When it comes to migrants themselves, the impacts of moving can be seen in terms of education, health, and employment, as well as vulnerability and the experience of isolation and xenophobia. Examined from these different perspectives, it becomes clear that international migration does not offer unmitigated blessings, as promising as they may be. There are tremendous gains to be reaped by promoting mobility, but governments also need to manage and compensate for the unevenly distributed costs.

[70] This debate may evolve as individuals who are clearly forced to flee their country (such as may be the case for Maldives citizens) at some future date perhaps win the right to relocate as "environmental refugees" (Boana, Zitter, and Morris, 2008).

6.4.1 IMPACTS ON RECEIVING COUNTRIES

At an aggregate level, immigration stimulates economic growth in receiving countries. Low-skilled foreign workers often take jobs that are considered less desirable by natives, or they provide services, such as home care or child care, that release skilled workers into the labor market. Highly skilled migrants typically work in growing sectors of the economy, or in areas such as health care, education, and information technology that are short of native workers.[71] In short, migration creates more opportunities for people to specialize in their work, which produces a net economic stimulus.

Macroeconomic studies of developed countries with significant foreign-born populations have consistently found that migration boosts and sustains growth. A recent longitudinal study of OECD countries found that increased immigration is accompanied by commensurate increases in total employment and GDP growth.[72] A government-sponsored study in the UK found that migrants contributed about £6 billion to the national economy in 2006.[73] George J. Borjas (1999) estimates that migrants make a modest net contribution of $10 billion a year to the US economy, a figure that other economists have suggested is at the low end of the range. Between 1995 and 2005, 16 million jobs were created in the United States, and 9 million of them were filled by foreigners.[74] During the same period, migrants made up as many as two-thirds of new employees in Western and Southern European countries.

While economists agree that immigration produces net benefits for the economy, they debate how to measure these effects. For example, Borjas finds that immigration boosts growth overall, but he cautions that the benefits are unevenly distributed and that those workers who are competing for jobs with migrants will lose from immigration through lower wages or crowding out. Others argue that the direct impacts on native workers are actually marginal, and migrants are meeting crucial gaps in the workforce.[75] Although foreigners make up around 10 to 15 percent of the workforce in the UK, about half of all new jobs are filled by migrants, either because they are in areas requiring particular skills (like plumbing or banking) or because natives do not want them (like fruit picking or elder care).[76] Other countries rely more heavily on migrants, without whom their economies would collapse. In some Gulf Cooperation Council countries, migrants constitute more than 90 percent of the labor force.

---

[71] Centre for Economics and Business Research (2007).
[72] Ortega and Peri (2009).
[73] McVeigh (2008).
[74] Castles and Miller (2009), p. 224.
[75] Peri and Sparber (2008).
[76] *The Economist* (2008a).

Migrants also tend to be more mobile than native workers, and their flexibility and willingness to move in response to labor market demands can help to stabilize economies. The authors of an OECD study found that higher levels of migration within the EU can "speed up adjustment to changing conditions" and "help soften the cost of structural change on the native population."[77] As old jobs and industries disappear and new ones are created, perhaps thousands of miles away, migrants move more quickly to new dynamic centers than a rooted native population. Although the aggregate contribution of migration to growth is now widely recognized, the benefits are diffuse and the costs of migration are felt through wage pressure pressures in certain low-skilled sectors and potential fiscal burdens and social pressures in communities experiencing a sudden influx of migrant labor.

The overwhelming conclusion of research on wages is that the impacts of immigration on native workers are very small at most, and may be irrelevant. Most work on the subject has focused on the United States, where relatively high numbers of undocumented workers exert greater downward pressure on overall wages because they often have to accept pay below minimum wage. In Europe and Australia, where levels of undocumented migration are lower, there is very little evidence that native wages are affected at all by immigration.[78] Following the 2004 EU Accession of Eastern European countries, the massive inflows of migrants to the UK and Ireland did not displace local workers or increase unemployment.[79] Borjas, who has been cited as a pessimist on the impact of immigration on wages, now concludes: "the measured impact of immigration on the wage of native workers fluctuates widely from study to study (and sometimes even within the same study) but seems to cluster around zero."[80]

Even if wages are slightly lower for the small share of the population competing directly with migrants for jobs (typically high school dropouts and other immigrants), these affected workers gain through lower prices for goods and services. In the late 1980s and 1990s, US cities that had higher levels of immigration saw reductions in the costs of housekeeping, gardening, child care, dry cleaning, and other labor-intensive services.[81] Lower prices benefit all consumers, with poor people benefiting the most, since a higher share of their consumption is affected by the prices of local goods and services. When US cities that have received larger numbers of migrants are compared with those experiencing lower migration rates, it is found that immigration produces no negative effects for US workers.[82]

The impact of migrants on wages is influenced by whether or not they are *complementary* to native workers.[83] This means that when migrants specialize

---

[77] Coppel, Dumond, and Visco (2001).   [78] Hanson (2008).
[79] Barrell, FitzGerald, and Riley (2007).   [80] Borjas (2003), p. 1335.
[81] Hanson (2008), p. 22.   [82] Card (2005).   [83] Smith and Edmonston (1997).

in jobs that would not otherwise have been created or filled, their work is beneficial for everyone. This could involve jobs that require longer hours and more physical work. Or, when they open restaurants and offer lawn care or elderly care, they create new jobs or release more highly skilled workers into the economy. These are small changes at the individual level, but they can aggregate into a general economic benefit. Migrants also make large and singularly notable contributions to the economy through innovation, creating new products, concepts, and businesses that are at the cutting edge of our global economy.

Knowledge, entrepreneurship, and technology are the driving force of a dynamic economy. Two reliable ways to generate ideas and innovation in an economy are to increase the number of highly educated workers and to introduce diversity into the workplace. Both of these objectives are advanced through immigration, and the experience of countries like the United States bears out the bold propositions of "new growth theory." While economic growth in the United States has been sluggish compared to other countries, its most dynamic industries have high concentrations of migrants.

Fareed Zakaria argues that the global "edge" of the United States and its "ability to invent the future" rest on high levels of immigration.[84] The United States has long benefited from the creative and intellectual contributions of its migrants. According to some sources, immigrants have made up more than three times as many Nobel Laureates, National Academy of Science members, and Academy Award film directors as have native-born Americans.[85] Migrants have been founders of firms like Google, Intel, PayPal, eBay, and Yahoo. More than a quarter of all global patent applications from the US are filed by migrants, although they are only about 12 percent of the population.[86]

Harvard researchers William Kerr and William Lincoln (2008) make a direct connection between US immigration policy that is open to skilled workers and information technology innovation. They find that higher rates of temporary high-skilled admissions "substantially increased" rates of invention. By 2000, migrants accounted for 47 percent of the US workforce with a science or an engineering doctorate, and they constituted 67 percent of the growth in the US science and engineering workforce between 1995 and 2006.[87] In 2005, a migrant was at the helm of 52 percent of Silicon Valley start-ups, and a quarter of all US technology and engineering firms founded between 1995 and 2005 had a migrant founder. In 2006, foreign nationals living in the United States were inventors or co-inventors in 40 percent of all international patent applications filed by the US government. Migrants file the majority of patents by leading science firms: 72 percent of the total at

[84] Zakaria (2009), p. 198.   [85] Putnam (2007).
[86] Wadhwa et al. (2009).   [87] Kerr and Lincoln (2008).

Qualcomm, 65 percent at Merck, 64 percent at General Electric, and 60 percent at Cisco.[88]

Higher rates of immigration also have second-order effects on innovation. Ethnic diversity plays a key role in attracting and retaining creative and talented people to cities. Economic geographer Richard Florida (2002) argues that diversity increases a region or city's ability to compete for talent.

Diversity becomes a stimulant to further innovation and growth. Using complex modeling, Scott E. Page (2007) shows that diverse perspectives can support innovation by enabling people to find novel solutions to problems. His theoretical observations are borne out empirically by Kerr and Lincoln (2008). They find that migrant innovation "crowds in" invention by residents, growth in a region's migrant population on an H-1B visa (for the high skilled) stimulates patent filings by natives. Another study by Hunt and Gauthier-Loiselle (2008) finds that in the long run, a 1 percentage point increase in US migrant university graduates increases patents per capita by 15 percent.

Exposure to disagreement from a minority stimulates thinking about problems from multiple perspectives, what social psychologists call "divergent thinking." Groups composed of similar people are more likely to engage in "convergent thinking," which reinforces the status quo. The different life experiences, social norms, and personal values of migrants contribute to more effective and creative decision making than consultation among similar people.

Cultural diversity is not only useful for decision making and production; it adds value to cities and boosts their economies. Migrant-run businesses may sell goods and services that introduce novel cultural amenities—such as new foods or art forms—into local economies, which are valued by natives of a receiving country. The development of cultural diversity, studied in US cities between 1970 and 1990, has been shown to boost local wages and the rental prices of housing.[89] While most of the benefits of diversity accrue at a national level, there are also local gains to be reaped in the long run.

To the extent that immigrants produce fiscal costs, they tend to be small, short run, and local.[90] In the United States and Europe, the fiscal impacts of migrants are well under 1 percent of the GDP. According to one economist, there is a "striking... degree of consensus" among scholars that high skilled migrants make a substantial fiscal contribution to their host economies and that low-skilled migrants who settle permanently impose a minor cost on taxpayers.[91] The costs are greater for states that have more progressive

---

[88] See Wadhwa (2009).

[89] Ibid.

[90] While some migrants can be a burden on public services in the short run, most will make a net contribution in the long run. See United Nations (2004), p. 121, and ILO (2004), p. 7.

[91] Rowthorn (2008), p. 577.

taxation systems, such as the Nordic countries. Overall, however, these impacts are not significant and are likely to be compensated for by the overall and dynamic contributions migrants make to national income.[92]

The migrants most likely to generate fiscal burdens are those who are unemployed (i.e. not paying income taxes) and drawing on social benefits. In general, labor force participation among foreign-born men actually exceeds that of the native born.[93] Those who are more likely to be outside the workforce are women who have migrated through family channels or asylum seekers whose participation in the labor market is limited by law or due to trauma or language barriers.

Paradoxically, given public concerns about the potential social burdens they bring, undocumented workers make significant contributions to the public purse. In the United States, they have a higher rate of labor market participation than native workers or other migrants, pay income tax through automatic deductions, often make social security payment (using fake personal details), and are unable to access welfare benefits due to their status.[94]

While the overall national fiscal burden of migrants is marginal, the concentration of migrants in localities or regions can strain local government resources. In some UK localities, the concentration of migrants is as high as 24 percent, which is far above the national migrant stock of 9.3 percent of the total population.[95] While localities can expect to reap long-term wage benefits from immigration, in the short term, many will experience increased congestion and infrastructure overload.[96] An influential study of migration in the United States found that while the fiscal impact of migration is "strongly positive at the national level," it can be "substantially negative at state and local levels."[97] Managing the fiscal costs of migration may require redistributing tax benefits to address the excess burden placed on particular local and regional authorities.

Overall, the economic impacts of immigration are positive for receiving countries. Growth is stimulated through both low-skill and high-skill migration, wages are only marginally affected (if at all), non-refugee migrants produce modest fiscal gains, and they have been shown to foster significant levels of innovation. While governments increasingly appreciate the economic benefits of immigration, the social effect of growing diversity is a recurrent policy challenge in receiving countries. We will briefly return to this theme in the final two sections.

---

[92] For a review of the available evidence see Goldin, Cameron, and Balarajan (2011), chapter 6. See also Baker and Benjamin (1995), Büchel and Frick (2003), ILO (2004), and Kerr and Kerr (2008).

[93] Jacoby (2006). See also IPPR (2007) and House of Lords (2008).

[94] See ILO (2004) and Jacoby (2006).

[95] See Goldin, Cameron, and Balarajan (2011), table 5.4.

[96] Nathan (2008), p. 24.

[97] Smith and Edmonston (1997), p. 12.

6.4.2 IMPACTS ON SENDING COUNTRIES

While most political and media attention on migration, and as a result funding for research remains focused on receiving countries, the impacts on sending countries are as deserving of inquiry. Although this imbalance remains, in recent years, increasing attention from researchers and multilateral organizations has been given to questions of migration that concern developing countries and migrants themselves.

In 2006, UN Secretary General Kofi Annan issued a report on "International Migration and Development," which drew on the Global Commission on Migration, the first global initiative on migration of its kind. The same year, the World Bank formalized its "international migration agenda," which has since focused on the role of remittances in development and the risks of brain drain. In 2007, over 150 states came together in the first Global Forum on Migration and Development (GFMD), and they continue to meet in a different country every year at the GFMD. In 2009, the United Nations Development Programme issued its Human Development Report on "Overcoming Barriers: Human Mobility and Development" (UNDP 2009). These initiatives at an international and multilateral level are the fruits of an encouraging increase in research and advocacy by a number of countries and civil society organizations.

Much of the optimism about "co-development" has been driven by the growing volume of international remittances flowing from migrants working in developed countries to their families living in developing countries. Annual remittances now exceed the value of official development assistance or portfolio investment for most developing countries, and they rival flows of foreign direct investment. The risks of migration for developing countries, on the other hand, are expressed in the question asked by the World Bank's 1995 *World Development Report*: "Can something be done to stop the exodus of trained workers from poorer countries?"[98] The specter of brain drain, it was proposed, threatens to depopulate struggling countries of their valuable human capital.

Sending countries are impacted by the two issues of remittances and "brain drain." The initial unguarded optimism around remittances has since been tempered by more realistic assessments of who they help and how they contribute to development. And long-held concerns about brain drain are now diminished by new research on human capital formation, "brain circulation," and the role of diasporas in development. In reviewing the evidence and debate over brain drain and remittances, we see that both produce costs that in certain respects are corrected in the long run.

---

[98] World Bank (1995), p. 64.

6.4.2.1 Brain drain and brain circulation

Examined on the surface, brain drain statistics paint a devastating picture of the impact of skilled emigration on some developing countries. More than 70 percent of university graduates from Guyana and Jamaica move to developed countries, and other countries have similarly high percentages of their graduates leaving: Morocco (65 percent), Tunisia (64 percent), Gambia (60 percent), Ghana (26 percent), Sierra Leone (25 percent), Iran (25 percent), Korea (15 percent), Mexico (13 percent), Philippines (10 percent).[99]

High-skilled emigration is depicted as the principal risk of mobility for developing countries. While Europe and East Asia actually send the highest *number* of educated migrants, Africa, the Caribbean, and Central America send the largest *proportions* of their educated population overseas–around 20 percent from sub-Saharan Africa (excluding South Africa) and more than 50 percent in most Caribbean and Central American countries. For sub-Saharan African countries, this loss is particularly significant because only 4 percent of the population possess university degrees.[100] Caribbean and Central American countries have such small populations that the mass departure of graduates can hollow out the skill base of both the public and private sectors. In Asia, on the other hand, skilled migration rates are low enough and populations generally large enough that the impacts of human capital depletion are not as great.

In addition to the general depletion of human capital, particular concerns are raised by the cost of emigrating health care professionals from developing countries.[101] For many less developed countries, the outflow of medical professionals has imperiled already weak public health systems. Malawi, for instance, lost more than half of its nursing staff to emigration over a recent period of just four years, leaving just 336 nurses to serve a population of 12 million. Meanwhile, vacancy rates stand at 85 percent for surgeons and 92 percent for pediatricians. In the face of the HIV/AIDS pandemic, health services have been hard to come by. Rates of perinatal mortality doubled from 1992 to 2000, a rise that is in part attributed to falling standards of medical care.[102]

The risks of brain drain are real for a subset of countries, but a closer look at why and how brain drain happens recasts it as a problem to be managed through migration policy rather than stopped altogether. As Hein de Haas et al. (2009) note, it is not clear that many of those migrating would have been

---

[99] These percentages reflect the proportion of a country's university educated population that emigrates. See Carrington and Detragiache (1999) and Adams (2003).

[100] See Ozden and Schiff (2006), especially pp. 10–11.

[101] See Bach (2006), p. 8, and Goldin, Cameron, and Balarajan (2011), table. 6.3.

[102] Dugger (2004).

as productive at home: "In the Maghreb, Egypt, Jordan and Yemen there is high unemployment among university graduates" (p. 33).

While the mass emigration of graduates may have short-term collective costs for some countries, research on the "new economics of brain drain" suggests that it may have medium- and long-term benefits. Global generalizations in this area are particularly hazardous, and the impact of migration of highly skilled individuals needs to be studied in relation to the particular time and context. Oded Stark (2005) observes that the problem of brain drain is rooted in the "leakage" of human capital from a country, but seen within a broader context, this concern is exaggerated. Without the prospect of migration, people generally underinvest in their education because the opportunities for putting it to use and the relative competition for jobs may not require much schooling. However, knowledge of the opportunity to migrate to a developed economy where wages are higher for skilled labor leads people to pursue more advanced education. While the country still loses a proportion of its human capital to emigration, it is left with a higher number of graduates within the country than it would have without "brain drain." Migration, Stark notes, is "a harbinger of human capital gain" and not "the culprit of human capital drain."[103]

Return migration can stimulate local development, and the transmission of "social remittances" in the form of "ideas, behaviours, identities and social capital that flow from receiving to sending country communities."[104] When migrants lost to "brain drain" return home, they bring with them social and cultural resources that sometimes influence entrepreneurship as well as family, social, and political life. Return migration rarely happens in large numbers, however, without the presence of other factors conducive to development. The return of skilled migrants is a significant phenomenon in China, for example, but it has yet to take hold in countries like Guyana.

The phenomena of "brain circulation" and return migration suggests that some migrants move overseas for education or early career development and later return home either permanently or episodically. The development of dynamic information technology industries in Taiwan and Israel has been a result of migrants returning home in the early 1980s from the United States and Silicon Valley. Return migrants brought capital, technical and operating experience, knowledge of business models, and networks of contacts in the United States. The two countries now boast leading firms in software, security, PC production, and integrated circuits. A similar process of return migration is now occurring in India, with skilled workers from Silicon Valley

---

[103] Stark (2005), p. 138. Studies show that Fiji and the Philippines have both ended up with more skilled workers at home due to emigration opportunities (Chand and Clemens 2008; Clemens 2008).

[104] Levitt (1998), p. 927.

bringing expertise and capital from abroad to develop the Bangalore IT industry.[105]

Members of a country's diaspora can play a "bridging" role in connecting their home countries with foreign expertise, finance, and contacts, overcoming what can be volatile political negotiations with foreign companies. "Network diasporas," Kuznetsov (2006) argues, "are but the latest bridge institutions connecting developing economy insiders, with their risk mitigating knowledge and connections, to outsiders in command of technical know-how and investment capital."[106] For countries to successfully tap into their overseas expertise there need to be conditions at home that are attractive for expatriates to return to or invest in. Migrants in a diaspora are unlikely to spontaneously fire up a flailing national economy; they are a resource that can reinforce or accelerate existing positive trends.[107]

Even when skilled expatriates do not return home, they may remain connected through diaspora networks that support development in the sending country.[108] Between 1985 and 2000, for example, overseas Chinese contributed about 70 percent of China's total foreign direct investment.[109] Taiwan has relied on diaspora networks for decades to promote the flow of ideas, goods, capital, skills, and technology. It serves as an intermediary between Chinese and Southeast Asian markets and American capital, skills, and ideas.[110] To capture the benefits of diasporas for national development, some countries are developing ad hoc "diaspora engagement policies."[111]

The political impact of diasporas can also be significant. In the short run, the loss of local and national leaders to migration can deprive a country of key visionaries and community builders, but their later return can ultimately help them chart a new path for their home countries. Consider, for example, the cases of Mohandas Gandhi, Kwame Nkrumah, Ho Chi Minh, or Ellen Johnson-Sirleaf, leaders who spent their young adult years overseas, where they assimilated new ideas that allowed them to later play crucial roles in nation building at home. In other cases, however, exile groups have sought to return to power at the expense of democracy or have been involved in genocide.[112]

---

[105] See Saxenian (2005), especially p. 3.

[106] Kuznetsov (2006), p. 4.

[107] de Haas (2009).

[108] Skilled migrants often take spontaneous interest in their home countries, and actively seek out ways of "giving something back." See Olivier (2009).

[109] World Bank (2005), p. 67.

[110] IOM (2005), p. 228.

[111] See Gamlen (2008).

[112] See Wallis (2009).

6.4.2.2 Remittances

As the number of migrants from developing to developed countries has grown in the past thirty years, they have contributed to the remarkable growth in the volume of recorded remittances to developing countries (see figure 6.5). From about US$31.1 billion in 1990, they are estimated to have reached about US$325 billion in 2010.[113] Whereas the share of remittances flowing to developing countries was 57 percent in 1995, it had risen to 72 percent by 2005.[114] Kofi

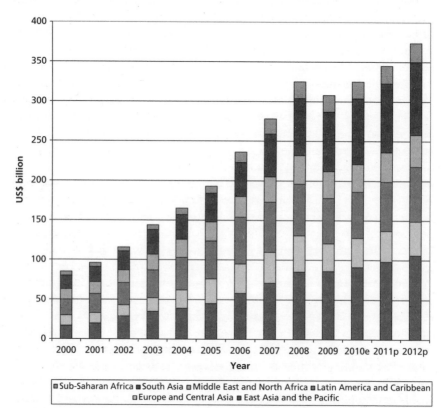

Figure 6.5. Flow and forecast of international migrant remittances to developing countries (2000–2012)

Notes/sources: e = estimated, p = projected. Numbers are World Bank staff calculations based on IMF balance of payments statistics. Data for 2010 is estimated and data for 2011–2012 is the World Bank baseline forecast. Data for 2000–2005 is from Ratha (2007), table 1, p. 2. Data for 2006 is from Ratha, Mohapatra, and Silwal (2010), table 1, p.18. Data for 2007–2009, 2010 (estimated), and 2011–2012 (forecast) is from Mohapatra, Ratha, and Silwal (2010).

---

[113] de Haas (2007b), p. 1. See also Mohapatra, Ratha, and Silwal (2010).
[114] United Nations (2004), p. 54.

Annan called remittances "the most immediate and tangible benefit of international migration."[115]

According to Dilip Ratha (2007), if informal and unrecorded channels of remittances to developing countries were included, they would show that remittances are "larger than foreign direct investment and more than twice as large as official aid received by developing countries."[116] The dramatic increase in recorded remittances in the past twenty years can be explained by a number of factors: better measurements of remittance flows; closer scrutiny of money transfers since the September 11, 2001, attacks; a reduction in remittances costs; the depreciation of the US dollar and relative rise in value of other currencies; and growth in the stock of migrants and their incomes.[117]

The World Bank reported a slight decline in the volume of remittances due to the 2008–2009 global recession. The drop in remittances was less severe than falling portfolio debt and equity flows and the sharp contraction in foreign direct investment because remittances are generally less volatile and less pro-cyclical.[118] The relative resilience of remittances is related to various factors that ensure their persistence over time: they flow from the accumulated stock of migrants so they withstand short-run changes in mobility; they constitute a relatively small part of the income of migrants, so they are expected to continue even in the face of hardship; fiscal stimulus packages in developed countries will likely create jobs for migrant workers; and migrants work longer hours or reduce their own consumption to send more when their dependents are most in need.[119] Nevertheless, recent evidence from the United States suggests that only a quarter of the Hispanic migrants who lost their jobs managed to keep sending remittances and that remittance flows from the United States to Latin America dropped 11 percent in 2009.[120]

The economic impact of remittances on migrants' countries of origin can be significant. Remittances make of a large share of the GDP in small developing countries, and in larger countries the annual flow can reach into the tens of billions (see Figure 6.6). The primary, and perhaps most important, impact of remittances is that they directly reduce poverty in the countries to which the remittances are sent. A study of 71 developing countries finds that "international migration and remittances significantly reduce the level, depth and severity of poverty in the developing world."[121] A 10 percent increase in per capita remittances can lead to a 3.5 percent decline in the proportion of people living on under $1 per day in the source

[115] Ibid., p. 54.
[116] Ratha (2007), p. 2.
[117] Ibid.
[118] de Haas (2007b), p. 9 and Mohapatra, Ratha, and Silwal (2010).
[119] Mohapatra, Ratha, and Silwal (2010) and Ratha, Mohapatra, and Silwal (2010).
[120] Mapstone (2009).
[121] Adams and Page (2005) cited in de Haas (2007b), p. 10.

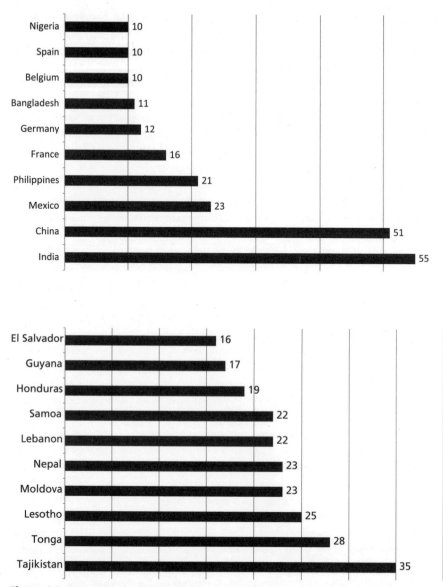

Figure 6.6. International remittances: Top ten countries in terms of total receipts (US$ billions) and as percentage of GDP, 2010

Note/source: estimates for 2010 form Mohapatra, Ratha, and Silwal (2010).

country.[122] Surveys in developing countries show that fewer remittance receiving households are below the poverty line than non-receiving households.[123] Most remittances are used for basic subsistence needs and for improving housing conditions. In Pakistan, Turkey, and Somalia, remittances help households to overcome short-term income fluctuations.[124] Recipients in Bangladesh count remittances as half of their household income, and in Senegal, the share is as high as 90 percent.[125] In Turkey, 80 percent of receiving households spend remittances on daily expenses. In Latin America and the Caribbean, more than 50 million people are supported by remittances.

Remittances sent home by asylum seekers can be vital to the survival of communities decimated by conflict in the source country. Remittances were sustaining so many communities in Somalia that the November 2001 closure of the al-Barakat *hawilad* money transfer network (due to alleged ties with al-Qaeda) led to a food crisis affecting about 300,000 people.[126] In El Salvador, remittances sent by refugees living in the United States are estimated to sustain 15 percent of domestic households. To sustain these flows, the Salvadoran government has gone so far as to offer legal assistance to Salvadorans in the United States to prolong "temporary protected status," a refugee-like status that allows them to remain legally in the United States.[127]

Country studies also show that remittances improve the health and education of children, and they have a positive influence on infant health, child mortality, and years of schooling.[128] Remittances also stimulate local development by providing funds to hire labor, improve crop production, and invest in small scale enterprises.[129] In other cases, remittances can take the form of significant collective transfers from migrant organizations that support development projects at home or contribute to disaster relief initiatives.[130] Even when households in source countries spend remittances on consumption, the expenditures can have multiplier effects that boost local and national economies. Every dollar in remittance spending creates two or three dollars of income in the source country, depending on whether remittances are spent on buying imported or locally produced goods.[131] Through

[122] Ratha (2007), p. 5. [123] Ibid., p. 5.
[124] de Haas (2007b), p. 8. [125] Ghosh (2006), p. 51.
[126] Koser and Van Hear (2003), p. 10.
[127] Thanks to Kathleen Newland for clarifying this example.
[128] See United Nations (2004), Ghosh (2006), de Haas (2007b), and Ratha (2007).
[129] See Ghosh (2006), Rapoport and Docquier (2005), and United Nations (2006), for example.
[130] See Castles and Miller (2009), p. 61, and Vertovec (2009).
[131] United Nations (2006), p. 55.

their multiplier effects, remittances have increased the average per capita income in many Central American countries by around 7 to 14 percent.[132]

The benefits remittances create for households and some communities indicate their unique potential for relieving poverty and promoting local development. There are a very small number of countries, however, for which remittance flows are substantial relative to the GDP, and in only eleven countries are remittances larger than merchandise exports.[133] The distribution of remittances is also uneven at an international level—the poorest countries (particularly in sub-Saharan Africa) tend to receive much lower flows than South Asian and Latin American countries. Even though for some African countries, such as Lesotho, remittances can be a very significant share of their total income, foreign aid to Africa is still three times the total volume of recorded remittances.[134] Those countries for which remittances are a significant source of external capital are the exception and not the rule. Even in areas receiving large transfers, remittances do not constitute an adequate independent stimulus to development.[135]

The primary benefit of remittances is that they reduce the burden of poverty for recipient households in the short run. They provide a modest boost to the economy in the medium run and build up the human capital base of a country in the long run. These significant benefits should be harnessed by receiving countries, but the potential effects on the economies of developing countries should not be unduly exaggerated. It is also worth remembering that remittances constitute the bright side of a system often characterized by suffering, where members of a household often have to spend long periods of time away from their families in order to provide for them.

6.4.3 IMPACTS ON MIGRANTS

The majority of migrants are economically better off for moving, especially those who move from developing to developed countries. Workers from developing countries who move to the United States earn four times as much as they would have at home. Studies of other countries have confirmed similar results, even when migrants do not move to OECD countries. Thai workers in Taiwan and Hong Kong earn at least four times more than they would make as low-skilled workers in Thailand.[136] In Tajikistan, the income

---

[132] United Nations (2004), p. 110.
[133] Ghosh, (2006), p. 54.
[134] World Bank estimates cited in IOM (2008), p. 533.
[135] Ghosh (2006), p. 57.
[136] Sciortino and Punpuing (2009).

of a seasonal out-migrant could easily cover the household expenses of a family for an entire year.

Research for the UN Human Development Report shows that high-skilled workers experience significant wage benefits from moving as well.[137] A doctor from the Ivory Coast will make six times as much working in France. A junior lecturer from China will earn more than five times more in Australia than at home. Moving from Malawi to South Africa will more than double the wages of a nurse. And software engineers get paid at least three or four times more in the United States than in India.

The wage benefits to migrants are in stark contrast to their peers at home, even if they may not be equal to the wages and employment opportunities of native workers in destination countries. Migrants to the United States typically have higher rates of employment than natives (although this is a trend that reversed in 2008–2009), but foreign-born employees, at all levels of education, earn less per week than native-born colleagues.[138] Migrants earned about 23 percent less than native-born workers in the United States in 2007.[139]

Female migrants occupy a particularly disadvantaged or precarious position in the labor markets of receiving countries. The OECD reports that "immigrant women are generally the group with the least favorable outcomes in the labor market... both in absolute terms and relative to children of natives of the same gender."[140] They also tend to be disproportionately represented in low-paid and casual work, such as care activities, cleaning, or domestic work.[141]

Migrant workers, in general, are more heavily concentrated in casual, temporary, and high-risk work. In Spain, for example, 56 percent of the foreign-born work in temporary jobs, compared with less than 30 percent of locals. This trend applies to every European country except for Austria and Switzerland.[142] It is symptomatic of the barriers migrants face when looking for paid work in receiving countries—they may encounter discrimination, language difficulties, and a lack of official recognition of their skills and credentials.[143] This phenomenon of "brain waste" may also be a product of skilled migrants moving to countries where their qualifications are not as relevant to labor market needs.[144] In either case, university educated migrants are more likely than natives to be employed in low-skilled jobs.

---

[137] See Clemens (2009), p. 63.
[138] Aged 25 years or older. See Camarota (2007) and Camarota and Jensenius (2009).
[139] Camarota (2007).
[140] Quoted in Castles and Miller (2009), p. 235.
[141] Castles and Miller (2009), p. 237.
[142] See OECD (2007), p. 76, and Goldin, Cameron, and Balarajan (2011), figure 6.4.
[143] In addition, low-skilled migrants are especially vulnerable in times of economic crisis. See *The Economist* (2008b), Boxell (2009), Walker (2009), and Perucca and Le Moël (2010).
[144] Mattoo, Neagu, and Özden (2008).

The relative gains in wage earnings experienced by most migrants are qualified by the obstacles they face in destination country labor markets. In terms of educational attainment and health care, however, the results are more generally positive. Because most migrants move to relatively more developed countries, access to higher incomes, better infrastructure, and public services contribute to relative improvements in their health and education and that of their children. Still, migrants may suffer more from particular conditions such as stress, depression, and anxiety, which can be traced to the circumstances or experiences of migration. In terms of education, the children of migrants show relatively high rates of achievement in destination countries. They acquire more education than they would have at home, but members of some groups have lower levels of achievement (compared to native students) because of factors related to social exclusion, language, and urban poverty.

The health outcomes of migrants to developed countries improve most directly because of their higher levels of income, relative to pay at home. A study using US data finds that the health of immigrants improves notably in their first year after moving.[145] Other studies point to a "healthy migrant" phenomenon, where migrants show better health outcomes than native-born citizens.[146] These effects are achieved through a combination of selection bias (people healthier than the norm are more likely to migrate) and recent migrants taking advantage of the higher incomes and health facilities that accompany moving to a more developed country.

The longer migrants stay in destination countries, however, the more their "health advantage" appears to dissipate. These short-lived dramatic health gains for migrants are explained by the adoption of unhealthy lifestyles and eating habits, the conditions of precarious and risky work, and the mental strains of being far from home.[147] The health of migrants relative to the native-born may tend to converge over the long term, but the relative health benefit of moving over staying is generally retained.

People who move under conditions of distress or political insecurity and end up living in precarious situations, however, will almost certainly not reap the same health benefits as most migrants. Migrants' health is most at risk when they are exposed to hazardous journeys, "warehoused" in refugee camps, or assume undocumented status and hesitate to seek medical assistance (or are excluded from access). On arrival in a destination country, undocumented migrants may live in crowded and unsanitary conditions that increase their vulnerability to other health risks. Refugees have a high risk of contracting diseases due to separation of families, break down of social

---

[145] Jasso et al. (2004).

[146] See Hyman (2001) and Minnesota Department of Health (2003).

[147] See Noh and Kaspar (2003), for example.

structures, and poor access to health care.[148] The World Health Organization has found that undocumented migrants and asylum seekers suffer from mental illness and are often excluded from treatment and therapy (WHO 2003). The welfare outcomes experienced by migrants are, to a certain extent, conditional upon their circumstances and background. Those who move for economic reasons to societies with accessible public services are likely to benefit the most. The circumstances and conditions of migration are no less important when it comes to educational achievement.

Migration improves educational attainment relative to those left behind, even if migrants do not always perform as well as the native-born. As with health care, the educational achievements of migrants are explained by their relatively higher incomes and greater access to facilities. School enrolment is consistently higher for children of families that migrate to a country with a higher Human Development Index (HDI) rating.[149] As expected, the gains are the largest for children moving from countries that score poorly on this development index.

At a national level, the educational gains from migration vary with the age of the migrant. Those who migrate to the United States as children (before 13) or as young adults (25–29) reap the greatest educational benefits from moving.[150] Arrival between ages 13 and 19 confers a relative disadvantage on migrants, however, because of obstacles with language and integration in schools, which are no easier to overcome in teenage years. Second-generation students acquire more education than both native-born and most first-generation migrants.[151] Government policy aimed at the education of new migrants, particularly those who arrive as teenagers, can make a significant impact on their welfare and social integration. Such policy measures include language training, social assistance, school selection processes, classroom settings, and early childhood education.[152]

Not all countries provide equal access to education for migrant children and youth. Developed countries almost universally provide access to schooling for all types of migrants (permanent, temporary, undocumented, or asylum seekers). Many developing countries, however, officially restrict access for certain types of migrants or present obstacles to attendance because of xenophobia and discrimination in schools. For example, more than one-third of school aged children of migrants in South Africa face obstacles attending school because of income restrictions and/or exclusion by school

---

[148] See IOM (2005), pp. 43, 334.

[149] As the UNDP (2009), p. 73 shows.

[150] Chiswick and DebBurman (2004).

[151] See Crul and Vermeulen (2003), Heath, Rothon, and Kilpi (2008), and Goldin, Cameron, and Balarajan (2011).

[152] Crul and Vermeulen (2003), p. 984.

administrators.[153] While the South African constitution does not permit discrimination against foreigners, migrants encounter systemic problems with accessing public services from low-level gatekeepers and bureaucrats.[154]

In general, migrants improve their health and education by moving. Most are better off than if they had stayed put. Where social mobility is restrained, however, disadvantage and poverty can perpetuate itself into the second and third generations.

6.5 **The highly vulnerable**

International migration is increasing in scale and diversity, which produces greater ethnic, religious, and cultural difference in host countries. The social costs are felt in localities experiencing rapid and concentrated immigration, which can be accompanied by deteriorating trust and sense of community.[155] While many countries have responded to growing diversity by embracing multiculturalism policies and anti-racism campaigns, migrants still experience xenophobia, hostility, and discrimination, particularly during times of economic crisis or insecurity. In its extreme form, xenophobia can lead to violence and direct attacks on migrants.

The endorsement of xenophobia by officials can lead to state-sponsored discrimination against migrants. In Russia, a prejudiced attitude toward ethnic groups from the Caucasus, Georgians, Armenians, Azerbaijanis, Chechens, and Dagestanis is perpetuated through depictions in the media and public statements by high officials.[156] Similarly, intolerance from employers toward migrants manifests itself in the less overt, but no less insidious, practice of workplace discrimination which includes unusually high rates of unemployment and brain waste amongst some ethnic groups.[157]

While xenophobia and discrimination may lessen over time as migrant groups become more integrated into society, it can also set the stage for generations of poverty. Portes (2008) describes the circumstances faced by many Mexican families in the United States (especially those who are undocumented), where poverty, discrimination, and racism disadvantage the second generation of migrants. This process of "downward assimilation" (in

---

[153] Landau and Kabwe Segatti (2009).

[154] Vigneswaran (2008).

[155] The widespread claim that "there is a tradeoff between diversity and community" (in the words of one influential social scientist—Putnam 2007) is controversial, and may not be able to withstand closer empirical scrutiny (see Goldin, Cameron, and Balarajan 2011, chapter 6).

[156] See Mereu (2001) and Amnesty International (2006), for example.

[157] See Hansen and McClure (1998), Zegers de Beijl (1999), Arai, Bursell, and Nekby (2008), and Oreopoulos (2009).

which successive generations of migrants move *down* in socio-economic status because of racism and social exclusion) has been well documented in the United States, although it has not been observed to the same degree among migrants to Europe.[158]

Although history suggests that societies' sustained exposure to difference tends to promote tolerance and acceptance in the long run, the costs of social exclusion can be severe. The persistent prejudices faced by many Africans, Turks, and Pakistanis in Europe, Latin Americans and Africans in the United States, and African foreigners in South Africa illustrate the need for a proactive state to promote integration, accommodation, and social mobility at local levels.

While for many people migration evokes the promise of opportunity, adventure, and new horizons, for others it can involve perilous journeys and a lack of control of their destinies. A scan of the media each week reveals the death toll associated with migration: those who have drowned in their attempt to cross into Europe, suffocated in compartments of goods vehicles trying to enter the UK, or dehydrated as they cross expanses of the US–Mexican frontier. While it is impossible to get an accurate count of these deaths, there is on average more than one death per day recorded on the US–Mexico border alone.[159] The number of people who have died crossing the US border has increased steadily over the past decades, more than doubling since 1995. It has been suggested that of the many thousands who annually take treacherous ocean routes from Africa to the Spanish Canary Islands or across the Mediterranean, as many as one in eight do not complete the crossing, with many of these missing persons presumed to have drowned.[160]

More stringent border controls often compel people to take greater risks involving more dangerous crossings. Those who arrive safely face new challenges and difficulties. Among the most vulnerable groups of migrants are the low skilled, the undocumented, and refugees.

6.5.1 EXPLOITATION OF LOW-SKILLED MIGRANTS

Low-skilled migrants often move to countries where they have limited legal rights (in the case of seasonal labor) or almost none at all, if they are undocumented. The nature of the work they undertake and the lack of adequate workplace protection generate particular risks. The United Nations

---

[158] Heath, Rothon, and Kilpi (2008), p. 229.

[159] Cornelius (2001).

[160] See Sweeney and Booth (2009). At the time of writing frequent reports of boats capsizing ("150 North African migrants feared dead") and boats missing ("UN says 400 African migrants feared drowned") fill the popular press, as civilians attempt to flee the conflict, violence, and dissent erupting in North Africa and the Middle East (see Kington 2011; Walker 2011).

reports that in Europe, the occupational accident rate for migrants is twice as high as for native workers, which is related to the "dirty, dangerous and difficult" jobs often reserved for migrants.[161] Migrant agricultural workers in both developed and developing countries suffer disproportionately from illnesses related to exposure to toxic pesticides.[162] Most of these migrants do not have access to health care because they lack insurance or are unaware or unable to access health facilities.

Low-skilled migrants and undocumented workers are also particularly vulnerable to exploitation by employers and recruiting agents. Migrants from South Asia often borrow heavily to pay the substantial fees charge by recruitment agencies to secure a job abroad.[163] Unaware of their rights or fearful of being sent home without earning any money, migrants are forced by their circumstances to endure such exploitation. Female migrant workers may also suffer degrading abuses. In the words of Human Rights Watch, "Some women workers [were so] traumatized from rape and sexual abuse at the hands of employers [that they] could not narrate their accounts without anger or tears. Living in forced confinement and extreme isolation, [it was] difficult or impossible for these women to call for help, escape situations of exploitation and abuse, and seek legal redress."[164] Without adequate legal protections or opportunities to unionize, low-skilled migrants in foreign countries too frequently become victims of deception and abuse.

The investigation into the death of 18 cockleshell pickers trapped by a rising tide in England's Morecambe Bay in February 2004 revealed that they were undocumented migrants who could not speak English and were working for an organized gang.[165] Public reaction to the tragedy led to the regulation of the UK shell fishing industry by a Gangmaster Licensing Authority. However, as Oxfam notes in considering the lessons five years after the tragedy, "abuse of migrant workers continues."[166]

6.5.2 HUMAN TRAFFICKING

Human trafficking, or "modern slavery," is proliferating as transnational economic networks expand across increasingly open borders. The UN estimates that 2.5 million people are in forced labor (including sexual exploitation) at any time, as a result of trafficking.[167] The total trade in people (including trafficking and human smuggling) is worth US$7 to US$10 billion

---

[161] United Nations (2004), p. 160.
[162] Ibid., p. 160.
[163] Human Rights Watch (2004).
[164] Ibid., p. 3.
[165] BBC (2004).
[166] Oxfam (2009).
[167] ILO (2007).

a year.[168] Trafficking often involves deception and coercion of aspiring migrants by brokers who profit from the cross-border trade in people. An aspect of human trafficking is the sex trade, which is global in scope. The sex trade disproportionately involves women, who are often either kidnapped or lured under false promises of clerical work or jobs in the entertainment industry.[169]

Trafficking also emerges as a response to a growing demand for children or wives. In China, for example, the long-term effects of a one child policy and patterns of sex-selective abortion have produced a population with many millions more men than women. Chinese men living near the Vietnamese border are known to pay for brides from China's populous southern neighbor. The "bride trade" across the Vietnam–China border shares characteristics with other cases of human trafficking, where migration involves a complex combination of deception, coercion, economics, and constrained choice.[170]

Children are also trafficked for economic and sexual exploitation. Many large European cities host informal labor markets where young children, mainly boys, are used for peddling and begging and older children as cheap construction labor.[171] UNICEF (2006) estimates that about 1.2 million children are channeled into the sex trade every year, but much of the trade is underground and difficult to study. The impact of the trade on the mental and physical health of children is a matter of great concern. Children involved in prostitution are 6 to 16 times more likely to be infected with a sexually transmitted disease than adolescents worldwide.

6.5.3 REFUGEES

Refugees often go through protracted situations of uncertainty and insecurity, unable to return home, settle permanently either in their country of first asylum, or gain resettlement in a third country. They may be confined indefinitely in camps or holding areas near volatile border areas, where they are exposed to renewed violence.[172] Even where refugees do not face immediate threats to their security, they are vulnerable to arbitrary policy changes that place them at risk of destitution, arrest, or involuntary and premature repatriation.

In some countries, refugees remain confined to camps in remote locations, entirely dependent on the assistance of the international community for basic needs of sustenance, shelter, and other services. Denied freedom of movement, given little or no opportunity to develop economic self-sufficiency, and

---

[168] Naím (2005), p. 89.
[169] United Nations Office on Drugs and Crime (2009).
[170] Howard and Lalani (2008).
[171] IOM (2005), p. 335.
[172] UNHCR (2006), p. 129.

with scant information as to when or if they will ever be able to return, life is characterized by insecurity. Health and education indicators among encamped refugees are often poor due to limited opportunities and services. There are also high rates of suicide, alcoholism, abuse, and drug smuggling, and the trafficking of women and children occurs with alarming frequency.[173]

The experiences of refugees, trafficked persons, and low-skilled workers highlight the need for adequate legal and political protection for migrants. Other categories of migrants are exposed to similar risks and vulnerabilities when they move to new countries, often relying on strangers to assist their passage, unfamiliar with language and culture, and lacking information or access to legal systems. Without the protection of states, the impact of migration on people can be traumatic.

6.6 **Summary**

The post-World War II era has usherd in a new age of mass migration. The characteristics of migration can be summed up with three principles: the individual agency of a migrant, the social dynamics of migration processes, and political and economic structures. To the extent that the decision to migrate is a choice, it is one that is influenced and constrained by a variety of factors. Migration assumes different levels of cost and risk for each individual, depending on their level of education, financial resources, social capital, access to information, social networks, and other endowments. Furthermore, the "push" and "pull" factors associated with migration are products of the local or national context in both the home and destination countries. The dynamic interaction between individual goals and desires, networks, and macro-level factors helps to explain why some people migrate and others do not, but it does not amount to a general model or theory of migration.

While the migration decision itself is complex, contemporary globalization is leading to increasing pressures on the borders of developed countries. The migration policies of states reflect their dual desire to manage borders that are both more permeable and more highly regulated than ever before. While developed countries increasingly align the objectives of their immigration policies, if not their admissions procedures, they continue to face the challenge of undocumented migration. Despite the existence of immigration policies that are based on similar economic imperatives, borders are not impervious. The high numbers of undocumented migrants, an estimated 12 million in the United States alone, indicate that conventional border

[173] Ibid., p. 117.

control strategies are unsuccessful at limiting the presence of migrants who work outside the legal system. Labor demand and market pressures conflict with the inclinations of state control.

Migration promises tremendous potential benefits for sending and receiving societies as well as for migrants themselves. Some of these gains—higher wages for migrants and increased productivity for receiving societies, for example—are generated simply by opening borders to larger flows of people. More migration makes good economic sense. However, there are also costs and risks associated with migration, and these are typically felt in localities that experience a rapid and large increase in the foreign-born population. Recognizing that enabling more migration is in our collective longer-term interest, the orientation of governments toward "management" should shift away from the quest to control borders and toward harnessing the social and economic potential of migrants and offsetting short-run and local costs.

In response to these challenges several international organizations and forums have called for an international migration agenda. While a single institution does not govern migration, an increasing number of multilateral efforts have focused on how to bring it within a multilateral framework. Cameron and Goldin (2011) argue that "a global migration agenda should be centered on a clear long term objective of freer [labor] movement."[174] Like many others, they point to the economic gains from liberalizing capital and trade flows over the forty years, and turn to labor mobility as the next frontier where more openness can produce global economic benefits. Lant Pritchett (2006) writes what many others are thinking: "If everything else is globalised then why not labor?"[175]

---

[174] Cameron and Goldin (2011), p. 15   [175] Pritchett (2006), p. 31.

7　Ideas

In previous chapters, we examined trade, capital flows, aid, and migration and the interaction of these global flows with development. In each case, these dimensions of economic globalization had the ability to contribute to development *under certain conditions*. This chapter focuses on ideas, an often neglected dimension of globalization, despite often being the most important. Ideas involve generating and transmitting distinctive intellectual constructs in any field that can affect production systems, organizational and management practices, governance practices, legal norms, and technological trends. Our scope here is thus very wide. Nevertheless, as with the other dimensions of economic globalization, there are distinct if subtle connections between the realm of global idea generation and dissemination and the realm of poverty and development. We attempt to convey some of these connections here.[1]

7.1 **The power of ideas**

Ideas are the most powerful influence on history. Globalization is above all about the flow and intermingling of ideas among the countries of the world. Ideas inform the evolution of politics and economics. The ways in which ideas flow and are absorbed shapes globalization and its impact on poor people. This has been true since the first migrations of our early ancestors across Africa, the Americas, Asia, and Europe. That the global spread of ideas is not a new phenomenon is evident in the rise of the earliest civilizations and the development and adoption of language, early implements, and agricultural technologies.[2] The spread of languages and cultures, of religion, and of specialization and trade reflect the forces of globalization. Although the expansion and then contraction of the influence of the ancient African, Chinese, Greek, Mayan, and other civilizations may be interpreted as the rise and decline of their military power, this power reflected an underlying set of ideas and technologies that shaped and informed the waxing and waning of the empires.

---

[1] Some of the elements considered in this chapter have been previously identified by Meier (2001).
[2] These processes have been effectively described by Diamond (1997), who emphasizes the role of continental East–West axes in facilitating the early diffusion of agricultural technologies.

Development may be characterized as the application of better and smarter ways of dealing with key challenges. As a leading growth economist Paul Romer (1993a) has written, "Nations are poor because their citizens do not have access to the ideas that are used in industrial nations to generate economic value."[3] Development marks the evolution of newer and more effective ideas that replace those that no longer reflect the opportunities and policy choices available to individuals and societies. Consequently development requires a more rapid evolution, dissemination, and assimilation of ideas that allows *local* knowledge to complement and inform global knowledge.[4]

Not all ideas are good. Indeed, some of the most negative effects of globalization can be attributed to the adoption of inappropriate ideas. One extreme case of this—the idea of *mercantilism*—is considered in Box 7.1. However, creating barriers against the flow of ideas is not an appropriate response to the risk of adopting bad ideas. Insulating society from these flows, through intellectual autarky (intellectual self-sufficiency), is perhaps best illustrated by the Democratic People's Republic of Korea, which—after adopting and adapting the big, far reaching idea of Marxist Leninism—has virtually cut itself off from the world, with disastrous consequences for its population. We might imagine that if the Democratic People's Republic of Korea were to end its isolation and benefit from its proximity to its neighbors, the Republic of Korea and China, the dynamic effects of the new ideas flowing in would dwarf the development impact of foreign aid and even foreign investment flows.[5]

The challenge for countries and individuals is to create the capacity to identify, from the myriad idea flows, those that are most interesting and that offer the most potential, and to then evaluate and adapt them in a process that facilitates local innovation and progress. This is no small challenge. The evaluation and adaptation of ideas requires local capacity in the form of both skills and institutions.[6] It also requires a culture of learning and adaptation, of openness to ideas and to challenging past practices. In development projects, it requires the explicit recognition of the need for independent

---

[3] Romer (1993a), p. 543.

[4] In international economics, the importance of local knowledge was first emphasized by Pack and Westphal (1986). These authors noted that "the combination of technical knowledge with knowledge of local circumstances can lead to innovations that would, in all likelihood, not have been forthcoming otherwise. The resultant new (differentiated, adapted, or otherwise) products or processes are non-tradable in the sense that they could not have been created without their development in the local circumstances" (p. 109). The concept of local knowledge is well developed throughout the social sciences as well. See, for example, de Walt (1994).

[5] The authors are grateful to F. Halsey Rogers, who contributed this scenario in the course of our discussions on the role of ideas.

[6] Rodrik (2000) emphasizes that "large-scale institutional development by and large requires a process of discovery about local needs and capabilities" (p. 14).

assessments based on accurate data, followed by frank discussions of what works and what does not, what can be improved and how.

Although it is vital to stress the importance of the capacity to absorb ideas, at least as important is the capacity to adapt or even *reject* ideas. Developing countries have often suffered the burden of imposed, inappropriate ideas. Although this characterized the colonial period in an acute manner, it is also a modern phenomenon. For example, tied aid and inappropriate conditions associated with financial flows, and anti-development intellectual property regimes reflect an imbalance in bargaining strength in the realm of ideas, similar to that in other dimensions of globalization. The solution to this problem is not isolation but rather judicious and vigorous engagement on the part of the developing world in the evaluation of ideas.

The post-World War II period has been associated with an unprecedented increase and reach of the cross-border flow of ideas. It is no accident that this period also has been associated with unprecedented leaps in life expectancy and literacy, benefits brought by the spread and adoption of new policies and technologies. The combination of global knowledge and local innovation and adaptation and implementation has been particularly powerful. This is evident, for example, in the way that global knowledge about the relations between germs and diseases has been applied in local campaigns to encourage people to wash hands, and in how the biological advances in understanding HIV/AIDS have been combined with local knowledge to develop public health strategies that have saved hundreds of millions of lives. Similarly, the combination of global knowledge and local innovation provided the engine for the Green Revolution, which benefited hundreds of millions of poor people through dramatically raising agricultural productivity, particularly in Asia. The flow of ideas across borders has been underpinned by the rise of global governance, the expansion of civil society organizations (including international lobbying groups), and innovations in communication technologies that instantly transfer information from one locality to another.

Although the rapid spread and adoption of new ideas is behind the greatest leaps in development, ignorance and the failure to learn rapidly enough is behind some of the greatest development setbacks. For example, the failure to act earlier and more decisively against HIV/AIDS in a number of countries, such as Botswana and South Africa, has already reversed the gains of the life expectancy of the past 30 years.[7] However, the significance of ideas is not largely confined to health and technology. The implications of ideologies,

---

[7] Interestingly, the commitment of Bill Gates to provide unprecedented private support to combat HIV/AIDS and other preventable diseases also reflects the power of ideas. Gates, at the United Nations on May 9, 2002, stated "My personal commitment to improving global health started when I learned about health inequities...in the 1993 [World Bank] World Development Report...My wife Melinda and I were stunned to learn that 11 million children die each year from preventable diseases. That is when we decided to make improving health the focus of our philanthropy" (UNICEF, 2002).

BOX 7.1 MERCANTILISM

Mercantilism was one the most misguided development ideas of all time. In its myriad forms, mercantilism influenced development patterns from the mid-fifteenth century through the end of the nineteenth century. This influence ranged from mild to catastrophic among the various regions of what we now call the developing world. The basic notion of mercantilism was that wealth was to be found in precious metals, primarily gold. As an admiral of Christopher Columbus stated, "of gold is treasure made, and with it he who has it does as he wills in the world and it even sends souls to Paradise." Where gold was not to be acquired directly, through mining, it was to be acquired indirectly, by generating a trade surplus. As stated by Thomas Mun in an early mercantilist treatise, "The ordinary means . . . to increase our wealth and treasure is by Foreign Trade, wherein we must ever observe this rule; to sell more to strangers than we consume of theirs in value." Gold was seen as important in part for its role in paying armies. Indeed, trade and war were closely related in much mercantilist thinking and practice, perhaps most famously in the case of the Dutch East India Company, which at its height maintained a force of 30,000 soldiers. As one of its employees wrote, "We can't trade without war, nor make war without trade."

It was mercantilism that provided the intellectual structure of Spain's brutal colonial conquests and set the stage for the famous inflows of gold into the capital of its empire, Sevilla. The barren nature of mercantilist ideas became apparent with Iberian inflation and, ultimately, the collapse of the empire by the end of the seventeenth century. Spain itself gained few long-term benefits from its empire, no less its brutalized colonial subjects. As Adam Smith noted in his anti-mercantilist *Wealth of Nations*, "Wealth does not consist in gold and silver; but in what money purchases."

In the late 1700s, Spain locked up the documents of its colonial history in the Old Exchange Building in Sevilla. In 1862, the young King Leopold of Belgium spent a month in these archives, carefully studying Spain's application of mercantilist practice to its colonies. These he applied to his own colony in the Congo after the Berlin Conference of 1885. Again, the effect was brutal, resulting in the deaths of approximately 10 million Congolese from 1885 through 1920. Thus, the mercantilist idea extended its devastating reach across more than four centuries, with each imperial power seeking to run a trade surplus by locking its colonies into patterns of trade that prevented the colonies trading with other imperial powers or their colonies, choking what now is known as South–South trade.

Sources: Mun (1664/1924), Smith (1776/1937), Galeano (1997), *The Economist* (1998, 1999), and Hochschild (1999).

including ideas about religion and economics, have an even more powerful influence.

Ideas of destiny, right, and might, enacted in the crusades, colonial conquest, and communism, have massive and continuing implications for development. Globalization does not appear to have diluted such ideas. Although in some senses there has been what Bell (1960/2000) and Fukuyama (1992) heralded as "the end of ideology" and "the end of history," respectively, the tenacity of ideologies remains evident. Examples range from the growth of religious fundamentalism in many parts of the world to the dogged adherence in the richest countries to protectionist policies. As discussed in Chapter 3, protectionism in rich countries has a devastating impact on millions of poor people whose struggle to escape poverty is frustrated by the barriers that rich countries place on their exports.[8] Protectionism in rich country agriculture is an idea that a former Chief Economist of the World Bank has characterized as "politically antiquated, economically illiterate, environmentally destructive and ethically indefensible."[9] Yet it persists.

Ideas on development cannot be divorced from the broader context of ideas of humanity, freedom, culture, and religious belief. These shape and inform economic development and globalization and, in turn, they evolve in response to the changes in their operating environment. The spread of ideas about human rights, for instance, has driven development progress.[10] Important phases of this spread have included the movement for the abolition of slavery, the struggle for suffrage for woman, the anti-colonial movements, and the development of trade unionism. Today, thousands of international conventions and the development of hundreds of international organizations, not least the United Nations and Bretton Woods systems to which the great majority of the world's nations belong, have given institutional form to the globalization of ideas about rights and the broadening of our understanding of development.

One extremely powerful idea that has spread across the globe from one country to another is the ideal of democracy. John Markoff (1996) charts the expansion of democracy from the mid-1970s in terms of a series of multi-continental "waves" which have swept across Europe, Latin America, Asia, and Africa. Most recently, the idea of democracy (or at least a strong reaction against autocratic rule) has spread throughout the Middle East and North Africa following the downfall of President Zine al-Abidine Ben Ali in Tunisia and President Hosni Mubarak in Egypt in the wake of political protests and pressure. While it is still too early to tell what sort of political system will replace these regimes in the medium to long term, the demand for change has rapidly moved to other Arab countries leading to UN and NATO intervention in Libya, civil unrest and violence in Yemen and Syria, and political protests for reform in Bahrain, Jordan, Morocco, and Oman.

What is remarkable about these developments is not just the speed and scale at which ordinary people have been prepared to take the streets, but the way in which ideas have contagiously spread and taken hold through informal

---

[8] Recall from Chapter 3 that estimates of the number of people kept in poverty by rich country protectionism is at least 65 million.

[9] Stern (2004), p. 5. Efforts to argue for agricultural protection in terms of the "multifunctionality" of agricultural production in the rich (but apparently not the poor) world (for example, Jules 2003) is no less an exercise of right and might than previous ideologies have exercised. See Peterson (2009).

[10] See, for example, Sen (1999), chapter 10, and Sen (2009) who revisits human rights in the context of considering the idea of justice. Ruggie (2008) provides additional perspectives on the relation of human rights to business.

networks, underground news organizations, and new technologies in countries in which the media and contact with the outside world are tightly controlled (see BBC 2011). Equally remarkable is the resolve of protesters in many of these countries, who have increasingly been motivated by the conviction that political reform and change is possible. In many cases, large-scale protests and demands for change have spontaneously ignited. Most opposition movements have no *de facto* leaders, but rely instead on grass roots activists to keep things moving.[11]

The spread of democracy (and reactions against autocracy) shows that ideas can be contagious and their flow unpredictable. Other notable examples include the collapse of the seemingly deeply entrenched communist regimes in Eastern Europe, the fall of apartheid in South Africa, and the rise of religious fundamentalism. The advent of mass communication technologies, particularly global television channels and the Internet has lifted the globalization of ideas to new heights. In addition to transferring ideas that weaken government and other national monopolies over information, mass communication has profound implications for patterns of production and consumption. This is one of the defining features of the latest wave of globalization. As John Stuart Mill in the mid-nineteenth century observed,

It is hardly possible to overrate the value ... of placing human beings in contact with persons dissimilar to themselves, and with modes of thought and action unlike those with which they are familiar. ... Such communication has always been and is peculiarly in the present age, one of the primary sources of progress.[12]

7.2 **Growth and development**

An honest assessment of idea formulation and reformulation would acknowledge both its frequency and somewhat random character. Arndt (1987), like many others, captures the multidimensional nature and evolution of the idea of development as well as its tendency toward what Santiso (2006) calls the "endless waltz of paradigms."[13] There are good reasons for both of these characteristics. With regard to the first, it is simply the case that development

---

[11] See Ghattas (2011). One noteworthy development is the rise of "cyber activism" to coordinate protests and share information between localities. The "Syrian Revolution 2011" Facebook page has more than 120,000 fans while the Twitter account "@SyRevoSlogans" (created April 18, 2011) offers a range of slogans to use during protests.

[12] Mill (1846), III.17.14.

[13] As noted by Szirmai (2005), there is a *time element* inherent in this process: "A common characteristic of ... recipes for development is their short-term perspective. Time and again, proposals have been put forward in order to achieve certain goals. ... In the meantime, developments that take place irrespective of the fashion of the day are ignored or disregarded. ... But when the immediate

cannot be divorced from the broader human context that shapes and informs it. With regard to the second, the complex nature of development processes does not lend itself once-and-for-all action-outcome mappings.[14] Rather, the increased dimensionality of development thinking has been an outcome of an increasingly nuanced understanding of what drives development.

The most durable notion of development has been in terms of *per capita income*. It has the virtues of being parsimonious and completely conformable to measures of income poverty, such as those of Ravallion, Chen, and Sangraula (2009). It is also readily subject to analytical treatment in the form of growth theory, an area of renewed theoretical and empirical research.

Development experience suggests that the economic growth remains a powerful force for reducing income poverty. As stated by the United Nations' Development Programme, "Although growth is not the end of development, the absence of growth often is."[15] The challenge, then, is sustaining growth over significant periods of time. Rapid growth episodes of a few years or a decade are not uncommon.[16] What has been much less common is sustained, rapid growth over a period of decades, exactly what is necessary to eliminate absolute poverty.[17] Since only a portion of growth is driven by increases in physical and human capital, countries need sustained productivity increases to reduce income poverty.

There is a great deal of accumulated evidence that institutions are central to growth and poverty reduction (for example, Rodrik 2000 and 2003a, and Rodrik, Subramanian, and Trebbi 2004).[18] By the mid-1990s, it became apparent that the purely "pro-market" school of development thinking was missing much of the development story. Macroeconomic stability, openness, and domestic market liberalization proved to be *necessary* but *not sufficient* for growth and poverty reduction. The free market view neglected the institutional foundations of effective private markets, what might be called soft infrastructure. The importance of institutions has been empirically underscored by continued growth and poverty reduction in China, a country that pursued market-oriented reforms without excessive disruption of institutional foundations; a lack of growth and poverty reduction in the former Soviet Union where a lack of institutional development led to disappointing

results are slow in materializing, disenchantment set in. The issue disappears from the public eye, and new and more appealing solutions and catch-phrases emerge" (pp. 2–3).

[14] See Denzau and North (1994).

[15] UNDP (1991), p. 13.

[16] For example, countries that successfully emerge from civil war often experience relatively rapid economic rebounds for several years. See, for example, Collier and Gunning (1995).

[17] See Pritchett (2000) and Easterly (2001) for a discussion of why this is difficult to achieve.

[18] Indeed, Rodrik (2003a) argues that institutional quality and governance are the underlying variables that drive all of the other growth enhancing factors.

development outcomes; and the financial crisis in East Asia, to which institutional weaknesses contributed heavily.[19] While it performed a useful service by spotlighting government failure, the free market reaction minimized very real problems of market failure that are prevalent in the developing world.[20] As a result, growth performance in many parts of the world fell short of the expectations generated by free market lines of thinking.[21]

With regard to the role of ideas in growth processes, recent innovations in growth theory have drawn on Schumpeter (1949) to emphasize the role of the evolution of ideas at the micro-level in processes of firm innovation.[22] In this line of thinking, ideas produce innovations in productive methods, including organization, sources of supply, and quality. As emphasized by Romer (1993b), for example:

Ideas should be our central concern. . . . In a world with physical limits, it is discoveries of big ideas, together with the discovery of millions of little ideas, that make persistent economic growth possible. Ideas are the instructions that let us combine limited physical resources in arrangements that are ever more valuable.[23]

The Schumpeterian vision is that of development being accelerated through an increase in the supply of ideas and their translation into innovations. For this to happen, the transmission and acceptance of ideas must be in a form that can be translated into realized capabilities. Increases in rates of growth and poverty reduction thus require *both* an acceleration of idea transmission *and* the adoption of ideas through innovations contributing to technical and societal change. We return to this issue below when we take up the topic of learning.

Despite the centrality of per capita income and growth in the idea of development, a conceptual reorientation away from these notions has taken place.[24] This had its origins in Sen (1987 and 1989) amongst others.[25] The key concept here is the neo-Aristotelian notion of *capabilities*.[26] Sen (1987) noted that "it is reasonable to argue that while well-being is related to being well off, they are not the same and may possibly diverge a good deal."[27] More to the

---

[19] See Stiglitz (2000) and Rajan and Bird (2001).

[20] Some of these ideas are taken up in Lindauer and Pritchett (2002).

[21] We invite the reader to revisit World Bank (1993 and 1994a) as examples of these sorts of claims.

[22] For an overview, see Alcouffe and Kuhn (2004).

[23] Romer (1993b), p. 64.

[24] See Seers (1972), Chenery et al. (1974), and Streeten et al. (1981).

[25] Sen's concept of "development" can be traced back to his 1979 Tanner Lecture at Stanford University, "Equality of What?" (Sen 1980). See also Sen (1984, 1985, and 2009).

[26] The neo-Aristotelian literature springs in part from Aristotle's assertion in *Nicomachen Ethics* (Crisp 2000) that "wealth is clearly not the good we are seeking, since it is merely useful, for getting something else" (p. 7). The capability approach also has strong connections with John Rawls, Adam Smith, John Stuart Mill, and Karl Marx (see, for example, Clark 2006).

[27] Sen (1987), p. 15.

point, Sen (1989) argued that "Countries with high GNP per capita can nevertheless have astonishingly low achievements in the quality of life."[28] While strongly emphasizing the role of capabilities, however, Sen is somewhat agnostic as to compiling a complete, objective list of the most relevant ones.[29] Nevertheless, it was Sen's thinking that helped to support the evolution of the idea of *human development*.[30]

The link between the capabilities idea and that of human development was clearly articulated in the 1998 *Human Development Report*, which defined human development as follows:

Human development is a process of enlarging people's choices. Enlarging people's choices is achieved by expanding human capabilities and functionings. At all levels of development the three essential capabilities for human development are for people to lead long and healthy lives, to be knowledgeable and to have access to the resources need for a decent standard of living.[31]

This conception of human development was codified in the Human Development Index (HDI) by Mahbub ul Haq who emphasized the need for a *single measure* to contrast against per capita income.[32] Despite some detractors, the HDI and its components have taken a central place in development policy deliberations and have strongly influenced the current Millennium Development Goals (MDG) vocabulary. The most lasting contribution of the capabilities framework, however, has been to expand the dimensionality of development thinking, conceptions of poverty or deprivation, and development policy. Central capabilities in the form of health, education, and empowerment have taken their place alongside per capita income as key development indicators.

Finally, there have been some important convergences between growth in per capita income investigations and human capabilities. For example, Pio (1994) advocated devoting "particular attention...to the role of human capital with an emphasis on the adjective human; that is to say, on the levels

---

[28] Sen (1989), p. 42.

[29] He writes: "The problem is not with listing important capabilities, but with insisting on one predetermined canonical list of capabilities, chosen by theorists without any general social discussion or public reasoning. To have such a fixed list, emanating entirely from pure theory, is to deny the possibility of fruitful public participation on what should be included and why... public discussion and reasoning can lead to a better understanding of the role, reach and significance of particular capabilities" (Sen 2004, pp. 77, 81; quoted in Clark 2006, p. 38). Nussbaum (2000) is much more specific, providing and defending a universal list of central capabilities. Alkire (2002), Clark (2002), and Saith (2007) explore the various lists of capabilities, needs, and rights advanced in the literature.

[30] The idea of human development is closely related to the neo-Aristotelian notion of *human flourishing*. See Rasmussen (1999), Alkire (2002), and Qizilbash (2006).

[31] UNDP (1998), p. 14.

[32] See Sen (1999), Fukuda-Parr (2003), and Clark and Hulme (2010). Sen (2006a), p. 257 maintains that "the breadth of the human development approach must not be confused with the slender specificity of the Human Development Index."

of health, education, and nutrition of the population and the implications of changes in such levels for long term growth."[33] He concluded that "the inclusion of a broader definition of human capital (encompassing health and nutrition as well as education) seems useful both in the construction of models and in their empirical verification."[34] Subsequently, there has been empirical work and policy debate supporting the role of human development and capability expansion in promoting growth.[35] It is therefore becoming more apparent that the income and capability dimensions of development and poverty alleviation are mutually supporting, an example of the role of learning in the formulation of ideas of development.

7.3 **Managing knowledge**

As suggested above, the deficiency of knowledge can be a more pervasive handicap to development than the scarcity of any other factor. Knowledge, however, is in many respects a *public good*. Once something is known, that knowledge can be used by anyone, and its use by any one person does not preclude its use by others. This characteristic of knowledge is precisely the hallmark of a public good, and suggests that knowledge, like other public goods, will be underprovided by market systems. The challenge, then, is the effective development and management of knowledge, recognizing its public good nature.[36]

The *World Development Report* noted that "Knowledge is like light. Weightless and intangible, it can easily travel the world, enlightening the lives of billions of people everywhere. Yet billions of people live in the darkness of poverty—unnecessarily."[37] The World Bank went on to distinguished between *knowledge gaps* in know-how or technical knowledge (such as birth control, software engineering, and accountancy) and *information gaps* in areas such as product quality, creditworthiness, and other types of incomplete information that lead to market failures.

For developing countries to address the problem of knowledge gaps, the authors of the *World Development Report* recommended three key actions: (1) *Acquiring knowledge* by tapping into and adapting knowledge available

---

[33] Pio (1994), p. 278.

[34] Ibid., p. 297.

[35] See, for example, Birdsall and Londono (1998).

[36] In the terminology of microeconomics, the benefits of knowledge are "non-excludable," and its consumption is "non-rival." As pointed out by Stiglitz (1999), knowledge is actually a *global* public good. We consider global public goods later in this chapter.

[37] World Bank (1999), p. 1.

elsewhere in the world—for example through trade, foreign investment, and licensing—as well as by creating knowledge locally through research and development and building on indigenous knowledge; (2) *Absorbing knowledge* by ensuring universal basic education, creating opportunities for lifelong learning, and supporting tertiary education; and (3) *Communicating knowledge* by taking advantage of new information and communications technology. This requires that poor people have access and that information flows be promoted, using vibrant media and modern technologies, among other methods.

To address information gaps, the World Bank report recommended that priority be given to ensuring transparency and accountability in financial flows, reducing the risk of capture and corruption, and increasing knowledge of opportunities. It also highlighted the need to overcome information deficits that discriminate against poor people and isolate them from markets, as well as those that lead to failing to account for the environment.

7.3.1 DISSEMINATION OF KNOWLEDGE

Access to ideas is a key issue for the effective dissemination of knowledge in a globalized world. This involves issues of technology, education, and the media. One measure of technological access is communications connectedness, which indicates that low-income countries are at a significant disadvantage compared to middle-income countries and even more so compared to high-income countries (Figure 7.1). However, mobile phone subscriptions

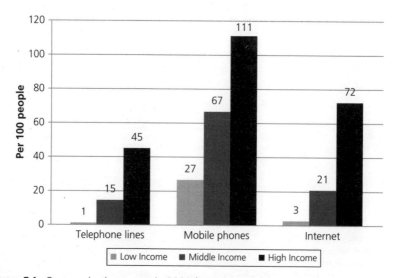

Figure 7.1. Communication access in 2009 (per 100 people)

Source: World Development Indicators (http://databank.worldbank.org), April 28, 2011.

have expanded rapidly in low-income countries since the turn of the century (from 0.3 percent in 1999 to 26.6 percent in 2009), even though the overall number remains well below half that of middle-income countries. Little progress has been made in terms of landline or internet connections in low-income countries, although modest progress has been made in middle-income countries over the last decade.[38]

In terms of knowledge, networks, and scientific research, the latest Royal Society (2011) report observes that "the traditional scientific superpowers," the United States, Western Europe and Japan continue to lead the world, although "science in 2011 is increasingly global."[39] One major development, however, is the rapid expansion in the number of scientific papers authored by researchers in developing countries like Brazil, China, India, Korea, South Africa, and Mexico. As Figure 7.2 shows, the annual growth of publications in many of these countries has consistently outpaced that of the leading G-8 economies. Although the global share of citations for publications produced by researchers located in developing countries is small, it is expanding with China now ranked among the top ten global leaders (Figure 7.3). International scientific collaborations amongst researchers have also increased in both global and regional terms in recent years. For example, collaboration between African countries grew substantially after 2000 with South Africa, Egypt, and Sudan acting as crucial networking bridges linking North and sub-Saharan Africa (see Figure 7.4). Although these are positive and welcome developments, bottlenecks in communication technologies and scientific connectivity that reflect a lack of infrastructure continue to prevent poor people from sharing in the global exchange of ideas.

Education and training in all their forms support the diffusion of knowledge. The education of children and adults, in both formal and informal settings, is vital to the global flow of ideas. In particular, literacy, numeracy, and the ability to absorb and evaluate information are central. In the important phrase of development economics, education and training are all about "learning to learn." Without this capacity, ideas have no vitality.[40] Education is also a central part of translating global ideas into local variations. However, as noted by Root (2006), "despite a strong record of productivity gains, political obstacles often prevent the adequate delivery of education. Inequality affects the strategies of the rulers by influencing the disbursement of public

---

[38] A measure of the actual *use* of capacity is international voice traffic in minutes per person. Unfortunately recent aggregate data is not available for country groups. Goldin and Reinert (2010) report the following figures for 2002: Low-income countries (5 minutes per person), middle-income countries (17 minutes per person), and high-income countries (149 minutes per person). In recent year the expansion of international voice traffic has slowed as new technologies (most notably, Skype) have taken an increasing share of the market (Telegraphy 2010).

[39] Royal Society (2011), p. 5.

[40] See, for example, Stiglitz (1987).

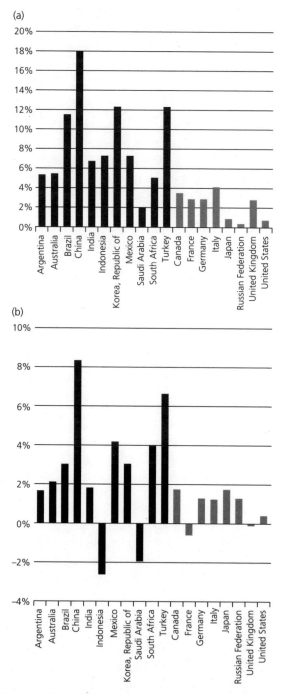

Figure 7.2. Science in the G-20. (a) Annual growth in publications, 1996–2008. (b) Annual growth in GDP spending on R&D 1996–2007.

Note: G-8 labeled in lighter grey bars.

Source: Royal Academy (2011).

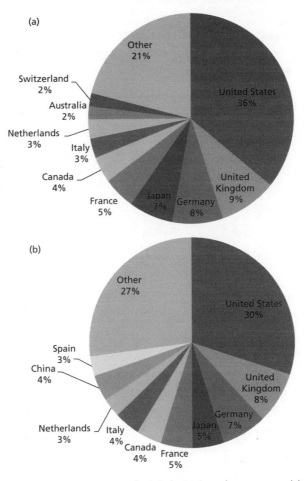

(a)

(b)

Figure 7.3. Comparative proportion of global citations by country. (a) 1999–2003 (b) 2004–2008

Source: Royal Academy (2011), figure 1.3, p. 25.

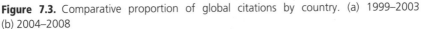

expenditures away from the poor and toward a select few in the form of private benefits."[41] Consequently, harnessing the flow of ideas is tied up with the political economy of globalization and development.

7.3.2 THE MEDIA AND REFORM

A vibrant media can play a vital role in disseminating knowledge. Higher literacy rates, lower printing costs, and new broadcast technologies (including

[41] Root (2006), p. 24.

the Internet) can promote the potential of the media to inform citizens and create global constituencies and commerce. At the global level, media can move currency markets and influence international trade. At the other end of the spectrum, however, are the local, vernacular media. These can help develop market opportunities for poor farmers through daily radio broadcasts of prices, for example. They can also increase awareness of local threats and opportunities, considerably improving local health and knowledge.

New information can change people and cultures and create demand for new institutions as well as facilitate debate and collective action. The combination of providing information and voice (the ability to access views and

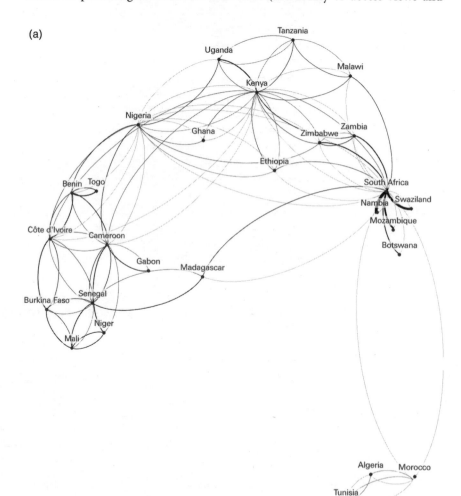

Figure 7.4. Collaboration between African countries. (a) 1996–2000.

Source: Royal Academy (2011).

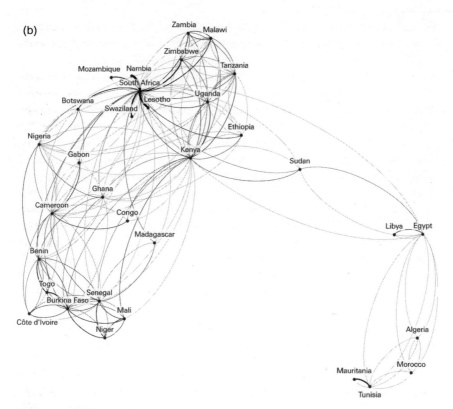

Figure 7.4. (b) 2004–2008.

express them effectively) can and does facilitate social change, albeit for the better or worse. This point has been emphasized by Amartya Sen (1999) who argues that:

The reach and quality of open discussions can be helped by a variety of public policies, such as press freedom and media independence (including the absence of censorship), expansion of basic education and schooling (including female education), enhancement of economic independence (especially through employment, including female employment), and other social and economic changes that help individuals to be participating citizens. Central to this approach is the idea of the public as an active participant in charge, rather than as a passive and docile recipient of instructions or of dispensed assistance.[42]

[42] Sen (1999), p. 281.

Among other things, Sen has argued that the media can play a vital role in preventing famines in functioning democracies like India, by providing "political incentives generated by elections, multiparty politics and investigative journalism."[43] Moreover, the rise of new media which provides access to interactive digital content on demand almost anywhere can have significant impacts on events (as the Middle East and North Africa experience considered above illustrates). Some have taken a fairly negative view of the media, arguing that the flow of information and ideas reflect global power relations.[44] On occasions the media has also been used to help prop up oppressive regimes, promote xenophobia, and even ferment genocide in the case of Rwanda.

The role of the media in improving governance depends on both their ability to provide relevant information and their willingness to reflect diverse points of view. Too often, the capture of the media by narrow political or financial interests, coupled with weak capacity and heavy constraints on journalism, lead to the media not rising to their potential. Diversity of perspective, as well as financial and editorial independence, is vital for both state and private media. This is a major regulatory challenge, which, in the age of increasing global concentration, needs ongoing and increased attention. This challenge is not simply confined to the poorest societies, where lack of capital and capacity and the constraints placed on markets by the poverty and illiteracy of readerships and advertisers undermine the potential for the use of media in addressing knowledge deficits. In the most advanced societies, a plethora of choice and availability, as is evidenced in the hundreds of channels available on satellite TV and the unprecedented access offered by broadband Internet, is coupled with a homogenization of content. Consumers typically choose among a widening range of similar products owned and operated by a narrowing set of major multinational corporations.

Although the potential to learn about the world and develop a global citizenry has never been greater than it is now, the irony is that global and national polls do not appear to reflect a rising knowledge among consumers who spend hours a day watching television, "surfing" the Internet, or reading newspapers and journals. Clearly, content is at least as important as capacity.

7.3.3 CHALLENGES FOR KNOWLEDGE MANAGEMENT

Following Goldin and Reinert (2010), it is possible to identify three broad elements relating to effective knowledge management for development. The first of these involves increasing the voice of developing countries and their

---

[43] Ibid., p. 178.
[44] See, for example, MacBride (1980). This issue is briefly considered by Murphy (2006).

citizens.[45] This is an essential ingredient of inclusive globalization and is especially important in global consultation and decision making with direct consequences for the citizens of developing countries. It is also important to enhance developing country participation in global institutions in order to ensure their legitimacy. The governance of the United Nations (at least at the Security Council level), the World Bank, and the International Monetary Fund reflects the balance of power 60 years ago.[46] There is widespread recognition of the need for enhancing the participation of developing countries. Although some progress has been made in areas related to program formation, the structural issues of voting rights and board representation remain intractable. As stated by Bhattacharya and Griffith-Jones (2004), it is "important to go beyond consultation to *full representation* of developing countries in bodies that deliberate and set international norms and action plans."[47] The principles of transparency, accountability, and good governance that the global institutions advocate for developing countries should also be embraced by these institutions themselves. The requisite reforms are indeed daunting, but failure to undertake the challenge will undermine any chances of an effective, multilateral system for managing globalization and development.

A second element of knowledge management for development is broad access. In addition to investing in education and research, governments can facilitate the sharing of knowledge and make special efforts to overcome the exclusion of poor communities from ideas. A particular challenge is to make knowledge available in ways and languages that can be understood by wide audiences such as local development practitioners who do not speak English. Timely and effective information flows on issues important to poor communities can both mitigate risks and expand opportunities. Such efforts include providing market prices to poor farmers via village mobile phones, broadcasting weather information and disaster warnings on local radios, and highlighting the risks of HIV/AIDS and the benefits of public health measures in community information campaigns. In these sorts of cases, knowledge helps to empower poor people.

A third element of knowledge management for development is increased technology transfer to developing countries. Article 66.2 of the Agreement on Trade Related Aspects of Intellectual Property Rights (TRIPS) of the World

---

[45] This theme has been recently taken up by Sen (2006b), chapter 7, who states that "the preeminent practical challenges today include the possibility of making use of the remarkable benefits of economic connections, technological progress, and political opportunity in a way that pays adequate attention to the interests of the deprived and the underdog" (pp. 131–2).

[46] As Derviş (2005) notes, "without greater legitimacy at the supranational level, progress in solving global problems will be very difficult" (p. 3). Derviş makes very specific proposals for changing the governance structures of these institutions that deserve careful consideration.

[47] Bhattacharya and Griffith-Jones (2004), p. 205 (emphasis added).

Trade Organization, for example, commits developed countries to providing "incentives to enterprises and institutions in their territories for the purpose of promoting and encouraging technology transfer" to the least developed countries. This commitment needs to be implemented *in practice* and applied to a wider set of countries. As outlined by Hoekman, Maskus, and Saggi (2004), this can occur through a variety of measures. These include:

- Incentives for corporations and non-governmental organizations to transfer mature patent rights or to provide technical assistance.
- Public support for research into the specific technology needs of developing countries.
- University training for students from the low-income countries in science and technology.
- Finance for participation of developing country representatives in standard setting bodies.
- Public purchase of patents on certain technologies for free use in developing countries.

These and other steps can better assure that knowledge in the form of international technological development is more broadly spread in the developing world.

7.4 **Intellectual property**

Trade in goods and services and flows of capital are often packaged with ideas and innovations, and there is an extensive literature on the role of technology transfer in foreign direct investment.[48] Here we go beyond the arguments of chapter 3 to discuss the particular questions of trade in knowledge products.

As stated above, knowledge has strong public good characteristics. For this reason, it tends to be underprovided by a market based system. This is because, "the innovator's inability to obtain adequate compensation for his effort would, under a competitive system, cause too few resources to be allocated to research."[49] This problem is typically addressed in the co-evolution between markets and governance systems through various types of intellectual property protection, a key form of knowledge management.

The area of *intellectual property rights* is among the most controversial in economics. One area of intense debate concerns the role of intellectual

---

[48] See Hoekman, Maskus, and Saggi (2005) as well as Chapter 4.
[49] Leach (2004), p. 174.

property rights in growth. The common argument is that the presence of strong intellectual property rights spurs innovation, which leads to higher rates of economic growth and increasing benefits for all. The kernel of the argument is that, if strong property rights provide good incentives for the production of things, they must also provide appropriate incentives for the production of ideas. Boldrin and Levine (2002, 2004a, and 2004b) question this, arguing that intellectual property has come to mean not only the right to own and sell ideas, but also the right to regulate their use, which can create a socially inefficient monopoly.[50] They agree that for efficiency reasons ideas should be protected and available for sale, just like any other commodity. They object, however, to the idea of an intellectual monopoly, arguing that monopoly is neither needed for, nor a necessary consequence of, innovation and that intellectual property is *not* necessary for innovation and growth. In fact it can hurt more than help. Boldrin and Levine suggest that, although the producers of a new product or service should have the right to benefit from its sale, they should not be able to appropriate the right of others to learn from the ideas embodied in that product (just as the producers of potatoes or French fries cannot monopolize the ideas embodied in their production).[51]

Table 7.1 Potential effects of intellectual property on poor people

Area of Concern	Potential Costs	Potential Benefits
Health	Increased prices of essential drugs.	Greater innovation of drugs of importance to developing countries.
Food and Agriculture	Loss of self-reliance for poor farmers. Increased privatization of genetic materials and biological resources.	Increased use of geographical indications to promote commercialization of products.
Traditional Knowledge, Folklore, and Culture	Piracy of traditional knowledge in the form of medicinal plants, agricultural products, and forest products.	Increased protection of and royalties for music industries. Provision of intellectual property registration systems to indigenous peoples.
Access to Knowledge and Innovation	Restrictions of fair use of digital information.	Support of knowledge generation and diffusion.
		Promotion of inflows of private capital, especially FDI.
	Increased licensing costs.	Increased protection of textile designs and emergent software industries.

Source: International Centre for Trade and Sustainable Development (2003).

[50] See also Shapiro (2004), who argues that excessive issuing of patents in the United States restricts competition and harms innovation.

[51] The authors are grateful to Jean-Jacques Dethier for highlighting a number of the points in this paragraph.

Intellectual property rights are designed to increase innovation by offering incentives to those who develop new techniques. As Wolf (2004) has noted, "given the role of innovation, intellectual property is not a marginal feature of the property rights regime of a modern market economy, but its core. It is the most important example of property that only a powerful state can protect. The reason that such action is needed is because ideas are public goods."[52] The problem for developing countries is that intellectual property rights are a legally sanctioned restraint of trade. They can lead to the monopolization of ideas and innovation by first comers and those with the most well-endowed research and legal systems. Not surprisingly, their application requires careful analysis of both benefits and costs on the part of the development community if they are not to lead to further inequities, and to ensure both growth and more equitable development, benefiting poor people and poor countries.

How this can best be done is a question to which answers greatly diverge. As noted by the International Centre for Trade and Sustainable Development (2003), "since the early 1990s, Intellectual Property (IP) policy has become one of the most economically and politically contentious issues in the international arena, whether in discussions on public health, food security, education, trade, industrial policy, traditional knowledge, biodiversity, bio-technology, the Internet, or the entertainment and media industries."[53] In each of these areas, consensus of the development community members on correct policy is often elusive.

As the above list of issue areas suggests, the range over which intellectual property protection can help or harm poor people is large. A summary of some of these areas, including potential costs and benefits, is presented in Table 7.1.

7.4.1 PATENTS

Patents are a central concern with regard to the impact of intellectual property protection on poor people, affecting three of the four areas described in Table 7.1: health, food and agriculture, and access to knowledge and innovation. As stated by Leach (2004), "The essential trade off in choosing the patent life is that a longer patent life raises the rate at which discoveries occur, but reduces the social benefits of each discovery."[54] The proponents of stronger patent protection in developing countries argue that this protection will promote domestic innovation as well as the flow of ideas through increased FDI and exports. There is not complete agreement on this matter, however. For example, Kash and Kingston (2001) argue that, in the case of complex technologies, patent protection can actually inhibit innovation. To some extent,

---

[52] Wolf (2004), p. 51.
[53] International Centre for Trade and Sustainable Development (2003), p. 1.
[54] Leach (2004), p. 175.

then, the ability of increased patent protection to deliver access to knowledge and innovation is uncertain.[55] One suggested reform of current intellectual property arrangements is to modify rules governing patents under the TRIPS agreement to allow for *patent ladders*, in which the minimum extent of patent protection varies according to the level of per capita income. Although designing such a system is not straightforward, this is a way to avoid what, in the case of environmental or labor standards, is called a "one-size-fits-all" approach to standardization of governance systems.

One key area regarding patent protection and the poor is in the field of pharmaceuticals and the extension of patent rights to developing countries as required by TRIPS. Although some argue that the extension of intellectual property rights may lead to more research on drugs to address developing country needs, the evidence on the short experience since this extension remains hotly contested. For many commentators, the relatively small size of the purchasing power in developing countries and the apparent lack of commercial interest by the pharmaceutical companies (rather than patent issues) explain the tiny portion of research devoted to diseases prevalent in tropical and other low-income developing countries. Whereas the average health expenditure per person in the United States is about US$7,160, in sub-Saharan Africa it averages US$75 per person and in rural areas it is even lower.[56] With the cost of bringing a new drug to market currently running at around US$1.3 billion, the incentives for the major drug companies are overwhelmingly skewed in favor of the primary problems facing rich countries.

Recent years have seen a number of highly significant efforts to boost investment in research and its application in developing countries. The Measles Initiative, started in 2001 with significant support from the World Health Organization (WHO), the Red Cross, and media entrepreneur Ted Turner has contributed to reductions of 78 percent in the global measles mortality rate. Vaccination campaigns over the past ten years are estimated to have saved 4.3 million people.[57] Despite these remarkable gains, the ongoing limited access of many people to the vaccine, which costs under $1 per dose and has been available since 1963, still results in 164,000 deaths per year, mostly among children under five in Africa and India. The Global Alliance for Vaccines and Immunizations (GAVI) is an impressive example of public–private partnership, bringing together donor and developing country governments, established and emerging vaccine manufacturers, non-governmental

---

[55] See Goldin, Stern, and Dethier (2003).

[56] In 2009 the average expenditure on health per person was US$148 in East Asia and the Pacific, US$182 in the Middle East and North Africa, US$386 in Europe and Central Asia, and US$543 in Latin America and the Caribbean. See World Bank (2011b).

[57] These figures relate to the period 2000 to 2008. See www.measlesinitiative.org

organizations (NGOs), research institutes, UNICEF, the World Health Organization, the World Bank, and the Bill & Melinda Gates Foundation. The devastating impact of malaria has received increasing attention over the last decade. While the number of new infections remains high (around 250 million each year), the number of malaria deaths have been reduced to less than one million since the Roll Back Malaria partnership was launched. Malaria remains an especially serious problem in Africa, where one in five childhood deaths is due to the effects of the disease.[58] Malaria alone is estimated to cost sub-Saharan Africa up to US$12 billion per year in lost productivity and is closely correlated with poverty. This is both because it is most rampant where the associated drugs, bed nets, and public health systems are least affordable, and because malaria itself undermines productivity, clogs public health systems, and undermines the economic and technical capacity of countries to cope with it as well as with other diseases such as HIV/AIDS.

With 2.6 million new infections each year (down from 3.1 million in 1999) and 1.8 million AIDS related deaths (lower than the 2.1 million deaths in 1999), international efforts to combat HIV/AIDS are finally starting to have some impact. The magnitude of the task, however, is daunting. Since the beginning of the epidemic, more than 60 million people have been infected and nearly 30 million have died from AIDS related illnesses. In 2009 there were 33.3 million new infections. Sub-Saharan Africa remains the worst affected region with two-thirds—22.5 million—of all new cases. While the HIV incidence rate has declined by more than 25 percent in sub-Saharan Africa since 2001, the number of African children orphaned by the disease has continued to rise reaching around 16.6 million in 2009.[59]

The key to combating HIV/AIDS is forthright national leadership, widespread public awareness campaigns, and intensive prevention efforts, including the availability of affordable drugs. The debate on intellectual property and incentives for innovation is being severely tested in this area. Work continues on vaccine development, and the number of people with access to anti-retrovirals has increased to 5.2 million—up from 700,000 in 2004.[60] Given the scale of the problem, this response remains inadequate.[61] Research and its application remains a critical stumbling block, with questions of affordability and availability of drugs and the timing of their development, as well as the availability of skilled professionals and health care systems for their application, posing key constraints. The case of the governments of Brazil, India, and South Africa challenging US patents on HIV/AIDS drugs,

[58] See http://www.who.int/features/factfiles/malaria/en/index.html
[59] See UNAIDS (2010a), (2010b), p. 114.
[60] 3.9 million of these people were located in sub-Saharan Africa (UNAIDS 2010a).
[61] Anti-retroviral therapy coverage in 2009 was estimated at 37 percent in sub-Saharan Africa, 50 percent in Latin America and the Caribbean, 31 percent in East, South, and South East Asia, 19 percent in Europe and Central Asia, and 11 percent in the Middle East and North Africa (UNAIDS 2010a).

which raised the costs of these drugs to AIDS patients in these countries, received widespread attention.

In 2001, WTO members gathered in Doha Qatar for the fourth Ministerial Conference of the WTO. At this meeting, pressure over the HIV/AIDS issue was intense. As a result, the members issued a special declaration allowing for measures "to protect public health." More specifically, the declaration reaffirmed certain "flexibilities," including the following statement: "Each member has the right to determine what constitutes a national emergency or other circumstances of extreme urgency, it being understood that public health crises, including those related to HIV/AIDS, tuberculosis, malaria and other epidemics, can represent a national emergency or other circumstances of extreme urgency." This was a victory for those in developing countries with a concern for AIDS and other public health issues. However, ten years after the Doha declaration UN agencies remain concerned about the long-term capacity of developing countries to maintain and scale up antiviral treatment through TRIPS flexibilities.[62]

There appear to be two approaches to dealing with the ongoing issue of intellectual property and public health, namely the Lanjouw (2006) proposal on regional declarations in patent applications and compulsory licensing under a permanent amendment to the TRIPS. Lanjouw (2006) proposed that developed country patent systems allow for patent enforcement only in one of two regions of the world: developed countries or developing countries.[63] In the case of what Lanjouw terms "global" diseases such as cancer or heart disease, developed country pharmaceutical companies would choose to ensure patent protection in developed countries where markets are significantly larger, allowing for less costly delivery of generic pharmaceutical to the developing world. In the case of "tropical" diseases such as malaria, the pharmaceutical companies would choose to ensure patent protection in the developing countries, hopefully spurring innovation. Thus, the trade-offs between innovation and low cost would hopefully break out in the desired fashion across "global" and "tropical" diseases.

This is an important proposal that has consequently received a good deal of attention. It may, however, not adequately cover some important diseases such as HIV/AIDS that have both "global" and "tropical" characteristics. There could indeed be cases where compulsory licensing proves to be required in order to adequately address public health crises. As noted, the 2001 Doha declaration on TRIPS reconfirmed certain "flexibilities" available to protect public health, which includes compulsory licensing. This declaration did not,

---

[62] See UNAIDS/UNDP/WHO (2011). UNAIDS (2011) is exploring ways in which developing countries can use TRIPS to increase access to HIV treatment.

[63] Presumably, this would be according to ongoing classification in the World Bank's World Development Indicators.

however, address the issue of the right of countries without domestic capacity to import non-patent pharmaceuticals.[64] A 2003 WTO decision on this issue allowed poor countries to import off-patent, generic drugs under specified conditions, and directed the WTO TRIPS Council to prepare an amendment based "where appropriate" on the decision.[65] An agreement regarding this amendment was reached in 2005 and this is due to be ratified by the end of 2011 (following postponements in 2007 and 2009).[66] It remains, however, both for supporting legislation in WTO member countries to be fully enacted and for the provisions of the amendment to be tested in practice. It has become clear that capacity building is necessary to support an effective use of the system by developing countries.[67]

7.4.2 TRADITIONAL KNOWLEDGE

To enhance development, it is important that intellectual property protection be extended to what Table 7.1 calls "traditional knowledge, folklore, and culture," or what Finger (2004) calls "poor people's knowledge." It is not only vital that intellectual property regimes allow developing countries to benefit from ideas developed in rich countries, but also that their own indigenous ideas are suitably protected. The key issue here, as expressed by Finger, is that of "enhancing the commercial value of poor people's knowledge in which there are no worries about this use being culturally offensive to members of the community or about this use undermining the traditional culture of the community."[68] Examples include the protection of the craft designs of the nearly 10 million artisans in India, Congolese wire toy designs, the recordings of the Senegal Musicians' Association, *Kente* designs in Ghana, and many, many others. By enhancing the returns on these types of knowledge, intellectual property protection could help poor communities. Individual country governments can help in this process by following the lead of India in constructing Traditional Knowledge Digital Libraries (TKDL) containing formal inventories of all cultural property its citizens might rightfully exploit in the future.[69]

The crowding out of local ideas and culture by global brands—such as McDonalds, Nike, and Coke—is of particular concern to many who worry

---

[64] This issue arises because Article 31(f) of TRIPS limits the use of pharmaceuticals produced under compulsory licenses to the *domestic* markets of producing countries.

[65] See Matthews (2004, 2006).

[66] See WTO (2011).

[67] See Adusei (2011).

[68] Finger (2004), p. 3.

[69] The Indian TKDL contains 24 million pages and will be available to patent offices in the United States, the European Union, and Japan. Moahi (2007) refers to it as a "benchmark" for other countries to follow in order to prevent theft of their cultural patrimony. See also Sahai (2003) and Singh (2007).

that this undermines local cultures and products. The appeal of many global products transcends national borders and ideologies. To the extent that they crowd out consumption of traditional or local products or are seen as a symbol of US or "Western" economic and cultural domination, they have become rallying points for anti-globalization protests.[70] This presents some cause for concern. As expressed by Sen (1999), "Equity in cultural as well as economic opportunities can be profoundly important in a globalizing world."[71] However, Sen concludes that "The one solution that is *not* available is that of stopping globalization."[72] Rather, what is required is that people, including poor people, be empowered enough to take part in social decisions about cultural issues. In the case of poor people, deprivations of access, information, participation, and education make this very difficult. Sen casts this issue in terms of "human rights in the broadest sense."[73]

7.4.3 POLICIES ON RESEARCH AND DEVELOPMENT

Throughout the second and third phases of globalization discussed in Chapter 1, there was a strong tendency on the part of multinational enterprises (MNEs) to conduct R&D in their home bases. The only small role for R&D in developing countries was in product adaptation. In recent years, this historical pattern has begun to change. One reason for this is the information and communication (ICT) developments that took place in the third phase of globalization, also discussed in Chapter 1. A second reason is the rise of emerging markets and the need to better tailor products to these markets. A third reason is that talent and creativity for effective R&D is no longer confined to the traditional MNE home bases: the United States, Western Europe, and Japan. To name just two countries, China and India have emerged as sources of scientific and engineering talent.[74] MNEs that want to tap into this talent can either recruit it by bringing it to their home bases and other R&D sites or begin to relocate their R&D. Many MNEs have chosen to relocate some aspects of their R&D.

From an economic perspective, relocating R&D to these new sources of scientific and engineering talent can make a great deal of sense. As reported by

---

[70] On concerns over cultural homogenization, see Barber (1996). Klein (2000) has become core reading for those opposing globalization, and Wolf (2004) marshal many of the economic arguments for the proponents of globalization. Held and McGrew (2007) provide a balanced overview of the arguments for and against globalization and attempt to move beyond this divide. Chua (2003) raises concerns about globalization in the context of what she terms "market-dominant minorities." See also, for example, Mander and Goldsmith (1996) and Helleiner and Pickel (2005) on more "market-dominant minorities."

[71] Sen (1999), p. 241.
[72] Ibid., p. 240 (emphasis added).
[73] Ibid., p. 242.
[74] See, for example, Yusuf, Nabeshima, and Perkins (2006).

Khurana (2006), "both China and India offer dramatic cost advantages of 30–60 percent, even after accounting for training and coordination costs."[75] These realities have forced MNEs to rethink the role of R&D in their global production networks (GPNs), choosing to locate specific kinds of R&D outside of the home base and developing *regional R&D facilities* that they link together in coordinated networks. If a trend can be identified, it is for basic research (the R in R&D) to remain in the home base, with more applied research (the D in R&D) moving abroad.

Dicken (2007, chapter 5) noted that the R&D element that is most likely to be dispersed throughout MNEs GPNs is the *support laboratory*. The purpose of this R&D unit is to "adapt parent company technology to the local market and to provide technical backup."[76] There is a tendency to locate these in association with production facilities. Less often, but increasingly, MNEs chose to set up the aforementioned regional R&D laboratories with more responsibilities than support laboratories, including a focus on new product development. Asia is a common location for these laboratories.[77]

The significance of these changes is that the global production of ideas via innovation is beginning to shift to the developing world. All indications are that this trend will grow in importance. One type of innovation taking place in some developing countries with significance to poor people is *frugal innovation*. Frugal innovation is one aspect of adapting products to make them more appropriate for lower-income consumers.[78] It involves reducing costs and profit margins significantly in an effort to reach a broader customer base. While the archetype of frugal innovation is Tata Motors Nano car, which sells for just over US$2000, there are many other examples, including water filters, tiny refrigerators, and inexpensive medical devices. The importance of frugal innovation is that it can help to support poor people's access to basic goods and services. As such, it is a welcome trend. It is part of the adaptation of ideas to developing country contexts that is so important.

---

[75] Khurana (2006), p. 50.

[76] Dicken (2007), p. 144.

[77] *The Economist* (2010d) wrote that "the world's biggest multinational are becoming increasingly happy to do their research and development in emerging markets. Companies in the *Fortune* 500 list have 98 R&D facilities in China and 63 in India. Some have more than one" (p. 4).

[78] See, for example, Prahalad and Hart (2002) and Prahalad and Mashelkar (2010). *The Economist* of April 15, 2010, carried a special report on innovation in emerging markets which included a useful introduction to some of the dimensions of frugal innovation.

7.5 **Ideas about the role of states, markets, and institutions**

How governments and societies organize themselves and how they absorb ideas and allow their citizens and firms to operate is a key determinant of growth and poverty reduction. Much of the intellectual property debate is about the private appropriation of ideas, and hence is vital in considering the role of ideas embodied in technologies and processes that are developed and adopted by private firms and individuals. Prior to the 1990s, the very idea of a private market based economic system was foreign to many countries and firms. Through the absorption and adaptation of ideas, new economic systems have evolved, which in turn, over time, fundamentally change the way in which ideas are generated, transmitted, and absorbed.

The development community's understanding of the most effective way to achieve development objectives has evolved over time with the accumulation of evidence and experience. Approaches that once appeared to be both correct and obvious have been shown not to work by experience and closer analysis. In the same way, our current ideas will no doubt give way to others as experience accumulates and thinking evolves. This surely reminds us to beware of simplistic solutions or "silver bullets" in development thinking. Perhaps the most important questions on which our understanding has deepened over the past decades are: What are the respective roles of governments and markets in spurring development? How do institutions fit into the picture? At the risk of oversimplification, we can identify at least three major phases in the evolution of our answers to these questions.

In practice, we recognize that there is a continuum of approaches, both in developed and in developing countries, and that the phases described here do not match precisely the evolution of thinking in any particular region. Instead, the discussion of these phases is intended to capture the broad shifts in the thinking of the development community and development practitioners. It is also the case that successful countries throughout this post-World War II period have seen both state and market play positive roles. With those caveats, this broad brush picture can nevertheless provide a useful context for a discussion of development assistance by suggesting where that assistance is most likely to be effective.

The first of these phases, dating back the 1950s and 1960s, reflected a period of great confidence on the part of the development community. Development practitioners and thinkers trusted government both for its intentions and for its ability to make economic progress happen, in both the richer and the poorer countries. Development thinking focused on market failures, which were especially prevalent in developing countries and seemed to provide a strong rationale for state intervention. The private sector was thought to be too uncoordinated, too poorly developed, and too focused on private interests to allow it to serve as the locomotive for growth. In Africa, newly independent countries searched for a postcolonial model of development and a strengthened leadership role for the national state. In many countries around the world, the confidence in government was reflected in the heavy role of central planning and in the relatively closed (import substitution) trade policy.[79]

This state-led approach had some initial development successes. Leading economies of Latin America, where state economic management did not completely crowd out the private sector, grew rapidly for decades under the *import substitution model*. And even in some "tiger economies" of East Asia, industry managed to grow and become more productive behind high trade barriers, thanks to otherwise good economic management. Nevertheless, the costs of state economic control became clearer over time. State planners were not omniscient: they could not possibly acquire all the information needed to make decisions that reflected both efficiency considerations and people's differing preferences.

Worse, governments revealed themselves to be collections of interests rather than disinterested and benevolent "social planners." Even had they been effective in their role as social planners, government officials would not have been able to create the entrepreneurial dynamism essential for sustained development and change. Behind protective barriers, firms in many countries (India and Mexico, to name just two) became less efficient as they focused on obtaining government favors rather than improving productivity. Finally,

Table 7.2 Idea changes in development thinking

Dimension	State-Led Approach	Pro-Market Approach
Government	Plays a central role; acts as the driving force behind development.	Plays a central role, but acts as the main obstacle to development.
Accumulation	Is central to development process; coordination and scale problems require government involvement.	Is central to development process; private sector investment is the key.
Trade and Integration	Has no particular advantage beyond the import of capital goods and the purchase of necessary inputs.	Exports bring dynamic advantages; import competition is necessary for disciplining domestic producers.
Foreign Capital	FDI is to be avoided, but government borrowing is acceptable, preferably from foreign sources.	Government borrowing is to be avoided, but FDI is encouraged.
Development Assistance	Provide project-based lending of foreign exchange and resources to governments.	Quick disbursing; policy-based lending to establish conditions for FDI and domestic investment.

Source: Lindauer and Pritchett (2002).

[79] The import substitution idea is skilfully reviewed by Bruton (1998).

fiscal and macro instability rose with the oil price shocks of the 1970s and early 1980s, contributing to the debt crisis and revealing the weaknesses in the statist model.

As a consequence of the disappointing results of the state-led approach, the 1980s and early 1990s saw a strong reaction that stressed the primacy of markets in development.[80] This second phase in thinking was a necessary corrective in many ways: it refocused attention on production efficiency and market signals, and it inspired the move to lower trade barriers as a way to spur productivity. Macro stability and balanced fiscal accounts were seen as fundamental building blocks for development and became early priorities for reform. This period saw substantial improvements in both macroeconomic stability and openness to trade and financial and other flows through much of the developing world. This important change in development thinking was summarized by Lindauer and Pritchett (2002) along the dimensions of Table 7.2. These include the role of government, encouragement of savings, trade and integration, foreign capital, and development assistance. Development policy changed in each of these dimensions to reflect new thinking.

By the mid-1990s, it became widely recognized that this purely "pro-market" school of development thinking failed to address some key points. Once countries began to achieve macro stability and greater openness to trade, it became clear that these elements were *necessary* but *not sufficient* for growth and poverty reduction. In particular, the free market view tended to neglect the institutional foundations of effective private markets. The importance of institutions reflected a third wave of thinking underscored by major shifts: the economic decline in the countries of the former Soviet Union; the continued growth in China, a country that moved forward with market-oriented reforms without excessive disruption of institutional foundations; and, later in the 1990s, the financial crisis in East Asia, to which institutional weaknesses contributed heavily. Furthermore, even as it performed a useful service by spotlighting government failure, the free market reaction had minimized very real problems of market failure that are prevalent in the developing world. As a result, growth performance fell short of expectations in many parts of the developing world.

Recent years have seen a greater recognition in the policy debate of the complementarities between markets and governments. Clearly, experience shows that the private market economy must be the engine of growth; but it shows also that a vibrant private sector depends on properly functioning state institutions to build a good investment climate and deliver basic services competently.

---

[80] Wolf (2004) is a modern advocate of this point of view.

This view of complementarities draws heavily on what we have learned from the more successful cases of income growth, such as East Asia and Chile. It also draws on learning from the transition process in the former Soviet Union, where a lack of institutional development combined with excessively optimistic expectations led to disappointing development outcomes and demonstrated clearly the importance of a sound state in providing the environment for growth. It leads to a pragmatic approach that Santiso (2006) refers to as the "political economy of the possible."

We have also learned more about the diversity of approaches among countries that have been effective in accelerating growth and reducing poverty.

- Evidence from past successes and failures suggests strongly that neither the more statist approach of the 1950s and 1960s nor the more minimal government, free market approach that dominated policy debate in the 1980s and early 1990s will achieve these goals.

- Effective approaches will be led by the private sector, but with effective government to provide the governance framework as well as the physical infrastructure and human capital investments necessary for growth and poverty reduction. In fact, to set state and market against each other is to miss the central question: How can they best complement each other to promote growth and reduce poverty?

- A public–private development partnership is essential, especially in the area of health and education. Institutional development has too often been neglected in the development policy debate, but strong institutions are now recognized to be essential to sustained poverty reduction.

The intermingling of ideas evidenced over the past decade has meant that even the more orthodox economic leaders are seeking to go beyond the standard ideas, such as what came to be known as the *Washington Consensus*.[81] In certain dimensions, such as capital account liberalization and privatization, there is a widening appreciation of the need for a differentiated approach—one that takes account of vulnerabilities, not least in institutional development.[82] The importance of institutions and governance, as Goldin and Reinert (2007) emphasize, has increasingly been seen as a vital element of development. Key elements of the political economy of reform include: (1) good governance and better institutions; (2) empowerment and democratic representation; (3) ownership of the development agenda; (4) improved infrastructure, health, and education; and (5) gender equality including voice and rights for women. Putting these factors together to spur

---

[81] See Williamson (1990, 2009), often cited as the author of the Washington Consensus.
[82] See, for example, Stiglitz (2000, 2010) and Goldin and Vogel (2010).

sustained growth is a challenge: it requires proper sequencing and selection of reforms, as well as consistency over time, neither of which is easy to achieve.

Although some sequencing problems are easy to identify, finding the best sequence of steps to sustain growth in a particular country is a great challenge, and it remains an area where our knowledge needs to expand. Rapid growth episodes of a few years or a decade are not uncommon. For example, countries that successfully emerge from civil war often experience relatively rapid economic rebounds for several years.[83] What has been much less common is sustained rapid growth over a period of decades, which is what is necessary to eliminate absolute poverty.[84] The need for consistency underlines the importance of attaining sustained productivity growth. Only a portion of growth is driven by increases in physical and human capital intensity of production, which can be difficult to sustain over long periods. Countries also need rapid growth in productivity.

Development thinking evolves continually, and this evolution has accelerated over the past 50 years.[85] In response to the lessons of experience and analysis, development practitioners have adapted their approaches to promoting development, and even the goals of development work. We have learned that strategies that seemed obvious to many at some point—for example, both the heavily statist and minimal government free market approaches—have had to be reconsidered and changed as part of a continuous learning process. This is one reason why a careful and measured look at experience is so important and why the extent of openness to the flow of ideas is vital for growth.

7.6 **Global public goods**

Global action is a vital complement to national and local level policies. One important area of action is in the provision of global public goods. Public goods have benefits that are *non-excludable* and consumption that is *non-rival*. These types of goods (for example, traffic safety) may be underprovided by market systems. Global public goods have benefits that extend across all countries.[86]

---

[83] See Collier and Gunning (1995).

[84] See Pritchett (2000) and Easterly (2001) for a discussion of why this is difficult to achieve. Strategies for achieving sustainable growth have been advanced by the Commission on Growth and Development (2008).

[85] See Goldin, Stern, and Dethier (2003) and Stern, Dethier, and Rogers (2004) for further discussion.

[86] See Kaul, Grunberg, and Stern (1999) and Kaul et al. (2003). The latter authors advocate a very general definition of global public goods: "Global public goods are goods with benefits that extend to all countries, people, and generations" (p. 23).

Demand for global public goods has grown rapidly with globalization, but supply is constrained by the difficulty of putting in place coordinating mechanisms to pay for the benefits or recoup costs. At international conferences held in Monterrey and Johannesburg, global leaders established firm poverty reduction targets and highlighted the need for a clear strategy to strengthen the provision of global public goods. In five areas of particular interest, concerted international action can yield very large benefits across borders and contribute to individual country poverty reduction.

- *Fighting Infectious and Communicable Diseases.* As indicated above, infectious diseases in developing countries kill millions of people, exacerbating poverty and severely disrupting economic life. The benefits to individuals of advances in this area are vast and go beyond any attempt at measurement. These benefits, in terms of enhancing the quality of life, reducing lost workdays, and raising productivity are widely shared, even in countries or communities where other interventions or investments are ineffective. Infectious diseases are carried more and more frequently across borders through trade and travel, so fighting them is increasingly becoming a direct need for all countries.

- *Improving the Global Environment.* Our water, our land, our atmosphere, our forests, and our biodiversity are vital assets, with potentially catastrophic losses if international protective action is inadequate. Tropical countries in particular are vulnerable to projected climate change and environmental degradation, including loss in food production resulting from global warming, and an expanding range of tropical diseases. Global action must be complemented by environmental policies on national and local levels. Rich countries have a special contribution to make here because they dominate energy use and because they are the largest consumers for most natural resources and they generate the most pollutants. The demographic and growing economic weight of developing countries—together with their share of environmental resources and challenges—means that their participation in global compacts on the environment is essential (see Goldin and Winters 1995).

- *Promoting Orderly Cross-Border Movement of Goods and Services.* The fall in international transportation and communication costs has led to a rapid growth in cross-border trade in goods and services. International markets provide tremendous opportunity to developing countries to expand trade flows, provided they have market access. The WTO is dedicated to removing barriers to trade but it faces an uphill battle against protectionist interests in both developed and developing countries.

- *Encouraging Global Financial Stability.* As discussed in Chapter 4, the integration of global capital markets greatly increased the volume of international private capital flows. This has helped support a rapid expansion of economic activity in developing countries, but it has also brought heightened vulnerability to financial shocks and market contagion, the social burden of which often falls most sharply on the urban poor. The point is underlined by the 2008–2010 financial crisis, which reflects new kinds of systemic risk and the failure of global governance and institutions to keep pace with the increasing integration, technological innovations, and complexities that characterize the "current tidal wave of globalisation" (see Goldin and Vogel 2010). In particular, governance gaps within and between global, national institutions, inadequate regulation of financial markets and the corporate sector, the need for greater competition, issues of regulatory capture, and massive increases in government spending all need to be addressed within the context of "more transformative global action."[87]

- *Creating and Disseminating Knowledge on Development Issues.* Multilateral development agencies must play a lead role in research on development and in disseminating the lessons of development experience. Initiatives such as the Development Gateway, which provides local to global connectivity, have the ability to empower local communities, build knowledge networks, and serve citizenry more effectively through enhanced and low-cost information.[88] Such gains through disseminating knowledge are most effective when knowledge is a public good accessible to all.

The challenge to all of the above pressing priorities is one of cooperation.[89] As noted by Kaul, Grunberg, and Stern (1999), "billions of people do not negotiate directly with each other. In many instances their governments do it on their behalf, reducing the number of negotiating partners to about 185—still an unwieldy group for creating cooperative arrangements."[90] Unwieldy though this process may be, fulfilling the important promise of the global public goods idea requires the international community to forge ahead with these efforts.

7.7 **Summary**

To ignore the development and flow of ideas as a component of economic globalization is to miss a central feature of the globalization process, a feature that has important implications for poverty alleviation. Poverty responds to

---

[87] Goldin and Vogel (2010), p. 9.
[88] See www.developmentgateway.org
[89] The problem of cooperation is discussed by Martin (1999).
[90] Kaul, Grunberg, and Stern (1999), p. 15.

effective development, and effective development is, in large measure, the deployment of appropriate ideas in appropriate ways. As we have repeatedly emphasized here, there is no single model of how this can be done. Rather, effective development from the point of view of ideas is largely about tailoring existing, global knowledge to evolving local circumstances in ways that directly and indirectly benefit poor people.

Important connections exist among the global flows of ideas and the other globalization elements considered in this book: trade, capital flows especially in the form of foreign investment, aid, and migration. Trade, as we have shown in Chapter 3, embodies ideas reflected in technologies and processes. The benefits of foreign investment involve both basic and deep learning. These, in turn, require threshold levels of skills and education. In the case of migration, international movements of labor and experts facilitate the less formal processes of knowledge transfer. The effective deployment of ideas is therefore facilitated by the global movements of goods, services, capital, and people.

Ideas for development are always emerging in processes of formation and reformation. If one looks hard enough, however, there is a middle ground among past ideological divisions in development thinking. For example, there is now a better appreciation than in the past of the roles of institutions, history, the public sector, and human welfare in development processes and policy.[91] The emerging middle ground does not offer any simple, one-size-fits-all prescriptions. Indeed, in some ways, we have arrived at a stage in which "we know that we do not know,"[92] and there is some measure of ironic comfort in this. It provides the intellectual room for multiple, successful routes to development that involve large measures of local learning and experimentation.

One important theme to emerge from this chapter is the theme of knowledge management. There is a fundamental tension here that remains largely unresolved from a policy perspective. As we emphasized, knowledge is a global public good that has great potential to help the poor. However, there has been a growing tendency, supported by WTO agreements, to advance the privatization of knowledge. In some respects, this can help the poor. In other respects, this is cause for alarm.

This chapter has sought to highlight the central role of learning and ideas in development. Policy makers and practitioners require opportunities to understand what works and what does not, based on evidence and on analysis that draws on the widest possible data, experience, and skills. By reducing the constraints posed by information, education, language, and access, policy makers at the global, national, and local levels can make a significant contribution to improving the chances that globalization will offer more opportunities for growth and poverty reduction.

---

[91] See Rodrik (2007).   [92] Hoff and Stiglitz (2001), p. 428.

8   Toward a policy agenda

Globalization is held out by competing groups as both the only means by which global poverty can be reduced and as the very cause of that poverty. Neither of these contrasting claims is helpful. First, they fail to adequately distinguish among the many aspects of globalization discussed in previous chapters. Second, they fail to recognize that most dimensions of globalization have both positive and negative potential for eliminating poverty. Third, they fail to adequately address the role of policy in influencing outcomes.

In this book, we have brought together the key flows that underpin economic globalization, namely trade, finance, aid, migration, and ideas. In examining the links between poverty reduction and these flows, we have sought to clarify whether and how economic globalization can work for poor people. In this chapter, we consider the potential role for *policy* in making possible that economic globalization helps poor people. These policies address the globalization processes discussed in previous chapters, as well as larger issues of the global commons discussed in Chapter 2. These global commons issues include climate change, fisheries, water resources, food security, pandemic threats, biodiversity, and human security.

8.1 Globalization for poor people?

To the question "Can globalization work for poor people?" our answer is "Yes." If we rephrase this question as "Does globalization work for poor people?" we need to modify the answer to "Maybe." We have shown that globalization can help poor people, but this potential is *far from automatic*. Whether globalization works for poor people depends crucially on the policies that accompany it. In our view, these policies are of utmost importance in helping to determine whether globalization helps or hurts poor people. Further, however, increased connectedness or interdependency is a key factor to consider in making globalization work for development. Developing resilience to what Goldin and Vogel (2010) and others have termed "systemic risk" will be increasingly important to ensure that globalization helps poor people. These systemic risks can be economic in nature as in the case of financial crises discussed in Chapter 4, but they can also arise in the areas of health (e.g.

pandemics) or environment (e.g. climate change) and a set of related issues concerning the global commons.

Given all of these concerns, the relevant policy agenda is large. While this can be daunting, it is important to remember that progress in any area is helpful in and of itself. Not being able to do everything should not be an excuse to do nothing! While they do not constitute a panacea, the policies recommended here can contribute to an accumulation of "small wins" that make a significant difference over time.[1]

We do not claim that our policy suggestions are original. They draw on the sources referenced and are "in the air" at conferences or in conversations among development practitioners and international economists. Our value added is in bringing together a broad range of policy suggestions in one place and linking them to the dimensions of globalization and poverty reduction considered in this book.

8.1.1 LEVELS OF POLICY ENACTMENT

Policies can be enacted at four levels: global, regional, national, and local or community. Policies should not be considered as only part of global and national agendas that ordinary people in both developing and developed countries cannot affect. Examples of policies in favor of a pro-poor globalization are presented in Table 8.1, which illustrate the multiple levels at which policies are made.

For example, if developed countries commit to reducing their agricultural subsidies as part of multilateral trade negotiations under the WTO, they engage in a global policy change. If members of a regional trade agreement issue temporary visas to guest workers among member countries, they effect a regional policy change. If a country engages in an effort to ensure universal primary education, it exercises national policy making. Finally, if a firm or individuals in a local community seek to reduce their pollution, or to increase the incentives for children to attend school, they are making local policies that will contribute over time to investment and growth. All of these policy levels are potentially important in influencing globalization processes in ways that might be beneficial to poor people. The room for action, therefore, is larger than is often appreciated.[2]

---

[1] On small wins in the social sciences, see Weick (1984). Weick noted that "it seems useful to consider the possibility that social problems seldom get solved because people define these problems in ways that overwhelm their ability to do anything about them. Changing the scale of a problem can change the quality of resources that are directed at it. Calling a situation a mere problem that necessitates a small win moderates arousal, improves diagnosis, preserves gains, and encourages innovation. Calling a situation a serious problem that necessitates a larger win may be when the problem starts" (p. 48).

[2] On the local policy perspective in globalization and development, see for example, Boisier (2005).

Table 8.1. Examples of policies affecting globalization processes and outcomes

	Policy Levels			
Globalization Dimension	Global	Regional	National	Local or Community
Trade	Multilateral trade agreements	Regional trade agreements	Trade-related capacity building	Business best practice centers
Capital Flows	A plurilateral investment agreement[a]	Regional investment agreements	Sequenced liberalization of various components of the capital account	Development of effective banking systems and other forms of financial intermediation
Foreign Aid	Increased multilateral and bilateral foreign aid disbursements	Regional capacity building programs	Ensuring that policies benefit poor people, donors are coordinated, and corruption eliminated	Improved needs assessment, impact evaluation and service delivery
Migration	A multilateral agreement on migration A GATS "Mode-4" visa program[b]	Mobility of labor provisions in common markets	Changes in national visa and citizenship requirements, fair treatment of foreigners	Refugee support Savings mobilization for increased remittances
Ideas	Increased technology transfer to developing countries	Increasing the research capacity of regional development institutions	Increased government funding of basic research, openness to ideas	Inventories of traditional knowledge
Other	Multilateral efforts to fight the spread of infectious diseases	Regional infrastructure investment coordination	Universal primary and secondary education	Municipal water supply and sewerage upgrades

[a] "Plurilateral" in the terminology of the WTO implies that members are free not to take on the negotiated commitments.
[b] "Mode-4" in the terminology of the WTO refers to the provision of services through the temporary movement of natural persons.
Source: Authors.

Policy making at the global, regional, national, and local or community levels interacts in significant ways. For example, developing an effective banking regulatory system at the national level could support increased liberalization of trade in financial services at the multilateral or global level. National educational advancements can support learning from foreign direct investment, which in turn can be supported by regional investment agreements. And when certain rich countries refuse to make concessions on global trade talks, saying that farmers at the local level will protest, they are undermining the opportunities for poor people in local communities of poor countries. Because the various levels of policy making interact, it is often important to pay attention to the timing and sequencing of policy changes. In some cases, such as universal primary education, the fight against infectious diseases, and actions to reduce greenhouse gas emissions, "timing" comes down to making dramatic changes as quickly as possible.[3]

8.1.2 GLOBALIZATION AND POLICY FORMATION

Many people believe that globalization has significantly eroded the abilities of countries and citizens to form national and local policies. We believe this is an unhelpful characterization. Although it is true that globalization does place some new and significant restrictions on policy, it also creates new opportunities and spaces for policy engagement. Globalization changes the ways policies at various levels can be deployed. It poses constraints but also presents opportunities. Policy still matters for poverty alleviation. National governments can still tax and then spend revenues, and the effectiveness with which they do so matters a great deal to the poor people of the world.[4] Indeed, some international economists rightly view effective government expenditures as a *prerequisite* for global integration.[5]

The diversity of experience (for both countries and individuals) in addressing globalization constraints and opportunities points to the need to focus on the specific questions of how globalization can be made to work for poor people. The fact that these experiences are indeed diverse shows that we need to focus on how to make globalization work better than it often does for marginalized individuals and communities. We also need to focus on how to better insulate these individuals from different types of systemic risk, whether economic, health oriented, or environmental.

We believe that policies outlined here help to determine the ways in which globalization processes affect poor people. In the remainder of this chapter, we will be primarily focused at the global level. However, we want to emphasize that, because poor people live in countries, regions, and localities, policies at all these levels can have a significant impact. The role of national policies is particularly vital. How governments tax and spend; what they do about corruption; and how they encourage private investment and provide opportunities for individuals to get educated, be healthy, and participate in the choices affecting their lives make an enormous difference to poor people.

[3] This would be the case for what Reinert (2011) calls "basic goods," for example. On the issue of basic services (a particular type of basic good), see Devarajan and Reinikka (2004) and Nazmul and Devarajan (2006).

[4] For the case of the OECD countries, for example, see chapter 12 of Wolf (2004). For the case of oil-rich developing countries, see Devarajan, Le, and Raballand (2010).

[5] This point is made by Rodrik (1998), for example. Rodrik stated that "The scope of government has been larger, not smaller, in economies taking greater advantage of world markets" and suggests that "the reasons have to do with the provision of social insurance" (p. 1028).

We will proceed by taking up each of our economic globalization dimensions and identifying policy changes associated with them. These policy recommendations are summarized in the form of a global policy checklist in Table 8.2.

8.2 **Trade: Proposed policy changes**

The first dimension of globalization considered in this book is international trade, the exchange of goods and services among the countries of the world economy. The policy changes we propose for international trade fall into the following areas:

- market access
- trade-related capacity building
- arms trade
- forced labor

We consider each in turn.

8.2.1 MARKET ACCESS

An urgent policy change that would make the international trade dimension of economic globalization friendlier to poor people is the *substantial* increase in market access for goods and services from the developing countries. This is particularly, but not exclusively, important for labor-intensive manufactured goods, including processed food products, agricultural products, and services.

There needs to be a *significant* reduction in the agricultural subsidies of the developed countries. As we noted in Chapter 3, producer-support payments alone in agriculture are approximately the same as foreign aid. Agricultural subsidies are often justified in terms of various external benefits to agricultural production.[6] Such arguments are spurious for at least three reasons. First, nearly all economic activity has external benefits of one kind or another. Second, to the degree that agriculture does have these external benefits, they are present in *all countries*, not just the rich countries. Subsidies to support agriculture in the rich world undermine the most important external benefit of agriculture in developing countries: poverty alleviation. Third, agriculture in developed countries also generates external costs in the form of pesticide and fertilizer run-off into watersheds. Consequently, as noted by Peterson

[6] The term generally employed to describe the external benefits of agricultural production is *multifunctionality*. See, for example, Jules (2003).

Table 8.2 A global policy checklist

Globalization Dimension	Policy Area	Description
Trade	Market access	A sharp increase in market access for labor-intensive goods and services from developing countries, including the commitment to a rapid reduction in tariff escalation and agricultural subsidies in the rich countries of the world.
Trade	Trade-related capacity building	The continued promotion of trade-related capacity building for low-income countries that is explicitly linked to increases in market access. This capacity building needs to address meeting WTO commitments, full WTO representation, the effective negotiation of regional agreements, and supply side constraints.
Trade	Arms trade	The adoption of a multilateral Arms Trade Treaty to create legally binding arms controls and ensure that all governments control the arms trade according to the same internationals standards, which restrict exports to countries with significant records of human rights abuses, to criminal organizations, and to conflict zones.
Trade	Forced labor	The extension of the World Trade Organization's general exception of commitments for the case of prison labor (Article XXe) to all forms of forced labor.
Finance	Heterodox capital account reform	The maintenance of a heterodox approach to capital account reform in the absence of consensus on best practice. There should not be a one-size-fits-all approach to capital account liberalization, and allowance must be made for market friendly capital controls.
Finance	Macro-prudential policies to reduce systemic risk	Continued strengthening of the Basel III standards, particularly the requirements for Tier I and Tier II bank capital.
Finance	Standards for multinational enterprises	The development of norms for corporate social responsibility and the application of standards that encourage best practice by multinational enterprises such as has been the case with the OECD Guidelines. The current review of these guidelines needs to consider an enhanced role of National Contact Points.
Foreign Aid	Meeting commitments on aid flows	The OECD countries need to implement their commitments and increase foreign aid in real, per capita terms.
Foreign Aid	Untying aid	Decoupling aid commitments from requirements to purchase consultancy or other goods or services from donor countries and end the blurring of aid and military/strategic flows.
Foreign Aid	Harmonization and alignment	The coordination and harmonization of aid flows with those of other donor countries, and the alignment of these with recipient governments' own priorities.
Foreign Aid	Evaluation and knowledge sharing	Including impact evaluation in projects and transparency in sharing results in order to ensure that lessons of development are widely shared.
Foreign Aid	Debt relief	Maintaining debt relief efforts to ensure that all developing countries that have the necessary commitments to sustainable policies benefit, with this debt relief funded by additional financial commitments from the rich countries.
Migration	Multilateral coordination of migration policy	Reform and harmonization of the global migration system on a multilateral basis to protect migrants' rights and

		improve efficiency and security. Particular areas of concern include dual citizenship and voting rights, low skill migration programs, pension portability, managing remittances, and the enforcement of human, health and safety, and other rights for migrants.
Migration	Temporary movement of persons	The establishment of a multilateral system of identifying individuals seeking temporary movement, providing national security clearance to them, and granting multi-entry visas to them under the WTO General Agreement on Trade in Services.
Migration	Brain drain	The adoption and expansion of measures by destination countries to limit the recruitment of highly skilled professionals from countries facing shortages in these areas, particularly those facing public health emergencies. Ensuring greater coherence between aid and migration policies by increasing incentives to retain vital skills.
Migration	Brain waste and diaspora	Increasing the matching of skilled personal with opportunities by increasing the rights of employment. The promotion of diaspora networks and encouragement of return investment, technology transfer, and brain circulation.
Migration	Remittances	Increase competition in remittance services, ending monopolies, and encourage entry into money transfer systems that facilitate migrants' use of officially recorded channels, including through electronic smart cards and other technologies.
Migration	Research and data	Increased funding for research and data collection, with view to understanding costs and benefits of migration and enhancing development impacts.
Ideas	Knowledge management	Support countries' efforts to develop coherent knowledge strategies, focused on acquisition, absorption, and communication of ideas and information. Use of knowledge assessment methodologies can help identify weaknesses across key dimensions, including hardware (telecommunications, infrastructure) and software (education, web access, media access, etc).
Ideas	Intellectual property harmonization	Evaluation of the costs and benefits to developing countries of the current intellectual property negotiations in the TRIPS and to build common agreement to ensure that intellectual property rules support access for developing countries to key health and other technologies.
Ideas	Access to medicines	The swift and permanent establishment of the right of countries without pharmaceutical manufacturing capacity to access generic pharmaceuticals in order to fight AIDS, tuberculosis, and malaria. This would include a fast-track procedure for national health emergencies that will not be subject to unilateral action by developed countries.
Ideas	Increased technology transfer to developing countries	The extension of developed country TRIPS commitments on technology transfer to a larger number of developing countries and an honoring of this commitment through a variety of specific means.
Global Commons	Insurance for climate change related risks	The study of potential insurance schemes for climate related risks, possibly including multiple tiers of climate change related risk insurance. The principle of better

(*Continued*)

Table 8.2 Continued

Globalization Dimension	Policy Area	Description
		preparing the most vulnerable to foreseeable risks needs to be established and institutionalized.
Global Commons	Combating anti-microbial resistance	An increased commitment to the WHO's Directly Observed Treatment Short course (DOTS) to prevent anti-microbial resistance in tuberculosis and an increased commitment to addressing other evolving AMR risks such as in the cases of malaria and staph infections.
Global Commons	Agricultural development for food security	The inclusion of agro-ecology science in developing attempts to sustain agricultural yields in the face of increased global population as a complement to biotechnology, and the resistance to further "agro-investment" in Africa.
Global Commons	Enhancing human security	The recognition that illicit trade and conflict trade can pose threats to human security and need to be addressed through international law enforcement and peacekeeping efforts.

Source: authors.

(2009), "the concept of multifunctionality fails as a justification for farm subsidies."[7]

What do we mean by "substantial" and "significant?" Any improvement in market access and reduction in agricultural subsidies is a step in the right direction. Given the scale of existing distortions and their negative impacts on poor people, however, bold actions are needed. We make three recommendations:

- First, there should be immediate and full market access for the low-income countries.

- Second, there should be the elimination of all tariff peaks and tariff escalation for the developing countries as a whole.

- Third, the *total* agricultural protection (*both* producer-support payments *and* market price support) of the high-income countries should be reduced to the level of total foreign aid contributions.

These changes would help to ensure that the trade dimension of globalization better helps poor people. In rich countries, agricultural protection costs the average consumer around US$1,000 per year through increased prices and

---

[7] Peterson (2009), p. 244.

taxes. As lower-income people spend a higher share of their income on food, these policies are highly regressive. In poor countries, the policies penalize rural producers and communities.

Increases in market access will have a number of salutary impacts. First, reductions of agricultural subsidies will allow more competitive suppliers (e.g. African cotton producers and Latin American sugar producers) to begin to compete fairly in the world trading system.

Second, removing tariff escalation (by which more processed products face higher tariff levels) will make it easier for developing countries to escape their dependence on exporting raw materials and to vertically diversify their exports toward processed commodities that have more value.

Third, reducing protection levels for non-traditional agricultural goods (such as flowers and fruit) and for manufactured goods will reduce the pressure on developing countries to concentrate production in primary commodities, such as coffee and cotton, where they have market access. By making it easier for developing countries to diversify horizontally into a wider variety of goods and to diversify along the value chain into processed goods (coffee powder rather than beans, or chocolate rather than cacao and sugar), the risks associated with fluctuations in the primary production of prices and markets will be reduced.

Finally, increases in market access according to legally binding multilateral rules will reduce the uncertainty that all developing countries face about potential future protection and indiscriminate actions that can close access to markets. This uncertainty undermines investor confidence and raises the barriers to many potential investments, both in primary commodities and in non-traditional exports in developing countries.

At the time of this writing, the Doha Round is in a "final countdown" stage. While the Round as currently under negotiation will not go as far as we recommend in the realm of market access, it is nonetheless significant. As noted by Hoekman, Martin, and Mattoo (2010), the Doha Round would eliminate agricultural exports subsidies and reduce the scope for agricultural domestic support.[8] There would also be significant reduction in agricultural tariffs. Notable as well is the proposal for tariff and quota free entry for products from the least developed countries. For these reasons, the Doha Round is very much worth concluding for its contribution to market access.

8.2.2 TRADE-RELATED CAPACITY BUILDING

Substantial increases in market access must be combined with efforts to promote export *capacity* in low- and middle-income countries. Market access

---

[8] In the case of domestic support, there is less than meets the eye due to the gap between bound and applied levels.

without capacity undermines the growth and poverty potential of trade reform. Conversely, if countries have the capacity to compete but are prevented from doing through restricted market access, they cannot realize their potential. As discussed in Chapter 3, capacity constraints are multidimensional and include infrastructure, market information, skills, and credit. Capacity building in all these areas can also help developing countries to implement WTO commitments, to be properly represented at the WTO, to overcome trade barriers in the form of standards, to effectively negotiate regional commitments, and to overcome supply side constraints. As emphasized by Brenton et al. (2009), capacity building needs to focus on services exports as well as goods exports.

There are a number of efforts underway in the area of trade-related capacity building. One is the Integrated Framework (IF) or Enhanced Integrated Framework (EIP), discussed in Chapter 3. Another is a cooperative effort between the OECD and the WTO focused on developing the Doha Development Agenda Trade Capacity Building Database. As reported in Hoekman, Martin, and Mattoo (2010), spending on "aid for trade" is also on the rise but much greater investment in this crucial area is required. These worthwhile activities provide much needed support for the trade and development agenda.

Countries should be supported in building the "behind the border" hardware, such as infrastructure (including ports, roads, airports, equipment, and transport), and software, such as customs and marketing and market intelligence capacity.[9] Firms also require reliable electricity, water supply, and other infrastructure. This is particularly the case for small firms and family enterprises, which cannot afford their own generators or other basic infrastructure to take advantage of new opportunities. Translating these improvements in trade capacity into widespread employment and growth opportunities requires addressing broader countrywide constraints. In particular, improvements in the investment climate, including in the legal and judicial system, in the regulatory environment, and in the overall levels of education and health of the population may be necessary.

Although often overlooked, the capacity to engage and negotiate in bilateral, regional, and multilateral trade is a key requirement for a more equitable globalization. The negotiating playing field is highly uneven. Further effort should be made to improve the capacity of developing countries, particularly

---

[9] In a detailed study of bilateral trade flows, for example, Francois and Manchin (2007) found that "variation in infrastructure relative to the expected values for a given income cohort is strongly linked to exports. Indeed, sample variation in base infrastructure (communications and transportation) explains substantially more of the overall sample variation in exports than do the trade barriers faced by developing countries. This points to a more nuanced/diversified strategy, focused not just on WTO related market access conditions but trade facilitation (infrastructure and institutions) linked to trade performance" (p. 22).

the smaller and poorer countries, to enter into negotiations on an informed and equitable basis. Too often, whether in bilateral trade agreements or in Geneva at the WTO, teams of highly qualified and seasoned trade civil servants and expert consultants from one of the richest countries confront a handful of junior, relatively inexperienced civil servants from one of the poorer countries.

In the WTO, the increasing complexity and breadth of the negotiations—many of which take place simultaneously, especially during the crucial final days of negotiations—make it all but impossible for the majority of developing countries to even attend all the sessions, let alone negotiate on a fully informed and capable basis. To help developing countries engage more effectively in trade negotiations, efforts need to be made both to prevent the overload of the negotiations across an ever-widening span of issues and to support developing country trade policy staff in data gathering, understanding complex texts, analyzing the implications of different options, and negotiating with other WTO members.

One small but important step in assisting developing countries' representation in some aspects of the WTO is the Advisory Center on WTO Law (ACWL). Founded in 2001, the purpose of the ACWL is to provide assistance to developing countries on WTO legal matters, particularly dispute settlement. Evidence presented in Brown (2009) suggests that it has made a difference, although not for all developing countries. As such, its efforts should be supported and expanded if possible.

8.2.3 ARMS TRADE

The notion of gains from trade and the benefits trade expansion can bring to poverty reduction do not apply to trade in arms.[10] In 2008, three-quarters of global arms sales were to developing countries, accounting for over US$40 billion in sales. This is one third of foreign aid for that year and an increase of nearly three times since 2001.[11] These figures account for only legal arms sales, and it is likely that illegal arms sales add significantly to them. It is estimated that these trade flows contribute to the deaths of more than 300,000 persons each year and fuel civil conflicts that set back development processes for up to decades at a time.[12] This is particularly true for human development, because expenditures on arms rival expenditures on health or education in many

---

[10] This point was made by Wolfensohn (2002) and Reinert (2004).

[11] See Grimmett (2003, 2009). The five largest exporters of arms to the developing world in 2008 were, in order of importance, the United States, Russia, France, China, and the United Kingdom.

[12] In its first *World Report on Violence and Health,* the World Health Organization (WHO 2002) estimated that there were 320,000 deaths due to civil conflict in 2000. This report has not yet been updated. See also Collier and Sambanis (2003), Naím (2005), and Control Arms Campaign (2006).

developing countries.[13] Beyond development issues, the proliferation of small arms has even stymied the world's military forces, a testament to their destructive power.[14]

What is required is an international Arms Trade Treaty, for which the 1997 Ottawa Treaty on land mines (or more formally, the Convention on the Prohibition of the Use, Stockpiling, Production and Transfer of Anti-Personnel Mines and on their Destruction) serves as an example. The idea of an Arms Trade Treaty was endorsed by the Foreign Secretary of the United Kingdom and the Commission for Africa (2005). It has also been discussed in the First Committee of the United Nations and endorsed by Nobel Laureate Amartya Sen (2006c). The purpose of the treaty would be to tightly control weapons exports to countries with significant records of human rights abuses, to criminal organizations, and to conflict zones. Efforts of this nature, which provide a multilateral, legal framework to international arms trade, are not a panacea, but could have substantial positive effects by reducing mortality rates from armed conflict in the developing world. For this reason, control of the global arms trade through the development of an Arms Trade Treaty is an important area for global cooperation.

8.2.4 FORCED LABOR

The benefits of any market transaction, including international trade, presume that the participants in the transaction are engaged as a result of choice, not coercion.[15] If coercion is present, the market transaction is unlikely to be beneficial. This is most certainly the case with forced labor. It is true that workers in many poor countries are pressured by circumstances to find jobs that pay very poorly, but choose to remain thus employed by force of circumstance. However, forced labor is entirely different because freedom of choice has been infringed upon through a violation of human rights. The WTO has a general exception for the case of prison labor (Article XXe). This general exception should be extended to all forms of forced labor in order to expand the global commitment to human rights. Trade should not be permitted with employers who produce goods made by individuals who are coerced into employment.

---

[13] See Control Arms Campaign (2006).

[14] For example, Chivers (2011) noted: "Entire regions of the world, flooded with excess stocks of government arsenals, have become simmering conflict zones and areas out of any government's control. These are places where even the world's best military forces operate with difficulty and local populations suffer from the presence of armed and lawless groups" (p. 110).

[15] The importance of freedom in market transactions was emphasized by Sen (1999) who noted that "a denial of opportunities of transaction, through arbitrary controls, can be a source of unfreedom in itself" (p. 25).

With regard to the issue of child labor, it is important to note that, as emphasized by Sen (1999), "the worst violations of the norm against child labor come typically from the virtual slavery of children in disadvantaged families and from their being forced into exploitative employment."[16] Our suggestions on forced labor address these worst violations. We do not call for an outright ban on all forms of child labor as part of the multilateral trade system because this has real risks of making the situation worse for the children involved. For example, it is entirely plausible that children removed from more conventional forms of child labor will end up poorer and that, as they and their families become increasingly desperate, they could end up working in sectors that are not part of international trade, such as prostitution. Non-forced child labor is much better dealt with by providing food programs and health services within school systems, subsidies for school attendance, and other means to increase the incentives and means to attend school, as well as by addressing the underlying economic and other factors that lead to child labor.[17]

8.3 Finance: Proposed policy changes

The second dimension of globalization considered in this book is finance in the form of capital flows. This includes foreign direct investment (FDI), equity portfolio investment, bond finance, and commercial bank lending. In Chapter 4, we compared these flows and demonstrated the extent to which private flows to developing countries have grown relative to other flows, currently accounting for the lion's share of capital flows to middle-income developing countries. Although a handful of the resource-rich low-income countries have had substantial private inflows, the majority of low-income countries are more dependent on remittance flows and aid flows than private investment. Attracting equity flows—investments in firms and productive capacity that creates jobs—and reducing the share of their budgets that go to debt repayment can greatly assist countries to benefit from globalization. The policy changes we propose for capital flows fall into the following three areas:

- a heterodox approach to capital account reform
- macro-prudential policies to reduce systemic risk
- standards for multinational enterprises.

We consider each in turn.

---

[16] Sen (1999), p. 30.
[17] One model of this approach is conditional cash transfer (CCT) programs such as Brazil's *Bolsa Familia* program. As discussed in Fiszbein and Schady (2009), these have proven to be effective.

8.3.1 A HETERODOX APPROACH TO CAPITAL ACCOUNT REFORM

Global capital flows take place on countries' capital/financial accounts, which record their transactions with the rest of the world involving productive and financial assets of various kinds. The policy of international financial institutions on capital accounts has evolved in recent years. In 1997, the International Monetary Fund (IMF) considered making capital account liberalization an explicit policy goal to be part of its articles of agreement. However, there is a distinct lack of consensus on the desirability of capital account liberalization among prominent international economists and among governments. Two of the economies that have been most effective in avoiding crises and that have seen the most stable and high levels of growth over the past decades have been China and India, and both have maintained controls on their capital accounts.

The recent financial crisis has strengthened the case for a cautious approach to capital account liberalization. To the surprise of many, after the 2007–2009 financial crisis, the IMF revisited capital controls and gave them an endorsement (Ostry et al. 2010). This study suggested that market-friendly capital controls can help countries cope with surges of capital inflows that can end in sudden stops and contribute to the crises discussed Chapter 4. It endorsed many of the observations concerning capital controls discussed in this book. The 1997 position of the IMF on capital controls is fortunately now a thing of the past. With both practical experience and theory indicating that the case for capital account liberalization is not proven for developing countries, the global policy community needs to maintain a tolerant and heterodox posture toward the issue.

Why does this matter to poor people? As we discussed in Chapter 4, and as has been seen in cases such as the Asian and Argentina crises, mistakes made in this area can have devastating consequences for poverty levels, education, and health. The identification, adoption, and diffusion of best practice here can play an important role in preventing future crises of this kind and can help reduce levels of flight capital. However, in the absence of best practice, it does not make sense to force countries into a one-size-fits-all mold. For capital account and accompanying financial sector liberalization, it makes sense to err on the side of caution to prevent costly crises. This would allow countries to adopt a carefully sequenced and prepared set of steps toward fully integrating their capital markets and capital accounts with the world markets.

8.3.2 MACRO-PRUDENTIAL POLICIES TO REDUCE SYSTEMIC RISK

As pointed out by Goldin and Vogel (2010) and Scott (2010), the recent financial crisis has reinforced the need for macro-prudential policies to reduce systemic risk. In particular, there is a growing governance gap as a result of the failure of governments and international financial institutions to respond to innovations and developments in particular parts of the financial sector. National treasuries, the IMF and the Bank for International Settlements (BIS) do not always have the necessary skills to fully understand the implications of new financial products. There is also a failure to assess developments at the international level in order to appreciate their systemic implications. The outcomes of the recent crisis may have even made this situation worse through consolidation processes. As stated by Goldin and Vogel (2010), "current global financial institutions are inadequate in their policy response to systemic risk and cannot keep pace with innovation and increasing system complexity in global finance."[18]

The international financial community took a recent step forward in the form of what is known as the Basel III standards.[19] Under these standards, "Tier I" bank capital will be strictly limited to equity capital, the amount of this required core capital will be increased from 2 percent to 7 percent, and risk adjustment will be less determined by banks' internal models than in previous versions of the standards. In late 2010 and early 2011, the Basel Committee set out standards for both Tier I and Tier II bank capital that, upon initial examination, seem to strengthen standards significantly. Consequently, Basel III now appears to be a significant first step toward collective action to lessen systemic risk in the financial system. That said, a number of fundamental problems continue to bedevil the global financial system. These include the failure to secure the participation of all key players in robust agreements and the virtual absence of a global executive and compliance capacity. The processes put in place are based on self-reporting and regulation and do not go far enough in preventing free riding or gaming of the system. Significant doubts also remain about the capacity of the regulators to keep pace with innovation in instruments and regulatory arbitrage is likely to remain a pervasive problem. Finally, doubts remain as to the levels and structure of capital adequacy agreed in Basel III and the slow pace of implementation. Not surprisingly, then, Basel III has some critics.[20] Our view is

---

[18] Goldin and Vogel (2010), p. 4.

[19] The previous Basel II standards proved to be totally insufficient. As noted by *The Economist* (2010c), "the definition of Tier I capital was far too lax. Many of the equity like instruments allowed were really debt. In effect, the fine print allowed banks' common equity, or 'core' Tier I, the purest and most flexible form of capital, to be as little as 2 percent of risk adjusted assets." Further, leaving the risk adjustment process to banks' own internal models proved to be a mistake. Finally, it relied too heavily on "market discipline" in the form of credit rating agencies. As noted by Rochet (2010), "By giving credit rating agencies quasi-regulatory powers, the Basel Committee immeasurably augmented the powers of these agencies and exacerbated the conflict of interest that arises from the fact that these agencies are paid by the issuers of structured securities, with the now familiar disastrous outcome" (p. 99).

[20] For example, Wolf (2010) suggested that the Basel III equity requirement "is far below levels markets would impose if investors did not continue to expect governments to bail out creditors in a crisis." By some reckonings (e.g. *The Economist*, 2010c), capital requirements on the order of 15 percent are necessary. See also Scott (2010).

that while providing a valuable and important development in managing systemic financial risk, much greater analytic and institutional progress is urgently required.

8.3.3 STANDARDS FOR MULTINATIONAL ENTERPRISES

The polarization of policy discussions about globalization and poverty appears with some intensity in the case of foreign direct investment and the role of multinational enterprises (MNEs). This is perhaps most apparent in the ongoing debate over sweatshops and minimum standards. As with the other dimensions of globalization, the actual relationship between FDI and poverty is more subtle and complex.[21] While FDI can provides new opportunities to host economies, the extent to which poor people benefit varies greatly by country, sector, and firm. One crucial question is the extent to which standards for MNE behavior can influence these outcomes.

For example, whereas in South Africa the mining industries originally colluded with the apartheid government to force vibrant rural communities off their land and introduced the world's most oppressive migrant labor system, the descendants of these same companies today have made some progress and, while there remains considerable scope for further positive changes, they are among the standard setters for foreign investors in developing countries. The South African case highlights the particular problems associated with mining and other extractive industries.[22]

In line with a recent major review of extractive industries, we recommend adopting widespread safeguards, revenue reviews, and transparency mechanisms to ensure decent employment conditions and the proper management of taxes and other public revenues. The International Finance Corporation of the World Bank has encouraged the adoption of the Equator Principles of good governance. Further, the Extractive Industries Transparency Initiative (supported by the British government) and the civil society initiative Publish What You Pay are indicative of the new attention focused on providing transparent means of accounting for revenues.[23] These initiatives and a growing range of corporate responsibility charters are examples of new standards of behavior for investors. These should be adopted more widely with the support of source and destination governments and international agencies.

[21] For a thorough review of the debate, see Part III of Dunning and Lundan (2008).

[22] As pointed out by Collier (2007), these problems can also be found in the construction sector.

[23] See Extractive Industries Transparency Initiative at www.eiti.org and Publish What You Pay at www.publishwhatyoupay.org At the time of this writing, the Extractive Industries Transparency Initiative had 17 supporting countries, 5 compliant countries, and 28 candidate countries. Publish What You Pay had 600 member organizations in nearly 70 countries.

More broad guidelines for the behavior of MNEs are to be found in the Organization for Economic Cooperation and Development (OECD) Guidelines for Multinational Enterprises (Guidelines). These were developed in 1976, with changes introduced in subsequent years. The current version dates to 2000, but the OECD has recently launched an effort to re-evaluate and update the guidelines. The 2000 revision of Guidelines covered human rights, local capacity building, labor relations, health and the environment, corporate governance, and science and technology.[24] There was also an increased emphasis on standards of conduct, closer connections to international law, and an increased global focus. The Guidelines apply to the OECD member countries themselves, but additional countries have agreed to adhere to the Guidelines. This, plus endorsements by the G-8 and the United Nations Secretary General's Special Representative on Business and Human Rights, have contributed to the evolving global reach of the Guidelines.

While the 2000 Guidelines are still not binding, two developments have contributed to their applicability. First, the Guidelines have an implementation mechanism known as National Contact Points (NCPs). The NCPs have proved to be useful for labor organizations, businesses, and NGOs to become involved in processes related to the Guidelines.[25] Second, in 2006, the OECD adopted a Risk Awareness Tool for Multinational Enterprises in Weak Governance Zones. This is important because many MNEs operate in environments where governance structures are quite weak, so the Guidelines are an important supplement to ILO standards where the latter are not enforced.

At the time of this writing, the OECD has launched an effort to re-evaluate and update the guidelines. The terms of reference for the update suggest that, while not of the order of the 2000 revision, useful extensions are under consideration. These include: elaboration of the guidelines on human rights; guidance on the application of the guidelines to supply chains (global production networks); revisiting the disclosure chapter in light of the 2004 OECD Principles of Corporate Governance; elaboration of the chapter on bribery; and the relationship between the Guidelines of the Extractive Industry Transparency Initiative. All of these considerations suggest that the Guidelines are moving forward in appropriate ways and will be of increased relevance.

In an ideal world, there would be binding, *de minimis* guidelines for MNE behavior. However, the imperfect Guidelines do provide a critical focus point for holding MNEs to account. They should be embraced to help ensure more positive outcomes in leveraging MNE activities for development. In order to

---

[24] An assessment of the 2000 revisions by Murray (2001) noted that the guidelines formed a useful complement to the core labor standards of the International Labor Organization and could serve as a point of reference for groups concerned with MNE behavior.

[25] See, for example, Bowman (2006) on potential indigenous use of National Contact Points.

enhance their role in ensuring better development outcomes, attention and capacity building should focus on enhancing the role of NCPs in the Guideline process.

8.4 **Foreign aid: Proposed policy changes**

The global citizen should be forgiven for any confusion with regard to best policies for foreign aid. Prominent economists themselves are in significant disagreement concerning this third dimension of globalization, with Sachs (2005) advocating significant expansions of flows and Easterly (2006) questioning its effectiveness altogether. Collier (2007) took an intermediate position, but this could still leave the global citizen wondering what to think. In keeping with the "small wins" perspective of this chapter, we advocate a set of moderate changes to the aid process that can help this money be spent more effectively. The policy changes we advocate for aid are

- increasing the volume of aid flows in real, per capita terms to meet the commitments entered into forty years ago and reaffirmed at the Millennium Summit in 2000 and again at Gleneagles in 2005
- untying aid
- harmonizing donors' activities and aligning aid to recipient countries' development goals
- the widespread use of evidence-based evaluation and learning processes to increase aid effectiveness and knowledge sharing
- continued efforts for debt relief.

We consider each in turn.

8.4.1 MAINTAINING AID FLOWS

Foreign aid flows have increased significantly in nominal terms in recent years, from approximately US$50 billion in 2000 to approximately US$130 billion in 2010. This, in our view, has been a positive change, overcoming stagnation in aid flows in previous years. In real (constant 2010 US dollars), per capita terms these aid flows increased from US$15 per capita in 2000 to US$22 per capita. However, the 1990 value was US$20 per capita and the 1980 value US$21 per capita, so we need to keep the increase in some perspective. It is imperative that current levels of aid flows be maintained in *real, per capita* terms.

We have noted that aid alone cannot bring development. Making aid effective requires further improvements in national policies, as well as supportive trade and other capacity-building policies at the global level to provide the greatest benefit. It is worth noting that developed countries spend approximately the same amount on agricultural subsidy payments (producer support) as on foreign aid and that developing countries spend about one third the amount of foreign aid on arms imports. Reducing both agricultural subsidies and arms imports would be real progress and make aid flows more effective.

8.4.2 UNTYING INTERNATIONAL AID

The stagnation of real, per capita aid flows in recent decades has come at precisely the time when the impact of benefits derived from it has significantly increased. If countries are willing to take the steps necessary to reform, assistance in the form of capacity building, financial assistance, and analytical support can yield strong results. A critical lesson of past decades is that the countries themselves must be responsible and be fully behind their actions: the commitment of the recipient countries is essential. This requires that aid be allocated without conditions requiring recipients to purchase inputs from donors. The process of tying aid to the exports of donor countries is contrary to the principles of the multilateral trade system.[26] Although empirical analysis of tied vs. untied aid is scarce, the work of Miquel-Florensa (2007) indicated that, conditional on policies, tying aid reduces its potential growth effect. Aid flows should be uncoupled from requirements that the recipient countries purchase items from donor countries, whatever these items might be. A vital part of this agenda is also to ensure that aid flows are less tied to political and other priorities and that aid goes to where it can be effectively used for poverty reduction. The allocation of a significant part of aid flows to Iraq and Afghanistan and the blurring of the boundaries between aid and military assistance is of particular concern when this involves an effective diversion of resources away from other deserving and previously committed destinations.

8.4.3 HARMONIZATION AND ALIGNMENT

Harmonization of aid programs across donors reduces the need of recipients to spend their very scarce resources and time to support individual donors' requirements. This management burden is considerable, with ministers and other key staff often spending too much of their time meeting donors' needs rather than their domestic constituents' needs. The harmonization agenda needs to be pursued vigorously to ensure that, instead of each donor requiring very burdensome reporting and chaperoning, these administrative requirements

---

[26] This has been pointed out by La Chimia and Arrowsmith (2009).

are done collectively. Wherever possible, this should be through reinforcing and building the recipient countries' own existing systems, rather than creating additional systems to satisfy donor requirements. This process must also ensure that the aid programs are aligned with recipient government development goals. The reinforcement of country systems should cover not only the accounting and fiduciary reports required by donors, but should also extend to the governance and environmental, social, and other safeguards that increasingly dominate the aid process.

Ensuring that the recipients share a concern with safeguards—and that part of the aid program transforms these safeguards from externally imposed to internally built processes—will support sustainability, reduce transactions costs, and build domestic capacity. Improving the quality of aid also requires that it be more timely, predictable, and support multi-year programs.[27]

8.4.4 INCREASED EVALUATION AND KNOWLEDGE SHARING

The often neglected but perhaps most important element in aid is the role that it plays in learning and the evolution of policy. This role has many dimensions. As we illustrated in Chapter 5, it has also been associated with some of the most controversial aspects of aid, as donors in past decades sought to use aid to promote their own ideologies and geopolitical agendas. Although this risk remains, Chapter 7 on ideas showed that there is a convergence around development ideas and an increasing recognition of the need for country specificity.

Policy makers and citizens are more effectively able to engage in policy discussions and make policy if they are informed by the wealth of experience of other countries. By providing access to these lessons of this experience— both successes and failures—donors can support the introduction of new perspectives and ideas. Equally vital, and similarly neglected, is assistance in establishing statistics and data, designing projects that can be assessed against their objectives, and incorporating the results of this assessment into future program and project design.[28]

We recommend that building evaluation and learning into aid programs be an explicit objective rather than an afterthought. Long menus of required steps, which are beyond the reach of even the wealthy countries, are not helpful. Rigorous analysis of what works and what does not and how things

---

[27] For example, support for investment in rural infrastructure such as roads and water, or for recurrent expenditures in education and health such as salaries for teachers and nurses, cannot be turned on and off year by year, with leads and lags that reflect donor-driven processes and priorities rather than recipients' needs. For a discussion of related issues in the context of Ghana, see Quartey (2005).

[28] For example, Banerjee and He (2008) called for the use of randomized evaluation of aid outcomes and Easterly (2006) called for evaluation to be truly independent.

can be improved, based on lessons of the countries' own experiences as well as on comparative data and the lessons of others, are vital tools. Globalization offers great potential in terms of drawing on the lessons of others and not repeating their mistakes. Realizing this potential requires a determined effort on the part of developing countries, and also of aid agencies and other international players.

8.4.5 DEBT RELIEF

Many poor countries continue to spend more of their budget on debt service than on water supply, rural roads, health and education, or other productive investments. This situation has real costs for the world's poor people and undermines these highly indebted countries' abilities to grow and reduce poverty. Although it is not difficult to pin blame on both the countries themselves and the public and private lenders for creating excessive debts, it is also the case that the current problems for many are the legacy of past regimes that today's leadership are trying to put behind them. The Heavily Indebted Poor Country (HIPC) initiative described in Chapter 5 offers the most comprehensive approach yet to support the poorest and most indebted countries that are prepared to make a fresh start.

As of the end of 2010, 40 countries were part of the HIPC process, with 32 of these reaching the "completion point," 4 reaching the "decision point," and 4 waiting to reach the decision point. HIPC debt relief reached over US$100 billion.[29] The evidence to date suggests that the HIPC has had positive fiscal outcomes and social outcomes (e.g. Cassimon and Van Campenhout 2007 and Dömeland and Primo Braga 2009). That said, HIPC is not a panacea. The evidence presented in Yang and Nyberg (2009) and Dömeland and Primo Braga (2009) suggest that HIPC countries face continued vulnerabilities even with regard to sustainably managing their debt levels. One issue identified by these authors is export diversification, and this is where the trade policies of market access and capacity building interact with finance policies. Additionally, it needs to be recognized that much of the HIPC evaluation to date has not accounted for the full effects of the recent financial crisis on low-income countries.

To the extent that the HIPC process can be extended to additional low-income countries (more formally, non-HIPC, Extended Credit Facility countries), this should be pursued. Also, to the extent that the HIPC process can be better tailored to fragile states, that would also be helpful. Following the Jasmine revolutions in 2010 in North Africa and the Middle East, the focus of donor attention has been on supporting the democratic transition

---

[29] This includes the 2005 Multilateral Debt Relief Initiative as well as the 1999 "enhanced" HIPC.

and shoring up the finances of the new leadership. This already has led to new commitments of rapidly disbursing loans, to the inclusion of Egypt in the portfolio of the European Bank for Reconstruction and Development and for considering a restructuring of liabilities. Given the evolution of the markets and needs, debt relief and aid is constantly requires revisiting and review.

8.5 **Migration: Proposed policy changes**

The fourth dimension of globalization considered in this book is migration, which we define as the temporary or permanent movement of persons between countries. Migration is an ancient globalization flow, and although over the ages its form and impetus have changed significantly, it remains a powerful driver of development. Indeed Goldin, Cameron, and Balarajan (2011) demonstrated that historically it has been the most significant source of poverty reduction, but that this potential has been eroded by increasing restrictions on migration. With increased restrictions on movements, the global community is at a policy crossroads, with research and policy debate dominated by the concerns of the rich countries. The challenge is to ensure that policies are developed to meet these concerns, but also to enhance the impacts of migration in poverty reduction and development. The policy changes we propose for migration fall into the following areas:

- multilateral coordination for migration policy
- temporary movement of natural persons
- managing the brain drain
- reducing brain waste and leveraging the diaspora
- managing of remittances
- research agenda

We consider each in turn.

8.5.1 MULTILATERAL COORDINATION OF MIGRATION POLICY

Three percent of the world's population can be characterized as migrant, falling into one of the categories of migration we presented in Chapter 6. However, as noted by Klein Solomon and Bartsch (2003), "there is no comprehensive and harmonized system regulating international migration through which the movement of people can be managed in an orderly and cooperative way."[30] As we noted in Chapter 6, international migration can

---

[30] Klein Solomon and Bartsch (2003), p. 2

offer substantial benefits to poor people, but it can also involve heavy costs, especially to vulnerable populations. Further, migration is attracting the participation of international criminal organizations in both smuggling and trafficking activities. Moves to reform and harmonize the global migration system on a multilateral basis can reduce the injustices and improve the efficiency of current, piecemeal arrangements. Particular areas of concern here include dual citizenship, low-skill migration programs, managing remittances, and enforcing human rights for migrants.

As the Global Commission on International Migration (2005) concluded, greater multilateral coordination of migration policy could proceed through a number of avenues. The Berne Initiative, launched in 2001 by the Swiss government, engaged in extensive consultation with a view to developing non-binding guidelines for best practice to manage the international movement of people "in a humane and orderly way." The Berne Initiative was followed by the Global Commission on International Migration (GCIM), which was established in 2003 by the UN Secretary General to investigate potential frameworks for formulating coherent global response to migration issues. Although this international commission was supported by an ad hoc alliance of countries rather than the UN as a whole, and although it excluded some key countries, it nevertheless reflected a growing recognition of the importance of migration as a neglected dimension of international politics and development policy.

The Berne Initiative and the GCIM were followed by the United Nations High Level Dialogue (HLD) on International Migration and Development in 2006. As assessed by Martin, Martin, and Cross (2007), the HLD was an important event for furthering multilateral communication on migration issues. It did not, however, translate into specific action items for increased global governance of migration. As such, there will be no quick fixes, but every effort should be made to build on this momentum to improve the multilateral system for migration.

One of the reasons why migration policy at the national and global level has lagged behind the evolution of other key dimensions of globalization is the fact that migrants are relatively disenfranchised.[31] Once they have left, they typically are unable to vote and have less influence on the politics of their home country than those who remain behind. Meanwhile, as new arrivals in their host country, they are usually excluded from the domestic politics of their host. Strengthening the voice of migrants is a key challenge. The voice of migrants is least heard when they are being abused, and for this reason, progress toward supporting migrant rights, including the Migrant Rights Convention, is important.

---

[31] This has contributed to what Pritchett (2006) termed "everything but labor globalization."

8.5.2 TEMPORARY MOVEMENT OF PERSONS

Under the auspices of the WTO, liberalization of trade in services has occurred in a number of areas of interest to developed countries. However, as
recognized a long time ago by Streeten (1995), "A consistent policy of free
trade in goods and services would remove all restrictions on migration of
people who can provide services, at least on temporary immigration while the
service is provided."[32] Under the WTO's General Agreement on Trade in
Services (GATS), this temporary movement of persons (TMNP) composes
Mode 4 of service delivery. Although there is a protocol under the GATS for
Mode 4 service delivery, this only addresses the movement of skilled personnel associated with international business operations. In other words, it is not
designed to benefit developing countries, which have a key interest in the
mobility of medium and less skilled service providers, as well as some skilled
service providers.[33]

What needs to be done in this area is to immediately pursue a multilateral
system of identifying individuals seeking temporary movement, provide them
with national security clearance, and grant them multi-entry GATS visas.[34]
This is a necessary step to harness temporary migration for poverty alleviation; no doubt it will require a new GATS protocol dedicated to the issue. As
Walmsley and Winters (2005) demonstrated, the gains for developing
countries from an increase of only 3 percent in their temporary labor quotas
would exceed the value of total aid flows and be similar to the expected
benefits from the Doha Round of trade negotiations, with most of the benefits
to developing countries coming from increased access of unskilled workers to
jobs in developed countries. We need to ensure that developing countries have
access to these potential gains.

---

[32] Streeten (1995), p. 187.

[33] As pointed out by Puri (2004), there is an important gender element here: "For the majority of
women, Mode 4 provides the only opportunity to obtain remunerative employment with temporary
movement to provide services abroad. It has been found to have a net positive effect on the economy
and poverty reduction in the home country. There are dramatic examples of how remittances from
female domestic service suppliers from Bangladesh, Ethiopia, and Sri Lanka; nurses from Jamaica,
Malawi, and the Philippines; nurses and doctors from India and South Africa; agricultural service
suppliers from Honduras and Mexico; and personal care providers from Caribbean and Latin
American countries have substantially improved women's status in their home country and augmented their command over resources" (p. 8).

[34] Similar (and other) proposals are considered in Walmsley and Winters (2005) and Pritchett
(2006). Although this proposal might strike the average citizen as extreme, we need to emphasize that
the developing countries have negotiated to their advantage the liberalization of trade in services
through FDI. It stands to reason that, if Citibank can provide financial services in the Philippines, then
Philippine nurses should be able to provide nursing services in the United States.

8.5.3 MANAGING THE BRAIN DRAIN

As we discussed in Chapter 6, the widespread recognition that capacity constraints are a critical obstacle to development is reflected in growing attention to the need for education and training facilities and opportunities for developing country nationals. At the same time, high-income countries increasingly reach out globally in their search for much needed professional skills, offering new opportunities to precisely those who could provide leadership and scarce skills in their home countries. At the top end of the labor market, and in an evolving range of specialized areas—such as information technology and health—the restrictions imposed on migration are significantly reduced or even waived in favor of programs that seek to recruit foreign nationals. A range of financial and other incentives also provide magnets to skilled graduates. This "brain drain" has assumed a centrality in policy discussions and research on migration, which reflects the importance that high-income countries attach to attracting skilled labor.

The evidence on the impact of skilled migration is mixed, reflecting very different circumstances and policy responses. As Goldin, Cameron, and Balarajan (2011) discussed, countries such as the Philippines have built on the demand for their professionals to create a powerful source of employment and foreign revenue. Despite the recruitment of over 250,000 largely privately educated Filipino nurses abroad, the Philippines has a satisfactory supply of domestic nurses, a significant portion of which return from work abroad. By contrast, Malawi is suffering from a crippling health crisis as a result of the excessive recruitment of its small cadre of nurses who have been educated at the expense of taxpayers.

The selective admission of skilled migrants into high-income countries offers the recipient countries great benefits. The impacts on the donor countries are often but necessarily negative. The direct costs typically include the loss of skills and vibrant members of the community. From a source government perspective, education and training costs are not compensated for by the service of professionals, nor by their tax revenues. Donor counties also do not benefit directly from the impact of these skilled people on the dynamics of growth. As the reverse flows of ideas, money, and skilled people into the Indian high-tech sector show, these are not *necessarily* one-way losses.[35] Governments can also influence the decisions of skilled people not to leave and to keep their capital in the country to some degree by shaping the overall environment for skilled people, by providing a safe and secure working environment, by reaching out to their skilled people and seeking their involvement in decision making, and through other incentives. However, given

---

[35] See, for example, Saxenian (2005).

the gaps in earning power and the attractions of cosmopolitan environments, this holding power is limited, particularly for the small and poor countries.[36]

A British parliamentary investigation into migration and development concluded that "it is unfair, inefficient and incoherent for developed countries to provide aid to help developing countries to make progress . . . on health and education, whilst helping themselves to the nurses, doctors and teachers who have been trained in, and at the expense of, developing countries."[37] To increase the coherence between its aid and skilled migration policies, the British government has committed itself to restricting its recruitment of essential skilled health professionals. Our recommendation is that such policies be extended in the light of careful analysis of the costs and benefits of such skilled migration for the sending country. Where the extent of recruitment and the resulting critical shortages are shown to have a serious impact on development objectives, such restrictions on government recruitment could go beyond doctors and nurses. It is important also to include teachers, engineers, accountants, and others whose services are vital if developing countries are to achieve essential education, governance, and infrastructure improvements and create the virtuous circles that will encourage skilled people to stay at home or to return home in *brain circulation* processes.

For human liberty, economic, and enforceability reasons we do not believe that it is practical to include recruitment agencies or private firms in binding commitments, although for many skilled people they provide the bridge for migration. Consideration, however, should be given to developing tax and other incentives that serve to better capture the costs to the source country and the benefits to the destination country of recruitment of skilled people. In particular, the often extensive public investment in education and training could be calculated and reimbursed, at least in part, through additional aid or other transfers. For example, every surgeon recruited from abroad implies a saving of over US$1 million in education investments in the destination country and a significant cost to the donor country.[38] The best solution is for destination country governments to remit a portion of the income taxes paid by source country trained health professionals to the source country government.

It is also now inescapable that developing countries suffering from significant outflows of health professionals will be required to pursue two-tier health professional training programs. This involves the introduction of basic training programs that fall short of international standards but can

---

[36] For wage gaps between Malawi and the United Kingdom in the health professions, see Record and Mohiddin (2006).

[37] United Kingdom, 2004, House of Commons, Migration and Development, Paragraph 7.

[38] For estimates of the costs of lost health professionals in Kenya, for example, see Kirigia et al. (2006).

nevertheless have a positive impact on health outcomes. For example, in Malawi, a "clinical officer" program supports the country's anti-retroviral campaign.[39]

8.5.4 REDUCING BRAIN WASTE AND LEVERAGING THE DIASPORA

Although much needed attention has recently focused on the brain drain, a neglected dimension of this problem is the underutilization of the skills of migrants in rich countries or *brain waste*.[40] This is particularly the problem for migrants who are escaping persecution and refugees. In the United States, a minority (typically a third to a half) of migrants who entered the United States with a bachelor's degree undertake work requiring such a degree, and examining the relatively well educated among some categories of migrants, such as the Mexicans and Poles, the probability is only around 20 percent that they will enter a skilled job that matches their qualifications.[41] This reflects the issues of brain drain discussed above. It also reflects the incoherence of aid and migration policies in rich countries and their failure to develop appropriate policies to absorb migrants into the labor market and society.

Migrants can and sometimes do play a vital role in investing, transferring technology, and serving as informal and even formal marketing agents for their home countries. The evidence on this suggests that, although there is much spontaneous generation of such flows, policies in the host and home countries can make a significant difference to the beneficial impact of diasporas such as in the case of the Indian technology diaspora. Initial research suggests that countries that give more migrants tend to benefit most from return investment flows from the host countries.[42] Consequently, policies to support such formal and informal networks as well as to encourage such investment and technology flows are to be encouraged.

One particularly creative proposal for enhancing diaspora benefits is that of *diaspora bonds*. Ketkar and Ratha (2010), for example, presented a list of 25 developing countries that appear to be potential candidates to issue diaspora bonds.[43] As suggested by these authors, it would be better for the proceeds of these bonds to be earmarked for specific development projects in order to

---

[39] See Dovlo (2004), Record and Mohiddin (2006), and Skeldon (2009).

[40] See, for example, Debebe (2009).

[41] See Mattoo, Neagu, and Özden (2008).

[42] See Özden and Schiff (2006).

[43] These authors stated: "As many as eleven countries are currently believed to be thinking about this financing vehicle. These include Ethiopia, Ghana, Grenada, Jamaica, Liberia, Morocco, Nepal, Philippines, Rwanda, Sierra Leone, and Sri Lanka" (pp. 258–9).

increase their attractiveness to the diaspora and to leverage them as much as possible toward poverty reduction.

8.5.5 MANAGING REMITTANCES

Migrants' remittances are increasingly recognized as a highly significant financial flow, with officially recorded flows two and a half times aid flows and more than half of FDI in 2010. Although remittance flows, like other capital flows, are unevenly distributed among developing countries, they are more evenly distributed and more stable than other flows. To the extent that the supply of migrants increases in bad times and these migrants send back more money, remittance flows can also be countercyclical. Officially recorded inflows of remittances into developing countries reached over US$325 billion in 2010. All indications suggest that the growth in remittances will continue with the World Bank projecting that they will exceed $400 billion by 2013.

Increased competition and the provision of lower-cost remittance services would greatly benefit both the sender and the beneficiary of the transfer. Increased competition can be fostered in a variety of ways, including through a facilitative regulatory and compliance framework. The preclusion of exclusive bilateral monopolies between official remittance agents and the licensing of a wider variety of certified competitors is to be encouraged. New e-commerce technologies, including in foreign exchange markets and in electronic cards, offer great potential to reduce the overall transactions costs. Similarly, increased competition and scrutiny may be expected to reduce the highly regressive structure of the markets; the smaller the transaction, the greater the cost relative to the amount transferred, which discriminates against lower-income migrants and those who wish to make smaller but more frequent transfers. The availability of accessible remittance services near the workplace or residence of migrants and near the people to whom the funds are to be transferred, which offer simple processes in languages understood by the migrants, will also greatly facilitate remittance flows. Such services will also encourage the movement of remittances from unofficial, unregulated networks into regulated flows, which is important for addressing security as well as development priorities.

In addition to reducing costs and facilitating remittance flows in other ways, a range of possible policy measures may be expected to enhance the development impact of remittance flows. Before recommending tax measures, official savings associations, and other government-led mechanisms to increase the beneficial impact of remittances, care must be taken to ensure that these measures will be welcomed by the migrants themselves. If they are not welcome, migrants will reduce their remittances or revert to unofficial channels or other strategies. Remittances are private, person to person flows, and coordination and policy interventions should be formulated with this in mind.

Continued empirical research is needed before we can with certainty identify the exact extent to which remittances have grown or whether the net impact of migration on the donor countries is positive. The net impacts should not be measured in terms of remittances alone, but rather the overall context. This point is perhaps most starkly illustrated by the flow of remittances during the apartheid period in South Africa, when higher levels of remittances reflected the increasingly destructive impact of apartheid on the lives of families that were forcibly separated. Fortunately, such research is under way.[44]

8.5.6 RESEARCH AGENDA

As the British Parliamentary Investigation into Migration noted, "Policy should not be designed on the basis of hunches and anecdotes . . . the evidence base urgently needs improving."[45] The absence of reliable data and the paucity of research on migration are striking. Whereas there are literally thousands of researchers and research papers and a wide range of data sets focused on trade, capital flows, and aid, the number of researchers residing in developing countries dedicated to international migration issues is much smaller. This contrasts the rapid growth of academic work examining migration issues from the perspective of the rich countries.[46]

The promotion of a development perspective on migration is urgently needed. Recent efforts in the World Bank and in a number of developing countries to create capacity to analyze these issues require continued support if the necessary data and analysis are to be provided to inform much-needed policy reforms. With such research will also come a better understanding of the interrelationship of flows, and the extent and manner in which trade, capital flows, and aid are a substitute or complement to flows of migrants. Research on remittances has grown most rapidly, with the scale of these flows finally attracting deserved attention by both researchers and officials. However, much more work is needed to address the questions of who migrates and why; what the short- and long-term costs and benefits are to the home community and country; and how temporary migration, brain drain, brain waste, and the links between diasporas and trade and investment can be

---

[44] See Maimbo and Ratha (2005), Özden and Schiff (2006), and Pozo (2009).

[45] House of Commons, International Development Committee, 2004.

[46] For example, in the United Kingdom alone, a number of research institutes have been created in the past few of years to address European migration issues, with an investment that we estimate exceeds all the work being conducted in developing countries on cross-border migration issues.

enhanced to the benefit of poor people. Research to inform better policies is urgently required to realize this development potential.

8.6 **Ideas: Proposed policy changes**

Ideas are potentially the most powerful influence on development.[47] Globalization and technical progress have meant that ideas are transmitted and exchanged as never before. The key question is how this potential can be harnessed to accelerate poverty reduction. What policies should countries adopt to facilitate the evolution of ideas and their generation, transmission, adaptation, and adoption? Knowledge management is often seen as a particularly difficult challenge for firms; for countries it is even more daunting. However, ignoring or giving only passing attention to knowledge management and the transmission of ideas is not a solution. The policy changes we propose for ideas fall into the following areas:

- increasing the voice of developing countries
- knowledge management
- intellectual property harmonization
- access to medicines
- technology transfer

We consider each in turn.

8.6.1 INCREASING THE VOICE OF DEVELOPING COUNTRIES

An essential ingredient for ensuring a more inclusive globalization is that the ideas generated by developing countries must be given greater weight. This is especially important in global consultation and decision making forums where decisions with direct consequences for the citizens of developing countries are made.[48] Without adequate representation and voice, decisions reached are less informed, less legitimate, and less effective.

In addition to ensuring that global institutions more adequately represent the different participants, it is also vital to ensure that those institutions that are representative, such as the United Nations, are effective and strengthened. The importance of leveling the playing field in the negotiations at the WTO was stressed above. Despite recent changes, the governance of the World Bank and the

---

[47] See, for example, Lin (2009) and Goldin and Reinert (2010).
[48] This section draws extensively on conversations with Amar Bhattacharya and on Bhattacharya and Griffith-Jones (2004).

IMF still largely reflects agreements and the balance of power of 60 years ago. There is widespread recognition of the need for enhancing the participation of developing countries. Although progress has been made in increasing the participation of developing countries in formulating programs—as, for example, with the Poverty Reduction Strategy Paper approach—and in enhancing the capacity of the multi-stakeholder boards, the structural issues of voting rights and board representation remains.[49] While improvements in the effectiveness of the UN system and the Bretton Woods Institutions will contribute to more effective global management, the issue of more effective global governance goes well beyond these institutions and is a key challenge.

Over the past decade, the economic and political muscle of the developing countries has increased both because of their rapid economic growth and because of rising awareness of global fragility, interdependence, and consequent increased systemic risks. The need for inclusive solutions has been highlighted first by repeated economic crises and continued security threats. The expansion of the G-7 to include Russia and now also frequently China, and the creation of new forums such as the G-20 and G-24, has given more voice to large developing countries. These and other outreach efforts are useful, but as Bhattacharya and Griffith-Jones (2004) pointed out, "it is important to go beyond consultation to full representation of developing countries in bodies that deliberate and set international norms and action plans" that affect the global community.[50] Similarly, the current arrangements by which the richest countries agree among themselves the leadership appointments for key global institutions disenfranchise developing countries. The principles of transparency and good governance that governments apply with increasing frequency to themselves and at the corporate level should also apply in global governance, thereby reinforcing the legitimacy and effectiveness of the global institutions.

8.6.2 KNOWLEDGE MANAGEMENT

Knowledge management embraces a wide range of activities designed to enhance countries' abilities to acquire, absorb, and take advantage of new information and ideas. The range of approaches includes being open to ideas available elsewhere (for example, through trade, foreign investment, and licensing); creating knowledge locally through research and development; and building on indigenous knowledge. Greater openness to trade and investment,

---

[49] In the case of the IMF, some significant changes were made in 2008. Members agreed to institute a significant quota reform, involving: a new formula for calculating quotas; an additional "ad hoc" quota increases to selected countries that were "underrepresented" in the new quota formula; increasing the number of "basic votes" for low-income countries; and a decision to review quotas at a minimum of every five years.

[50] Bhattacharya and Griffith-Jones (2004), p. 205.

and ensuring that trade and investment are associated with the transfer of technologies and expertise, contribute to deepening knowledge acquisition. So too does closing the digital divide and the combination of open access to the Internet and developing a regulatory environment that allows competitive entry into the telecommunications sector, reducing connectivity charges. Creating and adapting knowledge locally—by investing in public sector research and creating incentives for private sector research and collaboration—is vital. It can be encouraged by establishing a facilitative intellectual property environment.

Absorbing information builds on the fundamentals of literacy and numeracy, but to generate adaptation and innovation also requires the development of an inquisitive spirit and the ability to evaluate ideas and information. Exposure to the experiences of others provides helpful insights to development practitioners. Equally important is the careful evaluation of the impact of those experiences. By diligently examining the extent to which policy initiatives and interventions reach or fall short of their objectives, and by promoting a culture of critical analysis and open admission of weaknesses and strengths, governments can set the standards for the acceleration of learning.

In addition to investments in education and research, governments can facilitate the sharing of knowledge and make special efforts to overcome the exclusion of poor people and poor communities from information. Global institutions and partners have a responsibility to assist with the distillation and dissemination of the wide-ranging lessons of experience and research. A particular challenge is to make this available to developing countries in ways and languages that can be understood not only by a small leadership group who read English but also by wider audiences, ranging from school children to development practitioners such as those who design and implement policies in provincial and local governments.

In recent years, the role of communication and knowledge in risk management has become better understood. Timely and effective information flows on issues important to poor people can help them to manage their risks and maximize their opportunities. Such practical efforts include providing market prices to poor farmers through village mobile phones, broadcasting weather information and disaster warnings on local radios, and highlighting the risks of HIV/AIDS and the benefits of public health measures in community information campaigns. In these and other respects, knowledge really does provide power to poor people to improve their lives.

8.6.3 INTELLECTUAL PROPERTY HARMONIZATION

Although knowledge has global public good aspects, there is an ongoing process of knowledge privatization in the form of increased intellectual property protection. This is taking place at the WTO under the Agreement on Trade Related Aspects of Intellectual Property Rights (TRIPS), at the World Intellectual Property Organization (WIPO), and in regional or bilateral trade agreement negotiations in "TRIPS-plus" formats. From a development perspective, the TRIPS Agreement is controversial. International economists and lawyers have significant disagreements on the long-run benefits of restricting knowledge transfer to developing countries. The majority of developing countries, supported by many leading scientists and academics, have argued that intellectual property protection needs to be applied in a manner that allows developing countries greater access to research and new technologies.

Given this lack of consensus on the benefits and the costs to developing countries of meeting TRIPS implementation requirements, an intensive examination of the issues by an independent panel accompanied by a temporary moratorium of further commitments demanded of developing countries is in order.[51] This should include regional and bilateral agreements where "TRIPS-plus" obligations are being negotiated that go beyond the existing commitments made by developing countries. Demands for harmonization are now ahead both of intellectual capacity in many countries and of demonstrated benefits. A moratorium will allow expert evaluation to enable policy decisions to be made on a more credible basis of considered research into the issues.

8.6.4 ACCESS TO MEDICINES

As we mentioned in Chapter 7, patents are a central concern for the impact of intellectual property protection on poor people, particularly in the case of pharmaceuticals for HIV/AIDS, tuberculosis, and malaria. In 2001, WTO members reaffirmed certain "flexibilities" with regard to access to pharmaceuticals needed to address public health crises. This included the production of generic drugs under compulsory licensing arrangements under Article 31 of TRIPS. However, Article 31(f) limits the use of these generic drugs to the domestic markets of the producing countries. A 2003 WTO decision on this issue allowed poor countries to import off-patent, generic drugs under specified conditions and directed the WTO TRIPS Council to prepare an amendment based "where appropriate" on the decision. An agreement regarding this amendment was reached in 2005, and this is being ratified. It remains, however, both for supporting legislation in WTO member countries to be fully enacted and for the provisions of the amendment to be tested in practice. Indeed, Matthews (2006) noted that "it is perhaps surprising that no developing country has yet used the new mechanism to allow the importation of generic medicines following the issuance of a compulsory license in a developed country prior to patent expiry."[52] It has become clear that capacity

---

[51] In 2004, a group of NGOs issued a "Geneva Declaration on the Future of the World Intellectual Property Organization" calling for a moratorium on new patent treaties.
[52] Matthews (2006), p. 130.

building is necessary to support use of the system, and the World Bank, among others, has been active in this regard.[53]

Perhaps the compulsory licensing option will ultimately prove to be helpful in harnessing knowledge in the form of pharmaceuticals to alleviate health crises and promote human development. Additionally, however, alternative policy options need to be investigated. Adusei (2011) outlined a more comprehensive approach based on the following elements: negotiation, compulsory licensing, parallel imports, public/private initiatives, patent pools, rejecting "TRIPS-Plus" stipulations in preferential trade agreements, competition law, expired patents, and enforcement lapses or targeted "piracy." Given the magnitude of the problem, and the failure of compulsory licensing efforts to date, this multi-pronged approach is more appropriate.

8.6.5 TECHNOLOGY TRANSFER

The global transfer of ideas in the form of technology is one of the most important development processes. For decades, the apparently growing gulf between developed and developing countries has raised concerns regarding a "technology divide." In recent years, leading developing countries such as Brazil, China, India, and South Africa have demonstrated that certain countries cannot only overcome but even leap ahead in selected areas. Partly as a result of these advances, developing countries increasingly are looking to each other for ideas and collaboration.

Although learning from the deliberate policies put in place by those countries that have increasingly developed and adapted technologies, the overwhelming majority of developing countries will remain dependent on technology transfer. Article 66.2 of the WTO TRIPS Agreement commits developed countries to providing "incentives to enterprises and institutions in their territories for the purpose of promoting and encouraging technology transfer" to the least developed countries. This commitment needs to be implemented *in practice* and applied to a wider set of countries. As outlined by Hoekman, Maskus, and Saggi (2005), this can occur through a variety of measures. These measures include the following:

- incentives for corporations and non-governmental organizations to transfer mature patent rights or to provide technical assistance
- public support for research into the specific technology needs of developing countries

---

[53] Rwanda became the first country to do this in 2007 in order to import HIV/AIDS anti-retroviral drugs from Canada under that country's Access to Medicines Regime. However, this regime was criticized by Goodwin (2008) for its over-complexity and inefficiency.

- university training for students from the low-income countries in science and technology
- finance to enable the participation of developing country representatives in standard setting bodies
- public purchase of patents on certain technologies for free use in developing countries.

In addition, we would suggest that the rich countries consider the possibility of creating incentives—for example, through negotiating patent extensions on technologies primarily destined for high-income groups in return for lowering or waiving patent fees and restrictions on technologies destined for low-income markets. These and other steps can better ensure that international technological development is more likely to help poor people.

8.7 **Global commons**

The policy agendas for trade, finance, aid, migration, and ideas are large. However, there are emerging global risks that can have devastating impacts on poor people that must be addressed to prevent advances in policy in the economic realms from being submerged beneath larger global issues, including climate change, fisheries, water resources, food security, pandemic threats, biodiversity, and human security. The agenda here is large, but we want to make some specific, "small wins" suggestions. These fall in the following categories:

- insurance for climate change related risks
- combating anti-microbial resistance
- re-envisioning agricultural development for food security
- enhancing human security.

We consider each in turn.

8.7.1 INSURANCE FOR CLIMATE CHANGE RELATED RISKS

Despite its recent politicization, the issue of climate change has been a question of scientific investigation for over a half century. In the terminology of Nordhaus (2010), reducing greenhouse gas (GHG) emissions is an "extreme global public good." Nevertheless, the 1997 Kyoto Protocol and the 2009 Copenhagen Accord appear to be insufficient to meet reasonable targets.[54]

---

[54] Nordhaus (2010) noted that "The reality behind the (Copenhagen Accord) is not encouraging. To begin with, even if the high income countries fulfilled their commitments, these would probably

Urgent global action is required to address climate change. Too little is being done too late. Consequently, certain developing countries need to be prepared for future slowly developing difficulties or sudden disasters associated with climate change. This is particularly the case given the likelihood that climate change will undermine human security through increased conflict.[55]

To help in this process, the global community needs to begin thinking about insurance schemes for climate related risks along the lines of those suggested by Linneroth-Bayer and Mechler (2006), among others. While details need to be worked out for what might constitute multiple tiers of climate change related risk insurance, the principle of better preparing the most vulnerable to foreseeable risks needs to be established and institutionalized.

8.7.2 COMBATING ANTI-MICROBIAL RESISTANCE

The World Health Organization (WHO) has rightly called attention to the developing issue of anti-microbial resistance (AMR). AMR is defined by the WHO as "resistance of a microorganism to an antimicrobial medicine to which it was previously sensitive. Resistant organisms (they include bacteria, viruses and some parasites) are able to withstand attack by antimicrobial medicines, such as antibiotics, antivirals, and antimalarials, so that standard treatments become ineffective and infections persist and may spread to others." AMR is becoming a significant threat as tuberculosis has taken on increasingly strong AMR characteristics, even evolving into what is known as extensively drug resistant (XDR) TB that is untreatable. There is therefore an increasing threat that an XDR TB strain will develop into a pandemic. To prevent this, increased commitment to the WHO's Directly Observed Treatment Short course (DOTS) is needed.[56] The DOTS is crucial because it ensures that there is no incomplete treatment that contributes to AMR.

Along with TB, other areas of AMR concern include malaria and staph infections. An increased commitment to DOTS and an increased awareness of these other evolving AMR risks is important to ensuring that poor people can maintain recent gained improvements in health and avoid future pandemics.

---

not achieve anything close to the 2°C target.... Meanwhile, progress on reaching a more binding target has been glacial at best. At present, a global agreement is waiting for the United States to take credible legislated steps. Continued delay in adoption of climate change policies by the United States may lead to a domino effect in which other countries follow the US inaction" (p. 11721).

[55] See, for example, Barnett and Adger (2007). These authors point to the potential for climate change to reduce either access to or compromise the quality of natural resource assets that support current livelihoods.

[56] The DOTS involves the elements of government commitment, case detection, standardized treatment of 6 to 8 months, an uninterrupted supply of TB drugs, and a standardized recording and reporting system.

8.7.3 RE-ENVISIONING AGRICULTURAL DEVELOPMENT FOR FOOD SECURITY

As is now evident, accommodating a further two billion individuals on planet earth between now and 2050 is going to put strains on the world food system. If the past is any guide, it will be the poorest that bear the burden of emerging food insecurity and its associated social tensions. In the past, we have relied on a particular combination of plant science and specific agricultural inputs (energy and chemicals) to increase yields in "Green Revolution" fashion. As is now becoming evident, yield gains from this process are declining, and constraints are emerging related to agricultural water and energy use. Without calling a halt to this biotechnology based approach to sustaining agricultural yields, we also need to turn attention to the possibilities of advances in agro-ecology.[57] The reasons to include this approach to agricultural development in food security strategies are multiple. First, there is a general principle of diversifying approaches to enhance exploration of alternatives and to reduce the risks of failure in a single approach. Second, agro-ecology involves reduced use of water and energy inputs, two increasingly binding constraints. Third, agro-ecology tends to hold more carbon in biomass than biotechnology based agriculture and therefore tends to limit agriculture's own contribution to global warming, which is substantial.

It is important to note that agro-ecology is not anti-science in the sense expressed by the father of the Green Revolution, Norman Borlaug (2000). It is simply a different form of science that might prove to be equally promising. This is an instance when travelling down more than one path at the same time could be very much worthwhile.

An additional measure required for genuine food security is resistance to "agro-investment" in Africa by foreign entities. These land grabs increase risks for the poorest rural citizens in Congo, Ethiopia, Ghana, Kenya, Madagascar, Malawi, Mali, Mozambique, Nigeria, Senegal, Sierra Leone, Sudan, Tanzania, Uganda, Zambia, and Zimbabwe. Their negative effects have been noted by the World Bank (2011a) and include the displacement of local peoples, giveaways at low values, and lack of representation.[58] Given the tendency for poor people to be marginalized, large-scale agro-investment projects pose a real threat.

---

[57] This was recognized by the Human Rights Council of the United Nations General Assembly. See Wezel et al. (2009) and De Schutter (2010).

[58] The World Bank (2011a) concludes that: "Large scale expansion of cultivated area poses significant risks, especially if not well managed. As the countries in question often have sizable agricultural sectors with many rural poor, better access to technology and markets, as well as improved institutions to improve productivity on existing land and help judiciously expand cultivated area, could have big poverty impacts. Case studies illustrate that in many instances outside investors have been unable to realize this potential, instead contributing to loss of livelihoods. Problems have included displacement of local people from their land without proper compensation, land being given away well below its potential value, approval of projects that were only feasible because of

8.7.4 ENHANCING HUMAN SECURITY

Each of the above three global commons related policy changes would help to improve human security broadly conceived. Additionally, however, the relationship between increased economic interdependence and conflict is in need of attention. While there is conflicting evidence on the nature of this relationship,[59] it is clear that aspects of globalization more broadly conceived can indeed exacerbate conflict. This is the case, for example, in global criminal and warlord networks.[60] Naím (2005) highlighted the extent to which illegal trade has accompanied globalization. Illicit trade of commodities for arms fuels conflicts and leads to development in reverse. Focusing attention on illegal flows that undermine development requires placing this in the context of managing globalizations benefits, rather than engaging in protectionism. These are issues that require attention.

Addressing these problems involves a concept we have touched upon at various points in this book: global public goods. As noted by Hamburg and Holl (1999) and Mendez (1999), the prevention of deadly conflict as part of efforts to provide peace and security inherently involves benefits that are non-excludable. Because they are non-excludable, there are no direct specific incentives for countries that are not part of the conflict, so these efforts tend to be underprovided. Ensuring the benefits of globalization for the poorest, then, will require substantially more efforts to provide this and other global public goods.

8.8 **A global policy checklist**

Having described our policy agenda in some detail, it is useful to present its elements in a more concise format. We do so in Table 8.2. Without significant progress toward the changes described by the entries in Table 8.2, it will be much less likely that we can count on the globalization dimensions discussed in this book bringing positive benefits to poor people. As such, we view Table 8.2 as a global policy checklist, challenges that must be addressed by the world community if globalization is to have a chance to help poor people. If we fail

---

additional subsidies, generation of negative environmental or social externalities, or encroachment on areas not transferred to the investor to make a poorly performing project economically viable" (p. xlii). For an entity that strongly supports foreign investment in general, this is a strong conclusion.

[59] For reviews and analysis, see Barbieri and Schneider (1999) and Gartzke, Quan, and Boehmer (2001).

[60] See, for example, Cooper (2002) on the role of conflict trade.

to address the issues in this table adequately, we should not continue to claim that globalization can be an unmitigated force for the good in the development realm.

8.9 Summary and assessment

Despite continued development challenges, the post-World War II period of accelerated global integration has been associated with unprecedented progress on key dimensions of development. This is mainly because of countries adopting better national policies and directing cross-border flows of ideas, people, capital, and goods to meet the challenges faced by their citizens. Some examples of these leaps in development include improvements in health involving unprecedented increases in life expectancies, albeit rolled back in some countries due to the HIV/AIDs pandemic; significant reductions (on the order of one half) in adult illiteracy; and rapid increases in incomes per capita in a number of countries such as China, India, and Vietnam.

This progress in health, education, and income has not been just accidental. Governments, with the support of the development community and civil society organizations, have accelerated growth and poverty reduction by improving their policies, institutions, and governance, and through well-designed projects and programs. Importantly, the successful policy and institutional improvements have not been blind copies of orthodoxy, but have involved what Santiso (2006) called "endogenous credibility," namely "institutions and economic policies that are connected to the social realities of their respective countries, not to economics textbooks that do not pay sufficient attention to countries marked by poverty and inequality."[61]

The challenge is to extend the progress that has already improved the well-being of so many people to all regions and countries. To do so, the development community must learn from past failures, and must understand the origins of the successes. Like aid recipients, who have often followed weak policies or allowed institutions to deteriorate, donors also have made mistakes that slowed development. We must design policies at the global, regional, national, and local or community levels that ensure that the benefits of globalization reach the billion and more people who are currently marginalized and who have not benefited from the fruits of globalization. The policies discussed in this chapter will make this outcome more likely.

[61] Santiso (2006), pp. 5–6.

Our recommendations are not novel. Nor do we consider them to be a panacea. However, through our analysis and prioritization of practical actions, we hope to contribute to ongoing discussions of globalization and poverty. Globalization can work for poor people if we pursue the right policies and ensure against systemic risks. Let us act to ensure that the huge opportunities globalization offers lead to a better life for all.

■ BIBLIOGRAPHY

Abella, M. I. 2004. "The Role of Recruiters in Labour Migration." In D. S. Massey and J. E. Taylor (eds), *International Migration: Prospects and Policies in a Global Market.* Oxford: Oxford University Press, pp. 201–11.

Adams, R. H. 2003. "International Migration, Remittances, and the Brain Drain: A Study of 24 Labor Exporting Countries." *Policy Research Working Paper Series 3069.* Washington, DC: The World Bank.

Adams, R. H. and Page, J. 2005. "Do International Migration and Remittances Reduce Poverty in Developing Countries?" *World Development,* 33 (10), pp. 1645–69.

Adelman, C. 2003. "The Privatization of Foreign Aid: Reassessing National Largesse." *Foreign Affairs,* 82 (6), pp. 9–14.

Adelman, C. 2009. "Global Philanthropy and Remittances: Reinventing Foreign Aid." *Brown Journal of World Affairs,* 14 (2), pp. 23–33.

Adelman, I. 2001. "Fallacies in Development Theory and Their Implications for Policy." In G. M. Meier and J. E. Stiglitz (eds), *Frontiers of Development Economics: The Future in Perspective.* Oxford: Oxford University Press, pp. 103–34.

Adusei, P. 2011. "Exploiting Patent Regulatory 'Flexibilities' to Promote Access to Antiretroviral Medicines in Sub-Saharan Africa." *Journal of World Intellectual Property,* 14 (1), pp. 1–20.

Aggarwal, A., Hoppe, M., and Walkenhorst, P. 2009. "Special Economic Zones and Economic Diversification: Some Evidence from South Asia." In R. Newfarmer, W. Shaw, and P. Walkenhorst (eds), *Breaking into New Markets: Emerging Lessons for Export Diversification.* Washington, DC: World Bank, pp. 223–36.

Aiken, L. H., Buchan, J., Sochalski, J., Nichols, B., and Powell, M. 2004. "Trends in International Nurse Migration." *Health Affairs,* 23 (3), pp. 69–77.

Aitken, B. J. and Harrison, A. E. 1999. "Do Domestic Firms Benefit from Direct Foreign Investment? Evidence from Venezuela." *American Economic Review,* 89 (3), pp. 605–18.

Alcouffe, A. and Kuhn, T. 2004. "Shumpeterian Endogenous Growth Theory and Evolutionary Economics." *Journal of Evolutionary Economics,* 14 (2), pp. 223–36.

Alesina, A. and Dollar, D. 2000. "Who Gives Foreign Aid to Whom and Why?" *Journal of Economic Growth,* 5 (1), pp. 33–63.

Alfaro, L., Chanda, A., Kalemli-Ozcan, S., and Sayek, S. 2004. "FDI and Economic Growth: The Role of Local Financial Markets." *Journal of International Economics,* 64 (1), 89–112.

Alfaro, L., Kalemli-Ozcan, S., and Sayek, S. 2009. "FDI, Productivity and Financial Development." *World Economy,* 32 (1), pp. 111–35.

Alfaro, L., Kalemli-Ozcan, S., and Volosovych, V. 2008. "Why Doesn't Capital Flow from Rich to Poor Countries? An Empirical Investigation." *Review of Economics and Statistics,* 90 (2), pp. 347–68.

Alkire, S. 2002. "Dimensions of Human Development." *World Development,* 30 (2), pp. 181–205.

Alkire, S. and Santos, M. E. 2010. "Acute Multidimensional Poverty: A New Index for Developing Countries." *Human Development Research Paper 2010/11.* New York: United Nations Development Program.

Amnesty International. 2006. *Amnesty International Report 2006—Russian Federation*, May 23, 2006.

Anderson, K. and Bjorn, L. 2008. "Free Trade, Free Labour, Free Growth." *Project Syndicate*. http://www.project-syndicate.org/commentary/anderson1/English (last accessed April 26, 2010).

Anderson, K., Martin, W., and van der Mensbrugghe, D. 2006. "Impact of Global Trade and Subsidy Policies on Developing Country Trade." *Journal of World Trade*, 40 (5), pp. 945–68.

Anson, J., Cadot, O., Estevadeordal, A., de Melo, J., Suwa-Eisenmann, A., and Tumurchudur, B. 2005. "Rules of Origin in North-South Preferential Trading Arrangements with an Application to NAFTA." *Review of International Economics*, 13 (3), pp. 501–17.

Arai, M., Bursell, M., and Nekby, L. 2008. "Between Meritocracy and Ethnic Discrimination: The Gender Difference." Working Paper. Stockholm: Stockholm University Linnaeus Center for Integration Studies.

Arndt, H. W. 1987. *Economic Development: The History of an Idea*. Chicago: University of Chicago Press.

Arnold, J. M. and Javorcik, B. S. 2009. "Gifted Kids or Pushy Parents? Foreign Direct Investment and Plant Productivity in Indonesia." *Journal of International Economics*, 79 (1), pp. 42–53.

Axworthy, L. 2001. "Human Security and Global Governance: Putting People First." *Global Governance*, 7 (1), pp. 19–23.

Bach, S. 2006. "International Mobility of Health Professionals Brain Drain or Brain Exchange?" UN-WIDER Research Paper No. 2006/82. Helsinki: World Institute for Development Economics Research United Nations University.

Bacon, C. M., Méndez, V. E., Gliessman S., Goodman, D., and Fox, J. A. (eds) 2008. *Confronting the Coffee Crisis: Fair Trade, Sustainable Livelihoods, and Ecosystems in Mexico and Central America*. Cambridge, MA: MIT Press.

Baker, M. and Benjamin, D. 1995. "The Receipt of Transfer Payments by Immigrants to Canada." *Journal of Human Resources*, 30 (4), pp. 650–76.

Baliamoune-Lutz, M. 2009. "Institutions, Trade and Social Cohesion in Fragile States: Implications for Policy Conditionality and Aid Allocation." *Journal of Policy Modeling*, 31 (6), pp. 877–90.

Baliamoune-Lutz, M. and Mavrotas, G. 2009. "Aid Effectiveness: Looking at the Aid-Social Capital-Growth Nexus." *Review of Development Economics*, 13 (3), pp. 510–25.

Banerjee, A. and Duflo, E. 2011. *Poor Economics: A Radical Rethinking of the Way to Fight Global Poverty*. New York: Public Affairs.

Banerjee, A. and He, R. 2008. "Making Aid Work." In W. Easterly (ed.), *Reinventing Foreign Aid*. Cambridge, MA: MIT Press, pp. 47–92.

Banerjee, A. and Iyer, L. 2005. "History, Institutions, and Economic Performance: The Legacy of Colonia Land Tenure Systems in India." *American Economic Review*, 95 (4), pp. 1190–213.

Barber, B. 1996. *Jihad vs. McWorld*. New York: Ballentine.

Barbieri, K. and Schneider, G. 1999. "Globalization and Peace: Assessing New Directions in the Study of Trade and Conflict." *Journal of Peace Research*, 36 (4), pp. 387–404.

Bardhan, P. 2006. "Globalization and Rural Poverty." *World Development*, 34 (8), pp. 1393–404.

Barnett, J. and Adger, W. N. 2007. "Climate Change, Human Security and Violent Conflict." *Political Geography*, 26 (6), pp. 639–55.

Barrell, R., FitzGerald, J., and Riley, R. 2007. "EU Enlargement and Migration: Assessing the Macroeconomic Impacts." Discussion Paper No. 292. London: National Institute of Economic and Social Research.

Barry, J. 2005. *The Great Influenza*. New York: Penguin.

Battat, J., Frank I., and Shen, X. 1996. *Suppliers to Multinationals: Linkage Programs to Strengthen Local Companies in Developing Countries*. Foreign Investment Advisory Service. Washington, DC: The World Bank.

BBC. 2004. "Tide Kills 18 Cockle Pickers". February 6, 2004, http://news.bbc.co.uk/1/hi/england/lancashire/3464203.stm (last accessed May 4, 2011).

BBC. 2011. "Middle East Protests: Country by Country." BBC News website, http://www.bbc.co.uk/news/world-12482295 (last accessed June 23, 2011).

Beath, A. L., Goldin, I., and Reinert, K. A. 2009. "International Migration." In K. A. Reinert, R. S. Rajan, A. J. Glass, and L. S. Davis (eds), *The Princeton Encyclopedia of the World Economy*. Princeton: Princeton University Press, pp. 764–70.

Beck, T., Levine, R., and Loayza, N. 2000. "Finance and the Sources of Growth." *Journal of Financial Economics*, 58 (1–2), pp. 261–300.

Behrman, J. R., Alderman, H., and Hoddinott, J. 2007. "Hunger and Malnutrition." In B. Lomborg (ed.), *Solutions for the World's Biggest Problems: Costs and Benefits*. Cambridge: Cambridge University Press, pp. 390–404.

Bell, D. 1960/2000. *The End of Ideology*. Cambridge, MA: Harvard University Press.

Bénassy-Quéré, A., Coupet, M., and Mayer, T. 2007. "Institutional Determinants of Foreign Direct Investment." *World Economy*, 30 (5), pp. 764–82.

Benton, B., Bump, J., Sékétéli, A., and Liese, B. 2002. "Partnership and Promise: Evolution of the African River-Blindness Campaigns." *Annals of Tropical Medicine and Parasitology*, 96 (1), pp. 5–14.

Bergman, J. 2011. "Setting Rivalry Aside: China Responds to Japan's Plight." *The Times*, March 11.

Bhattacharya, A. and Griffith-Jones, S. 2004. "The Search for a Stable and Equitable Global Financial System." In J. J. Teunissen and A. Akkerman (eds), *Diversity in Development: Reconsidering the Washington Consensus*. The Hague: FONDAD.

Bhinda, N., Griffith-Jones, S., Leape, J., and Martin, M. 1999. *Private Capital Flows to Africa*. The Hague: Fonda.

Bigsten, A., Collier, P., Dercon, S., Fafchamps, M., Gauthier, B., Gunning, J. W., Oduro, A., Oostendorp, R., Pattillo, C., Söderbom, M., Teal, F., and Zeufack, A. 2004. "Do African Manufacturing Firms Learn from Exporting?" *Journal of Development Studies*, 40 (3), pp. 115–41.

Birdsall, N. and Londono, J. L. 1998. "No Tradeoff: Efficient Growth via More Equal Human Capital Accumulation." In N. Birdsall, C. Graham, and R. H. Sabot (eds), *Beyond Tradeoffs: Market Reforms and Equitable Growth in Latin America*. Washington, DC: Brookings Institution, pp. 111–45.

Blalock, G. and Gertler, P. J. 2008. "Welfare Gains from Foreign Direct Investment through Technology Transfer to Local Suppliers." *Journal of International Economics*, 74 (2), pp. 402–21.

Blanton, R. G. and Apodaca, C. 2007. "Economic Globalization and Violent Conflict: Is Openness a Pathway to Peace?" *Social Science Journal*, 44 (4), pp. 599–619.

Blomström, M. 1986. "Foreign Investment and Productive Efficiency: The Case of Mexico." *Journal of Industrial Economics*, 35 (1), pp. 97–110.

Blomström, M. and Kokko, A. 2003. "The Economics of Foreign Direct Investment Incentives." *NBER Working Paper 9489.* Cambridge, MA: National Bureau of Economic Research.

Blomström, M. and Persson, H. 1983. "Foreign Investment and Spillover Efficiency in an Underdeveloped Economy: Evidence from the Mexican Manufacturing Industry." *World Development,* 11 (6), pp. 493–501.

Blomström, M. and Sjöholm, F. 1999. "Technology Transfer and Spillovers: Does Local Participation with Multinationals Matter?" *European Economic Review,* 43 (4–6), pp. 915–23.

Boana, C., Zitter, R., and Morris, T. 2008. "Environmentally Displaced People." *Forced Migration Policy Briefing 1.* Oxford: Refugee Studies Centre.

Boccanfuso, D. and Savard, L. 2007. "Poverty and Inequality Impact Analysis Regarding Cotton Subsidies: A Mali-Based CGE Micro-Accounting Approach." *Journal of African Economies,* 16 (4), pp. 629–59.

Boisier, S. 2005. "¿Hay espacio para el desarrollo local en la globalización?" *Revista de la CEPAL,* 86, pp. 47–62.

Boldrin, M. and Levine, D. K. 2002. "The Case Against Intellectual Property." *American Economic Review,* 92 (2), pp. 209–12.

Boldrin, M. and Levine, D. K. 2004a. "The Case Against Intellectual Monopoly." *International Economic Review,* 45 (2), pp. 327–60.

Boldrin, M. and Levine, D. K. 2004b. "Rent-Seeking and Innovation." *Journal of Monetary Economics,* 51 (1), pp. 127–60.

Bolt, J. and Bezemer, D. 2009. "Understanding Long-Run African Growth: Colonial Institutions or Colonial Education?" *Journal of Development Studies,* 45 (1), pp. 24–54.

Boone, P. 1996. "Politics and the Effectiveness of Foreign Aid." *European Economic Review,* 40 (2), pp. 289–329.

Borjas, G. J. 1999. "Immigration," *NBER Reporter,* Fall. http://www.nber.org/reporter/fall99/borjas.html (last accessed March 1, 2011).

Borjas, G. J. 2003. "The Labour Demand Curve is Downward Sloping: Reexamining the Impact of Immigration on the Labor Market." *Quarterly Journal of Economics,* 118 (4), pp. 1335–74.

Borjas, G. J. and Bronars, S. J. 1991. "Immigration and the Family." *Journal of Labour Economics,* 9 (2), pp. 123–227.

Borlaug, N. 2000. "Ending World Hunger. The Promise of Biotechnology and the Threat of Antiscience Zealotry." *Plant Physiology,* 124 (2), pp. 487–90.

Bourguignon, F. and Morrisson, C. 2002. "Inequality among World Citizens: 1820–1992." *American Economic Review,* 92 (4), pp. 727–44.

Bourguignon, F. and Sundberg, M. 2007. "Aid Effectiveness: Opening the Black Box." *American Economic Review,* 97 (2), pp. 316–21.

Bowman, H. 2006. "If I Had a Hammer: The OECD Guidelines for Multinational Enterprises as Another Tool to Protect Indigenous Rights to Land." *Pacific Rim Law and Policy Journal,* 15 (3), pp. 703–32.

Boxell, J. 2009. "Recession Spurs Migrant Workers to Leave." *Financial Times,* May 21.

Brautigam, D. 2009. *The Dragon's Gift: The Real Story of China in Africa.* Oxford: Oxford University Press

Brautigam, D. and Knack, S. 2004. "Foreign Aid, Institutions and Governance in Africa." *Economic Development and Cultural Change,* 52 (2), 255–86.

Brenton, P., Newfarmer, R., Shaw, W., and Walkenhorst, P. 2009. "Breaking into New Markets: Overview." In R. Newfarmer, W. Shaw, and P. Walkenhorst (eds), *Breaking into New Markets: Emerging Lessons for Export Diversification*. Washington, DC: World Bank, pp. 1–35.

Brown, C. P. 2009. *Self-Enforcing Trade: Developing Countries and WTO Dispute Settlement*. Washington, DC: Brookings Institution Press.

Brown, M. and Goldin, I. 1992. *The Future of Agriculture in Developing Countries*. Paris: OECD Development Centre.

Brown, O. 2007. "Climate Change and Forced Migration: Observations, Projections and Implications." Human Development Report Office Occasional Paper 2007/17. New York: United Nations Development Program.

Bruton, H. J. 1998. "A Reconsideration of Import Substitution." *Journal of Economic Literature*, 36 (2), pp. 903–36.

Bruton, H. J. and Fairris, D. 1999. "Work and Development." *International Labour Review*, 138 (1), pp. 5–30.

Buchan, N. R., Grimalda, G., Wilson, R., Brewer, M., Fatas E., and Foddy, M. 2009. "Globalization and Human Cooperation." *Proceedings of the National Academy of Sciences*, 106 (11), pp. 4138–42.

Büchel, F. and Frick, J. 2003. "Immigrants' Economic Performance Across Europe: Does Immigration Policy Matter?" EPAC Working Paper 42. Colchester: University of Colchester.

Burns, J., Holman, M., and Huband, M. 1997. "How Mobutu Built Up His $4 Billion Fortune: Zaire's Dictator Plundered IMF Loans." *Financial Times*, May 1.

Burnside, C. and Dollar, D. 2000. "Aid, Policies, and Growth." *American Economic Review*, 90 (4), pp. 847–68.

Calvo, G. A., Leiderman, L., and Reinhart, C. M. 1996. "Inflows of Capital to Developing Countries in the 1990s." *Journal of Economic Perspectives*, 10 (2), pp. 123–39.

Camarota, S. A. 2007. "Immigrants in the United States 2007: A Profile of America's Foreign-Born Population." *Center for Immigration Studies Backgrounder*, November. Washington, DC: Center for Immigration Studies.

Camarota, S. A. and Jensenius, K. 2009. "Immigrant Unemployment at Record High: Rate now Exceeds Native-Born, a Change from Recent Past," *Center for Immigration Studies Announcement*, April. Washington, DC: Center for Immigration Studies.

Cameron, G. and Goldin, I. 2011. "Global Migration: Key Drivers and Policy Implications." Mimeo for submission to Global Policy, October.

Card, D. 2005. "Is the New Immigration Really so Bad?" *Economic Journal*, 115 (507), pp. 300–23.

Carrington, W. J. and Detragiache, E. 1999. "How Extensive is the Brain Drain?" *Finance and Development: A Quarterly Magazine of the IMF*, 36 (2), pp. 46–9.

Cassimon, D. and Van Campenhout, B. 2007. "Aid Effectiveness: Debt Relief and Public Finance Response: Evidence from a Panel of HIPC Countries." *Review of World Economics*, 143 (4), pp. 742–63.

Castles, S. 1989. "Migrant Workers and the Transformation of Western Societies." Western Societies Program Occasional Paper No. 22. Ithaca: Centre for International Studies, Cornell University.

Castles, S. 2002. "Environmental Change and Forced Migration: Making Sense of the Debate." Working Paper No. 70, UNHCR New Issues in Refugee Research. Geneva: UNHCR Policy Evaluations Unit.

Castles, S. 2006. "Guestworkers in Europe: A Resurrection?" *International Migration Review*, 40 (4), pp. 741–66.

Castles, S. and Miller, M. J. 2009. *The Age of Migration: International Population Movements in the Modern World* (4th edn). New York: Palgrave MacMillan.

Caves, R. E. 1974. "Multinational Firms, Competition, and Productivity in Host-Country Markets." *Economica*, 41 (162), pp. 176–93.

Caves, R. E. 2007. *Multinational Enterprise and Economic Analysis.* Cambridge: Cambridge University Press.

Centre for Economics and Business Research (CEBR). 2007. *Future Flows: Forecasting the Current and Future Economic Impact of Highly Skilled Migrants.* London: CEBR.

Chambers, R. 2008. *Revolutions in Development Inquiry.* London: Earthscan.

Chand, S. and Clemens, M. A. 2008. "Skilled Emigration and Skill Creation: A Quasi-Experiment." CGD Working Paper Number 152. Washington, DC: Center for Global Development.

Chappell, L., Sriskandarajah, D., and Swinburn, T. K. 2008. "Building a New Home: Migration in the UK Construction Sector." Economics of Migration Project, Working Paper 2. London: Institute for Public Policy Research.

Chen, M. X., Wilson, J. S., and Otsuki, T. 2008. "Standards and Export Decisions: Firm-Level Evidence from Developing Countries." *Journal of International Trade and Economic Development*, 17 (4), pp. 501–23.

Chen, S. and Ravallion, M. 2004. "How Have the World's Poorest Fared since the Early 1980s?" *World Bank Researcher Observer*, 19 (2), pp. 141–70.

Chenery, H., Ahluwahlia, M., Bell, C., Dulow, J., and Jolly, R. 1974. *Redistribution with Growth.* Oxford: Oxford University Press.

China Daily 2010. "China-Africa Trade Brings Mutual Benefit." *China Daily*, December 24. http://www.chinadaily.com.cn/cndy/2010-12/24/content_11748391.htm (accessed March 30, 2011).

Chiswick, B. R and DebBurman, N. 2004. "Educational Attainment: Analysis by Immigrant Generation." *Economics of Education Review*, 23, pp. 361–79.

Chivers, C. J. 2011. "Small Arms, Big Problems: The Fallout of the Global Gun Trade." *Foreign Affairs*, 90 (1), p. 110.

Christensen, B. V. 2010. "China in Africa—A Macroeconomic Perspective." CGD Working Paper 230. Washington, DC: Center for Global Development.

Chua, A. 2003. *World on Fire.* New York: Random House.

Chuang, Y-C. and Lin, C-M. 1999. "Foreign Direct Investment, R&D and Spillover Efficiency: Evidence from Taiwan's Manufacturing Firms." *Journal of Development Studies*, 35 (4), pp. 117–35.

Chudnovsky, D. and López, A. 2007. "Inversión extranjera directa y desarrollo: la experiencia del mercosur." *Revista de la CEPAL*, 92, pp. 7–23.

Claessens, S., Klingebiel, D., and Schmukler, S. L. 2002. "The Future of Stock Exchanges in Emerging Economies: Evolution and Prospects." In R. Litan and R. Herring (eds), *Brookings-Wharton Papers on Financial Services.* Washington, DC: Brookings Institution, pp. 167–202.

Clapp, J. 2001. *Toxic Exports: The Transfer of Hazardous Waste from Rich to Poor Countries.* Ithaca: Cornell University Press.

Clapp, J. 2009. "Basel Convention." In K. A. Reinert, R. S. Rajan, A. J. Glass, and L. S. Davis (eds), *Princeton Encyclopedia of the World Economy.* Princeton: Princeton University Press, pp. 124–6.

Clark, D. A. 2002. *Visions of Development: A Study of Human Values.* Edward Elgar: Cheltenham.

Clark, D. A. 2006. "Capability Approach." In D. A. Clark (ed.), *The Elgar Companion to Development Studies.* Cheltenham: Edward Elgar, pp. 32–45.

Clark, D. A. and Hulme, D. 2010. "Poverty, Time and Vagueness: Integrating the Core Poverty and Chronic Poverty Frameworks." *Cambridge Journal of Economics,* 34 (2), pp. 347–66.

Clemens, M. A. 2008. "Immigrants are an Engine of Prosperity." *Atlanta Journal-Constitution,* November 27. http://www.ajc.com/services/content/printedition/2008/11/27/clemensed.html (last accessed September 20, 2011).

Clemens, M. A. 2009. "Skill Flow: A Fundamental Reconsideration of Skilled-Worker Mobility and Development." UNDP Human Development Report 2009 Background Paper 8. New York: United Nations Development Programme.

Clemens, M., Radelet, S., and Bhavnani, R. 2004. "Counting Chickens When They Hatch: The Short-Term Effect of Aid on Growth." Working Paper 44. Washington, DC: Center for Global Development.

Cohen, D. 2001. "The HIPC Initiative: True and False Promises." *International Finance,* 4 (3), pp. 363–80.

Cohen, D. and Soto, M. 2007. "Growth and Human Capital: Good Data, Good Results." *Journal of Economic Growth,* 12 (1), pp. 51–76.

Collier, P. 2007. *The Bottom Billion: Why the Poorest Countries are Failing and What can be Done About it.* Oxford: Oxford University Press.

Collier, P., Devarajan, S., and Dollar, D. 2001. "Measuring IDA's Effectiveness." Unpublished. Washington, DC: World Bank.

Collier, P. and Dollar, D. 2002. "Aid Allocation and Poverty Reduction." *European Economic Review,* 46 (8), pp. 1475–500.

Collier, P. and Dollar, D. 2004. "Development Effectiveness: What Have We Learned." *Economic Journal,* 114, pp. 244–71.

Collier, P. and Gunning, J. W. 1995. "War, Peace and Private Portfolios." *World Development,* 23 (2), pp. 233–41.

Collier, P., Hoeffler, A., and Pattillo, C. 2001. "Flight Capital as a Portfolio Choice." *World Bank Economic Review,* 15 (1), pp. 55–80.

Collier, P. and Sambanis, N. 2003. *Understanding Civil War.* Washington, DC: World Bank.

Collier, P. and Venables, A. J. 2007. "Rethinking Trade Preferences: How Africa Can Diversify Its Exports." *World Economy,* 30 (8), pp. 1326–45.

Commission for Africa. 2005. *Our Common Interest.* London: Commission for Africa.

Commission on Growth and Development. 2008. *The Growth Report: Strategies for Sustained Growth and Inclusive Development.* Washington, DC: World Bank.

Control Arms Campaign. 2006. *Arms without Borders: Why a Globalised Trade Needs Global Controls.* Amnesty International, International Action Network on Small Arms, and Oxfam. http://controlarms.org/wordpress/wp-content/uploads/2011/02/Arms-Without-Borders-why-a-global-trade-needs-global-controls.pdf (last accessed September 20, 2011).

Cooper, N. 2002. "State Collapse as Business: The Role of Conflict Trade and the Emerging Control Agenda." *Development and Change,* 33 (5), pp. 935–55.

Coppel, J., Dumond, J.-C., and Visco, I. 2001. "Trends in Immigration and Economic Consequences." OECD Economics Department Working Paper No. 284. Paris: OECD.

Cornelius, W. 2001. "Death at the Border: The Efficacy and 'Unintended' Consequences of the US Immigration Control Policy 1993–2000." Working Paper No. 27. San Diego: Center for Comparative Immigration Studies, University of California.

Crafts, N. 2001. "Historical Perspectives on Development." In G. M. Meier and J. E. Stiglitz (eds), *Frontiers of Development Economics: The Future in Perspective*. Oxford: Oxford University Press, pp. 301–34

Cragg, M. I. and Epelbaum, M. 1996. "Why Has Wage Dispersion Grown in Mexico? Is It the Incidence of Reforms or the Growing Demand for Skills?" *Journal of Development Economics*, 51 (1), pp. 99–116.

Crisp, R. (ed.) 2000. *Nicomachean Ethics*. Cambridge: Cambridge University Press.

Crul, M. and Vermeulen, H. 2003. "The Second Generation in Europe." *International Migration Review*, 37 (4), pp. 965–86.

Curtis, M. 2001. *Trade for Life: Making Trade Work for Poor People*. London: Christian Aid.

Dadush, U. and Falcau, L. 2009. "Migrants and the Global Financial Crisis." Policy Brief No. 83. Washington, DC: Carnegie Endowment for International Peace.

Dasgupta, D., Nabli, M. K., Pissarides, C., and Varoudakis, A. 2007. "Making Trade Work for Jobs: International Evidence and Lessons for MENA." In M. K. Nabli (ed.), *Breaking the Barriers to Higher Economic Growth: Better Governance and Deeper Reforms in the Middle East and North Africa*. Washington, DC: World Bank, pp. 329–54.

Dauvergne, C. 2008. *Making People Illegal: What Globalization Means for Migration and Law*. Cambridge: Cambridge University Press.

de Ferranti, D., Perry, Lederman, G. E., and Maloney, W. F. 2002. *From Natural Resources to the Knowledge Economy: Trade and Job Quality*. Washington, DC: World Bank.

de Haas, H. 2007a. "North African Migration Systems: Evolutions, Transformations, and Development Linkages." Working Paper No. 6. Oxford: International Migration Institute, James Martin 21st Century School, University of Oxford.

de Haas, H. 2007b. "Remittances, Migration and Social Development: A Conceptual Review of the Literature." Social Policy and Development Programme Paper No. 34. New York: United Nations Research Institute for Social Development.

de Haas, H. 2008a. "Migration and Development: A Theoretical Perspective." Working Paper No. 9. Oxford: International Migration Institute, James Martin 21st Century School, University of Oxford.

de Haas, H. 2008b. "The Internal Dynamics of Migration Processes." IMSCOE Conference on Theories of Migration and Social Change, 1–3 July 2008, Oxford University.

de Haas, H. 2009. "Mobility and Human Development." Human Development Research Paper No. 2009/01. Washington, DC: United Nations Development Programme.

de Haas, H., Bakewell, O., Castles, O, Jónsson, G., and Vezzoli, S. 2009. "Mobility and Human Development." Working Paper No. 14. Oxford: International Migration Institute, James Martin 21st Century School, University of Oxford.

de la Torre, A. and Schmukler, S. 2007. *Emerging Capital Markets and Globalization: The Latin American Experience*. Palo Alto, CA: Stanford University Press.

De Schutter, O. 2010. "Report Submitted by the Special Rapporteur on the Right to Food." New York: Human Rights Council, United Nations General Assembly.

de Walt, B. R. 1994. "Using Indigenous Knowledge to Improve Agricultural and Natural Resource Management." *Human Organization*, 53 (2), pp. 123–31.

Deaton, A. 2004. "Health in an Age of Globalization." *Brookings Trade Forum*, pp. 83–130.

Debebe, G. 2009. "Brain Waste." In K. A. Reinert, R. S. Rajan, A. J. Glass, and L. S. Davis (eds), *The Princeton Encyclopedia of the World Economy*. Princeton: Princeton University Press, pp. 138–41.

Denzau, A. T. and North, D. C. 1994. "Shared Mental Models: Ideologies and Institutions." *Kyklos*, 47 (1), pp. 3–31.

Derviş, K. 2005. *A Better Globalization: Legitimacy, Governance, and Reform*. Washington, DC: Center for Global Development.

Desai, R. M. and Hermias, J. 2008. "Millennium Development Goals: Enhance Public Policy with Private Donors." *The Brookings Institute (Opinions)*, web editorial, September 25. http://www.brookings.edu/opinions/2008/0925_mdgs_desai.aspx (last accessed April 21, 2011).

Devarajan, S., Dollar, D., and Holmgren, T. (eds) 2001. *Aid and Reform in Africa*. Washington, DC: World Bank.

Devarajan, S., Le, T. M., and Raballand, G. 2010. "Increasing Public Expenditure Efficiency in Oil-Rich Economies: A Proposal." Policy Research Working Paper No. 5287. Washington, DC: World Bank.

Devarajan, S. and Reinikka, R. 2004. "Making Services Work for Poor People." *Journal of African Economies*, 13 (S1), pp. 142–66.

Diamond, D. and Dybvig, P. H. 1983. "Bank Runs, Deposit Insurance, and Liquidity." *Journal of Political Economy*, 91 (3), pp. 401–19.

Diamond, J. 1997. *Guns, Germs, and Steel*. New York: Norton.

Dicken, P. 2007. *Global Shift: Mapping the Changing Contours of the World Economy*. Guilford: Guilford Press.

Dobson, W. and Hufbauer, G. C. 2001. *World Capital Markets: Challenge to the G-10*. Washington, DC: Institute for International Economics.

Docquier, F. and Marfouk, A. 2006. "International Migration by Education Attainment, 1990–2000." In C. Ozden and M. Schiff (eds), *International Migration, Remittances and Brain Drain*. Basingstoke: World Bank and Palgrave MacMillan.

Dollar, D. and Kraay, A. 2004. "Trade, Growth, and Poverty." *Economic Journal*, 114 (493), pp. 22–49.

Dömeland, D. and Primo Braga, C. A. 2009. "Introduction." In D. Dömeland and C. A. Primo Braga (eds), *Debt Relief and Beyond: Lessons Learned and Challenges Ahead*. Washington, DC: World Bank, pp. 1–8.

Doucouliagos, H. and Paldham, M. 2009. "The Aid Effectiveness Literature: The Sad Results of 40 Years of Research." *Journal of Economic Surveys*, 23 (3), pp. 433–61.

Dovlo, D. 2004. "Using Mid-Level Cadres as Substitutes for Internationally Mobile Health Professionals in Africa: A Desk Review." *Human Resources for Health*, 2 (7), pp. 1–12.

Dugger, C. W. 2004. "Where Doctors are Scarce, Africa Deploys Substitutes." *New York Times*, November 23.

Dunning, J. H. and Lundan, S. M. 2008. *Multinational Enterprises and the Global Economy*. Cheltenham: Edward Elgar.

Duvell, F. 2009. "Irregular Migration in Northern Europe: Overview and Comparison." *Clandestino Project Conference*, London, March 27.

Easterly, W. 2001. *The Elusive Quest for Growth.* Cambridge, MA: MIT Press.

Easterly, W. 2006. *White Man's Burden.* New York: Penguin.

Easterly, W., Levine, R., and Roodman, D. 2004. "Aid, Policies, and Growth: Comment." *American Economic Review,* 94 (3), pp. 774–80.

Economist, The. 1998. "A Taste of Adventure." December 17. http://www.economist.com/node/179810 (last accessed September 20, 2011).

Economist, The. 1999. "The East India Companies." December 23. http://www.economist.com/node/347231 (last accessed September 20, 2011).

Economist, The. 2008a. "Of Bedsheets and Bison Grass Vodka." January 3. http://www.economist.com/node/10286177 (last accessed April 14, 2011).

Economist, The. 2008b. "Migrant Labour: Tough Times." November 29. http://www.economist.com/node/12689805 (last accessed June 30, 2011).

Economist, The. 2010a. "Brazil's Foreign-Aid Programme: Speak Softly and Carry a Blank Cheque." July 15. http://www.economist.com/node/16592455 (last accessed March 29, 2011).

Economist, The. 2010b. "Mexico's Economy: Bringing NAFTA Back Home." October 28. http://www.economist.com/node/17361528 (last accessed March 21, 2011).

Economist, The. 2010c. "Reforming Banking: Base Camp Basel." January 21. http://www.economist.com/node/15328883 (last accessed April 17, 2011).

Economist, The. 2010d. "The World Turned Upside Down." April 15. http://www.economist.com/node/15879369 (last accessed July 1, 2011).

Edmonds, E. V. and Pavcnik, N. 2005. "The Effects of Trade Liberalization on Child Labor." *Journal of International Economics,* 65 (2), pp. 401–19.

Edwards, L. 2004. "A Firm Level Analysis of Trade, Technology and Employment in South Africa." *Journal of International Development,* 16 (1), pp. 45–61.

Edwards, S. 1998. "Openness, Productivity and Growth: What Do We Really Know?" *Economic Journal,* 108 (447), pp. 383–98.

Eichengreen, B. 1996. *Globalizing Capital: A History of the International Monetary System.* Princeton: Princeton University Press.

Eichengreen, B. 1999. *Towards a New International Financial Architecture: A Practical Post-Asia Agenda.* Washington, DC: Institute for International Economics.

Eichengreen, B. 2004. "Financial Instability." In B. Lomborg (ed.), *Global Crises, Global Solutions.* Cambridge: Cambridge University Press, pp. 251–80.

Eichengreen, B. 2008. *Globalizing Capital: A History of the International Monetary System.* Princeton: Princeton University Press.

Epstein, G. S. 2008. "Herd and Network Effects in Migration Decision-Making." *Journal of Ethnic and Migration Studies,* 34, pp. 567–83.

Evans, S. 2005. "America's Generous Aid to Africa." BBC News, June 14. http://news.bbc.co.uk/1/hi/business/4091528.stm (accessed April 21, 2011).

Fernandez-Arias, E. and Montiel, P. J. 1996. "The Surge in Capital Inflows to Developing Countries: An Analytical Overview." *World Bank Economic Review,* 10 (1), pp. 51–77.

Financial Times. 2004. "How Dirty Money Binds the Poor." *Financial Times,* October 13.

Financial Times. 2008. "The Year the God of Finance Failed." *Financial Times,* December 26.

Finger, J. M. 2004. "Introduction and overview." In J. M. Finger and P. Schuler (eds), *Poor People's Knowledge: Promoting Intellectual Property in Developing Countries*. Washington, DC: World Bank, pp. 1–36.

Finn, M. 2007. "Stay Rates of Foreign Doctorate Recipients from U.S. Universities, 2005." Division of Science Resources Statistics of the National Science Foundation. http://orise. orau.gov/files/sep/stay-rates-foreign-doctorate-recipients-2005.pdf (accessed August 10, 2009).

Fiszbein, A. and Schady, N. 2009. *Conditional Cash Transfers: Reducing Present and Future Poverty*. Washington, DC: World Bank.

Florida, R. 2002. "The Economic Geography of Talent." *Annals of the Association of American Geographers*, 92 (4), pp. 743–55.

Fofack, H. and Ndikumana, L. 2010. "Capital Flight Repatriation: Investigation of Its Potential Gains for Sub-Saharan African Countries." *African Development Review*, 22 (1), pp. 4–22.

Fosu, A. K. 1996. "Primary Exports and Economic Growth in Developing Countries." *World Economy*, 19 (4), pp. 465–75.

Francois, J. and Manchin, M. 2007. "Institutions, Infrastructure, and Trade." World Bank Policy Research Working Paper No. 4152. Washington, DC: World Bank.

Francois, J. and Reinert, K. A. 1996. "The Role of Services in the Structure of Production and Trade: Stylized Facts from a Cross Country Analysis." *Asia-Pacific Economic Review*, 2 (1), pp. 35–43.

Francois, J. F. and Hoekman, B. 2010. "Services Trade and Policy." *Journal of Economic Literature*, 48 (3), pp. 642–92.

Francois, J. F. and Martin, W. 2002. "Binding Tariffs: Why Do It?" In B. Hoekman, A. Mattoo, and P. English (eds), *Development, Trade, and the WTO*. Washington, DC: World Bank, pp. 540–7.

Francois, J. F. and Woerz, J. 2008. "Producer Services, Manufacturing Linkages, and Trade." *Journal of Industry, Competition and Trade*, 8 (3–4), pp. 199–229.

Frenkel, M. and Menkhoff, L. 2004. "Are Foreign Institutional Investors Good for Emerging Markets?" *The World Economy*, 27 (8), 1275–93.

Friedman, M. 1958. "Foreign Economic Aid: Means and Objectives." *The Yale Review*, 47 (4), 500–16.

Fukuda-Parr, S. 2003. "Operationalizing Sen's Capability Approach", *Feminist Economics*, 9 (2–3), pp. 301–17.

Fukuyama, F. 1992. *The End of History and the Last Man*. New York: Free Press.

Fukuyama, F. 2002. "Social Capital and Development: The Coming Agenda." *SAIS Review*, 22 (2), pp. 23–37.

Fukuyama, F. 2004. *State-Building: Governance and World Order in the 21st Century*. Ithaca: Cornell University Press.

Gala, P. 2008. "Real Exchange Rate Levels and Economic Development: Theoretical Analysis and Econometric Evidence." *Cambridge Journal of Economics*, 32 (2), pp. 273–88.

Galeano, E. 1997. *Open Veins of Latin America*. New York: Monthly Review Press.

Gamlen, A. 2008. "Why Engage Diasporas?" COMPAS Working Paper No. 63. Oxford: Centre on Migration, Policy and Society, University of Oxford.

Gartzke, E., Quan, L., and Boehmer, C. 2001. "Investing in the Peace: Economic Interdependence and International Conflict." *International Organization*, 55 (2), pp. 391–438.

Ghattas, K. 2011. "Syria's Spontaneously Organised Protests." BBC News, April 22. http://www.bbc.co.uk/news/world-middle-east-13168276 (accessed April 27, 2011).

Ghosh, B. 2006. *Migrants' Remittances and Development: Myths, Rhetoric and Realities*. Geneva: IOM.

Gindling, T. H. and Robbins, D. 2001. "Patterns and Sources of Changing Wage Inequality in Chile and Costa Rica During Structural Adjustment." *World Development*, 29 (4), pp. 725–45.

Global Commission on International Migration. 2005. *Migration in an Interconnected World: New Directions for Action*. Geneva: Global Commission on International Migration.

Goldar, B. and Aggarwal, S. C. 2005. "Trade Liberalization and Price-Cost Margin in Indian Industries." *The Developing Economies*, 43 (3), pp. 346–73.

Goldberg, P. K. and Pavcnik, N. 2004. "Inequality and Poverty: What Do We Know? Evidence from Recent Trade Liberalization Episodes in Developing Countries." *Brookings Trade Forum*, pp. 223–69.

Goldin, I. 2011. "Future Development of Global Migration and the Impact of Environmental Change." Paper prepared for UK Government Department of Business Innovation and Skills, Foresight Global Environmental Migration Project.

Goldin, I., Cameron, G., and Balarajan, M. 2011. *Exceptional People: How Migration Shaped Our World and Will Define Our Future*. Princeton: Princeton University Press.

Goldin, I. and Reinert, K. 2007. *Globalization for Development: Trade, Finance, Aid, Migration and Policy* (2nd edn). Basingstoke: Palgrave MacMillan.

Goldin, I. and Reinert, K. 2010. "Ideas, Development and Globalization." *Canadian Journal of Development Studies*, 29 (3–4), pp. 329–48.

Goldin, I., Rogers, H. F., and Stern, N. 2002. "The Role and Effectiveness of Development Assistance: Lessons from World Bank Experience." In *A Case for Aid: Building a Consensus for Development Assistance*. Washington, DC: World Bank, pp. 25–183.

Goldin, I., Rogers, H. F., and Stern, N. 2006. "We Must Tackle Development Problems at the Level of the Economy as a Whole." *Boston Review*, 31 (4), July/August. http://bostonreview.net/BR31.4/goldin.php (last accessed September 20, 2011).

Goldin, I., Stern, N., and Dethier, J-J. 2003. "Development as Learning." Unpublished, Washington, DC: World Bank.

Goldin, I. and Vogel, T. 2010. "Global Governance and Systemic Risk in the 21st Century: Lessons from the Financial Crisis." *Global Policy*, 1 (1), pp. 4–15.

Goldin, I. and Winters, L. A. 1995. *The Economics of Sustainable Development*. Cambridge: Cambridge University Press.

Goldsmith, A. 2001. "Foreign Aid and Statehood in Africa." *International Organization*, 55 (1), pp. 123–48.

Goldstein, M. and Turner, P. 2004. *Controlling Currency Mismatches in Emerging Markets*. Washington, DC: Institute for International Economics.

Goldstein, M., Kaminsky, G. L., and Reinhart, C. M. 2000. *Assessing Financial Vulnerability: An Early Warning System for Emerging Markets*. Washington, DC: Institute for International Economics.

Goodwin, P. E. 2008. "Right Idea, Wrong Result—Canada's Access to Medicines Regime." *American Journal of Law and Medicine*, 34 (4), pp. 567–8.

Greenaway, D., Morgan, W., and Wright, P. 1999. "Exports, Export Composition and Growth." *Journal of International Trade and Economic Development*, 8 (1), pp. 41–51.

Greenland, D. J. 1997. "International Agricultural Research and the CGIAR System: Past, Present and Future." *Journal of International Development*, 9 (4), pp. 459–82.

Grether, J. M. 1997. "Estimating the Pro-Competitive Gains from Trade Liberalization: An Application to Mexican Manufacturing." *Journal of International Trade and Economic Development*, 6 (3), pp. 393–417.

Grimmett, R. F. 2003. *Conventional Arms Transfers to Developing Nations, 1995–2002*. Washington, DC: Congressional Research Service, U.S. Library of Congress.

Grimmett, R. F. 2009. *Conventional Arms Transfers to Developing Nations, 2001–2008*. Washington, DC: Congressional Research Service, US Library of Congress.

Guardian, The. 2011. 'Aid from OECD Countries—Who Gives the Most and How Has It Changed?" April 7.

Haddad, M. and Harrison, A. 1993. "Are There Positive Spillovers from Direct Foreign Investment? Evidence from Panel Data for Morocco." *Journal of Development Economics*, 42 (1), pp. 51–74.

Haider, M. Z. 2007. "Competitiveness of the Bangladesh Ready-Made Garment Industry in Major International Markets." *Asia-Pacific Trade and Investment Review*, 3 (1), pp. 3–27.

Hallaert, J. and Munro, L. 2009. "Binding Constraints to Trade Expansion: Aid for Trade Objectives and Diagnostic Tools." OECD Trade Policy Working Paper No. 94. Paris: Organization for Economic Cooperation and Development.

Hamburg, D. A. and Holl, J. E. 1999. "Preventing Deadly Conflict: From Global Housekeeping to Neighbourhood Watch." In I. Kaul, I. Grunberg, and M. A. Stern (eds), *Global Public Goods*, Oxford: Oxford University Press, pp. 366–81.

Hansen, H. and Tarp, F. 2000. "Aid Effectiveness Disputed." *Journal of International Development*, 12 (3), pp. 375–98.

Hansen, H. and Tarp, F. 2001. "Aid and Growth Regressions." *Journal of Development Economics*, 64 (2), pp. 547–70.

Hansen, N. E. and McClure, I. 1998. "Protecting Migrants and Ethnic Minorities From Discrimination in Employment: The Danish Experience." ILO International Migration Papers No. 25. Geneva: ILO.

Hanson, G. H. 2008. "The Economic Consequences of the International Migration of Labour." NBER Working Paper No. 14490. Cambridge, MA: NBER.

Hanson, J. A., Honohan, P., and Majnoni, G. 2003. "Globalization and National Financial Systems: Issues of Integration and Size." In J. A. Hanson, P. Honohan, and G. Majnoni (eds), *Globalization and National Financial Systems*. Washington, DC: World Bank, pp. 1–32.

Harzig, C., Hoerder, D., and Gabaccia, D. 2009. *What is Migration History?* Cambridge and Malden: Polity Press.

Hatton, T. J. and Williamson, J. G. 1994. "What Drove the Mass Migrations from Europe in the Late Nineteenth Century?" *Population and Development Review*, 20 (3), pp. 533–57.

Hatton, T. J. and Williamson, J. G. 1998. *The Age of Mass Migration*. Oxford: Oxford University Press.

Haug, S. 2008. "Migration Networks and Migration Decision-Making." *Journal of Ethnic and Migration Studies*, 34 (4), pp. 585–605.

Hawkins, E. K. 1970. *The Principles of Development Aid*. Harmondsworth: Penguin.

Hayter, T. 1971. *Aid as Imperialism*. Harmondsworth: Penguin.

Heath, A. F., Rothon, C., and Kilpi, E. 2008. "The Second Generation in Western Europe: Education, Unemployment, and Occupational Attainment." *Annual Review of Sociology*, 38, pp. 211–35.

Held, D. and McGrew, A. G. 2007. *Globalization/Anti-Globalization: Beyond the Great Divide*. Cambridge: Polity.

Helleiner, E. and Pickel, A. (eds) 2005. *Economic Nationalism in a Globalizing World*. Ithaca: Cornell University Press.

Heo, Y. and Doanh, N. K. 2009. "Trade Liberalisation and Poverty Reduction in Vietnam." *World Economy*, 32 (6), pp. 934–64.

Hertel, T. W. and Ivanic, M. 2006. "Making the Doha Development Agenda More Poverty Friendly: The Role of South-South Trade." *Review of Agricultural Economics*, 28 (3), pp. 354–61.

Hertel, T. W. and Reimer, J. J. 2005. "Predicting the Poverty Impacts of Trade Reform." *Journal of International Trade and Economic Development*, 14 (4), pp. 377–405.

Heshmati, A. and Lee, M. 2009. "Information and Communication Technology." In K. A. Reinert, R. S. Rajan, A. J. Glass, and L. S. Davis (eds), *The Princeton Encyclopedia of the World Economy*. Princeton: Princeton University Press, pp. 628–35.

Hjertholm, P. and White, H. 2000. "Foreign Aid in Historical Perspective." In F. Tarp (ed.), *Foreign Aid and Development*. London: Routledge, pp. 80–102.

Hochschild, A. 1999. *King Leopold's Ghost*. Boston: Houghton Mifflin.

Hoefer, M., Rytina, N., and Campbell, C. 2007. "Estimates of the Unauthorized Immigrant Population Residing in the United States: January 2006." *Population Estimates 2007*. Washington, DC: Office of Immigration Statistics Policy Directorate.

Hoekman, B. M. and Kostecki, M. M. 2009. *The Political Economy of the World Trading System*. Oxford: Oxford University Press.

Hoekman, B. M., Martin, W., and Mattoo, A. 2010. "Conclude Doha: It Matters!" *World Trade Review*, 9 (3), pp. 505–30.

Hoekman, B. M., Maskus, K. E., and Saggi, K. 2005. "Transfer of Technology to Developing Countries: Unilateral and Multilateral Policy Options." *World Development*, 33 (10), pp. 1587–602.

Hoff, K. and Stiglitz, J. E. 2001. "Modern Economic Theory and Development." In G. M. Meier and J. E. Stiglitz (eds), *Frontiers of Development Economics: The Future in Perspective*. Oxford: Oxford University Press, pp. 389–459.

Homer-Dixon, T. F. 1991. "On the Threshold: Environmental Changes as Causes of Acute Conflict." *International Security*, 16 (2), pp. 76–116.

Hossain, M. and Karunaratne, N. D. 2004. "Trade Liberalization and Technical Efficiency: Evidence from Bangladesh Manufacturing Industries." *Journal of Development Studies*, 40 (3), pp. 87–114.

House of Lords. 2008. *The Economic Impact of Immigration*. London: The Stationery Office Limited.

Howard, N. and Lalani, M. 2008. "The Politics of Human Trafficking." *St Antony's International Review*, 4 (1), pp. 5–15.

Hudson Institute. 2009. *The Index of Global Philanthropy and Remittances 2009*. Washington, DC: Center for Global Prosperity.

Hudson Institute. 2010. *The Index of Global Philanthropy and Remittances 2010.* Washington, DC: Center for Global Prosperity.

Human Rights Watch. 2004. *Bad Dreams: Exploitation of Migrant Workers in Saudi Arabia.* New York: Human Rights Watch.

Human Security Centre. 2005. *Human Security Report.* Oxford: Oxford University Press.

Hunt, J. and Gauthier-Loiselle, M. 2008. "How Much Does Immigration Boost Innovation?" NBER Working Paper No. 14312. Cambridge, MA: National Bureau of Economic Research.

Hyman, I. 2001. "Immigration and Health." Health Policy Working Paper No. 01–05. Ottawa: Health Canada.

Hymer, S. 1976. *The International Operation of National Firms.* Cambridge, MA: MIT Press.

ILO. 2004. *Towards a Fair Deal for Migrant Workers in the Global Economy.* Geneva: International Labour Organization.

ILO. 2007. *Forced Labour Statistics Factsheet.* Geneva: International Labour Organization.

IMF. 1998. *External Evaluation of ESAF: Report by a Group of Independent Experts.* Washington, DC: International Monetary Fund.

IMF. 2008. "IMF Presses Donors to Maintain Aid Flows Amid Crisis." *IMF Survey Magazine Online,* November 28. http://www.imf.org/external/pubs/ft/survey/so/2008/new112808a.htm (accessed April 21, 2011).

IMF. 2009. *Heavily Indebted Poor Countries (HIPC) Initiative and Multilateral Debt Relief Initiative (MDRI)—Status of Implementation.* International Development Association and International Monetary Fund.

IMF. 2010. "Debt Relief Under the Heavily Indebted Poor Countries (HIPC) Initiative." IMF Factsheet, December 17. http://www.imf.org/external/np/exr/facts/hipc.htm (accessed March 29, 2011).

Inama, S. 2002. "Market Access for LDCs: Issues to Be Addressed." *Journal of World Trade,* 36 (1), pp. 85–116.

Institute for International Education. 2009. *Open Doors 2008: Report on International Education Exchange.* Washington, DC: Institute for International Education.

International Centre for Trade and Sustainable Development. 2003. *Intellectual Property Rights: Implications for Development.* Geneva: International Centre for Trade and Sustainable Development.

IOM. 2005. *World Migration 2005: Costs and Benefits of International Migration.* Geneva: IOM.

IOM. 2008. *World Migration 2008: Managing Labour Mobility in the Evolving Global Economy.* Geneva: International Organization for Migration.

IOM. 2011. "Definitional issues." International Organization for Migration. http://www.iom.int/jahia/Jahia/activities/by-theme/migration-climate-change-environmental-degradation/definitional-issues (accessed April 8, 2011).

IPPR. 2007. *Britain's Immigrants: An Economic Profile.* London: Institute for Public Policy Research.

Jacoby, T. 2006. "Immigration Nation." *Foreign Affairs,* November/December, pp. 50–65.

Jaffee, S. and Masakure, O. 2005. Strategic Use of Private Standards to Enhance International Competitiveness: Vegetable Exports from Kenya and Elsewhere.' *Food Policy,* 30 (3), pp. 316–33.

James, H. 1996. *International Monetary Cooperation Since Bretton Woods.* Oxford: Oxford University Press.

Jasso, G., Massey, D. S., Rosenzweig, M. R., and Smith, J. P. 2004. "Immigrant Health—Selectivity and Acculturation." In N. B. Anderson, R. A. Bulatao, and B. Cohen (eds), *Critical Perspectives on Racial and Ethnic Differences in Health in Late Life*. Washington, DC: The National Academies Press, pp. 227–66.

Javorcik, B. S. 2004. "Does Foreign Direct Investment Increase the Productivity of Domestic Firms? In Search of Spillovers through Backward Linkages." *American Economic Review*, 94 (3), pp. 605–27.

Jayanthakumaran, K. 2003. "Benefit-Cost Appraisals of Export Processing Zones: A Survey of the Literature." *Development Policy Review*, 21 (1), pp. 51–65.

Jenkins, M. 2006. "Sourcing Patterns of Firms in Export Processing Zones (EPZs): An Empirical Analysis of Firm-Level Determinants." *Journal of Business Research*, 59 (3), pp. 331–4.

Jenkins, R. 2004. "Vietnam in the Global Economy: Trade, Employment and Poverty." *Journal of International Development*, 16 (1), pp. 13–28.

Jeon, H-C. 2010. "Sound Macro Fundamentals Lead to Rapid Recovery of Korean Economy." *SERI Quarterly*, 3 (3), July, pp. 12–20.

Johansson, H. and Nilsson, L. 1997. "Export Processing Zones as Catalysts." *World Development*, 25 (12), pp. 2115–28.

Johnson, S., Ostry, J. D., and Subramanian, A. 2010. "Prospects for Sustained Growth in Africa: Benchmarking the Constraints." *IMF Staff Papers*, 57 (1), pp. 119–71.

Johnston, L. 2011. "The Rise of China and Africa: Old Lessons for New Normals." Mimeo (draft February 26). Washington, DC: World Bank.

Joyce, J. P. and Nabar, M. 2009. "Sudden Stops, Banking Crises and Investment Collapsed in Emerging Markets." *Journal of Development Economics*, 90 (2), pp. 314–22.

Jules, P. 2003. "The Externalities and Multifunctionality of Agriculture." *EuroChoices*, 2 (3), pp. 40–5.

Kabeer, N. 2004. "Globalization, Labor Standards, and Women's Rights: Dilemmas of Collective (In)Action in An Interdependent World." *Feminist Economics*, 10 (1), pp. 3–35.

Kabeer, N. and Mahmud, S. 2004. "Globalization, Gender, and Poverty: Bangladeshi Women Workers in Export and Local Markets." *Journal of International Development*, 16 (1), pp. 93–109.

Kakwani, N. and Silber, J. (eds) 2008. *The Many Dimensions of Poverty*. London: Palgrave Macmillan.

Kambhampati, U. S. and Parikh, A. 2003. "Disciplining Firms: The Impact of Trade Reforms on Profit Margins in Indian Industry." *Applied Economics*, 35 (4), pp. 461–70.

Kaminsky, G. L., Reinhart, C. M., and Végh, C. A. 2003. "The Unholy Trinity of Financial Contagion." *Journal of Economic Perspectives*, 17 (4), pp. 51–74.

Kanbur, R. 2006. "The Economics of International Aid." In L-A. Gérard-Varet, S-C. Kolm, and J. Mercier Ythier (eds), *Handbook on the Economics of Giving, Reciprocity and Altruism*. Amsterdam: North-Holland: Elsevier, pp. 1559–88.

Kapur, D. and Whittle, D. 2010. "Can the Privatisation of Foreign Aid Enhance Accountability?" *New York University International Journal of Law and Politics*, 42 (4), pp. 101–37.

Kash, D. E. and Kingston, W. 2001. "Patents in a World of Complex Technologies." *Science and Public Policy*, 28 (1), pp. 11–22.

Kassouf, A. L. and Senauer, B. 1996. "Direct and Indirect Effects of Parental Education on Malnutrition among Children in Brazil: A Full Income Approach." *Economic Development and Cultural Change*, 44 (4), pp. 817–38.

Kaufmann, D. 2009. "Aid Effectiveness and Governance: The Good, the Bad and the Ugly." World Bank Special Report. *Development Outreach*, February, pp. 26–9.

Kaul, I., Conceição, P., Le Goulven, K., and Mendoza, R. U. 2003. "How to Improve the Provision of Global Public Goods." In I. Kaul, P. Conceição, K. Le Goulven, and R. U. Mendoza (eds), *Providing Global Public Goods: Managing Globalization.* New York: Oxford University Press, pp. 21–58.

Kaul, I., Grunberg, I., and Stern, M. A. 1999. "Defining Global Public Goods." In I. Kaul, I. Grundberg, and M. A. Stern (eds), *Global Public Goods: International Cooperation in the 21st Century.* Oxford: Oxford University Press, pp. 2–19.

Kerr, S. P. and Kerr, W. R. 2008. "Economic Impacts of Immigration: A Survey." Harvard Business School Working Paper No. 09–013. Cambridge, MA: Harvard University.

Kerr, W. R. and Lincoln, W. F. 2008. "The Supply Side of Innovation: H-1B Visa Reforms and US Ethnic Invention." Harvard Business School Working Paper No. 09–005. Cambridge, MA: Harvard University.

Ketkar, S. L. and Ratha, D. 2010. "Diaspora Bonds: Tapping the Diaspora During Difficult Times." *Journal of International Commerce, Economics and Policy*, 1 (2), pp. 251–63.

Keynes, J. M. 1920. *The Economic Consequences of the Peace.* New York: Harcourt, Brace and Howe.

Kharas, H. 2007. "The New Reality of Aid." *Brookings Blum Roundtable 2007.* Washington, DC: Wolfensohn Center for Development at the Brookings Institution.

Khurana, A. 2006. "Strategies for Global R&D." *Research Technology Management*, 49 (2), 48–57.

Kim, S. J. and Reinert, K. A. 2009. "Standards and Institutional Capacity: An Examination of Trade in Food and Agricultural Products." *International Trade Journal*, 23 (1), pp. 54–77.

King, R. G. and Levine, R. 1993. "Finance and Growth: Schumpeter Might Be Right." *Quarterly Journal of Economics*, 108 (3), pp. 717–37.

Kington, T. 2011. "UN Says 400 African Migrants Feared Drowned in Mediterranean." *The Guardian*, April 4, p. 7.

Kirigia, J. M., Gbary, A. R., Muthuri, L. K., Nyoni, J., and Seddoh, A. 2006. "The Cost of Health Professionals' Brain Drain in Kenya." *BMC Health Services Research*, 6 (89), pp. 1–10.

Klein, N. 2000. *No Logo: Taking Aim at the Brand Bullie.* New York: Picador.

Klein Solomon, M. and Bartsch, K. 2003. *The Berne Initiative: Toward the Development of an International Policy Framework on Migration.* Geneva: International Organization for Migration.

Klump, R. 2007. 'Pro-Poor Growth in Vietnam: Miracle or Model? In T. Besley and L. J. Cord (eds), *Delivering on the Promise of Pro-Poor Growth.* Washington, DC: World Bank, pp. 119–46.

Kofman, E. and Meetoo, V. 2008. "Family Migration." *World Migration 2008: Managing Labour Mobility in the Evolving Global Economy.* Geneva: IOM.

Kohpaiboon, A. 2006. "Foreign Direct Investment and Technology Spillovers: A Cross-Industry Analysis of Thai Manufacturing." *World Development*, 34 (3), pp. 541–56.

Kokko, A. 1994. "Technology, Market Characteristics, and Spillovers." *Journal of Development Economics*, 43 (2), pp. 279–93.

Kokko, A. and Blomström, M. 1995. "Policies to Encourage Inflows of Technology Through Foreign Multinationals." *World Development*, 23 (3), pp. 459–68.

Kokko, A., Tansini, R., and Zehan, M. C. 1996. "Local Technological Capability and Productivity Spillovers from FDI in the Uruguayan Manufacturing Sector." *Journal of Development Studies*, 32 (4), pp. 602–11.

Kose, M. A., Prasad, E.S., Rogoff, K., and Wei, S.-J. 2009. "Financial Globalization: A Reappraisal." *IMF Staff Papers*, 56 (1), pp. 8–62.

Kose, M. A., Prasad, E. S., and Terrones, M. E. 2003. "Financial Integration and Macroeconomic Volatility." *IMF Staff Papers*, 50 (S), pp. 119–42.

Koser, K. and Van Hear, N. 2003 "Asylum Migration and Implications for Countries of Origin." WIDER Discussion Paper No. 2003/20. Helsinki: World Institute for Development Economic Research, United Nations University.

Kostecki, M. 2001. "Technical Assistance Services in Trade Policy: A Contribution to the Discussion on Capacity Building in the WTO." ICTSD Resource Paper No. 2. Geneva: International Centre for Trade and Sustainable Development.

Krishna, K. 2009. "Rules of Origin." In K. A. Reinert, R. S. Rajan, A. J. Glass, and L. S. Davis (eds), *Princeton Encyclopedia of the World Economy*. Princeton: Princeton University Press, pp. 980–2.

Krueger, A. B. and Lindahl, M. 1999. "Education for Growth in Sweden and the World." *Swedish Economic Policy Review*, 6 (2), pp. 289–339.

Krueger, J. 2001. "The Basel Convention and the International Trade in Hazardous Wastes." In *Yearbook of International Co-operation on Environment and Development 2001/02*. London: Earthscan, pp. 43–52.

Kugler, M. 2006. "Spillovers from Foreign Direct Investment: Within or Between Industries?" *Journal of Development Economics*, 80 (2), pp. 444–77.

Kuznetsov, Y. N. (ed.) 2006. *Diaspora Networks and the International Migration of Skills: How Countries Can Draw on Their Talent Abroad*. Washington, DC: World Bank Institute.

La Chimia, A. and Arrowsmith, S. 2009. "Addressing Tied Aid: Towards a More Development-Friendly WTO?" *Journal of International Economic Law*, 12 (3), pp. 707–47.

Lall, S. 1998. "Exports of Manufactures by Developing Countries: Emerging Patterns of Trade and Location." *Oxford Review of Economic Policy*, 14 (2), pp. 54–73.

Lall, S. and Teubal, M. 1998. "Market-Stimulating Technology Policies in Developing Countries: A Framework with Examples from East Asia." *World Development*, 26 (8), pp. 1369–85.

Landau, L. B. and Wa Kabwe Segatti, A. 2009. "Human Development Impacts of Migration: South Africa." UNDP Human Development Report 2009 Background Paper No. 05. New York: United Nations Development Programme.

Landes, D. S. 1998. *The Wealth and Poverty of Nations: Why Some Are So Rich and Others So Poor.* New York: Norton.

Lanjouw, J. 2006. "A Patent Policy Proposal for Global Diseases." *Innovations*, 1 (1), pp. 108–14.

Leach, J. 2004. *A Course in Public Economics*. Cambridge: Cambridge University Press.

Lederman, D. and Maloney, W. F. 2009. "Trade Structure and Growth." In R. Newfarmer, W. Shaw, and P. Walkenhorst (eds), *Breaking into New Markets: Emerging Lessons for Export Diversificiation*. Washington, DC: World Bank, pp. 39–54.

Lee, Y. S. 2006. *Reclaiming Development in the World Trading System*. Cambridge: Cambridge University Press.

Lehr, D. 2008. "Dialing for Development." *Stanford Social Innovation Review*, Fall, pp. 44–9.

Levin, A. and Raut, L. 1997. "Complementarities between Exports and Human Capital in Economic Growth: Evidence from Semi-industrialized Countries." *Economic Development and Cultural Change*, 46 (1), pp. 155–74.

Levine, R. and Zervos, S. 1998. "Stock Markets, Banks, and Economic Growth." *American Economic Review*, 88 (3), pp. 537–58.

Levinson, M. 2006. *The Box: How the Shipping Container Made the World Smaller and the World Economy Bigger.* Princeton: Princeton University Press.

Levitt, P. 1998. "Social Remittances: Migration Driven Local Level Forms of Cultural Diffusion." *International Migration Review*, 32 (4), pp. 926–94.

Levitt, P. 2001. *The Transnational Villagers.* Stanford: University of California Press.

Lin, J. Y. 2009. *Economic Development and Transition: Thought, Strategy, and Viability.* Cambridge: Cambridge University Press.

Lindauer, D. L. and Pritchett, L. 2002. "What's the Big Idea? The Third Generation of Policies for Economic Growth." *Economia* (Journal of the Latin American and Caribbean Economic Association), 3 (1), pp. 1–28.

Lindley, A. 2008. "Conflict-Induced Migration and Remittances: Exploring Conceptual Frameworks." Working Paper Series No. 47. Oxford: Refugee Studies Centre, University of Oxford.

Linnerooth-Bayer, J. and Mechler, R. 2006. "Insurance for Assisting Adaptation to Climate Change in Developing Countries: A Proposed Strategy." *Climate Policy*, 6 (6), pp. 621–36.

Lipumba, N. H. I. 1994. *Africa Beyond Adjustment.* Washington, DC: Overseas Development Council.

Little, I. M. D. and Clifford, J. M. 1965. *International Aid.* London: George Allen and Unwin Ltd.

Liu, Z. 2002. "Foreign Direct Investment and Technology Spillover: Evidence from China." *Journal of Comparative Economics*, 30 (3), pp. 579–602.

Looy, van der, J. 2006. "China and Africa: A Strategic Partnership?" ASC Working Paper No. 67/2006. Leiden: African Studies Centre.

Lowell, L. 2008. "Highly Skilled Migration." *World Migration 2008: Managing Labour Mobility in the Evolving Global Economy.* Geneva: International Organization for Migration.

Lucas, R. 1990. "Why Doesn't Capital Flow from Rich to Poor Countries?" *American Economic Review*, 80 (2), pp. 92–6.

Lucas, R. 2005. *International Migration and Economic Development: Lessons from Low Income Countries.* Cheltenham, UK: Edward Elgar.

MacBride, S. 1980. *Many Voices, One World.* Paris: International Commission for the Study of Communication Problems, UNESCO.

McKinnon, R. I. and Pill, H. 1997. "Credible Economic Liberalization and Overborrowing." *American Economic Review*, 87 (2), pp. 189–93.

McLaughlan, G. and Salt, J. 2002. "Migration Policies Toward Highly Skilled Foreign Workers." Report to the UK Home Office, March. London: Migration Research Unit, Geography Department, University College London.

McVeigh, K. 2008. "Skilled Migrants are Vital to Economy, Study Says." *The Guardian*, March 25, p. 10.

Maddison, A. 2001. *The World Economy: A Millennial Perspective.* Paris: OECD Development Centre.

Maddison, A. 2007. *Contours of the World Economy: Essays in Macro-Economic History.* Oxford: Oxford University Press.

Maertens, M. and Swinnen, J. F. M. 2009. "Trade, Standards, and Poverty: Evidence from Senegal." *World Development,* 37 (1), pp. 161–78.

Maimbo, S. M. and Ratha, D. 2005. *Remittances: Development Impact and Future Prospects.* Washington, DC: World Bank.

Mander, J. and Goldsmith, E. (eds) 1996. *The Case Against the Global Economy.* San Francisco: Sierra Club.

Mapstone, N. 2009. "Remittance Flows to Latin America Fall Sharply." *Financial Times,* August 12.

Marin, A. and Bell, M. 2006. "Technology Spillovers from Foreign Direct Investment (FDI): The Active Role of MNC Subsidiaries in Argentina in the 1990s." *Journal of Development Studies,* 42 (4), pp. 678–97.

Market Intelligence. n.d. "Nairobi Stock Exchange." Document on the Market Intelligence (Kenya) website. http://www.mi.co.ke (accessed 2005; website no longer available).

Markoff, J. 1996. *Waves of Democracy: Social Movements and Political Change.* London: Pine Forge Press.

Markusen, J. R. 1981. "Trade and the Gains from Trade with Imperfect Competition." *Journal of International Economics,* 11 (4), pp. 531–51.

Markusen, J. R. 1995. "The Boundaries of Multinational Enterprise and the Theory of International Trade." *Journal of Economic Perspectives,* 9 (2), pp. 169–89.

Marten, R. and Witte, J. M. 2008. "Transforming Development? The Role of Philanthropic Foundations in International Development Cooperation." Research Paper Series No. 10. Berlin: Global Public Policy Institute.

Martin, L. L. 1999. "The Political Economy of International Cooperation." In I. Kaul, I. Grundberg, and M. A. Stern (eds), *Global Public Goods: International Cooperation in the 21st Century.* Oxford: Oxford University Press, pp. 51–64.

Martin, P. 1993. *Trade and Migration: NAFTA and Agriculture.* Washington, DC: Institute for International Economics.

Martin, P. 2008. "Low and Semi-Skilled Workers Abroad." *World Migration 2008: Managing Labour Mobility in the Evolving Global Economy.* Geneva: International Organization for Migration.

Martin, P., Martin, S., and Cross, S. 2007. "High Level Dialogue on Migration and Development." *International Migration,* 41 (1), pp. 7–25.

Martin, P. and Taylor, J. E. 2001. "Managing Migration: The Role of Economic Policies." In A. R. Zolberg and P. M. Benda (eds), *Global Migrants Global Refugees: Problems and Solutions.* Oxford: Berghahn Books, pp. 95–120.

Martin, W. and Mitra, D. 2001. "Productivity Growth and Convergence in Agriculture versus Manufacturing." *Economic Development and Cultural Change,* 49 (2), pp. 401–22.

Massey, D. S., Arango, J., Hugo, G., Kouaouci, A., Pellegrino, A., and Taylor, J. E. 1993. "Theories of International Migration: A Review and Appraisal." *Population and Development Review,* 19 (3), pp. 431–66.

Massey, D. S., Arango, J., Hugo, G., Kouaouci, A., Pellegrino, A., and Taylor, J. E. 2002. *Worlds in Motion: Understanding International Migration at the End of the Millennium.* Oxford: Oxford University Press.

Massey, D. S. and Taylor, J. E. 2004. "Back to the Future: Immigration Research, Immigration Policy, and Globalization in the Twenty-First Century." In D. S. Massey and J. E. Taylor (eds), *International Migration: Prospects and Policies in a Global Market*. Oxford: Oxford University Press, pp. 373–87.

Matthews, D. 2004. "WTO Decision on Implementation of Paragraph 6 of the Doha Declaration on the TRIPS Agreement and Public Health: A Solution to the Access to Essential Medicines Problem?" *Journal of International Economic Law*, 7 (1), pp. 73–107.

Matthews, D. 2006. "From the August 30, 2003, WTO Decision to the December 6, 2005, Agreement on Amendments to TRIPS: Improving Access to Medicines in Developing Countries?" *Intellectual Property Quarterly*, 10 (2), pp. 91–130.

Mattoo, A. 2009. "Exporting Services." In R. Newfarmer, W. Shaw, and P. Walkenhorts (eds), *Breaking into New Markets: Emerging Lessons for Export Diversification*. Washington, DC: World Bank, pp. 161–82.

Mattoo, A. Neagu, I., and Özden, C. 2008. "Brain Waste? Educated Immigrants in the US Labor Market." *Journal of Development Economics*, 87 (2), pp. 255–69.

Meier, G. M. 2001. "Introduction: Ideas for Development." In G. M. Meier and J. E. Stiglitz (eds), *Frontiers of Development Economics: The Future in Perspective*. Oxford: Oxford University Press, pp. 1–12.

Mendez, R. P. 1999. "Peace as a Global Public Good." In I. Kaul, I. Grunberg, and M. A. Stern (eds), *Global Public Goods*. Oxford: Oxford University Press, pp. 382–416.

Mereu, F. 2001. "Russia: Moscow Markets Present Troubled Tableau of Life of City's Immigrants." *Radio Free Europe/Radio Liberty*, November 14.

Mill, J. S. 1846. *The Principles of Political Economy*. London: Longmans, Green and Co.

Minnesota Department of Health. 2003. *Eliminating Health Disparities Initiative: 2003 Report to the Legislature*. Minnesota: Office of Minority and Multicultural Health, Minnesota Department of Health. http://www.health.state.mn.us/ommh/publications/legrpt012103.pdf (accessed August 10, 2009).

Minot, N. and Goletti, F. 2000. "Rice Market Liberalization and Poverty in Vietnam." IFPRI Research Report No. 114. Washington, DC: International Food Policy Research Institute.

Miquel-Florensa, J. 2007. "Aid Effectiveness: A Comparison of Tied and Untied Aid." Working Paper No. 2007/2. York: Department of Economics, York University.

Mishkin, F. S. 1999. "Global Financial Instability: Framework, Events, Issues." *Journal of Economic Perspectives*, 13 (4), pp. 3–20.

Moahi, K. H. 2007. "Globalization, Knowledge Economy and the Implications for Indigenous Knowledge." *International Review of Information Ethics*, 7, pp. 55–62.

Mohapatra, S., Ratha, D., and Silwal, A. 2010. "Outlook for Remittance Flows 2011–2012." Migration and Development Brief No. 13. Washington, DC: Migration and Remittances Unit, World Bank, November 8.

Moran, T. H. 1998. *Foreign Direct Investment and Development*. Washington, DC: Institute for International Economics.

Moran, T. H. 2001. *Parental Supervision: The New Paradigm for Foreign Direct Investment and Development*. Washington, DC: Institute for International Economics.

Mun, T. 1664/1924. "England's Treasure by Foreign Trade." In A. E. Munro (ed.), *Early Economic Thought*. Cambridge, MA: Harvard University Press, pp. 171–97.

Murphy, R. 2006. "Media Communications and Development." In D. A. Clark (ed.), *The Elgar Companion to Development Studies*. Cheltenham: Edward Elgar, pp. 357–62.

Murray, J. 2001. "A New Phase in the Regulation of Multinational Enterprises: The Role of the OECD." *Industrial Law Journal*, 30 (3), pp. 255–70.

Naím, M. 2005. *Illicit: How Smugglers, Traffickers, and Copycats are Hijacking the Global Economy*. Doubleday: New York.

Naím, M. 2007. "Rogue Aid." *Foreign Policy*, 159, March/April, pp. 95–6.

Nathan, M. 2008. *Your Place or Mine? The Local Economics of Migration*. London: Institute for Public Policy Research.

National Foundation for American Policy. 2006. "Nearly 40 Asian American and Pacific Island Organizations Unite to Demand Fair and Humane Integration Program." Press Release, May 19. http://www.apalc.org/pdffiles/Immigration%20Reform%20Press%20Release%200506. pdf (accessed August 10, 2009).

Nazmul, C. and Devarajan, S. 2006. "Human Development and Service Delivery in Asia." *Development Policy Review*, 24 (S), 81–97.

Ndikumana, L. and Boyce, J. K. 1998. "Congo's Odious Debt: External Borrowing and Capital Flight in Zaire." *Development and Change*, 29 (2), pp. 195–217.

Ndikumana, L. and Boyce, J. K. 2010. "Measurement of Capital Flight: Methodology and Results for Sub-Saharan Africa." *African Development Review*, 22 (4), pp. 471–81.

Ngugi, R., Murinde, V., and Green, C. J. 2002. "Does the Revitalization Process Really Enhance Stock Market Microstructure? Evidence from the Nairobi Stock Exchange." *African Finance Journal*, 4 (1), pp. 32–61.

Noh, S. and Kaspar, V. 2003. *Diversity and Immigrant Health*. Toronto: University of Toronto.

Nordas, H. K. 2003. "The Impact of Trade Liberalization on Women's Job Opportunities and Earnings in Developing Countries." *World Trade Review*, 2 (2), pp. 221–31.

Nordhaus, W. D. 2010. "Economic Aspects of Global Warming in a Post-Copenhagen Environment." *Proceedings of the National Academy of Science*, 107 (26), pp. 11721–6.

North, D. C. 1990. *Institutions, Institutional Change and Economic Performance*. Cambridge: Cambridge University Press.

Nunnenkamp, P. 2004. "To What Extent Can Foreign Direct Investment Help Achieve International Development Goals?" *World Economy*, 27 (5), pp. 657–77.

Nussbaum, M. C. 2000. *Women and Human Development: The Capabilities Approach*. Cambridge: Cambridge University Press.

O'Rourke, K. H. and Williamson, J. G. 1999. *Globalization and History: The Evolution of a Nineteenth-Century Atlantic Economy*. Cambridge, MA: MIT Press.

Obstfeld, M. 1998. "The Global Capital Market: Benefactor or Menace?" *Journal of Economic Perspectives*, 12 (4), pp. 9–30.

Obstfeld, M. 2009. "International Finance and Growth in Developing Countries: What Have We Learned?" *IMF Staff Papers*, 56 (1), pp. 63–111.

Ocampo, J. A. and Martin, J. 2003. *Globalization and Development: A Latin American and Caribbean Perspective*. Stanford: Stanford University Press.

Ocampo, J. A. and Parra, M. A. 2003. "The Terms of Trade for Commodities in the Twentieth Century." *CEPAL Review*, 79, pp. 7–35.

OECD. 2007. *International Migration Outlook 2007—SOPEMI*. Paris: Organization for Economic Cooperation and Development.

OECD. 2008a. *International Migration Outlook 2008—SOPEMI.* Paris: Organization for Economic Cooperation and Development.

OECD. 2008b. *The Paris Declaration on Aid Effectiveness and the Accra Agenda for Action.* Paris: Organization for Economic Cooperation and Development. http://www.oecd.org/dataoecd/11/41/34428351.pdf (accessed March 24, 2011).

Olivier, L. 2009. "Giving Something Back: Exploring Making a Contribution at a Distance: Policy and Practice." *ResIST Thematic Paper* 1, January.

ONS. 2010. *Migration Statistics 2009.* Statistical Bulletin, November 25. Cardiff: Office for National Statistics. http://www.statistics.gov.uk/pdfdir/miga1110.pdf (accessed May 4, 2011).

Oreopoulos, P. 2009. "Why Do Skilled Immigrants Struggle in the Labor Market? A Field Experiment with Six Thousand Resumes." Metropolis Working Paper No. 09–03. Vancouver: Metropolis British Columbia.

Ortega, F. and Peri, G. 2009. "The Causes and Effects of International Migrations: Evidence from OECD Countries 1980–2005." NBER Working Paper No. 14833. Cambridge, MA: National Bureau of Economic Research.

Osmani, S. and Sen, A. 2003. "The Hidden Penalties of Gender Inequality: Fetal Origins of Ill-Health." *Economics and Human Biology,* 1 (1), pp. 105–21.

Osterhammel, J. and Petersson, N. P. 2005. *Globalization: A Short History.* Princeton: Princeton University Press.

Ostry, J. D., Ghosh, A. R., Habermeier, K., Chamon, M., Qureshi, M. S., and Reinhardt, D. B. S. 2010. "Capital Inflows: The Role of Controls." IMF Staff Position Note SPN 10/04, February 19. Washington, DC: International Monetary Fund.

Otsuki, T., Wilson, J. S., and Sewadeh, M. 2001. "Saving Two in a Billion: Quantifying the Trade Effect of European Food Safety Standards on African Exports." *Food Policy,* 26 (5), pp. 495–514.

Ouattara, B. and Strobl, E. 2008. "Aid, Policy and Growth: Does Aid Modality Matter?" *Review of World Economics,* 144 (2), pp. 347–65.

Owens, T. and Hoddinott, J. 1998. "Investing in Development or Investing in Relief: Quantifying the Poverty Tradeoffs Using Zimbabwe Household Panel Data." Working Paper No. WPS/99–4. Harare: Centre for the Study of African Economies.

Oxfam. 2002. *Rigged Rules and Double Standards: Trade, Globalization and the Fight against Poverty.* Oxford: Oxfam.

Oxfam. 2005. *Paying the Price: Why Rich Countries Must Invest Now in a War on Poverty.* Oxford: Oxfam.

Oxfam. 2009. "Morecambe Bay 5 Years On—Abuse of Migrant Workers Continues". February 5. http://www.oxfam.org.uk/applications/blogs/pressoffice/?p = 3541 (accessed May 4, 2011).

Özden, C. and Schiff, M. (eds) 2006. *International Migration, Remittances, and the Brain Drain.* Basingstoke: Palgrave MacMillan.

Pack, H. and Westphal, L. E. 1986. "Industrial Strategy and Technological Change: Theory versus Reality." *Journal of Development Economics,* 22 (1), pp. 87–128.

Pagano, M. 1993. "Financial Markets and Growth: An Overview." *European Economic Review,* 37 (2–3), pp. 613–22.

Page, S. E. 2007. *The Difference: How The Power of Diversity Creates Better Groups, Firms, Schools, and Societies.* Princeton: Princeton University Press.

Papademetriou, D. 2003. "Managing Rapid and Deep Change in the Newest Age of Migration." *Political Quarterly,* 74 (1), pp. 39–58.

Park, A. and Johnston, B. 1995. "Rural Development and Dynamic Externalities in Taiwan's Structural Transformation." *Economic Development and Cultural Change*, 44 (1), pp. 181–208.

Parsons, C. R., Skeldon, R., Walmsley, T. L., and Winters, L. A. 2007. "Quantifying International Migration: A Database of Bilateral Migrant Stocks." World Bank Policy Research Working Paper No. 4165, March. Washington, DC: World Bank.

Paul, R. 2006. "True Foreign Aid." May 2. http://antiwar.com/paul/?articleid=8926 (last accessed April 19, 2011).

Peri, G. and Sparber, C. 2008. "Task Specialization, Immigration, and Wages." CReAM Discussion Paper Series No. 02/08. London: Centre for Research and Analysis of Migration (CReAM), University College London.

Perucca, B. and Le Moël, M.-M. 2010. "Foreign Labour Levels Squeezed as Financial Crisis Shrinks Job Market." *Guardian Weekly* (online), July 20.

Peterson, E. W. F. 2009. *A Billion Dollars a Day: The Economics and Politics of Agricultural Subsidies*. Oxford: Wiley-Blackwell.

Pettersson, J. 2007. "Foreign Sectoral Aid Fungibility, Growth and Poverty Reduction." *Journal of International Development*, 19, pp. 1074–98.

Pio, A. 1994. "New Growth Theory and Old Development Problems." *Development Policy Review*, 12 (3), pp. 277–300.

Plender, J. 2004. "A Big Squeeze for Governments: How Transfer Pricing Threatens Global Tax Revenues." *Financial Times*, July 22.

Pogge, T. W. 1999. "Human Flourishing and Universal Justice." *Social Philosophy and Policy*, 16 (1), pp. 333–61.

Pomerantz, P. R. 2004. *Aid Effectiveness in Africa: Developing Trust between Donors and Governments*. New York: Lexington Books.

Portes, A. 2008. "Migration and Development: A Conceptual Review of the Evidence." In S. Castles and R. Delgado Wise (eds), *Migration and Development: Perspectives from the South*. Geneva: IOM, pp. 17–41.

Portes, A. and DeWind, J. 2004. "A Cross-Atlantic Dialogue: The Progress of Research and Theory in the Study of International Migration." *International Migration Review*, 38 (3), pp. 828–51.

Porto, G. G. 2006. "Using Survey Data to Address the Distributional Effects of Trade Policy." *Journal of International Economics*, 70 (1), pp. 140–60.

Pozo, S. 2009. "Remittances." In K. A. Reinert, R. S. Rajan, A. J. Glass, and L. S. Davis (eds), *The Princeton Encyclopedia of the World Economy*. Princeton: Princeton University Press, pp. 963–8.

Prahalad, C. K. and Hart, S. 2002. "The Fortune at the Bottom of the Pyramid." *Strategy + Business*, 26, pp. 54–67.

Prahalad, C. K. and Mashelkar, R. A. 2010. "Innovation's Holy Grail." *Harvard Business Review*, 88 (7–8), pp. 132–41.

Prasad, E. S., Rajan, R. G., and Subramanian, A. 2007. "Foreign Capital and Economic Growth." *Brookings Papers on Economic Activity*, 1, pp. 153–230.

Prasad, E. S., Rogoff, K., Wei, S-J., and Kose, M. A. 2005. "Effects of Financial Globalization on Developing Countries: Some Empirical Evidence." In N. Roubini and M. Uzan (eds), *New International Financial Architecture, Volume 2*. Cheltenham: Edward Elgar, pp. 491–576.

Preston, S.H. 1975. "The Changing Relation between Mortality and Level of Economic Development." *Population Studies*, 29 (2), pp. 231–48.

Pritchett, L. 2000. "Understanding Patterns of Economic Growth: Searching for Hills Among Plateaus, Mountains, and Plains." *World Bank Economic Review,* 14 (2), pp. 221–50.

Pritchett, L. 2006. *Let Their People Come: Breaking the Gridlock On Global Labor Mobility.* Washington, DC: Center for Global Development.

Psacharopoulos, G. 1985. "Returns to Education: A Further International Update and Implications." *Journal of Human Resources,* 20 (4), pp. 583–97.

Psacharopoulos, G. 1994. "Returns to Investment in Education: A Global Update." *World Development,* 22 (9), pp. 1325–43.

Psacharopoulos, G. and Patrinos, H. A. 2004. "Returns to Investment in Education: A Further Update." *Education Economics,* 12 (2), pp. 111–34.

Puri, L. 2004 "The Engendering of Trade for Development: An Overview of the Main Issues." In A. Tran-Nguyen and A. B. Zampetti (eds), *Trade and Gender Opportunities and Challenges for Developing Countries.* New York: United Nations, pp. 55–76.

Putnam, R. D. 2007. "E Pluribus Unum: Diversity and Community in the Twenty-First Century, The 2006 Johan Skytte Prize Lecture." *Scandinavian Political Studies,* 30 (2), pp. 137–74.

Qizilbash, M. 2006. "Human Development." In D. A. Clark (ed.), *The Elgar Companion to Development Studies.* Cheltenham: Edward Elgar, pp. 245–50.

Quartey, P. 2005. "Innovative Ways of Making Aid Effective in Ghana: Tied Aid versus Direct Budgetary Support." *Journal of International Development,* 17 (8), pp. 1077–92.

Radelet, S., Clemens, M., and Bhavnani, R. 2005. "Aid and Growth." *Finance and Development,* 43 (3), pp. 16–20.

Rajan, R. G. and Subramanian, A. 2008. "Aid and Growth: What Does the Cross-Country Evidence Really Show?" *Review of Economics and Statistics,* 90, pp. 643–65.

Rajan, R. G. and Subramanian, A. 2011. "Aid, Dutch Disease and Manufacturing Growth." *Journal of Development Economics,* 94 (1), pp. 106–18.

Rajan, R. G. and Zingales, A. 1998. "Financial Dependence and Growth." *American Economic Review,* 88 (3), pp. 559–86.

Rajan, R. S. and Bird, G. 2001. "Still the Weakest Link: The Domestic Financial System and Post 1998 Recovery in East Asia." *Development Policy Review,* 19 (3), pp. 355–66.

Rapoport, H. and Docquier, F. 2005. "The Economics of Migrants' Remittances." IZA DP No. 1531E. Bonn: Institute for the Study of Labor.

Rasmussen, D. B. 1999. "Human Flourishing and the Appeal to Human Nature." *Social Philosophy and Policy,* 16 (1), pp. 1–43.

Ratha, D. 2007. "Leveraging Remittances for Development." *Migration Policy Institute Policy Brief,* June. Washington, DC: Migration Policy Institute.

Ratha, D., Mohapatra, S., and Silwal, A. 2010. "Outlook for Remittance Flows 2010–2011." Migration and Development Brief 12, November 8. Washington, DC: Migration and Remittances Unit, World Bank.

Ravallion, M. 2006. "Looking Beyond Averages in the Trade and Poverty Debate." *World Development,* 34 (8), pp. 1374–92.

Ravallion, M. 2011. "On Multidimensional Indices of Poverty." Policy Research Working Paper No. 5580. Washington, DC: World Bank.

Ravallion, M., Chen, S., and Sangraula, P. 2009. "Dollar a Day Revisited." *World Bank Economic Review,* 23 (2), pp. 163–84.

Raynolds, L. T. 2000. "Re-Embedding Global Agriculture: The International Organic and Fair Trade Movements." *Agriculture and Human Values*, 17 (3), pp. 297–309.

Reality of Aid Network. 2010. *South-South Cooperation: A Challenge to the Aid System? The Reality of Aid.* Special Report on South-South Cooperation 2010. Quezon City, Philippians: IBON Books.

Recchi, E., Tambini, D., Baldoni, E., Williams, D., Surak, K., and Favell, A. 2003. "Intra-EU Migration: A Socio-Demographic Overview." Working Paper No. 3, Pioneur Project. http://www.obets.ua.es/pioneur/documentos_public.php (last accessed September 20, 2011).

Record, R. and Mohiddin, A. 2006. "An Economic Perspective on Malawi's Medical 'Brain Drain.'" *Globalization and Health*, 2 (12), pp. 1–8.

Redding, S. and Venables, A. J. 2004. "Geography and Export Performance: External Market Access and Internal Supply Capacity." In R. E. Baldwin and L. A. Winters (eds), *Challenges to Globalization: Analyzing the Economics.* Chicago: National Bureau of Economic Research and Chicago University Press, pp. 95–127.

Reinert, K. A. 1998. "Rural Non-Farm Development: A Trade-Theoretic View." *Journal of International Trade and Economic Development*, 7 (4), pp. 425–37.

Reinert, K. A. 2004. "Outcomes Assessment in Trade Policy Analysis: A Note on the Welfare Propositions of the 'Gains from Trade'." *Journal of Economic Issues*, 38 (4), pp. 1067–73.

Reinert, K. A. 2011. "No Small Hope: The Basic Good Imperative." *Review of Social Economy*, 69 (1), pp. 55–76.

Reinert, K. A. 2012. *An Introduction to International Economics: New Perspectives on the World Economy.* Cambridge: Cambridge University Press.

Reinhart, C. M. and Rogoff, K. S. 2009. *This Time Is Different: Eight Centuries of Financial Folly.* Princeton: Princeton University Press.

Reisen, H. and Soto, M. 2001. "Which Types of Capital Inflows Foster Developing-Country Growth?" *International Finance*, 4 (1), pp. 1–14.

Robbins, D. and Gindling, T. H. 1999. "Trade Liberalization and the Relative Wages for More-Skilled Workers in Costa Rica." *Review of Development Economics*, 3 (2), pp. 140–54.

Robinson, J. A., Torvik, R., and Verdier, T. 2006. "Political Foundations of the Resource Curse." *Journal of Development Economics*, 79 (2), pp. 447–68.

Rochet, J. C. 2010. "The Future of Banking Regulation." In M. Dewatripont, J. C. Rochet, and J. Tirole (eds), *Balancing the Banks: Global Lessons from the Financial Crisis.* Princeton: Princeton University Press, pp. 78–106.

Rodrigo, G. C. 2001. *Technology, Economic Growth and Crises in East Asia.* Aldershot: Edward Elgar.

Rodríguez, F. and Rodrik, D. 2001. "Trade Policy and Economic Growth: A Skeptic's Guide to the Cross-National Evidence." In B. Bernanke and K. S. Rogoff (eds), *Macroeconomics Annual 2000.* Cambridge, MA: MIT Press.

Rodrik, D. 1998. "Why Do More Open Economies Have Bigger Governments?" *Journal of Political Economy*, 106 (5), pp. 997–1032.

Rodrik, D. 2000. "Institutions for High-Quality Growth: What They Are and How to Acquire Them." *Studies in Comparative International Development*, 35 (3), pp. 3–31.

Rodrik, D. (ed.) 2003a. *In Search of Prosperity: Analytic Narratives on Economic Growth.* Princeton: Princeton University Press.

Rodrik, D. 2003b. "Introduction: What Do We Learn from Country Narratives?" In D. Rodrik (ed.), *In Search of Prosperity: Analytic Narratives on Economic Growth*. Princeton: Princeton University Press, pp. 1–19.

Rodrik, D. 2007. *One Economics Many Recipes: Globalization, Institutions and Economic Growth*. Princeton: Princeton University Press.

Rodrik, D. 2008. "The Real Exchange Rate and Economic Growth." *Brookings Papers on Economic Activity*, Fall, pp. 365–412.

Rodrik, D. and Subramanian, A. 2009. "Why Did Financial Globalization Disappoint?" *IMF Staff Papers*, 56 (1), pp. 112–38.

Rodrik, D., Subramanian, A., and Trebbi, F. 2004. "Institutions Rule: The Primacy of Institutions over Geography and Integration in Economic Development." *Journal of Economic Growth*, 9 (2), pp. 131–65.

Romer, P. 1993a. "Idea Gaps and Object Gaps in Economic Development." *Journal of Monetary Economics*, 32 (3), 543–73.

Romer, P. 1993b. "Two Strategies for Economic Development: Using Ideas and Producing Ideas." *Proceedings of the World Bank Annual Conference on Development Economics 1992*. Washington, DC: World Bank, pp. 63–91.

Root, H. L. 2006. *Capital and Collusion*. Princeton: Princeton University Press.

Rousseau, P. L. and Wachtel, P. 2000. "Equity Markets and Growth: Cross-Country Evidence on Timing and Outcomes, 1980–1995." *Journal of Banking and Finance*, 24 (12), pp. 1933–57.

Rowthorn, R. 2008. "The Fiscal Impact of Immigration on the Advanced Economies." *Oxford Review of Economic Policy*, 24, pp. 560–80.

Royal Society. 2011. "Knowledge, Networks and Nations: Global Scientific Collaboration in the 21st Century." RS Policy Document 03/11. London: Published by the Royal Society.

Rudra, N. 2008. *Globalization and the Race to the Bottom in Developing Countries: Who Really Gets Hurt*. Cambridge: Cambridge University Press.

Ruggie, J. 2008. "Protect, Respect and Remedy: A Framework for Business and Human Rights." *Innovations*, 3 (2), pp. 189–212.

Sachs, J. D. 2005. *The End of Poverty*. New York: Penguin.

Sachs, J. and Warner, A. 1995. "Economic Reform and the Process of Global Integration." *Brookings Papers on Economic Activity*, 1, pp. 1–118.

Sagasti, F. and Timmer, V. 2008. *A Review of the CGIAR as a Provider of International Public Goods*. System-wide review of CGIAR. Washington, DC: CGIAR. http://www.cgiar.org/pdf/ir_sagasti_timmer.pdf (accessed March 28, 2011).

Sahai, S. 2003. "Indigenous Knowledge and Its Protection in India." In C. Bellmann, G. Dutfield, and R. Meléndez-Ortiz (eds), *Trading in Knowledge: Development Perspectives on TRIPS, Trade and Sustainability*. London: Earthscan, pp. 166–74.

Saith, R. 2007. "Capabilities: The Concept and its Implementation." In F. Stewart, R. Saith, and B. Harriss-White (eds), *Defining Poverty in Developing Countries*. Basingstoke: Palgrave, pp. 55–74.

SAMIRAD. 2011. "Saudi Aid to the Developing World." http://www.saudinf.com/MAIN/l102.htm (accessed April 21, 2011).

Santiso, J. 2006. *Latin America's Political Economy of the Possible*. Cambridge, MA: MIT Press.

Sarno, L. and Taylor, M. P. 1999. "Hot Money, Accounting Labels and the Permanence of Capital Flows to Developing Countries: An Empirical Investigation." *Journal of Development Economics*, 59 (2), pp. 337–64.

Saxenian, A. 2005. "From Brain Drain to Brain Circulation: Transnational Communities and Regional Upgrading in India and China." *Studies in Comparative International Development*, 40 (2), pp. 35–61.

Schelling, T. 2009. "International Coordination to Assess the Climate Challenge." *Innovations*, 4 (4), pp. 13–21.

Schrank, A. 2001. "Export Processing Zones: Free Market Islands or Bridges to Structural Transformation?" *Development Policy Review*, 19 (2), pp. 223–42.

Schultz, T. P. 2002. "Why Governments Should Invest More to Educate Girls." *World Development*, 30 (2), pp. 207–25.

Schumpeter, J. 1934/1949. *The Theory of Economic Development*. Cambridge, MA: Harvard University Press.

Schwalbenberg, H. M. 1998. "Does Foreign Aid Cause the Adoption of Harmful Economic Policies?" *Journal of Policy Modeling*, 20 (5), pp. 669–75.

Sciortino, R. and Punpuing, S. 2009. *International Migration in Thailand 2009*. Geneva: IOM.

Scott, H. S. 2010. "Reducing Systemic Risk through the Reform of Capital Regulation." *Journal of International Economic Law*, 13 (3), pp. 763–78.

Seers, D. 1972. "What Are We Trying to Measure?" *Journal of Development Studies*, 8 (3), pp. 21–36.

Sen, A. 1980. "Equality of What." In S. M. McMurrin (ed.), *The Tanner Lectures on Human Values*. Salt Lake City: University of Utah Press, pp. 195–220.

Sen, A. 1984. *Resources, Values and Development*. Oxford: Basil Blackwell.

Sen, A. 1985. *Commodities and Capabilities*. Oxford: Elsevier Science Publishers.

Sen, A. 1987. *The Standard of Living*. Cambridge: Cambridge University Press.

Sen, A. 1989. "Development as Capability Expansion." *Journal of Development Planning*, 19, pp. 41–58.

Sen, A. 1999. *Development as Freedom*. New York: Knopf.

Sen, A. 2004. "Capabilities, Lists and Public Reason: Continuing the Conversation." *Feminist Economics*, 10 (3), pp. 77–80.

Sen, A. 2006a. "Human Development Index." In D. A. Clark (ed.), *The Elgar Companion to Development Studies*. Cheltenham: Edward Elgar, pp. 256–60.

Sen, A. 2006b. *Identity and Violence: The Illusion of Destiny*. New York: Norton.

Sen, A. 2006c. "It's Time for Global Control of Small Arms." *International Herald Tribune*, June 26.

Sen, A. 2009. *The Idea of Justice*. London: Allen Lane.

Sen, B., Mujeri, M. K., and Shahabuddin, Q. 2007. "Explaining Pro-Poor Growth in Bangladesh: Puzzles, Evidence, and Implications." In T. Besley and L. J. Cord (eds), *Delivering on the Promise of Pro-Poor Growth*. Washington, DC: World Bank, pp. 79–117.

Shapiro, C. 2004. "Patent System Reform: Economic Analysis and Critique." *Berkeley Technology Law Journal*, 19 (3), pp. 1017–47.

Simanis, E. and Hart, S. 2006. "Expanding Possibilities at the Base of the Pyramid." *Innovations*, 1 (1), pp. 43–51.

Singa Boyenge, J. P. 2007. "ILO Database on Export Processing Zones." Working Paper No. 251. Geneva: International Labor Office.

Singh, S. 2007. "From Exotic Spice to Modern Drug?" *Cell*, 130 (5), pp. 765–68.

Skeldon, R. 2009. "Of Skilled Migration, Brain Drains and Policy Responses." *International Migration*, 47 (4), pp. 3–29.

Smith, A. 1776/1937. *The Wealth of Nations*. New York: Modern Library.

Smith, J. P. and Edmonston, B. (eds) 1997. *The New Americans: Economic, Demographic and Fiscal Effects of Immigration*. Washington, DC: National Academy Press.

Sobhee, S. K. 2009. "The Economic Success of Mauritius: Lessons and Policy Options for Africa." *Journal of Economic Policy Reform*, 12 (1), pp. 29–42.

Sorel, E. and Padoan, P. (eds) 2008. *The Marshall Plan: Lessons Learned for the 21st Century*. Leeds: OECD Publishing.

Stark, O. 2005. "The New Economics of Brain Drain." *World Economics*, 6 (2), pp. 137–40.

Stark, O. and Bloom, D. E. 1985. "The New Economics of Labour Migration." *American Economic Review*, 75 (2), pp. 173–78.

Steil, B. 2001. "Creating Securities Markets in Developing Countries: A New Approach for the Age of Automated Trading." *International Finance*, 4 (2), pp. 257–78.

Stern, N. 2004. "Scaling Up Poverty Reduction." Paper presented at the Scaling Up Poverty Reduction: A Global Learning Process Conference, Shanghai, May 25–27.

Stern, N., Dethier, J.-J., and Rogers, H. 2004. *Growth and Empowerment: Making Development Happen*. Cambridge, MA: MIT Press.

Stewart, F. 1995. *Adjustment and Poverty: Options and Choices*. London: Routledge.

Stiglitz, J. E. 1987. "Learning to Learn, Localized Learning and Technological Progress." In Dasgupta and P. Stoneman (eds), *Economic Policy and Technological Performance*. New York: Cambridge University Press, 125–53.

Stiglitz, J. E. 1999. "Knowledge as a Global Public Good." In I. Kaul, I. Grundberg, and M. A. Stern (eds), *Global Public Goods: International Cooperation in the 21st Century*. Oxford: Oxford University Press, pp. 308–25.

Stiglitz, J. E. 2000. "Capital Market Liberalization, Economic Growth, and Instability." *World Development*, 28 (6), pp. 1075–86.

Stiglitz, J. E. 2002. *Globalization and Its Discontents*. New York: Norton.

Stiglitz, J. E. 2010. *Freefall: Free Markets and the Sinking Global Economy*. London: Allen Lane.

Stiglitz, J. E. and Weiss, A. 1981. "Credit Rationing in Markets with Imperfect Information." *American Economic Review*, 71 (3), 393–410.

Streeten, P. 1979. "From Growth to Basic Needs." *Finance and Development*, 16 (3), pp. 28–31.

Streeten, P. 1995. *Thinking About Development*. Cambridge: Cambridge University Press.

Streeten, P., Burki, S., Haq, M., Hicks, N., and Stewart, F. 1981. *First Things First: Meeting Basic Needs in Developing Countries*. Oxford: Oxford University Press.

Subramanian, A. and Roy, D. 2003. "Who Can Explain the Mauritian Miracle? Meade, Romer, Sachs, or Rodrik?" In D. Rodrik (ed.), *In Search of Prosperity: Analytical Narratives on Economic Growth*. Princeton: Princeton University Press, pp. 205–43.

Sumner, A. 2010. "Global Poverty and the New Bottom Billion: Three-Quarters of the World's Poor Live in Middle Income Countries." IDS Working Paper No. 359. Brighton: Institute of Development Studies.

Suryahadi, A., Sumarto, S., and Pritchett, L. 2003. "Evolution of Poverty During the Crisis in Indonesia." *Asian Economic Journal*, 17 (3), pp. 221–41.

Sweeney, C. and Booth, J. 2009. "Hundreds of Migrants Feared Drowned as Boat Sinks off Libya." *The Times*, March 31.

Szirmai, A. 2005. *The Dynamics of Socio-Economic Development*. Cambridge: Cambridge University Press.

Taylor, A. M. and Williamson, J. G. 1994. "Capital Flows to the New World as an Intergenerational Transfer." *Journal of Political Economy*, 102 (2), pp. 348–71.

Taylor, L. 1993. "Stabilization, Adjustment, and Reform." In L. Taylor (ed.), *The Rocky Road to Reform*. Cambridge, MA: MIT Press, pp. 39–94.

te Velde, D. W. 2001. *Government Policies toward Inward Foreign Direct Investment in Developing Countries*. Paris: OECD Development Centre.

te Velde, D. W. and Morrissey, O. 2003. "Do Workers in Africa Get a Wage Premium If Employed in Firms Owned by Foreigners?" *Journal of African Economies*, 12 (1), pp. 41–73.

Telegraphy. 2010. "International Phone Traffic Growth Slows, while Skype Accelerates." January 19. http://www.telegeography.com/products/commsupdate/articles/2010/01/19/international-phone-traffic-growth-slows-while-skype-accelerates/ (accessed April 28, 2011).

Tembon, M. and Fort, L. 2008. *Girls' Education in the 21st Century*. Washington, DC: World Bank.

Thomson, G. 2003. "Behind Roses' Beauty, Poor and Ill Workers." *New York Times*, February 13.

Transatlantic Trends. 2008. *Transatlantic Trends: Immigration*. Washington, DC: German Marshall Fund of the United States.

Transparency International. 2004. *Global Corruption Report 2004*. London: Pluto Press.

Tremblay, K. 2005. "Academic Mobility and Immigration." *Journal of Studies in International Education*, 9 (3), pp. 196–228.

Tsang, E. W. K., Nguyen, D. T., and Erramilli, M. K. 2004. "Knowledge Acquisition and Performance of International Joint Ventures in the Transition Economy of Vietnam." *Journal of International Marketing*, 12 (2), pp. 82–103.

Tsou, M.-W. and Liu, J.-T. 1994. "The Spillover Effects for Foreign Direct Investment: Empirical Evidence from Taiwan Manufacturing Industries." *Taiwan Economic Review*, 25 (2), pp. 155–81.

Tsunami Evaluation Coalition. 2007. *Synthesis Report*. London: Tsunami Evaluation Coalition.

UNAIDS. 2010a. "Global Report: Fact Sheet" (23 November), "Sub-Saharan Africa: Fact Sheet." November 23. Geneva: United Nations Program on HIV/AIDS. http://www.unaids.org/en/resources/presscentre/factsheets/ (accessed April 30, 2011).

UNAIDS. 2010b. *UNAIDS Report on the Global AIDS Epidemic 2010*. Geneva: United Nations Programme on HIV/AIDS.

UNAIDS. 2011. "Using TRIPS Flexibilities to Improve Access to HIV Treatment." *UNAIDS, WHO, UNDP Policy Brief*. http://www.unaids.org/en/media/unaids/contentassets/documents/policy/2011/JC2049_PolicyBrief_TRIPS_en.pdf (accessed May 1, 2011).

UNAIDS/UNDP/WHO. 2011. "UNAIDS/UNDP/WHO Concerned Over Sustainability and Scale Up of HIV Treatment." March 15. http://www.who.int/hiv/mediacentre/trips_20110315/en/index.html (accessed May 1, 2011).

UNCTAD. 2001. *World Investment Report*. Geneva: United Nations Conference on Trade and Development.

UNCTAD. 2004. *The Least Developed Country Report 2004*. Geneva: United Nations Conference on Trade and Development.

UNCTAD. 2005. *World Investment Report: Transnational Corporations and the Internationalization of R&D*. Geneva: United Nations Conference on Trade and Development.

UNDP. 1991. *Human Development Report 1991: Financing Human Development*. New York: Oxford University Press.

UNDP. 1998. *Human Development Report 1998: Consumption for Development*. New York: Oxford University Press.

UNDP. 2009. *Human Development Report 2009: Overcoming Barriers: Human Mobility and Development*. New York: UNDP.

UNDP. 2010. *Human Development Report 2010: The Real Wealth of Nations*. New York: Palgrave Macmillan.

UNHCR. 2005. *State of the World's Refugees*. Oxford: Oxford University Press.

UNHCR. 2006. *State of the World's Refugees 2006*. Oxford: Oxford University Press.

UNHCR. 2008a. *2007 UNHCR Statistical Annex*. Geneva: United Nations High Commission for Refugees, December 30.

UNHCR. 2008b. *Asylum Levels and Trends in Industrialized Countries*. Geneva: United Nations High Commission for Refugees, March 24.

UNHCR. 2008c. *2007 Global Trends: Refugees, Asylum-Seekers, Returnees, Internally Displaced and Stateless Persons*. Geneva: United Nations High Commission for Refugees.

UNHCR. 2009. *2008 Global Trends: Refugees, Asylum-Seekers, Returnees, Internally Displaced and Stateless Persons*. Geneva: United Nations High Commission for Refugees.

UNHCR. 2010. *UNHCR Statistical Yearbook 2009*. Geneva: United Nations High Commission for Refugees.

UNICEF. 2002. "Speeches at the U.N. Secretary General's Luncheon United Nations—New York, NY." UNICEF online press centre, http://www.unicef.org/media/media_9465.html (last accessed September 19, 2011).

UNICEF. 2006. *State of the World's Children: Excluded and Invisible*. New York: United Nations Children's Fund.

United Nations. 2004. *World Economic and Social Survey 2004: International Migration*. New York: United Nations.

United Nations. 2006. "International Migration and Development: Report of the Secretary-General." UN General Assembly, 60th Session, UN Doc. A/60/871, May 18.

United Nations Food and Agriculture Organization. 2009. *The State of Food Insecurity in the World 2009*. Rome: FAO.

United Nations Office on Drugs and Crime. 2009. *The Global Report on Trafficking in Persons*. Vienna: UNODC.

United Nations Population Division. 2004. "Proceedings of the Seminar on the Relevance of Population Aspects for the Achievement of the Millennium Development Goals." New York: Department of Economics and Social Affairs, Population Division, November 17–19. http://www.un.org/esa/population/publications/PopAspectsMDG/PopAspects.htm (accessed April 13, 2011).

United Nations Population Division. 2006. *Trends in Total Migrant Stock: The 2005 Revision*. New York: Department of Economics and Social Affairs, Population Division. http://www.un.org/esa/population/publications/migration/UN_Migrant_Stock_Documentation_2005.pdf (last accessed September 20, 2011).

United States Department of Commerce. 2009. *An Aging World: 2008.* Washington, DC: US Department of Commerce.

van der Mensbrugghe, D. 2006. "Estimating the Benefits of Trade Reform: Why Numbers Change." In R. Newfarmer (ed.), *Trade, Doha and Development.* Washington, DC: World Bank, pp. 59–75.

van der Mensbrugghe, D. and Roland-Holst, D. 2009. "Global Economic Prospects for Increasing Developing Country Migration into Developed Countries." Human Development Research Paper No. 50. New York: United Nations Development Programme, Human Development Report Office.

Vertovec, S. 2009. *Transnationalism.* London: Routledge.

Vidal, J. 2011. "Private Firms Should Contribute More to Foreign Aid, says Bill Gates." *The Guardian Online,* April 5. http://www.guardian.co.uk/global-development/2011/apr/05/private-firms-money-to-poor-gates (accessed April 21, 2011).

Vigneswaran, D. 2008. "Enduring Territoriality: South African Immigration Control." *Political Geography,* 27, pp. 783–801.

Vincent-Lancrin, S. 2008. "Student mobility, Internationalization of Higher Education and Skilled Migration." *World Migration 2008: Managing Labour Mobility in the Evolving Global Economy.* Geneva: IOM.

Wacziarg, R. and Welch, K. H. 2008. "Trade Liberalization and Growth: New Evidence." *World Bank Economic Review,* 22 (2), pp. 187–231.

Wadhwa, V. 2009. "A Reverse Brain Drain." *Issues in Science and Technology,* 25 (3), pp. 45–52.

Wadhwa, V., Saxenian, A., Freeman, R. B., and Gereffi, G. 2009. "America's Loss is the World's Gain: America's New Immigrant Entrepreneurs, Part 4." Social Science Research Network, March 2. http://ssrn.com/abstract=1348616 (accessed August 20, 2009).

Walker, A. 2009. "Recession Moves Migration Patterns." BBC News, September 8. http://news.bbc.co.uk/1/hi/8244191.stm (accessed June 23, 2011).

Walker, P. 2011. "Migrant Boat Capsizes Near Italy." *The Guardian Online,* April 6.

Wallis, W. 2009. "Hutu Diaspora Fuels War Crimes in Congo." *Financial Times,* November 25.

Walmsley, T. L. and Winters, L. A. 2005. "Relaxing the Restrictions on the Temporary Movement of National Persons: A Simulation Analysis." *Journal of Economic Integration,* 20 (4), pp. 688–726.

Wang, J.-Y. 2007. "What Drives China's Growing Role in Africa?" IMF Working Paper No. 07/211. Washington, DC: International Monetary Fund.

Weekes, J. and Stein, H. 2006. "Washington Consensus." In D. A. Clark (ed.), *The Elgar Companion to Development Studies.* Cheltenham: Edward Elgar, pp. 676–80.

Wei, S. J. 2000. "Local Corruption and Global Capital Inflows." *Brookings Papers on Economic Activity,* 2, pp. 303–54.

Wei, Y. and Liu, X. 2006. "Productivity Spillovers from R&D, Exports and FDI in China's Manufacturing Sector." *Journal of International Business Studies,* 37 (4), pp. 544–57.

Weick, K. E. 1984. "Small Wins: Redefining the Scale of Social Problems." *American Psychologist,* 39 (1), pp. 40–9.

Wezel, A., Bellon, S., Doré, T., Francis, C., Vallod, D., and David, C. 2009. "Agroecology as a Science, a Movement and a Practice: A Review." *Agronomy for Sustainable Development,* 29 (4), pp. 503–15.

White, H. 2006. "Millennium Development Goals." In D. A. Clark (ed.), *The Elgar Companion to Development Studies*. Cheltenham: Edward Elgar, pp. 382–9.

WHO. 2001a. "FAO/WHO: Amount of Poor-Quality Pesticides Sold in Developing Countries Alarmingly High." Press Release WHO/04. Geneva: World Health Organization.

WHO. 2001b. *Macroeconomics and Health: Investing in Health for Economic Development.* Geneva: World Health Organization.

WHO. 2002. *World Report on Violence and Health.* Geneva: World Health Organization.

WHO. 2003. *International Migration, Health and Human Rights.* Geneva: World Health Organization.

WHO. 2007. *Revitalising Health Care Delivery in Sub-Saharan Africa.* African Programme for Onchocerciasis Control. Geneva: World Health Organisation.

Wikipedia. 2011. "International Response to Hurricane Katrina." http://en.wikipedia.org/wiki/International_response_to_Hurricane_Katrina (accessed April 21, 2011).

Williamson, J. 1990. *Latin American Adjustment: How Much Has Happened?* Washington, DC: Institute for International Economics.

Williamson, J. (ed.) 1994. *The Political Economy of Policy Reform.* Washington, DC: Institute of International Economics.

Williamson, J. 2000. "What Should the World Bank Think About the Washington Consensus?" *World Bank Research Observer*, 15 (2), pp. 251–64.

Williamson, J. 2009. "A Short History of the Washington Consensus." *Law and Business Review AM*, 15 (7), pp. 7–23.

Williamson, S. D. 1987. "Costly Monitoring, Loan Contracts, and Equilibrium Credit Rationing." *Quarterly Journal of Economics*, 102 (1), pp. 135–45.

Winters, L. A., McCulloch, N., and McKay, A. 2004. "Trade Liberalization and Poverty: The Evidence So Far." *Journal of Economic Literature*, 42 (1), pp. 72–115.

Wolf, M. 2004. *Why Globalization Works.* New Haven: Yale University Press.

Wolf, M. 2010. "Basel: The Mouse That Did Not Roar." *Financial Times*, September 14.

Wolfensohn, J. D. 2002. "A Partnership for Development and Peace." *A Case for Aid: Building a Consensus for Development Assistance.* Washington, DC: World Bank, pp. 3–14.

Woodruff, C. and Zenteno, R. 2007. "Migration Networks and Microenterprise in Mexico." *Journal of Development Economics*, 82 (2), pp. 509–28.

Woolcock, M. 2010. "The Rise and Routinisation of Social Capital, 1988–2008." *Annual Review of Political Science*, 13, pp. 469–87.

Woolcock, M. and Narayan, D. 2000. "Social Capital: Implications for Development Theory, Research, and Policy." *World Bank Research Observer*, 15 (2), pp. 225–49.

World Bank. 1993. *East Asian Miracle.* Oxford: Oxford University Press.

World Bank. 1994a. *Adjustment in Africa.* Oxford: Oxford University Press.

World Bank. 1994b. *Reducing the Debt Burden of Poor Countries: A Framework for Action.* Development in Practice Series. Washington, DC: World Bank.

World Bank. 1995. *World Development Report 1995: Workers in an Integrating World.* Oxford: Oxford University Press.

World Bank. 1998. *Assessing Aid: What Works, What Doesn't, and Why.* Washington, DC: World Bank.

World Bank. 1999. *World Development Report 1998/99: Knowledge for Development*. New York: Oxford University Press.

World Bank. 2001. *Finance for Growth: Policy Choices in a Volatile World*. Washington, DC: World Bank.

World Bank. 2002a. *Global Economic Prospects 2002: Making Trade Work for the World's Poor*. Washington, DC: World Bank.

World Bank. 2002b. *Globalization, Growth, and Poverty: Building an Inclusive World Economy*. Washington, DC: World Bank.

World Bank. 2004a. "Aid Agency Competition." Public Policy for the Private Sector Note No. 277. Private Sector Development, Vice Presidency, October. Washington, DC: World Bank.

World Bank. 2004b. *Global Development Finance: Harnessing Cyclical Gains for Development*. Washington, DC: World Bank.

World Bank. 2005. *Global Economic Prospects: Economic Implications of Remittances and Migration*. Washington, DC: World Bank.

World Bank. 2006. *The Enhanced HIPC Initiative—Overview*. World Bank, http://go.worldbank.org/67QOAKYDT0 (accessed March 29, 2011).

World Bank. 2010. *Global Development Prospects 2010*. Washington, DC: World Bank.

World Bank. 2011a. *Rising Global Interest in Farmland: Can It Yield Sustainable and Equitable Development?* Washington, DC: World Bank.

World Bank. 2011b. *World Development Indicators*. World Bank Databank. http://databank.worldbank.org/ddp/home.do

World Bank. 2011c. *World Development Report 2011: Conflict, Security, and Development*. Washington, DC: World Bank.

WTO. 2011. "Trips and Public Health." World Trade Organization. http://www.wto.org/english/tratop_e/trips_e/pharmpatent_e.htm#declaration (accessed May 1, 2011).

Yang, J. and Nyberg, D. 2009. "External Debt Sustainability in HIPC Completion Point Countries: An Update." International Monetary Fund Working Paper No. 09/128. Washington, DC: International Monetary Fund.

Yuan, K. 2005. "Asymmetric Price Movements and Borrowing Constraints: A Rational Expectations Equilibrium Model of Crises, Contagion, and Confusion." *Journal of Finance*, 60 (1), pp. 379–411.

Yusuf, S., Nabeshima, K., and Perkins, D. 2006. "China and India Reshape Global Industrial Geography." In L. A. Winters and S. Yusuf (eds), *Dancing with the Giants: China, India and the Global Economy*. Washington, DC: World Bank, pp. 35–66.

Zakaria, F. 2009. *The Post-American World*. London: W. W. Norton & Company.

Zegers de Beijl, R. 1999. *Migrant Discrimination in the Labour Market: A Comparative Study of Four European Countries*. Geneva: ILO.

Zlotnik, H. 2005. "International Migration Trends since 1980". *International Migration and the Millennium Development Goals: Selected Papers of the UNFPA Expert Group Meeting*. Marrakech, Morocco, May 11–12. New York: United Nations Population Fund.

Zohir, S. C. 2001. "Social Impact of the Growth of Garment Industry in Bangladesh." *Bangladesh Development Studies*, 27 (4), pp. 41–80.

INDEX

Note: Bold entries refer to figures, tables or boxes.